Urban Patronage and Social Authority

Lindsay J. Proudfoot

Urban Patronage and Social Authority

The Management of the Duke of Devonshire's Towns
in Ireland, 1764–1891

The Catholic University of America Press
Washington, D.C.

Publication of this book has been assisted by a grant from the
Publications Fund of The Queen's University of Belfast.

LIBRARY OF CONGRESS CATALOGING-IN-PUBLICATION DATA
Proudfoot, L. J. (Lindsay J.)
    Urban patronage and social authority : The management of the Duke
of Devonshire's towns in Ireland, 1764–1891 / by Lindsay J.
Proudfoot.
        p.   cm.
    Includes bibliographical references and index.
    ISBN 0-8132-0819-X
    1. Urbanization—Ireland—History.   2. City planning—Ireland—
History.   3. Administration of estates—Ireland—History.
4. Devonshire, Dukes of.   I. Title.
HT384.I66P76   1995
307.76'09415—dc20   94-22416

For Jenny, Gillian, and Robin

Contents

Figures

Tables

Acknowledgments

This book is based primarily on the various collections of Devonshire estate papers held at Chatsworth House, Derbyshire; at Lismore Castle, County Waterford; and at the National Library of Ireland, Dublin. My particular thanks are therefore due to His Grace, the Duke of Devonshire, and to the Trustees of the Chatsworth Settlement, for permission to use the material at Chatsworth and Lismore, and to the Council of Trustees of the National Library of Ireland, for the use of the Lismore Papers held in their care. I owe special thanks to a number of people associated with these institutions. At Chatsworth, Peter Day, the keeper of collections, and his assistant, Michael Pearman, made every effort to ensure that my visits were as profitable as possible. At Lismore, the duke's previous agent and his wife, Paul and Arabella Burton, were unfailingly generous in their help and hospitality. In Dublin, the staff of the National Library answered my numerous and frequently arcane requests concerning the Lismore Papers with patience and courtesy. In Belfast, Dr. Anthony Malcomson, director of the Public Record Office for Northern Ireland, was characteristically generous with his help, particularly in providing me with an introduction to the duke's agent at Lismore.

I also wish to thank the following people for allowing me to use papers held in their ownership or care: Lord Courtenay; the Earl of Portsmouth; the Earl of Roden; Lord Shannon; the late B. Y. McPeake, Esq.; James Villiers-Stuart, Esq.; the director of the British Library (Egmont Papers); the director of the Hampshire County Record Office; the director of the Devon County Record Office; and the deputy keeper of the Records for Northern Ireland (Chatsworth and Downshire Papers). The citation from the Cork and Orrery Papers is made by permission of the Houghton Library, Harvard University.

My intellectual debts are equally numerous. The earliest drafts of this work were read with great care but for different reasons by two of the leading Irish economic historians, Professor Leslie Clarkson, of Queen's University, Belfast, and Professor Louis Cullen, of Trinity College, Dublin. I owe a great deal to their comments and criticisms. I owe even more to my colleague, Dr. Brian Graham, of the University of Ulster, whose ruthless intellectual interrogation of my ideas concerning Irish landlords and their role in urban improvement was both stimulating and challenging.

This book would not have appeared in its present form were it not for the cooperation and efforts of various institutions and individuals. My thanks are due to the Academic Press (London) for permission to reuse figures 2.1 and 2.2, and to the Economic and Social History Society of Ireland for permission to reuse figures 3.1, 3.8, 5.1, and 5.2. The maps and diagrams were ably drawn by Gill Alexander and Maura Pringle of the Department of Geography, Queen's University, and the index compiled by Patricia Warke. I also wish to acknowledge the generous subvention toward the costs of publication provided by Queen's University.

My final debt is a personal one. Neither this book nor the doctoral thesis on which it is based would have appeared at all had it not been for the constant encouragement of my wife, Jennifer. To her my greatest debt is due.

Urban Patronage and Social Authority

CHAPTER I

Historians, Landlords, and Irish Towns

This book addresses two themes in Irish history that until recently have either been largely ignored by Irish historians, or else have been subject to analyses based more on the desire to reformulate a sense of national identity in post-Partition Ireland then to establish a nonjudgmental discourse with the past. The first theme is that of Ireland's urban history. More specifically, it concerns the widespread urban and village foundation and improvement that occurred throughout the country but particularly in the more commercialized eastern regions of Ulster, the east Midlands, and Leinster between the end of the "Williamite" land settlements circa 1703 and the Great Famine of 1845–1849. During this period more than 750 provincial towns and villages of all sizes and functions were either newly founded, refounded, or substantially rebuilt in a more or less formally planned manner, or were equipped with the appurtenances of modernity: market houses, dispensaries, mills, schools, and so forth.[1] A few of the more spectacularly formal of these places have figured in the geographical literature as examples of so-called estate or landlord towns. This terminology reflects the conventional view that such settlement modernization was largely carried out at the behest of Irish landlords, but in general the motivations, methods, and consequences involved in this phenomenon remain underresearched.[2]

This study explores these issues within the context of the towns wholly or partly owned by one of the major landed dynasties in eighteenth- and nineteenth-century Ireland: the Cavendishes, dukes of Devonshire. In so doing, the book engages its second theme, namely, the changing social and economic role of Irish landlords, particularly in their putative capacity as agents of modernization. The patronal activities of successive dukes of Devonshire are examined for the years between 1764 and 1891. This period encompassed their rise and fall as important Irish landowners, and coincided with the incumbency of the fifth, sixth, and seventh dukes. The actions of these dukes are examined with a view to illuminating the wider issue of the nature of the social authority enjoyed by the landed elite in Ireland, and how and why this authority changed during the eighteenth and nineteenth centuries. Much of the interest in these questions arises from the fact that, in common with other Irish landowners, successive dukes of Devonshire attempted to use their economic authority to pursue political objectives—arguably in defense of their property rights—at precisely the time when the structure of Irish society and politics was changing in ways that militated against this. Consequently there is a recurring fin de siècle flavor to the text that derives from the insistent need to discuss the growing *limitations* to this exercise of traditional property-based authority, as the landed elite themselves became increasingly vulnerable to the rising political and sectarian antagonisms that characterized nineteenth-century Irish society.

These themes are interrogated via a particularist narrative that was born of an—appropriately Whiggish—belief in the importance of the *individual* and his *locality* in any attempted discourse with the past. Arguably, human history can be read as the outcome of a myriad of individual decisions that were continuously being taken within an ever changing and inevitably imperfect information field concerning the surrounding human and physical environments. This relationship between the individual and his locality—his place—was an interactive one. Human activity undertaken in response to these imperfectly made decisions led to the continual modification of place, in effect continuously re-creating the spatial contexts—the geography—within which future decisions would be taken. Consequently, neither this nor any other historical analysis can afford to disregard the location and spatial context of its subject. Indeed, each community's spatiality was inherent in its identity, and provided a framework for individual human endeavor that was both constantly changing and always unique. Accordingly, throughout this study an attempt is made to explore the particularities of the relationship between people and place in each of the duke's Irish towns, and thereby illuminate the finer textural differences that existed in the structures of their everyday life. For it is clear that these differences were very real and played an important part in affecting the nature and direction of the patronal relationship that developed between successive dukes and their urban tenants in Ireland.

The agenda for this study is thus inherently particularist, and this particularism extends to its choice of subject. In many respects the Devonshires can hardly be said to have been representative of Irish landlords as a whole. Their very wealth both in England and Ireland set them apart in a superleague of magnate landowners, among whom Cannadine numbers the dukes of Bedford, Northumberland and Richmond and the marquess of Westminster, and who in Ireland included the earl of Fitzwilliam and the King-Harmans.[3] Between 1748, when the Devonshires inherited much of the rump of the extensive Irish estates of the earl of Cork and Burlington, and the 1890s, when large parts of their holdings were sold off under the aegis of successive Land Acts, the family owned more than sixty thousand acres in Counties Cork and Waterford, together with most or all of the towns of Bandon, Dungarvan, Lismore, Tallow, and Youghal. This property provided an income that averaged over £45,000 a year by the early nineteenth century, and which—initially at least—contributed handsomely to the family's current income. The latter rose from approximately £80,000 in the 1820s to a spectacular peak of £320,000 in the early 1870s, as a result of the early—but in the event transient—success of the family's industrial investments at Barrow-in-Furness.[4] In politics, too, the family stood apart from the Tory traditions of many Irish landowners. As confirmed Whigs and later, Liberals, the Devonshires supported both of the great reforming causes in early-nineteenth-century Ireland: Catholic Emancipation and borough reform. However, being generally moderate in their politics and mindful too of the rights as well as the responsibilities that attached to property ownership, their support did not extend to the Repeal of the Union or, later, to Home Rule. Nevertheless, for much of the early nineteenth century the sixth duke in particular enjoyed a reputation as a sympathetic and openhanded landlord and a generous employer, and for these reasons was perceived by contemporaries to be particularly humane in his dealings with his tenantry.

If the Devonshires were thus in some respects unusual among Irish
landowners, they nevertheless faced the same issues of principle as their
peers concerning the management of their property. Effective management required a compromise between the property interests of the landlord and those of his tenants. In particular, it was necessary for the
landlord's rent demand to leave enough of the property's value in the
tenant's possession to allow him to exploit this in an effective manner.
Clearly, this ideal was not always achieved. Lax or overexploitive attitudes on the part of the landowner or his agent, inefficiency on the part
of the tenant, and overextended tenurial structures might all combine to
dissipate the economic advantages of direct landlord-tenant dealings.
During the eighteenth and early nineteenth centuries, for example, the
tenurial relationships on many estates were no longer directly between
the landlord and his occupying tenants. Rather, they lay between the
landlord and a head tenant who represented only the first of many links
in a chain of tenurial dependency over which the landlord had virtually
no control. Each link in the chain was represented by a new tenant who
was one step further removed from direct landlord control, but who
nevertheless still sought to secure the conditions of his existence from
what was, when all was said and done, property of finite value. Consequently, the landlord's interest as the property's owner was in danger of
being squeezed as only one of an overlarge number of financial claims
upon it. At the very least, it was unlikely to reflect any upward movement in the property's real value. Not surprisingly, the later eighteenth
and early nineteenth centuries saw increasingly widespread attempts by
Irish landlords to reestablish direct, and therefore more profitable, relationships with their occupying tenants, as the earlier lengthy middlemen's leases fell in.

On most estates landlord-tenant relations were also characterized by
the extreme inequality of the wealth of each party. As Large and Curtis
have demonstrated, however, the landlord's capital and his liquid assets
were by no means necessarily unencumbered and easily accessible.[5]
Nevertheless, these inequalities frequently gave rise to the expectation
that the landlord might reasonably invest in the public capital of his
estate. This investment would not only secure the well-being of his tenantry but also further his own political and economic interests. However, political objectives were not always easily reconcilable with the

principles of sound estate management. Elections were likely to be won only after considerable expenditure. While this expenditure was usually limited to short-term payments of various sorts, it might also raise implications for the future long-term management of the property. Accordingly, on estates where landlords took an active political role, some prioritization of these potentially conflicting objectives was necessary. For tenants, a politically active landlord might be a mixed blessing, but his actions were likely to reflect the interdependencies on which the landlord-tenant relationship was based. On the one hand, the landlord's need of his tenants' votes might create opportunities for the latter to exact bribes and favors. On the other hand, the failure of a tenant to deliver his vote might result in his marginalization on the estate and his eventual loss of tenancy.

The principles underlying estate management on the Devonshire property as elsewhere were thus essentially those of equity and compromise, but also, ultimately, coercion. Equity was necessary because the tenants—the property *users* on the estate—required some recognition of *their* economic interests in order to operate with even minimal efficiency. Compromise was required because the landlord—the property *owner*—required the tenants' cooperation if *his* economic interest in the estate was to be realized. Finally, coercion could be used because ultimately, since the landlord could determine the conditions under which the tenants gained access to their property, he could if necessary bring pressure to bear to ensure that his own interests were preferentially protected. These relationships operated through a process of property delegation. Paradoxically, this process required the landlord to surrender some of his property rights to his tenants in order to ensure their continued participation in relations of production which, although ultimately coercive, functioned more efficiently with the tenants' cooperation then in its absence. Such delegation is held to have been expressed in various ways. Economically, it found formal expression through leaseholds and other types of tenure, and less formally through the landlord's financing of various public utilities. Socially, it operated through the landlord's paternalist support of local charitable, religious, and educational bodies. Politically, it was expressed in terms that could, if necessary, utilize the eventually coercive nature of the landlord's economic authority.

Historians and Irish Landlords

Prior to the appearance of the work of the so-called revisionist school of Irish economic historians in the 1970s, and indeed for some time afterward, conventional Irish historiography tended to emphasize the coercive nature of the landlord-tenant relationship and link this to a characterization of landownership that stressed its allegedly unchanging colonial character. Early analyses such as Pomfret's *The Struggle for Land in Ireland, 1800–1923,* Hooker's *Readjustments of Agricultural Tenure in Ireland,* and Palmer's *The Irish Land League Crisis* promulgated a predatory stereotype that portrayed landlords not only as an invariably English—and therefore culturally alien—class, but also as economically parasitic and intent on expropriating the maximum rent value from their tenants. Moreover, they were represented as being able and willing to indulge in a wide variety of brutal methods of coercion to achieve this goal.[6] These characteristics were also held to be part of a uniquely Irish phenomenon. Thus Jones Hughes echoed Aalen's earlier view when he asserted that Ireland "was unique in the Europe of the nineteenth century in that the overwhelming majority of the owners of property were aliens, and [that] this type of landlordism may therefore be viewed as part of an intrusive culture emanating mainly from England."[7]

The validity of these characterizations of Irish landownership is questionable. The "alien" epithet depends on an ethnically exclusive definition of Irish nationality that emphasizes the importance of one early —Celtic—phase of immigration at the expense of later, medieval and sixteenth- and seventeenth-century immigrant streams. In alleging the longevity of Gaelic social structures, this view denies the possibility that these later immigrant groups may have made an equally profound contribution to the progressive evolution of multifaceted Irish identities through the part they played in the continuous interaction of ideas, peoples, and places over time. Rather, proponents of the "immutability of the Celt" theory of Irish history envisage the island's cultural development as an assimilative process, in which successive external influences— be they people or ideas—were invariably absorbed and transformed into new varieties of (Celtic) Irishness by the strength of the underlying Gaelic culture. There is no place here for a sense of nationhood born of growing cultural diversity through fission rather than fusion.[8]

Equally, although widely applied, the colonial label has rarely been formally explained. In fact, the two phases of immigration from which most eighteenth-century landowning families originated—the Anglo-Norman settlement and sixteenth- and seventeenth-century plantations—were arguably both colonial in character. They involved the imposition or reimposition of an external authority over parts of Ireland in a relationship of economic dependence designed to exploit the country's resources for the benefit of the external power: the Anglo-Norman, later English, nation-state. The point in question, however, is whether these putative colonial *origins* provide an adequate explanation for the character of landownership as it existed in Ireland in the eighteenth and nineteenth centuries, after two hundred years or more of marriage, sale, and inheritance involving a progressively wider spectrum of Irish society. The corollary of these processes was the increasingly rapid deconstruction—informally for much of the eighteenth century and formally thereafter—of precisely those legal property codes that the seventeenth-century colonial elite had erected in an attempt to preserve their dominant position within Ireland. Had these codes survived, they *would* have lent an enduring colonial stamp to the pattern of eighteenth- and nineteenth-century landownership.[9] As chapter 2 demonstrates, this deconstruction was part of a broader process of modernization that increasingly eroded the colonial polarities of seventeenth-century society and replaced them with new and more complex patterns of social interaction, as Ireland's economic base broadened and social access to wealth widened.

Studies by revisionist historians, on the other hand, have been characterized by their willingness to shed such value-laden presuppositions and seek more objective assessments of the Irish landlords' socioeconomic role.[10] The results of this research have tended—partly at least—to rehabilitate landlords by demonstrating that they were at least as much the victims of socioeconomic circumstances beyond their control as the malign perpetrators of social injustice. Vaughan, for example, has argued plausibly that evictions were less frequent, rent increases lower, and insecurity of tenure less pervasive in post-Famine Ireland then adherents of the "predatory" theory of landlordism would allow.[11] Indeed, Crotty and Solow have argued that "bad" landlords were those who tolerated inefficient farming by undercapitalized or indolent tenants to the general detriment of rent and output. They imply that the portion of the full Ricardian rent not squeezed out of the tenant by the landlord was likely to be dissipated in some form of nonproductive expenditure.[12]

Subsequent studies by Curtis, Ó Gráda, and Vaughan have further refined our twentieth-century image of nineteenth-century Irish landlordism by exploring the financial constraints within which many post-Famine landlords operated. They have suggested that the generally low levels of investment that characterized many Irish estates—lower certainly than on many equivalent English properties—may have been linked to the landlords' failure to raise rents adequately in line with the rise in prices, a situation which Roebuck had previously identified in the later eighteenth century.[13] Other studies have provided variations upon these themes. Crawford has discussed the role of Ulster landlords in promoting the domestic linen industry,[14] while Lowe and subsequently MacCarthy have explored the rancorous relationship between the perpetuity tenants on the Trinity College estates and their institutional landlord.[15] This relationship revolved around precisely the same issue of rent levels that Maguire's earlier and exhaustive analysis of the Downshire estates also emphasized. He demonstrates that for landlords, the rents received were simply one factor in a complex equation of income and expenditure, in which the management of costs was equally important as the management of income, a conclusion supported by Large's more general assessment of Irish landed wealth.[16]

Revisionist views of post-Famine Irish landlordism have themselves come under critical scrutiny. Arguing on the basis of a reassessment of the changing aggregate value of agricultural rents, output, and labor costs between 1852 and 1874, Hoppen and Turner have challenged Vaughan's view of a post-Famine redistribution of agricultural value in favor of tenant farmers. According to their recalculation, rents and labor costs both rose by about one-fifth but gross farming profits remained virtually static. They therefore conclude that, far from seeing a substantial strengthening of the agricultural tenant interest, the twenty-five years following the Famine witnessed a major reassertion by landlords of their preferential property demands, paid for out of Irish agriculture.[17] Whether this newfound relative prosperity accounted for the contemporary recrudescence of landlord politicking in Ireland, as

Hoppen also suggests, remains unproven, but the coincidental timing is certainly suggestive.[18] What is more certain is that if the Hoppen-Turner thesis stands, it will throw the relative lack of landlord investment into post-Famine Irish agriculture into even sharper relief than Vaughan anticipated.

These broad contours in the continuing debate over the nature and role of Irish landlordism have been highlighted by a number of particularist studies by both historians and historical geographers that have examined individual landed families and their estates. Examples include Nolan's study of Fassadinin, County Kilkenny, and Neely's analysis of the Ponsonby estate at Kilcooley, County Tipperary.[19] Generally, these studies have utilized a chronological narrative that emphasizes the evolutionary nature of land ownership. Thus Nolan stresses the extent to which the pattern of eighteenth- and nineteenth-century property ownership was influenced by earlier—medieval—spatial structures, while Neely places similar emphasis on the spatial continuity between the medieval Cistercian estate at Kilcooley and the later eighteenth-century property.

Other geographical contributions to the estate-study genre have concentrated on the landscape impact and spatial distribution of estates, rather than on social, economic, or political questions relating to their ownership and management. Among the most substantive have been Horner's study of the demesne at Carton, County Kildare, and Smyth's analysis of the growth of the Shanbally estate, County Tipperary. Both of these provide a detailed spatial reconstruction of the processes involved in creating the landscaped parks that were to be found at the center of many estates.[20] Subsequent geographical studies have continued in much the same vein. O'Flanagan used successive estate surveys to reconstruct the pattern of rural settlement on part of the Devonshire estate between 1716 and 1851, and in so doing attempted to infer something of the socioeconomic processes giving rise to the changes he identified.[21] More broadly, Jones Hughes developed the concept of "estate cores"—identified as the proprietor's main Irish residence together with any associated village or town he built—and analyzed their distribution in the 1850s and 1870s at both the national and the regional levels.[22] His analysis is presented in straightforward colonial terms seemingly uninformed by the subtleties of Anglo-Irish identity.

Thus the areas he identifies as containing the most numerous of these cores—namely, southeast Ulster; the midland counties of Longford, Meath, and Roscommon; the Dublin hinterland; and the river valleys of south Leinster and east Munster—he typifies as "the most durable and persistent areas of English and Scottish colonisation and settlement in modern Ireland."[23]

Jones Hughes's work provides one example of the uncritical acceptance of the "alien and colonial" characterization of landownership that has typified geographical studies in the estate genre. Moreover, with the important exception of Horner's 1981 paper, this work has also frequently been characterized by an equally ready acceptance of the alleged abilities of landlords to re-create space unilaterally, without apparent regard for other social groups. Thus to quote Jones Hughes once more: "[T]he landowner was often the supreme arbiter of local life. . . . [He] thus effected and controlled some of the most significant modifications in the cultural landscape. . . . In this way the impact of the estate system is so overwhelming in places that it is difficult to decipher the type of landscape that immediately preceded it."[24] Orme has also stressed the role of landlords as "the main agents of change," this time in transforming the quality rather than the size of the Irish urban network. Significantly, he adds a sectarian dimension to their role, concluding that they created towns that were the "outward expressions of the wealth, security and creative ability of the *Protestant* ascendancy" (author's italics).[25] Daly is more explicit. She asserts that "Landlord-founded or remodelled towns had as their primary purpose the spread of Protestantism and industry," a view that seems to derive from Cullen's earlier and more cautious assessment of the encouragement given by Connacht landlords to Protestant textile workers from Ulster to settle on their estates.[26]

In his 1981 review paper, Horner warned against overemphasizing the discretionary nature of the landlords' actions, and thereby attaching too much importance to their ability to indulge in unilateral landscape transformations.[27] In Horner's view, the key factor determining the extent to which any landlord intervened in the management of his estate was its tenurial structure. Of crucial importance was the survival of extensive leases for lives, since these would normally prevent the landlord from taking direct action on a tenanted property. A lease for three lives might be expected to run for thirty or forty years, during which time the landlord had no legal right of intervention as long as the rent was paid and any leasehold covenants fulfilled. Although, as Vaughan has noted, certain nineteenth-century land agents had a reputation for being able and willing to break these sorts of lease, Horner marshalled a significant body of evidence in support of his view. He cites the duke of Abercorn's comment in 1774 that "long leases were the ruin of Ireland and every man in it," and Dickson's more recent (and more considered) conclusion that in early-eighteenth-century Munster "all types of landowner diminished their freedom of action by commiting the development of their properties to large tenants, who were themselves to delegate as the effects of the market were felt more deeply."[28] In Horner's view, therefore, the exercise by a landowner of his discretionary authority over his property was conditioned by the nexus of property rights he or his predecessors had previously delegated to the tenants. In effect, the bargains struck by one generation of landlords and tenants in the name of equity, compromise, and mutual self-interest necessarily determined the periodicity of those struck by the next generation.

Irish Urban History

Horner's cautious reappraisal of the limitations to landlord authority typified the new thinking that underscored revisionist attitudes toward Irish agrarian history and the role within it of the landed elite. As we have seen, this thinking has not gone unchallenged, but it has been challenged on grounds that in the main have been based on thought and argument rather than emotion and rhetoric. Consequently, after rather unpromising beginnings, it is now possible to feel more sanguine about the maturity of much of the debate in Irish agrarian history. The same cannot be said of Irish urban history. As an academic field this is still very much in its infancy. Daly ascribes this situation to the conventional concern of mainstream Irish history with the twin issues of nationalism and agrarian change, subjects for which urban studies seemed to offer few insights; and to a popular feeling, endorsed by some historians, that towns were somehow alien institutions within Irish culture.[29] Moreover, once urban historical research did commence in earnest in the 1970s, it engaged in a characteristically introspective debate over the colonial origins of Irish urbanism. This centered on the problems of urban classification and definition within Anglo-Norman and Gaelic Irish society. One consequence has been that many of the questions that are commonplace on the agenda of British urban history have yet to be asked in Ireland.[30] Thus while Daly rightly emphasizes the importance of studies that have delineated occupational and class structures, housing provision, public health legislation, and municipal government in Belfast, Dublin, and Cork during the eighteenth and nineteenth centuries, it must be stressed that these sorts of issue have yet to be explored for the much larger number of small market towns that constituted the bulk of the Irish urban network at this time.[31]

Consequently, the specifically urban content of this book finds its antecedents in English rather than in Irish scholarship, and in particular in that genre of urban estate studies that have concentrated on the activities of the creators and controllers of the built environment.[32] Conspicuous among these is Cannadine's study of the Devonshires' involvement at Eastbourne and the Calthorpes' development of their estate at Edgbaston.[33] In Sutcliffe's view, Cannadine's work effectively reset the agenda for urban estate studies by linking the study of land and social structure via the social and political aspects of the landed aristocracy's urban role.[34] The major theme in Cannadine's work is the complex and often contradictory relationship between aristocratic landowners and the towns they owned. This was characterized by successive periods of hostility (in the 1830s and 1840s and again in the 1870s and 1880s), and rapprochement (in the 1850s and 1860s). It led, however, to the gradual but inexorable displacement of aristocratic patrons as figures of real urban authority by the rising and politically assertive middle-class elites.[35] Subsequent studies have shown that in towns as diverse as Cardiff, Dudley, and West Bromwich the decline in aristocratic authority was signaled by a loss of control over both the parliamentary representation and local municipal bodies, and culminated in some cases in the territorial withdrawal of the aristocratic family from the town.[36] Trainor, for example, demonstrates that in Dudley and West Bromwich the decline in the political authority of the earls of Dudley and Dartmouth—the ground landlords—had already begun by 1850 and continued virtually unabated throughout the century. This process was hastened by the mobilization of working-class radicalism and middle-class liberalism alike, and was reflected in the eclipse of the earls' influence over these towns' representative municipal bodies. By the 1880s the earls' roles were reduced to those of locally important philanthropists, primarily concerned with funding school and church improvements.[37]

Other studies have established more general contexts for the exercise of aristocratic authority in urban promotion and regulation. Beckett stresses the pivotal importance of landowners in encouraging or retarding urban growth in eighteenth- and nineteenth-century Britain, not only in London but also in a wide variety of functionally specialized provincial towns. He emphasizes, however, the extent to which the participation of individual landowners depended on circumstances that were not always under their immediate control.[38] Some of course were, and thus the potential for intervention was greatest where a town was wholly or largely the property of one family, as at Whitehaven (owned by the Lowthers) or Huddersfield (owned by the Ramsdens). But such places were relatively few. Far more typical were towns such as Bath, Leeds, or Bradford, where in place of a substantial ground landlord numerous small freeholders existed to give the pattern of development a decidedly incremental air.[39] Even where the property was concentrated in a few hands, the pace and extent of landlord involvement still depended on other factors: the proprietor's investment strategy, for example, and the varying strength of market demand for housing. In some towns, notably Brighton, Leicester, Nottingham, and Portsmouth, proprietors sold the freehold of building land to the developers outright. The more general practice was to offer ninety-nine-year building leases—although this sometimes required breaking the entail on the estate. These leases were widely used during the development of various aristocratic estates in London during the eighteenth century, most notably on the Bedford and Portland estates during the 1770s. Here, as elsewhere, they offered the proprietor the prospect of a substantial income while retaining ultimate ownership of the property.[40]

Even the most favorable leaseholds could not by themselves generate the level of housing demand needed to make a success of these speculative developments unless the general economic conditions also encouraged this. As Lieven points out, British landowners were in fact the fortunate beneficiaries of a process of urban growth to which they had contributed very little, but which had the capacity to transform the value of strategically located agricultural estates. Moreover, with the notable exception of the development of London's West End during the seventeenth and eighteenth centuries, the most far-reaching of these transformations occurred during the nineteenth century, and involved a middle-class, provincial, and industrial housing market, rather than one which, like at London and Bath, was aristocratic and recreational.[41]

The financial rewards of urban property ownership for British landowners during Europe's first industrial revolution could be correspondingly enormous. For some landowners they far outweighed anything enjoyed by many of their European contemporaries. For example, the duke of Bedford's Bloomsbury and Covent Garden rents rose from £10,000 in 1732 to over £20,000 in 1775, while by the 1830s their total London rental was nearly £66,000, rising to over £104,000 in 1880 as existing leases fell in. The rise in the income of other London estates was even more dramatic. The return from the duke of Westminster's Mayfair estate rose from under £9,000 in the 1770s to £60,000 in 1835, when the family's total London income stood at £88,000. By the early 1890s the Westminsters' total London income had peaked at between £427,000 and £491,000.[42] By comparison, none of the nineteenth-century Prussian or Bavarian nobility owned congeries of urban property that could compare even with that of minor English landowners such as the Heskeths or Scarisbricks at Southport or Lord Radnor at Folkestone, let alone with the property owned by magnates such as the dukes of Bedford or Westminster. Lieven concludes that the only German magnate family whose wealth was based on urban property were the Tuckers of Nuremberg, who were part of the patriciate of that old imperial city rather than true aristocrats. In Russia, where the structure of nineteenth-century aristocratic landownership was in some respects similar to that in Britain, nobles with property in Moscow or Saint Petersburg tended to be urban rentiers rather than developers, and enjoyed correspondingly lower urban rents then their British counterparts.[43]

Arguably, therefore, the importance of aristocratic landownership to any understanding of eighteenth- and nineteenth-century urban growth in Britain derives precisely from this group's success in profiting from the secular social and economic processes that promoted such growth. As British society expanded and its economy industrialized, the property-owning elite were almost inevitably going to be beneficiaries of the growing demand for urban and industrial space. In Ireland, as chapter 2 demonstrates, the social and economic contexts for urban change were very different. The export-led agrarian economic expansion that characterized much of the country for most of the later eighteenth century, and which arguably encouraged landowner participation in urban improvement, gave way in the early nineteenth century to growing economic crisis. This was signaled by the collapse of Ireland's export markets following the end of the Napoleonic Wars in 1815, but had a more fundamental cause in the growing structural imbalance between the country's rapidly rising population and its essentially inelastic agrarian resource base. Between 1770 and 1841 Ireland's population almost doubled from around 4.3 million to over 8.25 million, but this growth was not accompanied by the sort of transformation of the resource base through the exploitation of coal and mineral reserves that had underpinned the English Industrial Revolution. The only region to experience industrialization in the nineteenth century on anything approaching the British scale was east Ulster, particularly around Belfast and its hinterland. Consequently, the resource ceiling imposed by the general reliance on agriculture continued. For many people, particularly in the more peripheral and less commercialized western districts, population growth led to growing poverty and social marginalization.

The widespread economic downturn was reflected in the condition of the urban network. Dublin remained a commercial and administrative city, despite losing its legislative role following the Act of Union in 1801, but lost its primate status as Belfast rapidly overtook it in size toward the end of the century. Cork and Limerick struggled to maintain their status as regional capitals in the face of the growing poverty of their hinterlands and the increasing competition from the products of the English Industrial Revolution. Finally, with very few exceptions, the processes of modernization that had been begun in many towns and villages under landlord direction or encouragement during the expansionist years of the mid- and late eighteenth century had petered out by the 1840s. They were replaced by contraction and stagnation, as

Ireland's provincial urban network sought to readjust to the loss of over
one-quarter of the country's population by 1851, and the continuing
hemorrhage of people to emigration and the contraction in the domestic market thereafter.

The diversity of this urban experience has been reflected in the eclec-
ticism of the writing on modern Irish urban history. No major theme
exists to parallel the colonial debate that dominated the discussion of
earlier periods. Despite the caveat entered above, a limited number of
studies have appeared that do shed some light on the workings of the
urban system during the eighteenth and nineteenth centuries and on
the role of landed patrons within it. This work is very far removed
from the anecdotal social and architectural history that characterized
early essays in the urban history of the period.[44] Maguire's careful analysis of the circumstances leading to the disengagement of the Donegalls
as ground landlords in Belfast in the mid-nineteenth century is adept
in its demonstration of both the internal complexities of patronal decision making and the limitations to patronal authority in large and
functionally complex urban communities.[45] Clarkson's census-based
examination of the economic and social structure of Armagh in 1770
emphasizes the town's functional role and the evidence for community
identity in the face of sectarian and economic divisions.[46] His later and
largely methodological study of the Carrick-on-Suir census of 1799 remains one of the few overtly demographic analyses to be carried out on
an early modern Irish town.[47] Similarly, few studies other than Connell's monograph on Navan have yet elaborated on Cullen's general
observation that the sharpest drop in urban population in the post-
Famine years occurred in Munster and Leinster. Here it resulted from
the loss of those impoverished rural-to-urban migrants who had
crowded into the towns in the immediate pre-Famine years.[48]

Clarkson's concern with community identity in small provincial
towns is mirrored in O'Flanagan's analysis of the changing confessional
structures in the Devonshire estate towns between 1659 and 1850. In
this study he demonstrates the relative completeness of the sectarian
transformation that had taken place by the mid-nineteenth century. In
virtually every town the original high-status Protestant "cores" had
either disappeared or were in the process of dissolution by 1850.[49] This
form of urban transformation clearly had implications for the political

representation of the remaining boroughs in post-Union Ireland. The whole issue of urban political representation both before and after the Union has been investigated by a number of historians as part of the mainstream concern with Irish political history. Thus work by Malcomson, Jupp, and Hoppen has explored the proprietorial attitudes displayed by landed families toward borough (and county) representation.[50] Much is now known about the changing emphasis patrons placed upon borough representation following the reduction in the number of boroughs at the Union, and about the strategies they adopted to defend their urban political interests in the face of franchise reform, the growth of nationalist sentiment, and the politicization of social elements who traditionally had been excluded from participation in the political process.

Other studies of provincial Irish urbanism have stressed regional patterns as much as process. For example, O'Flanagan's discussion of market foundation in Ireland between 1600 and 1800 is predicated on a trade-based model of urban growth that links the periodicity and locational shifts in market patterns to broader regional shifts in the focus of economic activity.[51] Similarly, Cullen's elaboration of the varieties of settlement form that were produced by interventionist landlord planning in the eighteenth and nineteenth centuries succeeds largely because these morphological issues are firmly located in their socioeconomic context.[52] Much the same applies to Clarkson's recent survey of urban growth in Ulster between 1821 and 1911, which successfully delineates regional differences in the growth rates experienced by towns in the province. Towns that experienced the most pronounced growth were either manufacturing centers such as Belfast, transport centers like Portadown, resorts such as Bangor, or dormitory suburbs like Holywood.[53] Curl's compendious study of the architectural history and settlement forms associated with the Londonderry Plantation between 1609 and 1914 complements the earlier geographical and historical analyses of Hunter and Philip and Olive Robinson, and provides an important record of the fast-eroding material legacy left by this uniquely important phase in Ireland's cultural history.[54] O'Connor adopted a similar regional framework for his analysis of urban development in Limerick and its environs between the seventeenth and the nineteenth centuries. He emphasizes the importance of both property ownership and property occupation in determining the pace and scale of urban development, as well as the continuing importance of the shifting pattern of regional trade in determining the relative success or failure of individual towns.[55]

Summary

Taken as a whole, however, these urban studies offer little in the way of a coherent methodological or theoretical stance, save in their shared—but invariably unspecified—assumption that towns were a distinctive historical phenomenon, with social, demographic, and economic characteristics that were peculiarly their own. Langton and Hoppe's critique of this approach is well known. They argue that this conceptualization of urbanism misrepresents the reality of human experience. They conclude that "in the early modern period, [the terms] 'urban' and 'rural' do not bind together and distinguish internally consistent and mutually opposed categories of experience. . . . Their experiences cannot be separated; neither had any wholeness." And, quoting Abrams, they note, "Within the analysis of a chosen social system the relationships concentrated spatially within towns present themselves for explanation. But if we are to avoid mystification, they should present themselves specifically in relation to our understanding of the systems in which they recur and not as examples of an autonomous urban reality."[56]

The discussion in the following chapters attempts precisely this form of contextual analysis. The evolving discourse between successive dukes of Devonshire and their Irish urban tenantry is explored in terms that recognize not only the inherent spatiality of this relationship, but also the continuum of the participants' life experiences. This linked them to a variety of worlds—urban and rural, local and national, and material and nonmaterial—in a continuously changing kaleidoscope of differently perceived reality. Thus chapter 2 explores the changing identity and role of the landed elite in eighteenth- and early nineteenth-century Ireland, and sets this exploration within the context of the accelerating processes of modernization that were themselves tempered by the consequences of rapid population growth. This provides a general context for the following, more closely focused, analysis of events on the Devonshire estate. Chapter 3 examines the acquisition and management of the Devonshire property and the financial return it offered successive dukes; emphasis is placed on the complexity of the managerial structures required for such a large and disparate estate. The negative financial, social, and political consequences of the structural inefficiencies of this system of management are considered in chapter 4. Chapter 5 discusses what was in many ways the pivotal period in the relationship between the Devonshires and their Irish estates, the phase of radical interventionist management in town and country alike between the Act of Union in 1801 and the Irish Reform Act of 1832. This sought to redress the inroads made on the family's property rights as a result of the earlier neglect. As the discussion demonstrates, however, the social and political contexts for such interventionism were rapidly changing. Chapter 6 examines the processes of patronal disengagement that took the place of such interventionism on the estate from the 1830s onward. Chapter 7 considers the nature and extent of the forms of authority that arose out of property ownership in Ireland, particularly in the light of the radical changes that occurred in the nature of Irish society as the nineteenth century progressed.

CHAPTER 2

Land and Society

Contexts for Urban Improvement, 1700–1850

Ireland circa 1900 bore few instantly recognizable traces of the "Williamite" Ireland of the late seventeenth century. A wide variety of changes, some of which were modernizing but others of which were clearly inimical to modernization, had combined in the interim to re-create Ireland's geography and society, not once, but continuously in a never-ending evolutionary process. The interactions between these forces were complex. Their outcomes reflected the regional variations in Ireland's resource base, in its inherited social structures and cultural norms, and in the development opportunities arising out of proximity to or distance from domestic and overseas markets and sources of investment or innovation. Foremost among the modernizing processes were the structural and technological changes that aided the progressive integration of Ireland's space-economy. These included agricultural improvement; the development of agrarian and nonagrarian industry; road, canal, and railway construction; and the general extension and refurbishment of marketing structures and systems. Paralleling these economic changes were equally important social and constitutional processes. The increasing use of English as a first language, the growth of literacy, the dismantling of disabling religious legislation, the extension of the franchise, and the state-aided provision of education—all combined to promote the continuous reconstruction of Irish society in ways that distanced it from the colonial edifices of the seventeenth century.

In the long term, however, the pace and extent of economic modernization in particular was affected by the fundamental structural weakness in the Irish economy, namely, its lack of extensive exploitable mineral resources. This argument has already been touched on in chapter 1 but it is worth reiterating here. Throughout the eighteenth and for much of the nineteenth century, Ireland relied upon agriculture to provide the resources necessary to feed the bulk of its population and to support most of its industries. The latter were dominated by textiles but also included a wide variety of food-processing and other manufactures utilizing agricultural products. This dependence created what was in effect a resource bottleneck. Any extension in the acreage devoted to industrial crops like flax could only be made at the expense of the area devoted to food crops. Thus it would also be at the expense of the population carrying capacity of Irish agriculture as a whole—unless the potential existed for further expansion of the cultivated area. Once this potential was exhausted, as it more or less was in Ireland by the early nineteenth century, the only way to improve *overall* agricultural productivity was either by increasing labor inputs—at the cost of reducing per capita productivity—or by substituting technology for labor. As the discussion below demonstrates, Irish agriculture in the eighteenth and early nineteenth centuries was not innovative, and for most tenant farmers and landlords the abundantly available cheap labor provided an obvious and preferred alternative to capital investment in new technology.

This increasing reliance on the progressively more intensive use of labor provided no solution to the growing imbalance between population and resources. Even on the best land, higher labor inputs effectively reduced the individual laborer's margin of subsistence. On the impoverished waterlogged soils of the west of Ireland, where for social and commercial reasons much of the pre-Famine population growth was concentrated but where agricultural yields were at best low and erratic, these productivity margins quickly evaporated. Thus the choice for a growing proportion of Ireland's expanding pre-Famine population was either poverty if they stayed put, or migration to urban employment in Belfast or Dublin, or emigration to Britain, Australia, or America. Had Ireland possessed an extensive nonagrarian resource base this surplus population might have been absorbed by the domestic economy. As in England, this alternate resource base would have been able to break through the agricultural resource ceiling by creating new forms of production geared toward reciprocal trading overseas and consequently higher levels of employment and rising standards of living at home. As it was, the absence of these resources led to a situation in which the rising population made some sort of neo-Malthusian adjustment inevitable—quite irrespective of the coincidental occurrence of *phytophthora infestans* in the potato crop in September 1845.

The argument here is that by the second quarter of the nineteenth century, the economic stress created by the growing imbalance between Ireland's population and its resources was proving to be inimical to the ethos of economic modernization and improvement that had characterized the expansionist years between circa 1750 and 1815. Paradoxically, however, we may argue that it was *precisely* this growing economic distress, coupled with the existing political tensions that it exacerbated, which created a climate of increasing government interventionism in the management of nineteenth-century Irish society. In turn, this interventionism spawned various important modernizing changes: a new system of education, the centrally organized relief of poverty, and electoral reform being among them. Both sets of processes were equally important in the continuous re-creation of Ireland's human geography, and in particular to the progressive erosion of the traditional sources of eighteenth-century social and political authority within the country. These were largely (although not entirely) Anglican, and as they decayed they were replaced with institutions that, while not necessarily more democratic, were perceived to be more representative of the aspirations of the majority of Ireland's population. These transformations were aptly symbolized by the fate of the Church of Ireland. This institution entered the nineteenth century in the same condition as it had existed for much of the eighteenth century: unreformed, yet still the Established Church, the spiritual bastion of a ruling minority who were as certain of their position and prestige as they were of their monopoly of political power and their control over Ireland's wealth. By the end of the nineteenth century the Church of Ireland had been disestablished and partly disendowed. It survived, marginalized from the centers of real political authority, to serve a diminishing community increasingly concentrated in south and east Ulster and in the Greater Dublin area. Elsewhere, particularly in the west of Ireland, its isolated and emptying parish churches signaled the progressive decline of the Anglican communities they served.

These changes in the Church of Ireland's status mirror the concerns of this chapter. It traces the changing role and identity of the land-owning minority within the general transformations in eighteenth- and nineteenth-century Ireland outlined above. Much of the discussion is concerned with an assessment of the landowners' modernizing role within the Irish economy, and with their investment in nonproductive forms of landscape modification such as the construction of demesnes and country houses.[1] The intention is to explore the diversity of land-ownership in eighteenth- and nineteenth-century Ireland and the diverse uses to which landed wealth was put, and thus provide a national context for the urban activities of successive dukes of Devonshire in Counties Cork and Waterford.

Patterns of Change: The Economy and Landownership, 1700–1850

At the end of the seventeenth century Ireland was still a relatively underdeveloped and underpopulated country. Rather less than two million people inhabited the island, and most of these lived in rural communities where the majority were supported by a predominantly pastoral agrarian economy.[2] The underdeveloped state of Ireland's economy was reflected in its spatial organization. Seventeenth-century state surveys suggest that by 1700 a pattern of regional differentiation had emerged characterized by distinctive east-west gradients in various indices of human activity, most notably in population densities and settlement patterns.[3] Thus Ireland's more fertile and accessible eastern districts were—relatively speaking—more highly populated and more heavily exploited than the more distant and environmentally difficult western districts.

These regional differences incorporated a distinctive pattern of ethnic variation. Foremost among the processes transforming the geography of sixteenth- and seventeenth-century Ireland had been the changes in landownership imposed by successive English governments between circa 1560 and 1703. These had been undertaken for a variety of political and economic reasons, but their net effect was to reduce the previous monopoly of landownership enjoyed by Catholic "Old" English and Irish proprietors to a mere residuum of some 14 percent of

profitable land.⁴ Moreover, these changes involved the deliberate transfer of many Catholic landowners from Leinster and Munster to smaller
properties in Connacht. Thus whereas in 1641 Catholics were the majority landowners in most counties and still owned approximately 60
percent of all profitable land, by 1703 many had been concentrated in
Sligo and Galway, where they owned no more than 25–49 percent of
the land.⁵

In other parts of Ireland successive generations of "New" English and
Scots landowners, merchants, soldiers, and government servants had
taken the place of the previous Catholic proprietors. These "new men"
formed the nucleus of a landed elite who were to dominate Irish politics and society throughout the eighteenth century, and whose subsequent marginalization was to form a major theme in Ireland's history
during the nineteenth century. The creation of this "replacement" elite
set up new dissonances and cleavages within Irish society. Although
separated from the majority of Ireland's population by their absolute
wealth and social authority, the displaced Irish and Old English elites
had nevertheless shared with the majority in their Catholicism and, increasingly, in the use of Irish as a common language. Moreover, despite
the survival of regional market economies throughout the immediate
preplantation period, economic exchange within Gaelic and Gaelicized
society still recognized the traditional complex web of status-based
mutual obligation between family and clan members.⁶ This can only
have reinforced the other linkages between the different echelons
within preplantation society. It was, quite literally, a world removed
from the commercial imperatives that underpinned the entrepreneurial
vision of the New English and Scots beneficiaries of the seventeenth-
century plantations and land confiscations.

In contrast, the English and Scots planters and their successors found
themselves separated from the rest of the population by the very same
traits of language, religion, and ethnicity that had earlier bound the
leaders and the led together. Thus most (but not all) of the landed elite
who emerged out of the political and social chaos of the seventeenth
century were alienated from the mass of Ireland's inhabitants by their
English language, Anglican religion, and Scots or English ethnicity, as
well as by their absolute wealth. In this regard, therefore, they may be
truly regarded as a colonial elite: the representatives and beneficiaries of

an external authority intent on exploiting Ireland's resources for its own benefit. Crucially, however, as time went on both the nature and role of this elite changed. As a class, it was first reconstructed and then subsequently marginalized by the discourse of modernization that occurred in Ireland during the eighteenth and nineteenth centuries.

Population Growth and Regional Diversity

Uniquely in Europe, the Irish experience of change after circa 1700 was characterized by massive population growth culminating in equally massive population decline during and after the Great Famine of 1845–1849. However, neither the pattern of population growth before the Famine, nor the pattern of population loss during or after it, was evenly distributed throughout the country. Rather, each phase displayed a diverse regionalism that reflected the differing capacity of the various regional economies in Ireland first to encourage rapid population growth and then to sustain high population levels. Population estimates for the period before the first Irish census of 1821 are notoriously unreliable, and for the moment we can probably do no better than accept Clarkson's reevaluation of K. H. Connell's original figures. These suggest that the total population rose slowly from just under 2 million in 1700 to around 2.25 million in 1753, when it had still not recovered from the excess mortality of between 250,000 and 400,000 caused by the famines of 1740–1741.[7] Thereafter, the population growth rate accelerated to take the total to between 4.2 and 4.6 million in the early 1790s, before slowing under the regionally varied impact of emigration, epidemics, and delayed marriage to carry the figure to perhaps 6.8 million in 1821 and (an estimated) 8.5 million in 1845.[8] Six years later, the 1851 census recorded Ireland's population at just over 6,552,000, representing a decline of nearly 20 percent since the 1841 census figure of 8,175,000, but of nearly one-quarter in barely six years if the 1845 estimate is correct.[9]

Freeman's map of the population distribution in 1841 indicates the extent of its regional variation (see figure 2.1). A major division existed between the east and the southeast, where rural densities were generally below two hundred people per square mile, and the rest of the country, where with the exception of the uninhabited bogs and mountains of west Ulster, Connacht, and Munster, densities were frequently twice

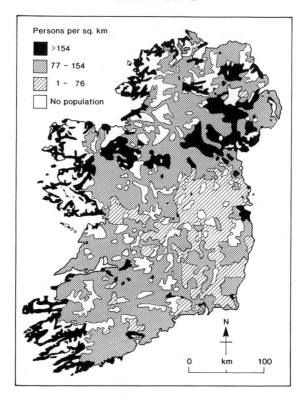

FIGURE 2.1   The Population Distribution in Ireland in 1841
(after T. W. Freeman, *Pre-Famine Ireland* [Manchester, 1957])

this figure. Clearly, any explanation for Ireland's pre-Famine population
growth has to take into account this marked regionality, and the possibility that in different parts of Ireland the similarly high (or low) population densities recorded in 1841 might have been the result of very
diverse evolutionary processes. As Ó Gráda notes, so great were the
regional variations in the demographic behavior that lay behind this
growth that any single explanation is probably misleading.[10]

For much of the western and southern zones of high population
density, some variant of Connell's classic neo-Malthusian explanation
would still seem to apply. Current versions of this model emphasize the
significance of food supply and dietary quality in reducing the effect of
subsistence crises in the later eighteenth century and in encouraging

early marriage and high marital fertility. Thus, the pronounced population growth in these districts, it is argued, was made possible by the growing availability of a nutritionally adequate and economically undemanding potato and dairy diet. This diet allowed laborers and smallholders to raise a family on a relatively small plot of land, which because it was also relatively cheap to rent was more easily acquired, and thus encouraged early nonprudential marriage. By increasing the demand for land, this led in turn to excessive land subdivision. In the environmentally difficult and commercially marginalized economies of the west and the southwest, many landlords encouraged this process as a means of increasing rent income from estates of otherwise limited commercial potential. By increasing the numbers of tenants on already cultivated land and by extending the cultivated area onto bog and hill land of—ultimately—limited productivity, rent rolls might be increased, at least in the short term. However, in the not-so-longer term, the inherent poverty of the soils in these districts turned this expanding "frontier" population into an impoverished peasantry living ever closer to the margins of subsistence. Supplementary sources of income, such as the textile industries which had been widespread in Counties Donegal, Sligo, Galway, and Mayo in the 1770s, had long ceased to be important by the 1840s, and thus the high population densities in these areas at this time were likely to truly reflect the deepening degree of misery of the poorest members of rural society there. Consequently, when the Famine struck, these districts saw some of the highest death rates, as the poorest peasantry were unable to afford the cost of emigration while their landlords—many of whom were encumbered by the selective burden of the Poor Rate as well as by collapsing rent rolls—could not afford to subsidize their flight either.[11]

Further to the northeast, in mid- and south Ulster, the equally high population densities recorded in 1841 were almost certainly a consequence of the presence of the rural-based domestic linen industry. The growth in importance of linen production had been one of the most significant features of the Irish economy during the eighteenth century. Linen exports had risen from 300,000 yards in 1700 to over 4.1 million yards in 1730, and to 20.5 million yards in 1770 and 35.6 million yards in 1800, when they formed part of Irish exports worth in all over £5 million.[12] The growth in linen production was paralleled by the progressive contraction of the industry to Ulster. Initially it was also widely distributed in Connacht, Leinster, and parts of Munster. However, a combination of factors, including the differential pace of infrastructural improvement, variations in the quality of labor and in the availability of capital and technology, but above all the entrepeneurial drive of the Ulster landowners, bleachers, and drapers who financed the industry in its domestic phase, helped to ensure the region's eventual dominance. By the 1840s a significant part of the Ulster linen industry was steam-powered, as linen yarn began to be produced by urban mills, utilizing wet-spinning technology transferred from Belfast's cotton industry after the latter's demise in the 1820s.[13] Even so, the continuing widespread availability of skilled hand weavers kept wage rates down and ensured that, for the moment, hand weaving was cheaper than factory weaving. It was these hand weavers who in 1841 constituted the bulk of the dense populations recorded in the Bann and Lagan valleys, and in Monaghan, Cavan, and south Armagh. As the linen industry progressively concentrated in Ulster from the mid-eighteenth century onward, so the linen weavers emerged as a "labor aristocracy," able and willing to pay a premium for smallholdings located close to brown linen markets such as Cootehill, Hillsborough, Lisburn, or Lurgan. This spatially selective demand encouraged precisely the same sort of excessive subdivision in these areas as in the far west and southwest, but in this instance as a response to the wider range of family employment that was available. This permitted many Ulster smallholders engaged in the dual economy of linen and agriculture to escape the worst consequences of the potato failures of 1845–1847, even though these were as severe as those in Connacht and west Munster. The additional income provided by weaving allowed families an alternative to starvation: emigration.

The much lower rural population densities recorded by the 1841 census in east and southeast Ireland reflected first, the more overtly commercial nature of agriculture in the region; second, the lack of sizeable areas of colonizable land onto which an excess rural population might be directed; and third, the existence of a more extensive urban network into which some surplus rural population might profitably be drawn. Generally speaking, this part of Ireland possessed a marginally drier climate and more fertile soils than many western districts. These encouraged the development of a more commercial agriculture that was sensitive to variations in market demand both at home and overseas, but which in consequence could not profitably support a large surplus labor force of marginal productivity. Accordingly, rural population growth in the southeast was limited by the operational demands of this agricultural system. While this required some increase in labor to meet the needs of the expansion in grain and livestock production prior to 1815, it was more generally characterized by tenurial and other constraints designed to keep such growth under control.[14] Thus while landowners attempted to maintain the economic viability of their tenants' farms by resisting pressure to permit subdivision, tenants proved willing to participate in a market for farm tenancies that became increasingly competitive during the agricultural boom years of the late eighteenth century. With comparatively little marginal land available for colonization and with tenurial structures still dominated by long leases for lives, age at marriage rose and marital fertility declined, as would-be tenants delayed marriage until a tenancy became available.[15]

For those unable or unwilling to wait, the developing urban network provided a wider range of employment opportunities than did the less numerous towns of the far west (see figure 2.2). In parts of Leinster and east Munster, for example, the woolen industry continued to provide urban employment until the closing decades of the eighteenth century. The weaving of "old draperies"—thick, heavy woolens such as broadcloths or frieze—was concentrated in Dublin and the surrounding towns until a decline in supplies of short-staple wool led to its demise from the 1780s. Production of the lighter and cheaper "new draperies" or worsteds remained concentrated in the towns of southern County Tipperary such as Clonmel and Carrick-on-Suir and in places such as Bandonbridge in County Cork.[16] As these traditional urban industries declined in the late eighteenth and early nineteenth centuries, largely as the result of increasing competition from the products of the British Industrial Revolution, so others were developed. Cotton production, for example, was widely introduced on a capital-intensive factory basis from the 1770s onward by landowners such as Henry Brooke at Prosperous, County Kildare (in 1780), or by industrialists such as the Quaker Malcomson family at Portlaw, County Waterford (in the 1820s). By the 1830s, however, these textile industries were generally in

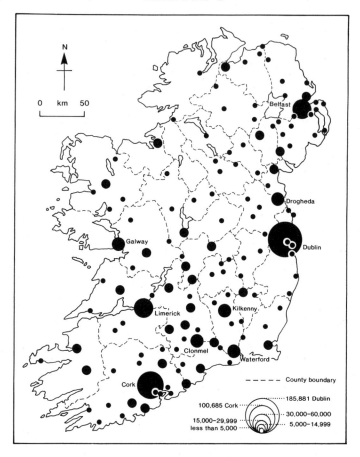

FIGURE 2.2 The Major Provincial Towns in Ireland, circa 1821
(after S. A. Royle, in B. J. Graham and L. J. Proudfoot, eds., *An
Historical Geography of Ireland* [London, 1993])

decline. They were replaced as important sources of urban employment by the growing array of retail and professional functions that
were to characterize the larger and more centrally located provincial
Irish towns for much of the nineteenth century. Conceivably, the continuing existence of this relatively extensive range of urban employment in Leinster and east Munster may have been among the
factors that helped curtail long-term pre-Famine rural population
growth in these areas. It should be noted, however, that as in other

parts of Ireland, many towns in these regions experienced massive but temporary population growth in the immediate pre-Famine years, as large numbers of impoverished rural peasants sought some form of urban existence, however marginal, in their peripheral cabin suburbs.[17]

The predominant element in the pattern of urban change in pre-Famine Ireland was Dublin's disproportionate growth throughout the eighteenth century. Between 1685 and 1800 the city's population probably more than trebled from around 65,000 to 200,000. Significantly, the city's share of Ireland's total population actually fell from 5 percent in 1750 to less than 3.5 percent in 1800. Dickson argues that this decline resulted from the absolute ceiling imposed by Ireland's agrarian economy on the size of the country's population, and therefore on the levels of demand this generated for the sorts of commercial, administrative, industrial, and financial services provided by a "consumerist" primate center such as Dublin. In these circumstances, neither Dublin nor any other town in the Irish urban network could look forward to open-ended growth.[18] In the absence of any research on the city's demography during this period, we can only speculate as to the sources of the growth that did occur, but it seems likely that in common with other European cities, Dublin operated as a "demographic sink," and relied on continuing rural-urban migration rather than natural increase to maintain its growth.[19] If this was the case, then clearly the city's growth would have been an important additional factor in syphoning off surplus rural population, again most probably from proximate rather than distant areas.[20]

Religion, Politics, and Social Adjustment

Such pronounced demographic growth and regional divergence inevitably had implications for the structure of Irish society. In numerical terms, the major beneficiary of this population growth was the Roman Catholic community. Despite continuing Scots Presbyterian migration into Ulster and subsequent though less extensive French Huguenot and German Palatine migration elsewhere into Ireland, it is probable that by the late eighteenth century Catholics comprised over three-quarters of the total population. By the time the Commissioners of Public Instruction reported on the denominational breakdown of Irish society in 1834, the Catholic proportion had risen still further to

an estimated 80.9 percent, compared to the 10.7 percent who were Anglican and the 8.2 percent who were Presbyterian.[21] At the same time,
of course, the vast bulk of this expanding Catholic population was
comprised of the very poorest members of rural society. These were
people who, in economic terms, were to be progressively marginalized
by the worsening imbalance between regional population growth and
resource allocation in the early nineteenth century. Some measure of
their deepening plight is provided by a comparison of the total Catholic population recorded in 1834 and 1861, the year of the first true religious census. During the intervening period their numbers fell by
nearly 30 percent from approximately 6.5 million to around 4.5 million. In fact, these figures probably underestimate the true extent of
the collapse in the Catholic population precipitated by the Famine.
The initial Catholic proportion is likely to have increased still further
between 1834 and 1845, since the continuing process of pre-Famine
population growth was concentrated in those areas and among those
social classes that adhered most completely to this confessional allegiance.[22]

The existence of such an uneven confessional divide was not unusual
in eighteenth-century Europe; nor, despite the Enlightenment, was the
discriminatory legislation, administrative action, and prejudice suffered
by the Irish Catholic community for much of the period as a legally
disadvantaged religious group. By the early eighteenth century different forms of religious homogeneity had been more or less established
over large parts of Europe. Spain, Portugal, and Italy were almost exclusively Catholic. Protestantism had been virtually extirpated in these
countries before the Catholic Reformation, and the small Jewish urban
communities were only tolerated—in Italy rather than Iberia—for
strictly commercial reasons. In Scandinavia, Lutherism was everywhere
in the ascendant, and it was not until 1781 that non-Lutheran foreign
Christians were allowed to build churches there; Jews were not allowed
to settle or build synagogues until a year later. In central Russia the
Orthodox church was predominant, although in the newly conquered
Baltic, Polish, and Ukranian provinces it gradually reached a series of
grudging accommodations with existing faiths. Thus mixed marriages
between Orthodox and Catholic believers were permitted from 1721
onward, so long as the children of these unions were brought up in the

Orthodox Church and no attempt was made to convert the Orthodox partner.[23]

Beyond these broadly homogenous zones, other countries contained a greater diversity of observance despite the existence of official state religions, both Protestant and Catholic. Thus while Catholicism was also the official faith in France, Poland, the Hapsburg territories, and in some of the Swiss cantons and German states, all of these countries also contained significant Protestant minorities. Similarly, while different varieties of Protestantism—Anglicanism, Calvinism, and Lutheranism—formed the official religion in Britain, the United Provinces, and other Swiss and German territories, as well as in Scandinavia, these countries too contained significant Catholic and Dissenting Protestant minorities. Crucially, however, they *were* minorities; the majority adhered to the official religion and were thus immune to attempts by the state to proscribe religious dissent on the grounds of its suspected association with political disloyalty.[24] In Ireland the situation was completely different. Arguably, the truly unusual feature of the developing sectarian divide in that country was that, unlike the general European experience, it separated an economically and politically marginalized dissenting *majority*, comprised of Catholics and Presbyterians, from a predominantly Anglican ruling *minority* who dominated most aspects of Irish life until the early years of the nineteenth century.

The origins of this division have already been shown to lie in the plantations and confiscations of the seventeenth century. By 1703 the overwhelming concentration of land into Anglican hands ensured that the adherents of this church had acquired a virtual monopoly of the means of production in what remained an overwhelmingly agrarian economy. This economic domination was matched by their control of the Irish legislature following the defeat of the Catholic Jacobite forces in 1691. Nevertheless, the Irish Protestant mind-set remained defensive. Not only were they a numerically small minority in their own country, but the political forces ranged against them in Europe remained immense. Both the French emperor, Louis XIV, and the Vatican continued to recognize the Stuart Pretender, James III, as the rightful claimant to the English throne. In the face of this hostility abroad and with the recurring fear of Catholic rebellion at home, the Anglican-dominated Dublin Parliament passed a series of measures between 1694 and 1728 designed to secure the Anglicans' position as a privileged ruling minority by further eroding the Catholic economic base in land-ownership and by destroying any possibility of their Church providing effective social leadership for the Catholic community at large. Earlier legislation predating the 1690s already prevented Catholics from effective participation in politics.[25]

The Penal Legislation   This "Penal Legislation," as these laws have come to be called, remained in force for much of the eighteenth century. They only began to be repealed from the 1760s onward, but considerable doubt remains over their impact and the extent to which they were enforced. The most important anticlerical measures were contained in the Banishment Act of 1697 (9 Will. III, c. 1), the Registration Act of 1704 (2 Anne, c. 7) and the Amending Act of 1709 (8 Anne, c. 3). The Banishment Act provided for the expulsion of all members of the Catholic diocesan hierarchies together with all priests in regular orders, and in eighteen months resulted in the departure from Ireland of over eight hundred Roman Catholic clergy.[26] The Registration Act required all remaining diocesan clergy to register with the county sessions and provide securities for their good behavior, but having done so, guaranteed them freedom to continue as practicing priests. However, following the renewed threat of a Jacobite invasion of England in 1708, an Amending Act was passed the following year that required all Catholic clergy to swear allegiance to Queen Anne and foreswear loyalty to the Stuart Pretender. In the event, less than one-tenth of the one thousand priests who had registered under the 1704 act took this Oath of Abjuration, rendering this part of the 1709 act unenforceable.[27]

The most far-reaching of the provisions against Catholic property ownership were contained in the "Popery Act" of 1704 (2 Anne, c. 6) and in the 1709 Amending Act. Earlier legislation passed by William III's second Irish parliament in 1695 had already sought to limit both the opportunities for Catholic education in Ireland and the right of Catholic gentry to bear arms, own horses, or otherwise display the trappings of their social status.[28] The Popery Act struck at the very basis of Catholic landownership itself. It forbade Catholics from buying land or from acquiring leases of more than thirty-one years or from paying rent of less than two-thirds the property's annual value. Moreover, existing Catholic landowners could no longer pass their entire estates on intact to their eldest son. Rather, they had to divide these estates equally among all their male offspring—unless the eldest son conformed to the Established Church. In such cases, the entire reversionary interest became the son's, and the father was reduced to the status of a tenant for life. Other provisions in the act required Catholic freeholders to take the Oath of Abjuration before elections, and Protestant Dissenters to take a sacramental test before they could receive an army commission, become an M.P., or sit in a municipal corporation.[29] These acts represented the high point of discriminatory legislation against Catholic property ownership in Ireland. Subsequent legislation passed between 1714 and 1728 was essentially reactive and designed to remedy any defects in the earlier laws. The only radical extension to Catholic disability was political and came in 1728, when the Act of 1 Geo. ii, c. g, s. 7 explicitly deprived Catholics of the parliamentary franchise.[30]

The question remains, however, of how effective the disabling provisions against Catholic property ownership were in practice prior to their progressive repeal beginning in the 1760s. Conventionally, historians have assumed that they were as draconian in reality as they were on paper. Wall, for example, has argued that they led to the widespread flow of (debarred) Catholic capital out of land ownership and into urban mercantilism, and sees this as the primary explanation for the allegedly growing Catholic domination of many urban merchant communities from the mid-eighteenth century onward.[31] More recent assessments have suggested that the Penal Legislation was already a "dead letter" by the 1730s, and that long before then, it had become clear that these laws were "neither going to eliminate Catholicism, nor bring about the mass conversion of Catholics nor [keep them] poor."[32] It is clear, moreover, that the prescriptions against Catholic landownership and Catholic tenancies could be—and were—circumvented. Catholic younger sons might be pressured into giving up their claim to a share of their father's estate under the provisions contained in the Popery Act, while Protestant landlords and Catholic tenants might collude in the manipulation of the leaseholds in order to preserve the latter's property interests. Perhaps the greatest constraint on the efficient operation of the Penal Legislation, however, was the general unwillingness of Irish lawyers to act illegally in its pursuit. Indeed, as the century progressed, many Irish Protestants appear to have been content to let these laws remain on the statute books as a potential rather than a real constraint on Catholic behavior. Thus for many Irish Catholics they remained a source of petty discrimination rather than serious oppression.[33]

Conceivably, therefore, while the Penal Laws hastened the decline in Catholic landownership in fee already begun by the seventeenth-century confiscations, they did not even begin to bring about the extirpation of Catholic agrarian wealth as such. Indeed, Cullen argues that the eighteenth century witnessed a remarkable growth in Catholic leasehold wealth in general. This thesis implies that whatever the formal disabilities suffered by Catholics due to their inability to take long leases, these were more than outweighed by their success in re-negotiating their tenancies. Thus, according to Cullen, the number of substantial "big farm" Catholic tenancies grew in line with the general expansion in the agrarian economy from the 1740s onward, particularly in the rich farmlands of south Leinster and east Munster.[34]

During the last four decades of the eighteenth century, formal state discrimination against the Irish Catholic community began to be rescinded. This appears to have been a response to the growing demands of empire for military manpower, the decline in anti-Catholicism among the British governing elite, and the latter's growing concern with the possible social ramifications of continued legislative discrimination against Catholics in Ireland. They were particularly alarmed at the growth in revolutionary fervor on the Continent and the influence this and events in America might have on radical Irish Catholics and Dissenters. Moreover, there was a growing body of opinion among the Anglo-Irish landed gentry themselves that a relaxation in the inheritance and property laws would be of general economic benefit. Accordingly, successive Catholic Relief Acts in 1761, 1778, 1782, and 1793 allowed Catholics to take 999 year leases, buy and inherit land on the same terms as Protestants (except in parliamentary boroughs), and finally, vote—subject to a property qualification.[35] If the recent reinterpretation of the true extent of the economic disabilities suffered by Irish Catholics prior to 1761 is correct, these Relief Acts did little more than remove formal penalties against Catholic property rights that had been honored in name only. Nevertheless, by doing away with the sort of collusive strategies that had previously been necessary and by making capital investment in leasehold property more worthwhile, the progressive removal of these disabilities can only have secured and enhanced Catholic property interests and encouraged Catholic participation in the economy at large.

The Political Rehabilitation of the Catholic Community   Equally important to the long-term constitutional position of Irish Catholics were the political provisions in the Relief Act of 1793. These gave a parliamentary vote to sections of the Catholic community for the first time in sixty years. The act extended the existing forty-shillings freeholder franchise to Catholics, and thereby effectively transformed what had been a nominal 40-shillings freehold electorate into a near-forty-shillings electorate. Under this franchise the freeholder had to show that his rented property was still worth at least this amount to him once he had paid his rent. As this was a minimum rather than an absolute value, many freeholders registering under this qualification prior to 1793 held tenancies worth a great deal more than the stipulated minimum. By extending this property qualification to the larger but generally much more impoverished Catholic community, the 1793 act reduced the average value of the freeholds registered in this way, for many of the newly enfranchised Catholic voters were hard put to meet even the forty shillings minimum. Moreover, this effect was exacerbated by the activities of landlords seeking to maximise the number of freehold tenant voters they could marshal in support of their candidates. By permitting the excessive subdivision of existing tenancies on their estates and by declaring each of the new tenancies to be worth the minimum value and letting them for one life, landlords might hope to create a docile and politically obedient army of voters, but only at the cost of economically inefficient property management.

The potential for this sort of electoral manipulation was greatest in the county constituencies, where there were large numbers of enfranchisable Catholic tenants. In the boroughs the franchise tended to remain exclusively in Protestant hands, as Catholics continued to be excluded from the electorate by a variety of legal or technical considerations.[36] By enhancing in this way the importance of the Catholic-dominated constituencies, the 1793 act had the potential to change the political map of Ireland, although this was not to be fully realized until the Catholic Emancipation act of 1829. As it was, the 1793 act was passed under British prompting by an Irish Parliament that had been granted considerable legislative independence by Lord Rockingham's Whig government in 1782, but which remained symbolic of an exclusively Anglican "Ascendancy" elitist nationalism.[37] Thus, in rather less of a paradox than might at first appear, the ruling minority acquiesced in the enfranchisement of part of a politically hostile majority, in order to defuse the—for them—more dangerous possibility of a revolutionary assault on society born out of the growth of radical Catholic and Dissenter political opinion. The act was, in short, an attempt to delegate authority in order to preserve that authority.

As events were to demonstrate, however, in the long term such delegation was insufficient to meet the radicals' demands for complete religious emancipation and political reform. Constitutional radicalism had first organized formally in Ireland in 1791, with the foundation of United Irishmen's Societies in Belfast and Dublin. Subsequently, the center of revolutionary activity shifted to east Ulster, where by 1795 a predominantly Presbyterian conspiracy was considering an offer of French help to foment a revolution in Ireland. A year later this group established links with the Defenders, a predominantly Catholic organization that had originated in the intense sectarian antagonisms among the weaving communities of County Armagh in the mid-1780s, but which had subsequently spread widely through Leinster and Munster as a revolutionary, sectarian nationalist secret society. By late 1796 both organizations had been absorbed by the newly reemergent Dublin United Irishmen as part of a more widespread revolutionary movement in southern Ireland.[38]

In the event, the revolutionary alliance between Ulster Presbyterians and Leinster and Munster Catholics proved unworkable in the face of the sectarian realities of the day. When the revolt finally broke out in May 1798, Presbyterian support in Ulster quickly collapsed in the wake of the early defeats at Antrim and Ballynahinch and as news of the sectarian massacres of Protestants in County Wexford by the United Irishmen reached the north. Despite the arrival of French help later the same year, the government had little difficulty in suppressing the rebellion. Only in County Wexford, where it had succeeded in attracting support from among the Catholic gentry and commercial classes as well as from laborers and the rural poor, did the revolt prove tenacious and protracted.[39]

The real significance of the rebellion lay in what it signaled for the future rather than in what it achieved for radical Irish politics in the short term. In the first place, it led to a reappraisal by Ulster Presbyterians of their aspirations for political independence, which in the following decades led them toward Unionism and a close alignment with the Anglican community. More importantly even then that, the uprising demonstrated beyond doubt the revolutionary potential that existed in Ireland so long as political representation remained the preserve of the elite minority. The economic rehabilitation of Roman Catholics had not been accompanied by their political emancipation. Catholic freeholders might vote—but not for Catholic M.P.'s. Indeed, if anything, the political monopoly of the Anglican minority had been enhanced after 1782. Thus when the Act of Union between Britain and Ireland became law on January 1, 1801, it followed a political debate which in Ireland had focused on the perspectives and concerns of the Anglican elite. For the proponents of the Union, its attractions were a closer constitutional alliance with the world's foremost economic power, coupled with the apparent—but in the event illusory—security it offered against future Catholic challenges to Anglican authority.[40]

The Act of Union was passed into law in the face of considerable opposition from ultra-Tory and reforming groups. Irish Tories like the marquis of Beresford feared that the Union would quickly be followed by Catholic Emancipation. The reformers had hoped that the constitutional changes of 1782 would have brought the Catholic propertied classes into an Irish parliament, and therefore saw the Union as an opportunity lost. The British government sought the Union as a counter both to further insurgency in Ireland and to continuing French hostility abroad. In order to secure the Catholic hierarchy's compliance in the measure, Pitt the Younger promised full Catholic Emancipation in the post-Union state. In the event, Pitt's failure to secure this, not the least because of George III's implacable opposition to it, ensured that "the Catholic Question" remained on the political agenda of the newly united kingdom for the foreseeable future. Royal opposition and government equivocation led to the defeat of successive Emancipation Bills in 1808, 1813, 1819, 1821, and 1825, and this in turn gave rise to increasingly Catholic militancy. The resulting radicalization of the Catholic political leadership centerd around the person of Daniel O'Connell. In 1823 he formed the Catholic Association, and in so doing created a movement that eventually succeeded in pressuring the government into granting Catholic Emancipation in 1829.

The significant development occurred in 1824, when associate membership in the movement was made available at a penny a month, rather than the annual guinea subscription the forty-six founding members paid. According to McCartney, this "transformed the Association from a middle-class political club into a mass-movement which politicised the countryside."[41] By paying this so-called Catholic Rent, large numbers of the relatively impoverished Catholic peasantry were able to participate, or at least were made to feel they participated, in the political process. As such, they constituted an impressively large and well-disciplined political body. The success of the Catholic Association's candidates in the elections for Counties Monaghan, Louth, Waterford, and Westmeath in 1826 and for County Clare in 1828, demonstrated its commitment to constitutional politics—but also the potential for disruption if its demands were ignored. These lessons were not lost on Peel's administration. Faced with the reality of a Catholic freeholder electorate that had shown that it could overturn traditional landed political authority, and conscious too of the danger of civil war, the government introduced the Catholic Relief Bill which was passed in 1829. For the first time in over 130 years Catholics were able to become members of Parliament, to be elected to borough corporations, and to hold the higher offices of state. The quid pro quo for the government was the introduction of a more exclusive property qualification in the predominantly Catholic county constituencies. This rose from forty-shillings to £10, and had the politically desirable effect from the government's point of view of reducing the predominantly Catholic electorate from 216,000 to 37,000. Existing forty-shillings freeholders were allowed to retain their vote for life.[42]

Property and Landownership   In the long term the accelerating pace of political change set in motion in Ireland by the Catholic Relief Act of 1793 and given added urgency by the Act of Union, the 1829 Relief Bill, and the Irish Reform Acts of 1832 and 1835, could only be to the detriment of the property-owning minority's exercise of their traditional social and political authority. In particular, the reduction in the number of Irish seats from three hundred to one hundred at the Act of Union and their transfer to Westminster—together with thirty-two seats for Irish peers and bishops—led to a reappraisal of traditional patronal attitudes in Irish politics. The proprietorial attitude previously displayed by many landowners toward the political representation of their property was only possible because of the "closed" nature of pre-Union Irish politics. Political aspirations and rivalries remained internalized within the ruling propertied class, who, while conscious of the potential challenge represented by the partial enfranchisement of the majority, retained effective political power. Consequently, patrons could trade their political influence on a pragmatic basis, secure in the knowledge that it was unlikely to result in a major *external* challenge to their authority.

The Union and subsequent reforming legislation changed matters entirely. Although landowners and other landlords retained their political dominance as the property-owning elite in the short term, they were now operating within a wider imperial arena. Here, the imperatives determining government action and policy were by no means necessarily consonant with the landlords' own social, economic, and political interests. Indeed, the Emancipation Bill seemed to demonstrate that when faced with the prospect of a radical, violent, and popular challenge to the fabric of the state, no British government would be prepared to face this down in defense of the traditional authority of the—mainly Protestant—Irish propertied class. In short, the prospect was for further change in Ireland's political landscape which would enhance majority aspirations at the expense of the traditional ruling elite. Thus, as chapter 5 demonstrates, in defending their increasingly precarious political position, these Ascendancy survivors of the Union had to rely increasingly on those—mainly urban—constituencies where their coreligionists remained predominant. But even here the tide of events was turning against them, as the Protestant electors in some of the unreformed corporations mounted a series of revolts in the 1820s against their erstwhile patrons. Paradoxically, these electoral

rebellions usually occurred because these patronal interests were perceived to be *too* supportive of Catholic rights in general.[43]

By the early nineteenth century, therefore, the ruling propertied elite
found itself being increasingly challenged on two fronts. First, by the
growing politicization of groups among the majority population who
had previously been politically marginalized, and second, by the consequences of the legislative changes put in place by the government in response to this. However, these external impositions formed only one
part of the evolutionary processes that affected landowners and other
members of the propertied elite during this period. Equally important
were the continuing internal adjustments within the class as it responded to economic change and the normal mechanisms of social mobility: birth, death, marriage, wealth accumulation, and debt. Between
them, these internal and external changes continuously re-created both
the number and social complexion of the propertied minority. It is thus
misleading to envisage this minority as being either static in size or
homogenous in character, and uniformly separated by a seamless array
of cultural attributes from the majority of the population. For example,
although the wealth of most property owners remained vested in landownership—given the agrarian nature of Ireland's economy it could
hardly be otherwise—as the nineteenth century progressed increasing
numbers of industrial capitalists joined their ranks as Ulster, in particular, industrialized. Significantly, these newcomers invariably sought to
buy the trappings of landed status through the purchase of residential
estates. This suggests that although the basis in wealth of property ownership may have become more varied, contemporary opinion still perceived the epitome of propertied status to be the possession of land and
the social cachet traditionally associated with this.

Numerically speaking, the propertied elite probably grew in parallel
with the total population, doubling from five thousand or so families
in the 1770s—when they represented less than 1 percent of the total
population but owned around 95 percent of the land—to perhaps ten
thousand families in the early 1840s.[44] This increase presumably resulted from the sort of social mobility just described and which Power
has identified in eighteenth-century County Tipperary. Here, the propertied minority doubled from around one hundred families in 1700 to
nearly two hundred a century later. This growth occurred largely as a

result of opportunistic land purchase by successful merchants, tenant farmers, and petty industrialists. These groups bought from the county's magnate landowners as the latter sold land in an attempt to solve their chronic indebtedness. The Tipperary sales included parts of the Ormond, Everard, and Dunboyne estates, but these were simply local examples of a wider phenomenon found throughout Munster and Leinster.[45]

It seems likely that the expansion in the number of genuinely landed proprietors ended with the Famine. Although the 1871 census lists some twenty thousand landowners, many of these were squatters, owning no more than an acre or two which they had carved out of common land and over which they had acquired freeholders' rights.[46] The impact of the Famine on more substantial landowners depended on whether they had let their estates to middlemen or to sitting tenants. Where estates were still let to middlemen, it was they rather than the landlords who bore the brunt of any financial loss, but where farms had been let to sitting tenants it was the landlords who faced collapsing rent rolls and bankruptcy.[47] Hoppen estimates that up to one-quarter of all land changed hands as a result of Famine-induced bankruptcy among landowners, which suggests that the long years of net admission to the ranks of landownership had been halted—at least temporarily.[48]

The growth in the size of the propertied class prior to the Famine was paralleled by its increasing social and cultural diversity. It is quite clear that the conventional depiction of this "landlord class" as a homogenous group, *uniformly* separated from the mass of the Irish people by politics, language, religion, and ethnicity is a gross oversimplification of a much more complex reality. Their politics ranged from the ultra-Toryism of Lord Bandon, the earl of Shannon and the marquis of Beresford, through the moderate Whiggish liberalism of the Villiers-Stuarts and Hely-Hutchinsons, to the radicalism of Daniel O'Connell, himself a minor Kerry landlord. Similarly, while the vast majority of landowners were Anglicans, a regionally varied minority of estates remained in Catholic ownership. These included the Bellew estate at Mount Bellew, County Galway, and Lord Kenmare's 118,000 acres in Counties Cork, Kerry, and Limerick. While some among this Catholic minority conformed to Anglicanism during the Penal era, others adopted a variety of strategies to retain effective control over their estates.[49]

The propertied minority were deeply divided, too, by the relative extent of their wealth. By the 1870s a small group of perhaps half a dozen magnate landowners, including the duke of Devonshire, stood out from the rest as owners of at least 60,000 acres. Others included the marquis of Landsdowne with 120,000 acres in Counties Dublin, Kerry, Laois, Limerick, Meath, and Offaly; and the duke of Abercorn with over 76,000 acres in Counties Donegal and Tyrone. Below this magnate elite were a group of some three hundred families who owned over 10,000 acres each; below these were a group of some 3,400 or so who owned between 1,000 and 10,000 acres. The vast majority of the landowning families—some 15,000 in all—owned far less than this, and—the freeholding squatters apart—merged imperceptibly with the ranks of the more substantial tenant farmers.[50] Significantly, in some parts of Ireland this size distribution had a discernibly ethnic flavor. By the 1850s in County Waterford, for example, landowning families of Old English or Gaelic Irish origin were significantly underrepresented in terms of the aggregate value of their estates when compared to New English or Scots properties. Estates in Gaelic Irish or Old English ownership constituted 58 percent of the total number, but accounted for only 46 percent of the total Poor Law valuation.[51]

These internal divisions indicate that the only true diagnostic of landlord status was the nature of the owner's title to his property. Language, religion, politics, ethnicity, and relative wealth all varied within the landlord class. The only constant was the landlords' status as owners of a sufficiently secure title to all or most of their property to allow them, in theory, extensive discretionary control over it. Obviously this control was not unbounded. Indeed, it is arguable that as Irish society became more complex, and as state intervention became increasingly commonplace throughout Irish life, this discretionary aspect of property ownership became progressively constrained. Thus while leases, jointures, and entails had always constituted potentially significant constraints on the landlord's freedom of action, in the nineteenth century these were supplemented by the legislative provisions of the state as it attempted to ameliorate the worst inequalities within Irish society. Thus, for the first time, property owners found themselves burdened with Poor Rates and other levies designed to support the incapable or impoverished, and challenged by the rival structures of authority set up by the state to administer this intervention. From the 1870s onward, of course, Gladstone's government struck at the very roots of the landed class in Ireland when it implemented legislation designed to transfer landownership to the tenant majority.[52] Prior to this, however, many landowners used their—admittedly constrained and perhaps diminishing—discretionary authority to promote the various modernizing transformations that characterized much of the Irish space-economy between circa 1700 and 1850. How was this achieved?

Property Ownership and Improvement

Daniels and Seymour have defined "improvement" in the eighteenth-century sense as the "restructuring of the landscape for social and economic as well as aesthetic ends and, by extension, restructuring the conduct of those who lived in, worked in, and looked upon it."[53] In both England and Ireland the involvement of landowners and other members of the propertied classes in this type of activity was always a matter for individual preference and judgment. Not every Irish landowner was interested in intervening in the reconstruction of the social and physical environment of those around him. Many were more than content to act as rentiers, receiving a suboptimal but more or less guaranteed rent income but doing nothing to maximize this income in the light of changing economic conditions. Even among those who were active interventionists in the cause of social or economic reconstruction, the extent of investment was generally lower than in England, though possibly comparable with that in other European countries, particularly France and Spain.

That said, we may nevertheless identify five main areas in the Irish space-economy where improving landowners made a significant contribution—directly or indirectly—to the process of modernization. These were in agriculture, industry, towns and marketing, communications, and finally—though less productively—in the ornamentation of the landscape. Significantly, in each of these areas save the last, landowners came to rely increasingly on the participation of other social groups in order to achieve their goals. In short, when it came to investment for reproductive purposes, landowners were prepared to delegate some of their economic authority to their tenants, arguably with the intention

of spreading some of the capital risks involved. The construction of demesnes and country houses was an entirely different matter. These
represented a much more personalized statement of the landowners'
social and world views, which did not depend for their realization on
the direct participation of other groups.

Agriculture   Although individual landowners were frequently active
promoters of agricultural improvement, the *overall* extent of landowner
involvement was surprisingly limited. Generally speaking, there is as
yet no reason to dispute Ó Gráda's view that few Irish landlords invested extensively on their agricultural estates either before or after the
Famine. Ó Gráda suggests that by the mid-nineteenth century, agricultural reinvestment in Ireland was running at no more than 3 percent
of gross rents, much lower than the comparable English figure.[54] The
reasons for this were threefold. First, unlike their English counterparts,
relatively few Irish landowners possessed *significant* external sources of
urban or industrial capital with which to finance agricultural improvement. In the main, this had to be financed from agricultural rents,
which made it vulnerable to the periodic deficiencies which occurred
in these rents even on the best-run estates.[55] Second, the predominantly pastoral nature of much Irish agricultural production may also
have acted to limit the need for extensive fixed-capital investment.
Prior to the expansion in tillage following Foster's Corn Law of 1784,
many of Ireland's regional economies were dominated by beef and
dairy production, neither of which demanded very much in the way of
structural investment. Moreover, in the rich grazing lands of south
Leinster and east Munster, it was the middlemen rather than the landowners who capitalized these livestock enterprises by acting as brokers
between their own subtenants and the cattle merchants.[56] Third, and
perhaps most importantly, the survival of lengthy leases for lives on
many Irish estates throughout the eighteenth and into the nineteenth
century provided a strong disincentive for landowner investment of
any kind. In many cases, the rents for these leases had been set at the
much lower levels prevailing in the 1730s and 1740s. Hence it was the
tenants rather than the landlords who had benefited from the rapid rise
in agricultural values in the second half of the century which culminated in the boom conditions of the Napoleonic War years. Moreover,

as long as the tenant paid his rent and fulfilled his leasehold obligations, his landlord had no legal right to intervene in the management of the land.

These constraints help to explain the timing and scale of the landlord involvement that did occur. Such evidence as there is suggests that this became more widespread from the late eighteenth century onward, as many landowners attempted to extract a greater financial return from their estates by shortening leases and raising rents, and as agriculture in general made a significant shift toward grain. These developments reduced the significance of the traditional tenurial constraint on landowner investment and at the same time provided an additional incentive for it. The most visible forms of improvement were seen in the modernization of demesne agriculture and in the spread of enclosure. Contemporary sources such as Young's *A Tour in Ireland*, published in Dublin in 1780, or the *County Statistical Surveys*, published by the Royal Dublin Society between 1801 and 1832, recorded the activities of individual "improving" landowners. Thus men such as Baron Foster at Collon, County Louth, or the Eccles and Richardson families in County Tyrone, set important local examples to their tenants and others by importing modern breeds of sheep and cattle, adopting new technology, and establishing new systems of integrated livestock /arable management.[57] In the event, many tenants were loath to adopt these innovations, preferring instead to retain traditional labor-intensive methods. It has recently been argued that these may have been more appropriate anyway to the difficult farming conditions found in many districts.[58]

If improving landowners enjoyed less than spectacular success in encouraging the adoption of modern technology in pre-Famine Irish agriculture, they were more successful in promoting structural efficiencies through engrossing and enclosure. The normal method of achieving this was through the enforcement of leasehold covenants, as for example on the Cork and Orrery estate at Caledon, County Tyrone, and the Midleton and Bernard estates in County Cork.[59] Thus in contrast to the English experience, in Ireland enclosure proceeded without significant recourse to legislation, providing eloquent testimony to the strength of the tenurial authority landowners might enjoy. Once again, a major regional distinction may be drawn between the predominantly "commercial" farming districts of the east and southeast and the more marginal environments of the western Atlantic littoral. In the former, formal engrossing and enclosure continued apace throughout the seventeenth and eighteenth centuries. It converted what had been a "champion" landscape of complex medieval and Tudor origins into a more efficient fieldscape held in severalty.

In the more marginal districts of western Ireland formal enclosure was more commonly a later, nineteenth-century phenomenon. It was closely associated with attempts by landowners to resolve the problems caused by the unprecedented pre-Famine population growth and associated excessive subdivision of holdings. By resettling the surplus tenants elsewhere or by encouraging them to emigrate, landowners might hope to reapportion the land on their estates among the remainder in such a fashion as to give each tenant a viable holding. One highly visible consequence of these proceedings were the so-called ladder farms that can still be found in western Ireland. Characteristically regular in shape, they formed part of an imposed geometric landscape designed to ensure that no tenant was unduly disadvantaged by the size and location of his tenancy.[60] This process of consolidation was greatly accelerated by the Famine, particularly in the smallholding districts of the west of Ireland. Faced with collapsing rentals and liable for the Poor Rate on behalf of their most impoverished tenants, landowners cleared their estates of people who were by now a complete drain on their resources. In consequence they opened the way for new relations of production with a reduced but, hopefully, economically viable tenant community.[61]

Industry   Landowner involvement in pre-Famine Irish industry took two forms: first, investment in widely dispersed but individually small primary extractive enterprises; and second, more widespread and successful investment in agrarian-related industry, particularly textiles. Mineral deposits were enthusiastically exploited by landowners as additional sources of income, but rarely sustained their initial profitability in the long term. One exception was the coal and iron ore mines operated by the Wandesworth family on their estate at Castlecomer, County Kilkenny. These were begun on a commercial basis in the late seventeenth century, and by the 1770s produced a profit of £10,000 a year.[62] Generally speaking, most Irish landowners' mining ventures were marked more by their owners' "insuppressible optimism" and the absence of sufficient external investment than by any sustained success. For example, the charcoal-based pig-iron production on the Petty and White estates in southwest County Cork dwindled in the face of fluctuating demand and fuel supply problems in the 1750s. Similarly, the copper mines that were opened on the Herbert estate in the same county at much the same time closed twenty years later.[63] Elsewhere in Ireland, coal continued to be mined in Counties Antrim, Tipperary, and Tyrone, while copper was worked in County Wicklow. But in the long term, increasing geological difficulties, combined with the high costs of extraction and transport, ensured the demise of these industries in the face of growing British competition in the mid-nineteenth century.[64]

Irish landowners were generally more successful in their promotion of the country's textile industries. The major example, in Ulster, has already been alluded to, and this was of course the local landowners' role in furthering the eighteenth-century domestic linen industry in that province. Individuals like Lord Hill of Hillsborough, County Down, or Arthur Brownlow at Lurgan, County Armagh, played an important entrepeneurial role in establishing brown linen markets by setting favorable leases to encourage weavers to settle, and if need be, by purchasing their production when demand fell.[65] Landowners played a similar role in encouraging textile production elsewhere in Ireland as well. In 1750, for example, Lord Grandison established Villierstown, in County Waterford, as a "Protestant Linen colony" populated by workers attracted from Ulster by the owner's offer of land and low rents. Linen production continued at Villierstown until the 1790s, partly protected by the restrictive covenants in the linen weavers' leases that required them to finish their linen using the facilities in the village. Like many other early linen ventures in Munster and Leinster, it declined thereafter.[66] The earl of Aldborough established a similar and, in the long term, similarly unsuccessful linen village at Stratford upon Slaney, County Wicklow, in 1780. Once again, the founder's express intention was to populate the "town" with Protestants. Six years later the earl transferred his interest in the linen manufactury to the Orr brothers from County Down. Forty years after that the industry was in decline, and the town was described as "poor and not improving."[67]

The Linen Board provided the means for many landowners to promote the industry on their own estates. The board had been established by act of the Dublin Parliament in 1711 and was comprised of
landowners and government representatives. It was charged with responsibility for encouraging linen production throughout Ireland by
means of education and subsidy.[68] The board's eventual failure as a
regulatory body and its disbandment in 1828 was partly the result of its
own inefficiency, but also reflected a more fundamental shift in the
balance of power within the industry. This transferred effective authority away from the landowners who had originally promoted it,
into the hands of the (Ulster) drapers and bleachers who had by then
long capitalized it.[69] This represented a significant stage in the transition from protoindustrial to factory-based production. In the first of
these phases, the industry had been largely financed by landed wealth.
During the second phase, industrial capitalists and wage labor were
linked in an entirely new set of production relationships in which
agrarian sources of capital were rendered insignificant.

Towns and Marketing   One notable feature of the changes in the
Irish space-economy during the eighteenth and early nineteenth centuries was the widespread modernization, foundation, or reconstruction
of over 750 provincial towns and villages of all sizes and functions, together with the extensive transformation of large parts of the major
cities, particularly Dublin, Cork, and Limerick. At one end of this spectrum of change were the newly planned "greenfield" settlements. Sometimes these were entirely new foundations, but frequently they replaced
earlier, decayed settlements. For example, John D'Arcy's new town at
Clifden, County Galway, was built between 1815 and 1835 as an entirely
new creation, whereas William Stewart's venture at Cookstown,
County Tyrone, was begun in the 1750s to replace a village destroyed in
the 1641 rebellion.[70] These newly founded or extensively transformed
towns and villages utilized a variety of formal planning elements. These
included orthogonal or linear street nets, squares, and crescents, as well
as architecturally important buildings treated as visual foci for proces-
sional vistas. The latter were particularly widespread, and can be seen,
for example, at Kingscourt, County Cavan, Lanesborough, County
Longford, and Strokestown, County Roscommon. Here, the vista leads

from the castellated demesne entrance to Strokestown House at one
end of the axis to the Anglican parish church at the other—a juxtaposi-
tioning of social icons that itself reflected the Anglican elite's dominance of contemporary Irish society. Similarly emphatic linear planning
occurs on a smaller scale at Summerhill, County Meath, and at Blessington, County Wicklow.

This formalism mirrored the far more grandiose Renaissance planning that occurred throughout urban Europe during the seventeenth
and eighteenth centuries.[71] However, the most immediate influence on
these Irish towns is likely to have been the extensive "Georgian" developments in Dublin and other Irish cities. Dublin's monopoly of the
apparatus of state in the post-Restoration period attracted a variety of
professional groups such as lawyers and bankers to the city, while the
presence of the Vice-Regal Court attracted the country's social and political elite. These elites created and "consumed" urban space in a
pattern which, as in other preindustrial European cities, was largely determined by the existing preurban cadastre of landownership.[72]

In the late seventeenth century the main expansion was to the south
of Dublin's old medieval core, where, for example, the earl of Longford's estate was rapidly developed from the 1660s onward.[73] For much
of the eighteenth century, however, most high-status residential growth
occurred to the north of the River Liffey, attracted there by the success
of speculators in creating fashionable and desirable developments. This
was especially true of the extensive Gardiner estate, which had been
amassed by Luke Gardiner from the 1720s onward. Throughout the
first half of the century Gardiner assiduously promoted and developed
his property to appeal to an aristocratic clientele. However, following
the construction of the Carlisle bridge in 1795, the area became more
closely integrated with the commercial districts to the south of the
Liffey. As a result both of this and the increasingly obvious inadequacy
of the infrastructural and amenity provision on the estate, the city's
aristocratic elite moved to more fashionable districts on the newly developed Fitzwilliam and Molesworth estates to the southeast of the city
center.[74] Although this piecemeal estate-based growth did not encourage the coherent organization of the city's development, attempts were
made to achieve this by corporation edict through the Wide Streets
Commissioners.[75] Moreover, the building controls exercised *within*

individual estates encouraged the architectural uniformity that remains characteristic of the "Georgian" districts around Merrion Square and St. Stephen's Green. As at Bath, Spa, Cheltenham, and other places of fashionable resort, these streets, squares, assembly rooms, and churches provided a stage on which the fashionable residential elite could parade their wealth and assert their status before their peers.[76]

The extensively and formally transformed settlements constituted but a part of the total number of Irish towns and villages that were improved during the eighteenth and early nineteenth centuries. In many other places change was much more limited, perhaps involving the reconstruction of individual buildings or streets no longer regarded as aesthetically pleasing or functionally adequate. These piecemeal transformations were frequently the consequence of the provision or extension of marketing, social, or industrial facilities, and involved the construction of marketplaces, courthouses, churches, schools, dispensaries, mills, or wharves. By definition, they were carried out in towns and villages of earlier—perhaps medieval or plantation—origin. As such they not only transformed but were also conditioned by the existing structures of inherited urban space.[77]

The balance between the inherited structures and those newly created during the eighteenth and nineteenth centuries varied in each town. For example, at Hacketstown, County Carlow, Boyle, County Roscommon, and Baltinglass, County Wicklow, the existence of formally planned public buildings and highly irregular property divisions suggests that a generally unplanned cadastre continued to exert a significant influence over what were relatively limited modernizing improvements. In other places the morphological impact of modernization was more formal and extensive, even though the towns and villages themselves were not totally transformed. Thus at Bailieborough, County Cavan, a small market square and adjacent market house define one end of the main visual axis and the Anglican parish church the other, but any overall sense of visual uniformity is lost because of the irregularity of the housing in between. At Cootehill, in the same county, it is precisely the uniformity in size and appearance of the buildings lining the main street that give rise to the town's striking visual coherence. At Athy, County Kildare, the formally laid-out eighteenth-century marketing complex built on the north bank of the River

Barrow by the town's patron, the duke of Leinster, provides a striking contrast with the irregular medieval street net running to the south.

The conventional assumption is that the main proponents of these changes were the property-owning elite themselves. Their very designation as *landlord* or *estate* towns and villages reflects this assumption. Thus Jones Hughes has identified a close relationship between the extent of such urban and village transformation and the size and value of the estates owned by their patrons. He argues that both were the expression of the "conformity and uniformity of landlord activity" in which "the estate operated as a kind of controlled environment within which there existed a strong ordering of elements, including settlement and community structures."[78] In the same vein, O'Connor envisages these towns as the material expression of "landlordism as a state of mind," a "controlled environment" in a "severely hierarchical world," in which "spatial order mirrored social order."[79] Inherent in these ideas is the assumption that the property owners involved were invariably agrarian landowners, an assumed congruity epitomized by Crawford's comment that "the heart of every estate was its town."[80]

In one sense, of course, the participation of members of the property-owning elite was inevitable. Given the private and exclusive nature of the Irish property code, the involvement of the enfeoffed or perpetuity landlord was axiomatic in the allocation of land for laying out a new settlement, as no other tenurial group had the authority to do this. Significantly, the known instances of settlement foundation by other agencies, for example the government's foundation of Williamstown, County Cork, or the so-called missionary settlements established by proselytizing Protestant societies in Counties Kerry, Limerick, and Mayo, occurred much later in the 1820s and 1830s. By then the accelerating pace of social, political, and economic change had already begun to undermine the landlords' social dominance and economic authority. Consequently, the towns and villages established by members of the propertied elite stand apart in the spectrum of settlement change. As specific instances of proprietorial initiative, they were perhaps more easily accomplished while their promoters' elite position within Irish society remained relatively secure.[81]

Where the processes of change were incremental and piecemeal rather than radical and transformative, landlord involvement was more likely to be indirect and exercised through the medium of building leases, rather than necessarily involving the outlay of substantial capital sums. If the proprietors took upon themselves the responsibility for constructing new institutional or infrastructural amenities, this sort of outlay did of course occur. But in many cases it seems that landlords were content to play an indirect role as *facilitators* of the improvements carried out by other, tenant, groups. The building leases used to achieve this offered the tenant a relatively long term of years or lives, but in return required him to bear most or all of the cost of constructing the property. These leases were in widespread though progressively diminishing use throughout Ireland until the early nineteenth century. They represented the delegation of some of the landlord's property rights to his tenant in what was intended to be a mutually advantageous bargain.[82] Whether one side subsequently gained more than the other depended on the future state of the economy. Crucially, however, it was this element of property *delegation* that enabled property-using rather than property-owning groups in Irish society to participate in urban and village improvement.

The identity of these other participants in urban and village improvement may well have grown increasingly varied as Ireland's society and economy modernized. Leasehold evidence suggests that in small eighteenth-century provincial market towns such as Cashel, County Tipperary, or Stranorlar, County Donegal, many of the tenants taking building leases were primarily either farmers or rentiers.[83] As time progressed these agriculturalists were increasingly supplanted in larger and functionally more complex towns by merchants and petty industrial capitalists. In ports such as Drogheda, County Louth, and textile towns such as Lurgan, County Armagh, "improving" tenants were increasingly drawn from the ranks of an urban bourgeoisie whose wealth was derived either from trade, from the professions, or from one of the agricultural processing industries.[84]

Further variation of a different sort was added by the progressive relaxation of the Penal Laws from the 1770s onward. The likely impact of this relaxation on the Catholic tenant community has already been discussed above. Although the real effect of this legislation has already been shown to be debatable, the formal rehabilitation of the Catholic tenants' rights of access to property can only have strengthened their participation in urban and village improvement. Although sizeable Catholic merchant communities may have existed in many towns prior to the 1760s, previous Catholic participation in urban improvement is likely to have been rendered more difficult—and less beneficial—by their formal tenurial disabilities.[85]

The repeal of the Penal Laws also opened up other avenues of participation in urban and village improvement for the Catholic community. The relaxation of the prohibitions against Catholic religious observance and the rehabilitation of Catholic property rights provided the Church with an opportunity to reestablish itself as a major institutional presence in many towns and villages. From the early nineteenth century onward, particularly in the historic hearthlands of Irish Catholicism in Leinster, east Munster, and the north midlands, the Church responded to the needs of its rapidly growing flock by constructing numerous chapels to service a parish network that was itself being steadily expanded.[86] The property transactions involved in this expansion remain unresearched. Each Catholic parish was theoretically responsible for erecting its own chapel, and it is thus probable that the acquisition of the site and funds for the subsequent building primarily involved the mobilization of the resources of the local Catholic community.

The extent of the landlords' participation in this programme of construction presumably depended on their attitude toward Catholicism in general. Some liberally disposed landlords sometimes gave the site for a chapel for nothing, as for example at Toor, County Waterford, and New Birmingham, County Tipperary.[87] Elsewhere, as at Dungarvan in 1809, landlords or their agents were more antagonistic. This may help to account for what Whelan has described as the "dialectical relationship" between estate villages and some of the four hundred or so informal hamlet-clusters that grew up around the new rural chapels, attracted by their nodality in parish life. Whelan envisages the former as indicative of social forces "unsympathetic to Catholicism," and implies that they were accordingly less likely to accommodate Catholic observance. Similar dialectical relationships have been argued to have existed in the towns. Jones Hughes has suggested that the new Catholic chapels were frequently located on the periphery of the towns, in a polar relationship with the centrally located icons of Anglican authority: the courthouse, the market house, and the Anglican church.

This too, he argues, reflected the subordinate status of the Catholic majority in Irish society.[88]

The Catholic Church was only one among a number of institutional agencies involved in the modernization of Irish towns and villages during the early nineteenth century. The growing legislative involvement of the British government in various aspects of Irish life left an increasing physical imprint on the urban environment. Various institutions of local government were established and were charged, among other things, with responsibility for public order, the provision of health and social welfare, and the regulation of urban communities. Each of these had to be accommodated within the fabric of the existing urban network. Under the Irish Constabulary Acts of 1822 and 1836, for example, police barracks were constructed in most towns and many of the larger villages.[89] The Poor Relief (Ireland) Act of 1838 created the system of Poor Law unions and led to the construction of numerous typically barracklike union workhouses. These formed new and visually dominant elements on the fringes of many Irish towns from the late 1830s onward, and provided an eloquent symbol of the changing nature of the forces promoting urban change in nineteenth-century Ireland.[90]

Significantly, in the early nineteenth century these innovative forces tended not to be generated by the most reactionary of the existing centers of municipal authority, the borough corporations. Prior to the Irish Municipal Reform Act of 1840, the thirty-three borough corporations that had survived the Act of Union continued to disburse their financial, social, and political patronage on a sectarian and divisive basis. McDonagh argues that these remaining corporations were essentially political institutions. Accordingly, unlike their English counterparts, they abdicated responsibility for the mundane business of paving roads, building sewers, and installing gas lighting.[91] Government legislation sanctioning these sorts of improvement had in fact been available to these corporations—as to other Irish towns—under the act for "lighting, cleansing and watching Irish cities and towns" of 1828. This had provided for the setting up of Town Commissions charged with overseeing these improvements, but few of the borough corporations had done anything to establish such commisions. However, following the abolition of the remaining borough corporations under the 1840 Municipal Reform Act, some twenty-five towns, including some of the ex-corporations subsequently elected commissioners under the 1828 act. Another twenty towns adopted essentially similar provisions under the 1854 Town Improvement (Ireland) Act.[92]

The motivations lying behind this urban and village improvement form the subject of much of the discussion in the remainder of this book. It may be noted here, however, that while the reasons for institutional involvement appear to be reasonably self-evident, those lying behind the intervention of individual landlords appear to have been more varied. Thus churches of all denominations were presumably concerned to provide accommodation for their members—and thereby assert or maintain ideological control over them—while the agencies of the state may be argued to have provided civic amenities that were perceived as socially stabilizing in their own right. On the other hand, landowners and tenants alike appear to have been driven by a variety of economic, social, and aesthetic imperatives. Only rarely were these explicitly stated, and it is therefore difficult to assess the relative importance of each. It seems probable, however, that economic motivations were paramount. Only by ensuring the reproduction of the existing economic system and their own advantageous position within it—through the control of marketing and redistribution—could landowners acquire the income necessary to pursue other social, political, or aesthetic goals. Viewed in this light, the extensive acquisition of market charters by landowners during the seventeenth and eighteenth centuries, and the widespread provision by landlords of market houses and shambles takes on a particular significance.[93] On the other hand, the morphological evidence for the functionally unnecessary architectural embellishment of the buildings in many "improved" towns, and the unequivocal evidence, discussed below, of politically motivated improvement, suggests that economic considerations were not the only reasons why landowners engaged in this form of modernizing activity. Arguably, these other social, political, and aesthetic goals also formed part of the property owners' attempted defense of their elite status, insofar as they either symbolized or helped reinforce the structures of authority that lay at its heart.

Communications   Landowners also attempted to improve local economic exchange by utilizing the system of county grand juries to pro-

mote improvements in inland transport. These juries had been set up
under an act of 1765 to finance and oversee the improvement and extension of Ireland's road and bridge network. Before this, local road improvements had been carried out on a parish basis. Each parish was
obliged by an act of 1613 to raise enough labor each year to maintain its
existing roads.[94] This responsibility did not extend to the construction
of new roads, and between the 1730s and 1750s most new arterial routes
were constructed by turnpike trusts. Set up as self-financing commercial ventures, their deficiencies soon became apparent. The income they
generated was rarely sufficient to cover the cost of maintaining the
roads, let alone to fund the capital cost of their construction. Consequently, there was little incentive to build turnpikes in the areas that
needed them most: the marginal districts inadequately served by existing transport and consequently barely integrated within the national
economy. Such places offered few prospects of future profit.

The 1765 act was designed to encourage road building by making it
less dependent on the probability of attracting minimum levels of traffic. Within each county, the proposals for new roads were submitted
for consideration by the grand jury. Those that were agreed to were
funded by an acreable cess paid by the baronies through which the
road was to pass. According to Arthur Young, this cess varied from between 3d and 6d per acre to as high as a 1/- an acre in County Meath.[95]
The grand juries were largely composed of local landowners newly appointed at each county court session by the county sheriff. Frequently
criticized as an unelected taxing body, from 1817 the grand juries were
only permitted to consider presentments once these had been first as-
sessed by local justices of the peace.[96] Nevertheless, long before its disbandment in 1898, the grand jury system had provided Ireland with a
road network that was generally adequate for the needs of its regional
economies.[97]

The much larger amounts of capital required for canal and railway
construction ensured that in Ireland both suffered from long-term
problems of capital availability. Canal construction began in Ireland
under the aegis of the Commissioners for Inland Navigation, set up by
act of the Dublin Parliament in 1729. The Newry Canal was begun in
1734 and was followed by the Grand Canal in 1756 and the Royal Canal
in 1786.[98] Within ten years, integrated canal and river navigations were

operating along most of the major river systems, including the Barrow, Munster Blackwater, Lagan, Shannon, Slaney, and Suir. Altogether, navigable waterways extended for over six hundred miles and in theory allowed for a major advance in the regional integration of the country's economy. The extent of landlord investment in these developments is difficult to assess. Cullen has argued that considerable "passive" land-lord investment occurred in canal stock during periods of rising income such as the 1740s and 1770s. As well as this, there is occasional evidence for more direct landowner involvement. The fifth duke of Devonshire's role in promoting the Lismore Canal between 1792 and 1796 is dis-cussed below, while in the same period the marquis of Abercorn spent £12,000 on the Strabane Canal.[99] Between 1801 and 1845 this sort of pri-vate investment in Irish canals may have amounted to over £1 million, when it was matched by the similar sum invested by the government.[100] Even with this additional funding, Ireland's canals never approached the success of those in England. For example, even at the height of their pre-Famine prosperity, the country's largest canals—the Grand and the Royal—carried no more than 350,000 tons of goods between them. Consequently both were vulnerable to the more efficient competition offered by the developing railway network. As in England, this compe-tition would eclipse the Irish canal system within a generation.

Ireland's "railway age" began with the standardization of the Irish gauge in 1846. The first proposal for an Irish railway had been made twenty-one years earlier in 1825, but the first line—between Dublin and Kingston—was not constructed until 1835. By 1850, over four hundred miles of track had been opened, including the main line from Dublin to Cork.[101] By 1854 the total network had expanded to over 860 miles and included the line between Belfast and Dublin. This had been completed with the construction of the viaduct over the River Boyne at Drogheda in 1853. Twelve years later the network had more than doubled to over 1,900 miles. By now, all of the potentially most profit-able routes had been completed, and the rate of investment corre-spondingly slowed, with only another 461 miles being added by 1880.[102] Initially, most of the capital required for these railways came from Eng-lish rather than Irish sources, and from speculative and business sources or from government.[103] Relatively little seems to have been pro-vided by Irish landowners, and thus the investment of over £200,000 by the seventh duke of Devonshire in Cork and Waterford railways appears to have been exceptional.

Landscape Ornamentation   The most extensive and visually striking of all the modernizing impacts on the Irish landscape brought about by the action of landowners and other members of the propertied class had relatively little to do with productive investment. These were the construction of numerous country houses and their associated landscaped parks. These parks formed part of the estate owner's demesne, that part of his land reserved for his exclusive use and which frequently included agricultural as well as recreational land. Estimates of the total number of houses and parks built in Ireland vary, and are rendered particularly imprecise by problems of definition. Bence-Jones suggests that over 2,000 "major" country houses were built in Ireland between 1660 and 1900.[104] The First Edition of the Ordnance Survey Six-Inch Maps, on the other hand, identifies over ten thousand individual country houses by name, but many of these lacked a demesne and were probably no more than substantial farmhouses.[105] More immediately comparable with Bence-Jones's estimate are likely to have been the 2,596 houses identified by these maps which stood in demesnes of fifty acres or more.

By the 1840s there was considerable regional variation in the distribution of these larger demesnes. They were least numerous in mid- and west Ulster and in west Connacht and Kerry in the far southwest, and most frequent in an eastern midland belt running from Counties Longford and Westmeath in the north through Laois and Offaly to Tipperary in the south. Previous research has demonstrated a strong positive relationship between the size of these demesnes and their parent estates.[106] Thus we may tentatively conclude that the areas characterized by numerous large demesnes were also characterized by the survival of significant numbers of relatively large estates. The apparent absence of many magnate estates in mid- and west Ulster may be a distant echo of the plantations. Theoretically, most planters had been limited to holdings of no more than 3,000 acres.[107] Significantly, some of the largest and most valuable Ulster estates, for example, the marquis of Downshire's 64,000 acres, Forde of Seaforde's 19,000 acres, or the earl of Clandeboye's 18,000 acres, were located in County Down, which lay beyond the limit of the formal plantation.

This investment by landowners in country house and demesne construction has conventionally been regarded as conspicuous consumption, designed to reaffirm the owner's membership within his peer group rather than to add anything to the growth of the productive economy.[108] In fact, their resource implications may have been less negative than this judgment implies. An analysis of the 134 demesnes in County Down indicated that in 1834 they accounted for only 14,820 acres, or less than 2.5 percent of the county's total agricultural land. Furthermore, many of the largest demesnes were located on marginal land with poor agricultural potential, and required relatively small amounts of capital for their construction. On some demesnes, this "ornamental" land also supported ancillary pastoral and forestry enterprises. In the case of the marquis of Downshire's park, built at Hillsborough between 1742 and 1800, the cost of construction amounted to under £4,800—less than 1 percent of the total income generated by the estate during the same period. On the Annesley's property at Castlewellan, sales of timber from the demesne averaged £320 a year during the 1790s, while at Tollymore, the earl of Clanbrassil's newly planted woods were thought to be worth over £2,500 in 1792.[109]

Irrespective of their resource implications, both demesnes and country houses had an important iconographic role to play in symbolizing and reinforcing the status differential between the property-owning minority and the rest of society. It was precisely because of this symbolic role that many successful urban merchants and industrialists bought country estates. In doing so, they enhanced their perceived social status.[110] This social distancing derived from the response of country-house and landed-park designs to changes in the aesthetic canon. By reconstructing his house or park in response to these changes, the landowner reaffirmed his social standing by signaling his adherence to his peers' aesthetic norms.

These ideals were Renaissance in origin, and hence, being of European provenance, they transcended the social milieu of landownership in Ireland. Just as in Europe, so too in Ireland, the formal garden designs of the late seventeenth century gave way to romantic reaction, the picturesque. By the 1730s the geometrical formality of earlier gardens, reflecting perhaps André le Nôtre's innovative work at Versailles in the 1650s, was replaced by increasingly naturalistic designs.[111] Consequently, few instances of the earlier formal style survive. Kilruddery, County Wicklow, provides a single almost complete example. Here, rectangular canals, radial walks, and focal statuary create a sense of "architectural" space linking the house and garden. Less completely formal gardens still survive in the grounds of Antrim Castle, while others now lost were to be seen in the 1840s at Mount Uniacke, County Cork, Grange House, County Kilkenny, and Golden Grove, County Offaly. The thoroughness with which the earlier designs were replaced by the new naturalism in the mid-eighteenth century bears eloquent witness both to the appeal—and the appropriateness—of the new style in Ireland. As in England, and despite utilizing the relatively greater textural variety of the Irish landscape, these later landscaped parks remained heavily contrived. Woodlands and vistas were artificially created and embellished with romantic shell houses, grottos, or classical statues, which in their contrast with the "natural" surroundings were intended to emphasize the "wildness" of nature and provoke awe at its sublimity.[112]

By the 1840s these features could be seen in numerous large demesnes throughout Ireland. Generally speaking, a consistent relationship existed between the size of a demesne and the extent of its ornamentation. In County Waterford, for example, larger demesnes tended to be almost exclusively ornamental, while smaller demesnes were much more likely to contain a significant amount of agricultural land. We may reasonably infer that only on larger estates could a significant area be devoted to predominantly noncommercial land uses, as the viability of smaller estates depended on the full utilization of the property's agricultural potential.[113]

The changing imperatives of fashion also dictated similarly frequent changes in country-house architecture. Consequently, few of the numerous houses built on the widespread rent boom of the 1720s and 1730s survive unaltered. The vast majority were either modified or replaced during the subsequent building boom generated by the agricultural expansion of the later eighteenth and early nineteenth centuries.[114] Accordingly, only a handful of early eighteenth-century Palladian houses survive to the present day, including Drumcondra House, County Dublin, and Strokestown, County Roscommon. On the other hand, the neoclassical houses built on the proceeds of the later boom remain well represented in the Irish landscape. Of relatively plain design, these later houses—aptly described as "Georgian boxes"—were distinguished from Palladian examples by their simpler ground plans and restrained detailing. Like the Palladian houses—and the "Gothick," "Tudor," and "Elisabethan Revival" houses that were subsequently built in the 1820s and after—they signaled the landowners' willingness and ability to affiliate to the changing norms of their peers and thereby distance themselves from the vast majority of Irish society.

Summary

The century and a half between the final flickering of politically inspired land confiscation in 1703 and the Great Famine of 1845–1849 has been shown to have been a period of profound social and regional adjustment in Ireland. Virtually no aspect of Irish life remained untouched by the diverse effects of the two most fundamental characteristics of the period: population growth and modernization. Moreover, these effects were by no means always benign. Thus, the worsening imbalance between a regionally diverse pattern of population growth and the resources available to support this growth created conditions of extreme and growing immiseration over much of western Ireland in the fifty or sixty years prior to the outbreak of potato blight in 1845. Elsewhere, historically different patterns of resource availability and exploitation created social conditions that tended to limit the extent of this population growth and mitigate its worst social, economic, and demographic consequences.

The development of Ireland's society and economy during these years may thus be characterized in terms of a dialectic between the negative impacts of this population growth on the one hand, and the very real advances made by the forces of modernization on the other. These have been shown to have included not only technological and structural improvements in economic production and marketing, but also a wide variety of social and political adjustments. Notable among the latter was the rectification of the marginalized position of significant numbers of Catholics with the repeal of the Penal Laws. However, with their readmission into the mainstream of Irish economic and political life, new cleavages opened up within pre-Famine society, as representatives of the Catholic majority sought to strengthen and extend their penetration of the structures of representative political authority.

This process was essentially one of democratization. Inevitably it brought a challenge to the position of the property-owning minority who had dominated Irish social, economic and political life throughout the eighteenth century. The challenge was initially political but presaged equally fundamental economic demands. With state support, these were ultimately to erode the elite's economic basis in landownership. The connection between the two was not coincidental. Ever since the fundamental land reallocations of the sixteenth and seventeenth centuries, economic and political authority in Ireland had reinforced each other in the hands of the propertied minority.

In contrast to the conventional stereotypes of Irish historiography, these property owners—landowners in the main—have been shown to have constituted a far from seamless cultural group. While it is true that they originated in large part in the colonial transformations of the plantations and after, they were increasingly riven by a variety of social, political, ethnic, and cultural divisions that deepened as time went on and their numbers increased. Even so, they remained set apart from the rest of Irish society by the particular benefits that accrued to them from their monopoly of property ownership. It is suggested here that foremost among these benefits was the extensive—but not untrammelled—discretionary authority they enjoyed to pursue social, economic, and political strategies which were to the benefit of their own class interests. The property owners' attempts to preserve their authority necessarily involved its partial delegation to other social groups. In the event, this proved insufficient to preserve it and them from the challenge posed by the political and economic mobilization of the property-using majority—backed by the state—in the nineteenth century.

The development of the duke of Devonshire's urban and other estates in Counties Cork and Waterford thus occurred against a rapidly changing demographic, economic, social, and political background. Events on the estate mirrored many of these changes. Although coming late into the family's ownership (in 1748), the property originated in the plantation of Munster, and in fact constituted a regionally important example of the continuing influence that phase of colonial settlement had on the subsequent cadastre of landownership in Ireland. The lands inherited by the Devonshires were very much the same as those initially acquired by Sir Walter Raleigh and subsequently bought by Richard Boyle. By the time of its acquisition by the Devonshires, the estate supported a diverse range of urban and rural communities, divided in their turn on sectarian as well as economic grounds. Accordingly, different parts of the estate posed very different management problems for the duke and his advisers. These problems became increasingly complex as the processes of modernization and population growth continued. Further complexity was added by changes in the attitude of successive dukes and their agents, and the diverse response these engendered from among the tenant community. Between them, these factors created urban communities that were distinctive in their character and organization and in their relationship with each duke. It is to these communities and this relationship and the questions they pose concerning patronage and social authority in Ireland that we now turn.

CHAPTER 3

The Origins, Administration, and Income of the Duke of Devonshire's Irish Estate, 1764–1891

The duke of Devonshire's property stood out as one of a small number of magnate estates in Ireland capable of generating very large incomes. By 1876 only sixteen other families in the country owned more than the 60,000 acres owned by the duke,[1] and only the Downshire, Fitzwilliam, King-Harman, Leinster, Longford, and Wallace estates produced a rent roll in excess of the £44,000 due to him in that year.[2] Nevertheless, even at its maximum extent (circa 1858), the Devonshires' Irish estate barely exceeded 30 percent of the family's total holdings in the British Isles, computed by Bateman in 1876 to be more than 198,000 acres.[3]

The Devonshires acquired their Irish estate in the mid-eighteenth century, but its origins lay in the Munster Plantation of the late sixteenth century. In 1586 Sir Walter Raleigh, one of the original plantation undertakers, acquired the reservation of three and a half seignories—about 42,000 statute acres—in east County Cork and west County Waterford.[4] After the grant was confirmed a year later, Raleigh held this abnormally large area as the seignory of Inchiquin for a "bargain" rent equivalent to that paid for a normal seignory of 12,000 acres.[5] Shortly thereafter Raleigh appears to have lost interest in the property, and by 1602 negotiations were underway for its sale to Richard Boyle, clerk of the Munster Council. The original agreement between Raleigh and Boyle stipulated that Boyle should pay £1,500 for the estate, but in 1603 the purchase was jeopardized by Raleigh's imprisonment and attainder for treason.[6] Raleigh's estates automatically reverted to the Crown, and Boyle only secured their release and his title to them by bribing Crown officials. Boyle's payment to Raleigh was for the inheritance of the seignory. In addition, he spent at least another £1,500 buying out the existing lessee together with his various subtenants, as well as 1,000 marks given to Elizabeth I to clear the land of "unwise estates and encumbrances."[7]

Raleigh's estate formed the nucleus of the vast property Boyle acquired in Munster over the next forty years. Ennobled as the earl of Cork in 1620, by 1641 Boyle owned part or all of ten Munster seignories in addition to Inchiquin, as well as extensive lands elsewhere in Ireland. He bought Ballymacdonnell seignory on the Dingle Peninsula (County Kerry) in the 1600s, and part of Cloghley seignory (County Waterford) together with substantial lands in Carberry and the Ivagh Peninsula a few years later. The latter were confirmed to Boyle by royal grant in 1620, and were divided into the manors of Ballydehob, Clonakilty, and Enniskean. At the same time Boyle was also active to the east of Enniskean in the Bandon valley. Between 1610 and 1619 he acquired the Castlemahony seignory from Phane Becher, and with it the town of Bandon, founded in the early 1600s under Henry Becher.[8] By 1623 Boyle had bought the adjacent Kinalmeaky seignory and, in County Waterford, the western half of Sir Christopher Hatton's original seignory of Knocknamona, near Dungarvan. The purchases continued. In 1628 Boyle acquired Skiddy's Castle in Cork and, in 1635, further lands in Corgrig seignory (County Limerick). He bought three-quarters of the Askeaton seignory in the same county shortly afterward. Further small acquisitions in the Kilmore and Clandonnell Roe seignories completed the Munster purchases by 1641. By this time Boyle also owned extensive property elsewhere in Ireland, including County Meath, King's County (Offaly), Queen's County (Laois), and Counties Clare, Tipperary, Roscommon, Mayo, Sligo, Dublin, Kildare, Wicklow, Wexford, and beyond.[9]

Not all of these enormous possessions descended to the duke of Devonshire. The first earl of Cork (the "Great Earl") bequeathed the greater part of his outlying estates together with some land in County Cork to his three surviving younger sons. His second son, Lewis, baron of Bandonbridge and viscount Boyle of Kinalmeaky, had been killed at

the battle of Liscarroll in 1642. Under the terms of the Great Earl's last
will, his third son, Roger, Baron Broghill (later first earl of Orrery), received virtually all the Kerry and Limerick estates, together with property in Cork and Dublin. The fourth son, Francis Boyle (later Viscount
Shannon), received numerous townlands in the barony of Barrymore
together with land in Devon. The fifth son, Robert Boyle, inherited the
estates in Connacht, together with land in Dublin, Kildare, King's and
Queen's Counties, Tipperary, Wicklow, and Wexford, as well as land in
the baronies of Orrery and Kilmore in County Cork. Thus the Great
Earl's eldest son, Richard, inherited a somewhat reduced Irish estate,
which nevertheless still included the bulk of the Cork and Waterford
seignories and amounted to over ninety thousand statute acres.[10] By the
time the estate had passed to the duke of Devonshire, it had been diminished still further. Between 1728 and 1738 the fourth earl of Cork
(and third earl of Burlington)[11] sold some £280,000 worth of land in
Cork and Waterford in order to continue his artistic and architectural
pursuits. Purchasers included Lord Duncannon, Henry Boyle, and Sir
William Heathcote, who bought more land from the estate in 1745.[12]

Despite these sales, the Burlington estates as they are properly
termed, remained among the foremost properties in Ireland. Moreover,
the family also retained extensive holdings in England, including estates at Londesborough and Castle Bolton in Yorkshire and property in
Chiswick and Piccadilly in London. Accordingly, when Lady Charlotte
Boyle, heiress of the fourth earl of Cork, married the marquis of Hartington, heir to the third duke of Devonshire in 1748, the match was regarded by many as an outstanding dynastic alliance. The bridegroom
and his father certainly thought so. The bridegroom's mother did not,
and the marriage only went ahead against the sustained and violent
opposition of the third duke's duchess.[13]

Lady Hartington survived her father by less than a year. He died in
December 1753, and she, prematurely in childbirth, in 1754. But by this
time the birth of three sons and a daughter to the Hartingtons had
secured the dynastic succession. Thus when Hartington succeeded as
fourth duke of Devonshire in December 1755, he brought with him the
vast Burlington inheritance. Admittedly, the Irish estate was initially
encumbered with a jointure for the Dowager Lady Burlington, but this
ceased with her death in 1758.

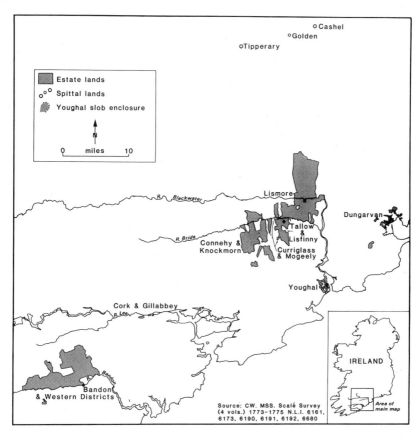

FIGURE 3.1   The Devonshire Estate at Its Maximum Extent, circa 1858

The fifth duke of Devonshire succeeded to the title as a minor in
1764, and came fully into his inheritance at his coming of age in 1769.
Despite the sales of land by his father, he inherited an Irish estate that
amounted to some 61,000 acres. Apart from the purchase of the small
Osborne estate in Dungarvan in 1809 and some property near Bandon
in 1873, successive dukes added little further land.[14] Consequently, the
estate inherited by the fifth duke was very much the same as that dis-
membered by the seventh duke in 1859 (see figure 3.1). The bulk of the
land, some 40,700 acres, lay in County Waterford in the valleys of the
Rivers Bride and Blackwater and on the adjacent Knockmealdown
mountains. A further 18,800 acres lay fifty miles to the southwest

around Bandon in south County Cork. The remainder consisted of small portions of spittal land[15] in County Tipperary, together with detached portions near Cork, Dungarvan, and Youghal. In addition, the duke also owned the tithes of twenty-six parishes.[16]

The Urban Estate in the 1770s

The urban estate consisted of the entire towns of Lismore and Tallow, the original plantation urban core at Bandon, approximately half the towns of Dungarvan and Youghal, Skiddy's Castle in Cork, and a house in Waterford. These places were of diverse origins. Bandon had been founded as a plantation "new town" between 1600 and 1610, while Tallow had been refounded as a plantation borough on the site of an earlier decayed town some years earlier.[17] Dungarvan was established as a port by the Anglo-Normans in the twelfth century, Lismore was founded as a monastic center in the seventh century and Youghal was created—possibly as a Viking longphort or defended harbor—in the ninth.[18] By the late eighteenth century the appearance of these towns mirrored the exigencies of their subsequent development. In function and morphology they were the result of the complex and continuing interplay between their own internal economic, social, and political structures and the broader processes of geohistorical change that provided the external context for these. Each of the towns had received a charter of incorporation from James I. These charters either confirmed earlier privileges, as at Youghal, or else created them for the first time, as at Bandon.[19] In every case, they established a form of local government based on a limited elective franchise that encouraged the growth of nonrepresentative oligarchies. By contrast, the towns' economic roles became more divergent as time progressed. Bandon's cloth industry increasingly set it apart as a manufacturing center,[20] while Youghal's gradually declining maritime trade and port-related industries were still sufficient to distinguish it from Dungarvan, itself officially accounted as one of Youghal's "creeks."[21] Tallow prospered in a modest way, initially as a cloth manufacturing center and later as an agricultural market, but Lismore declined into "a shadow of its former greatness."[22] Clearly, by the

1770s each town offered very different opportunities for future land-lord investment.

The Urban Population

Table 3.1 lists various population estimates for the estate towns in the period between 1773 and 1800. The figures indicate both the total population of each town and the tenant population on the Devonshire estate within it. O'Flanagan has recently suggested that while Dungarvan, Lismore, and Tallow experienced slight population growth between the 1650s and the 1770s, Bandon and Youghal may have lost population, although the influx of refugees into these towns after the 1641 rebellion may mean that this decline was more apparent than real.[23] A comparison with McCarthy-Morrogh's more precise population estimates for Munster towns in 1642 suggests that Bandon, Tallow, and Youghal all experienced significant growth by 1800. At Bandon and Tallow the population may have trebled to reach around 5,000–6,000 and 2,250, respectively, while at Youghal it may virtually

TABLE 3.1
The Estate Towns: Population Estimates, 1773–1800

	Bandon	Dungarvan	Lismore	Tallow	Youghal
Scalé 1773–1776 Houses	457	230	206	266	273
Tenants (houses x 4)	1,828	920	824	1,064	1,092
Tenants (houses x 5)	2,285	1,150	1,030	1,330	1,365
Tenants (houses x 5.5)	2,514	1,265	1,133	1,463	1,502
*Other total population estimates**					
1784	7,000	2,000	600+	1,000+	n.d.
1791	n.d.	480	780	1,180	n.d.
1798 houses	1,025	1,041	233	408	1,175
Population (houses x 4)	4,100	4,164	932	1,632	4,700
Population (houses x 5)	5,125	5,205	1,165	2,040	5,875
Population (houses x 5.5)	5,637	5,726	1,282	2,244	6,463
1800 houses	1,196	1,377	235	429	1,223
Population (houses x 4)	4,784	5,508	940	1,716	4,892
Population (houses x 5)	5,980	6,885	1,175	2,145	6,115
Population (houses x 5.5)	6,578	7,574	1,293	2,360	6,727

*See note 25.
n.d. = no data.

have quadrupled to reach about 6,000. At Dungarvan the population was probably marginally higher at about 7,500. Lismore remained the smallest of the settlements with no more than 1,300 inhabitants. Apart from this sort of general speculation, we know little about the nature of demographic change in these towns in the later eighteenth century, and at present cannot attempt to answer even the most basic questions currently comprising the agenda for demographic studies in English urban history.[24]

It is possible, however, to draw at least some conclusions from table · 3.1 about the relative size of the estate within the towns, and about the towns themselves as components in the Irish urban system in the later eighteenth century. Recent commentators have used the Hearth Money returns of 1798–1800 to reconstruct the urban system of the day, and have relied on estimated population size as the major criterion for categorization. Although the Hearth Money returns are incomplete and imperfect, they have been accepted as an adequate basis for an approximate ranking of Irish towns.[25] At the same time, writers have been aware of the need to apply as wide as possible a range of diagnostic criteria when defining urban status. While population estimates are often used for this purpose for sound pragmatic reasons, it is important not to assume that the complexity of each town's functional array was necessarily proportional to its population size.[26] Thus like Clarkson before him, Sheehan has stressed the usefulness to Irish urban history of Clark and Slack's earlier list of diagnostic features for the early modern town. As well as "an unusual concentration of population," these include a specialist economic function, a complex social structure, a sophisticated political order, and a distinctive influence beyond its boundaries.[27] In practice, however, published accounts of the Irish urban system circa 1798–1800 have been able to do little more than note the major functional characteristics attached to each size-category of town.

The picture that emerges is of a hierarchical urban system dominated by Dublin as a primate city, but which was also characterized by an extremely broad base comprised of numerous small market centers. Such a system is best described as a "primate hierarchy," that is, as an urban network in which the size distribution of the smaller towns adhered in some degree to the service principles delineated by central place theory, but in which the largest center, Dublin, performed a variety of national political, social, economic, and administrative roles that were reflected in its disproportionately large size. Carter has suggested that this sort of primate hierarchy existed in early modern England, and has postulated various determinant preconditions for its development that seem to apply to late-eighteenth-century Ireland. These include a mature political system and an advanced economy, but one in which "the prime urban role remains service for a countryside where the activities are agricultural and evenly spread rather than industrial and a consequence of point production."[28]

The most detailed reconstruction of the Irish urban system using the Hearth Money returns has been done by Clarkson, who identifies a six-rank hierarchy dominated by Dublin with an estimated population of about 200,000.[29] Next came Cork with a population of 80,000, and in the third rank the four major regional ports of Belfast, Drogheda, Limerick, and Waterford with perhaps 12,000–15,000 people each. The fourth rank comprised a dozen or so towns including Bandon, Dungarvan, and Youghal with populations in excess of 5,000–6,000, all but two of which were ports. Beneath these was a group of eighteen towns with populations of between 2,500 and 5,000; this group included many of the larger inland market centers such as Armagh and Kilkenny. Finally, forming the broad base of the hierarchy were a further seventy-three towns, each with a population of less than 2,500. This basal group included Lismore and Tallow. The duke of Devonshire's urban interests thus included property in three of the larger and more important provincial towns in Ireland, as well as in two centers of more modest size. Bandon, Dungarvan, and Youghal all figure in the highest quartile and were comparable in size with towns such as Galway, Kilkenny, or Londonderry. Tallow was larger than Dungannon, Naas, or Roscommon, and even Lismore, the smallest of the duke's towns, ranked sixty-fifth out of the 108 towns listed, and was larger than Wicklow or Cavan.

Clearly, however, this simple size comparison does not indicate the true extent of the duke's urban interests, since in the three largest towns his tenants constituted only a minority of the total population. The estimated percentage they represented obviously varies according to which household multiplier is employed and which population estimate chosen. Accordingly, it is probably most useful simply to note the

relative size order of the tenant population in each town. In Dungarvan and Youghal this varied between 17 and 25 percent, while at
Bandon it was of the order of 26–38 percent. At Bandon, the fifth duke
shared the role of urban patron with the Bernard family, much of
whose property in and around the town was in fact held from him
on a head lease. At Youghal, the corporation was the other major
property-owner, while Dungarvan was divided among a number of
proprietors, including the Hoares and the Osbornes.[30] In the larger
towns at least, the duke of Devonshire's influence as patron was therefore circumscribed by the existence of other proprietors whose objectives and attitudes toward their estates were frequently at variance
with his. These differences were most acutely realized in the political
arena, and it was here that the real limitations to the duke of Devonshire's patronal role in Bandon, Dungarvan, and Youghal were most
frequently made apparent.

The Morphology of the Urban Estate, circa 1773–1776

The social, political, and tenurial relations between the duke and his
urban tenants were played out within built environments of varying
complexity. Table 3.2 is derived from a survey carried out by Bernard
Scalé, a French surveyor employed to map the Devonshire estate be-

TABLE 3.2
The Urban Estate: Area and Housing Stock, 1773–1776

	Bandon	Dungarvan	Lismore	Tallow	Youghal
Area (stat. acres)*	134	28	52	60	37
Built-up area (stat. acres)	80	21	47	37	34
Total properties recorded by Scalé	468	241	211	277	287
Total residences recorded by Scalé	457	230	206	266	273
Total cabins recorded by Scalé	180	190	152	177	82
Cabins as a % of residences	39	83	74	67	30
% residences slated	8	10	11	23	40

*Excluding town lands and parks

tween 1773 and 1776, and highlights the variations in the urban estate in the different towns. Figures 3.2–3.6(a,b) reproduce Scalé's urban plans, and these reflect some aspects of each town's evolution. At Bandon, the largest of the duke's urban properties (see table 3.2), there is clear evidence of accretive suburban growth on the estate to the north of the river, and this was presumably a consequence of the town's pronounced population growth since the 1640s (see figures 3.2a, 3.2b). This expansion involved the demolition of part of the town's seventeenth-century defenses. These are shown in their entirety in a pictographic plan dated circa 1615, together with adjacent tenements that were themselves subsequently redeveloped.[31] This growth was reflected in other variations evident in the housing stock from the 1775 survey. Along the two main axes in the original plantation borough, Main Street and North Street, the building plots were markedly attenuated with breadth:length ratios of over 1:5, and contained "houses" rather than the presumably lower status "cabins" of the peripheral suburbs. The plot ratios in these outer areas were generally much lower— usually below 1:2, reflecting the fact that many were still only partly built-up. By contrast, the centrally located plots contained much rear development as well as formal gardens and frequent evidence of subdivision, particularly along Main Street. Indeed, as on the estate at Youghal but in contrast to the smaller towns, the vast majority of the duke's property in Bandon was of superior status. O'Flanagan has argued that as in other Irish towns, in Bandon social access to these different types of housing had a strong sectarian dimension.[32] Seventeenth-century bylaws had effectively excluded Roman Catholic Gaelic-Irish and Old English families from living within the plantation borough,[33] and the legacy of this discrimination continued into the 1770s. The high-status housing located in the center of the town and in the inner suburbs was occupied almost exclusively by Protestants, while the low-status housing on the periphery, where it frequently formed part of limited piecemeal developments that had not yet obscured the underlying agricultural field pattern, was largely tenanted by Roman Catholics.

The duke's estate at Dungarvan was the smallest and most fragmented of all his urban properties. Most of the estate lay scattered outside the original medieval borough. This had occupied the area to

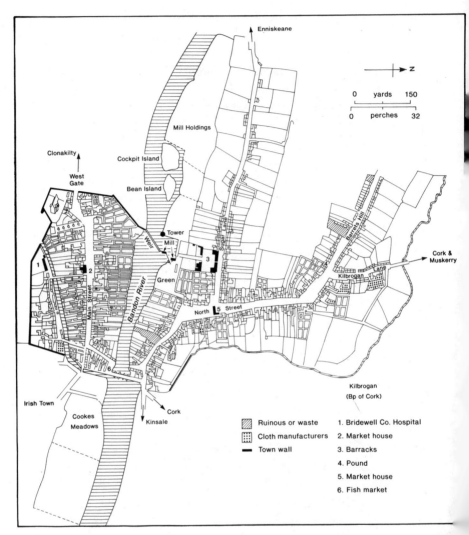

FIGURE 3.2A   The Urban Estate at Bandon in 1775: Property Boundaries

the east of Clubber's Lane as a *suburbium* to the Anglo-Norman castle, itself subsequently rebuilt as a barracks. Within this intramural nucleus, the duke owned only a scatter of houses at the end of Church Lane and Barrack Lane (see figures 3.3a, 3.3b). Beyond the town and its suburb across the River Colligan at Abbeyside, the estate included several rural

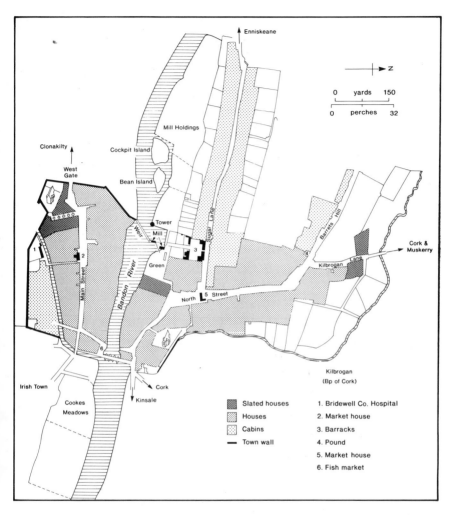

FIGURE 3.2B   The Urban Estate at Bandon in 1775: Housing Types

townlands and—reflecting the town's medieval origins—the lordship of the manor of Dungarvan and the tithe of all fish landed there.[34]

The schematic nature of Scalé's map of the Dungarvan estate makes it difficult to compare the type and quality of the duke's housing with that in the rest of the town. By the 1770s most of the duke's housing beyond the borough walls consisted of small cabins in poor condition, "built of mud, covered with straw [and] mostly old."[35] In fact over 80

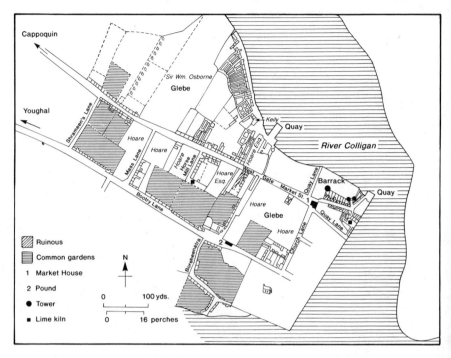

FIGURE 3.3A   The Urban Estate at Dungarvan in 1775: Property Boundaries

percent of the duke's housing was of cabin status—the highest proportion in any of his towns (see table 3.2). Many of these cabins shared
access to large communal gardens, suggesting a divisionary building
process in which initially quite large holdings were progressively subdivided by leaseholders to provide cheap housing—presumably for the
fishermen who constituted the bulk of Dungarvan's population. Most
of the duke's property within the walled nucleus appears originally to
have been of rather higher quality. Scalé designates this as slated
housing, frequently with extensive rear stores and often ruinous.
Neither the perspective view of the town published in 1748 nor the
map of the Hoare estate surveyed in 1760 indicate a similar degree of
dereliction in other properties in the town.[36] Accordingly, it seems
likely that, as in Lismore and Youghal, by the 1770s the duke's estate in
Dungarvan had been permitted to fall into an unusually dilapidated
condition.

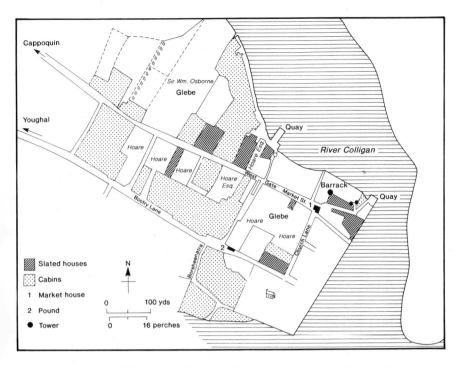

FIGURE 3.3B   The Urban Estate at Dungarvan in 1775: Housing Types

The dereliction at Lismore was widespread and belied the town's earlier importance. Nevertheless, traces of this significance were still to be found in its plan and morphology (see figures 3.4 a, 3.4 b). For example, the "cathedral" depicted by Scalé stood on the site of the early Christian monastery reputedly founded by Saint Carthage in A.D. 631, around which the original pre-Norman settlement had grown.[37] The castle was founded on its present site by John I in 1185, and was used as the residence of the bishops of Lismore until the see was united with Waterford in 1363.[38] No borough charter or any of the other trappings of legally defined urban status have been discovered for the medieval settlement, yet it is clear that when Lismore was enlarged and enfranchised in the early seventeenth century, both settlers and charter alike were attracted to an existing community.[39] However, additional clues concerning the nature of medieval Lismore can be derived from the placenames on Scalé's map. "The Warren" and "Spittle Field" indicate

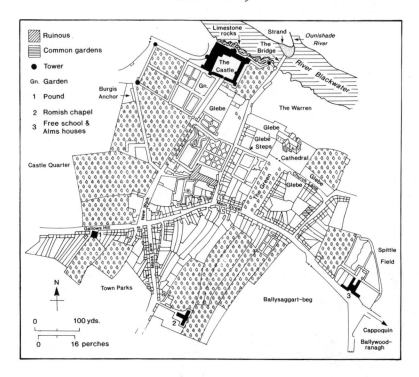

FIGURE 3.4A   The Urban Estate at Lismore in 1773: Property Boundaries

specific medieval land uses that were presumably reserved for the castle or one of the ecclesiastical institutions associated with the see. Indeed, the close proximity of the castle and the church aptly symbolize the dominant and mutually reinforcing social role of the Church and no-bility within feudal society in medieval Ireland.

By 1773 this relative grandeur was a thing of the past. Despite the relatively large average size of the properties in the town (see table 3.2), many were ruinous—and had been since at least the 1740s. In 1746 Smith commented "that instead of its ancient lustre, the cathedral, castle and a few tolerable houses intertwixt with cabbins are all that now appear [in Lismore]."[40] Fifty years later the agent was more specific. Writing after the depredations committed during William Conner's agency, Henry Bowman concluded that "the main street, and a few other houses in most of the other streets have been tolerably decent houses for the country, built with stone, clay, mortar, and covered with

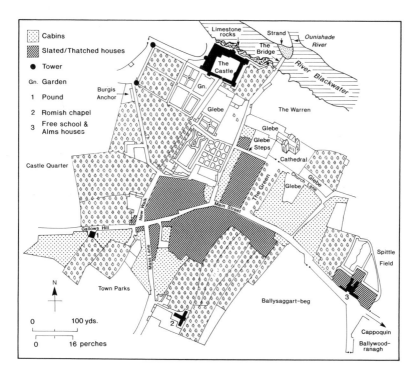

FIGURE 3.4B   The Urban Estate at Lismore in 1773: Housing Types

slates, but the rest are built with mud and covered with straw like cabins. At present the town (a few houses excepted) is almost in ruins."[41] Given this evidence for excessive dilapidation, it is probably unwise to place too much reliance on the housing differentials identified by Scalé in 1773. Nevertheless, if taken at face value, these indicate the existence of a crude centripetal status pattern. The properties on the south side of Main Street and on the west side of Ferry Lane were particularly large. Those at the eastern end of Main Street represent the only likely survivals of medieval burgages in the town; this area also contained the only slated housing as well as most of the thatched houses. As at Bandon, cabin development was peripheral, but accounted for nearly three-quarters of the housing stock—the highest proportion in any of the duke's towns except Dungarvan.

    The housing was located around an irregular street plan dominated by the road from Tallow to Cappoquin and by the castle, church, and green as major plan-form elements. The street names provide some circumstantial evidence for different phases in the town's development. Thus the "New Walk" leading to the castle entrance may be presumed to have been a relatively recent addition, possibly dating from the refurbishment of the town and castle in the early seventeenth century, when the free school and almshouses were built by the first earl of Cork. Ferry Lane no longer led to that particular facility but to the new bridge being built under the direction of Thomas Ivory.[42] Mass Lane led to the Roman Catholic chapel which had been built at the edge of the town. Jones Hughes suggests that the chapel's peripherality was typical of the location of chapels, ball parks, and fair greens in pre-Famine Irish towns in general. He argues that these represented the informal interests of the mass of the people, and that their siting provides an apt metaphor for the marginalized social position of most of the population. Sitting in opposition were the centrally located market house and courthouse, Anglican church, and the "polite" houses of the professional classes, which were consonant with, even if they did not fully represent, the interests of the Protestant landed elite. The idea has an attractive symmetry, but the existence of a substantial number of poor Protestant tenants living on the periphery of Lismore in Mass Lane is a timely reminder that even where they existed, such spatial polarities were rarely as neat as Jones Hughes implies.[43]

Originating in the Munster Plantation, Tallow shared none of Lismore's antiquity, and—the one exception on the duke's urban estate— little of its dereliction. An earlier settlement had existed on or near the same site, but by 1586 this had declined. The grant made in that year by Elizabeth I to Sir Walter Raleigh was of the "decayed town" of Tallow and the surrounding lands. Thereafter, Tallow reemerged as one of the foremost English settlements in the plantation, a position it was to retain for fifty years. In 1598 the town contained sixty English households but by 1622 this had risen to 150, perhaps the equivalent of some 750 people. Together with Bandon and Lismore, Tallow was one of the nine Munster towns enfranchised in 1613, although like Lismore it was temporarily disenfranchised on procedural grounds in the same year.[44]

By 1774 Tallow had evolved as one of the larger, more substantial, and most regularly ordered of the duke's Irish towns (see table 3.2

and figures 3.5 a, 3.5 b). In 1794, Bowman described it as "more extensive than Lismore, better built and [with] at present a better share of trade."[45] Cruciform in plan, Tallow lay on the main road from Lismore to Youghal at its junction with the road to Midleton and Cork. The various categories of property identified by Scalé displayed an almost perfect centripetal status pattern. The core of the town, around the market house and central marketplace and along West Street, consisted of slate houses with extensive stores and—in many cases—formal gardens. On Tallowbridge Street some of the stores were used by cloth merchants, a reminder of the town's early importance in this trade. Some thatched housing occurred in this area, but the contrast between this central "high-status" zone and the peripheral straggle of cabins along virtually every approach road was pronounced. As at Bandon, this variation in housing quality was paralleled by the confessional allegiance of their tenants. The majority of the superior houses in the town center were inhabited by Protestants, while most of the cabins were tenanted by Roman Catholics.[46] Thus in Tallow, as in most of the other estate towns, social space was structured in a sectarian fashion in ways that reinforced existing economic status differentials.

At the time of Scalé's survey in 1776, Youghal was benefiting from a period of trade-led prosperity that generated considerable refurbishment of the town's housing and commercial buildings. Against such a background, the neglect and decay of much of the Devonshire estate in the town was all the more apparent.[47] The duke's estate consisted of some 287 properties interspersed with corporation and other private property throughout the medieval walled core of the town and its adjacent suburbs (see figures 3.6 a, 3.6 b). Few of the duke's holdings included extensive agricultural land, and consequently his Youghal property was the most completely built-up of all his urban estates (see table 3.2).

The urban plan depicted by Scalé was essentially that of the medieval town together with some later accretive suburbs and quays. The medieval core consisted of two walled *encientes* (the "upper" and "lower" towns), together with two extramural religious foundations, the misnamed "South Abbey," founded as a Franciscan friary in 1224, and the "North Abbey," a Dominican friary established in 1278. By 1776 the site of the South Abbey had disappeared, although its general location was

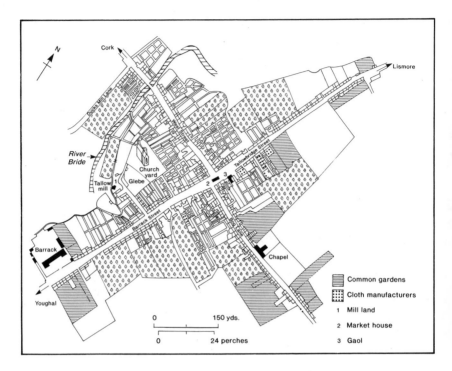

FIGURE 3.5A   The Urban Estate at Tallow in 1774: Property Boundaries

indicated by street names such as "Friar Street" and "The Abbey." The
ruins of the North Abbey survived, attached to a churchyard appropriated for use by the Roman Catholic chapel. Apart from the half-ruinous
Anglican parish church of Saint Mary (partly owned by the duke) and a
number of tower houses, the only other extensive medieval remains were
the town wall and turrets, which continued to exert a significant influence on the eighteenth-century town-plan. On the western side of the
medieval town, where the steeply rising flank of the Youghal plateau effectively precluded extensive suburbanization, the town wall continued
to delimit the edge of the built-up area. To the south, the wall had begun
to disappear under the impact of the sort of building process attested in
the Youghal Corporation's Council Book. The eighteenth-century entries in this book contain numerous references to corporation tenants

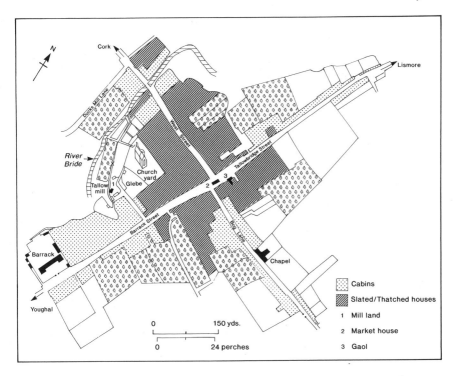

FIGURE 3.5B   The Urban Estate at Tallow in 1774: Housing Types

being permitted either to erect buildings against the medieval walls, or else to demolish these in order to improve access to their holdings.[48]

Despite short-term fluctuations, Youghal remained prosperous throughout much of the later seventeenth and early eighteenth centuries. In 1678 the town was the largest port in County Cork in terms of registered tonnage, and by the 1720s it enjoyed a particularly extensive trade with Bristol and other English ports, as well as with places further afield such as Bordeaux, Bilbao, Lisbon, Trondheim, and Cadiz. To facilitate this trade, the harbor facilities were gradually improved and extended from the early seventeenth century onward, although nothing could be done about the dangerous shoal at the mouth of the Blackwater estuary that prevented the passage of deep-drafted ships at low water.[49] Prior to 1776, most of the harbor improvement took place

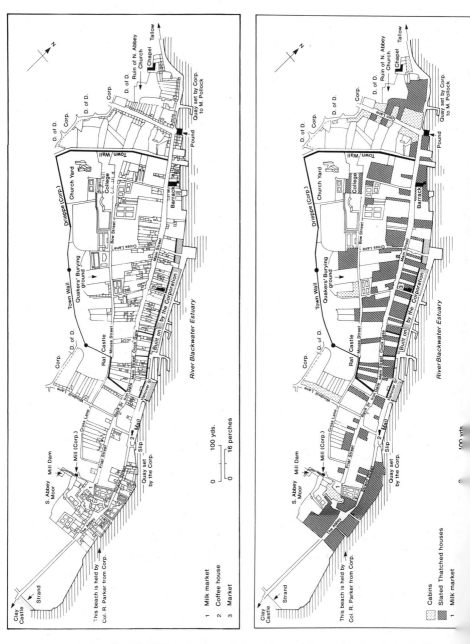

FIGURE 3.6A   The Urban Estate at Youghal in 1776: Property Boundaries (left)
FIGURE 3.6B   The Urban Estate at Youghal in 1776: Housing Types (right)

at the corporation's behest on parts of the Blackwater strand which were in disputed ownership with the duke. Ultimately, this dispute was resolved in the sixth duke's favor, and provided him with the opportunity to regain political control of the borough. In 1776, however, this land was still firmly in the corporation's control and represented a significant part of their property which they were anxious to use to further the town's trade. From the 1760s onward, the Youghal Corporation Council Book contains frequent references to grants of favorable building leases on the strand, made in order to encourage the extension of the town's wharves.[50]

As well as classifying the housing in Youghal according to type, Scalé's plan also indicates the relative age of many of the buildings, and whether they were in good, middling, or poor condition. The overall impression is of a consistent pattern of spatial variation in both the age and condition of the duke's property (see figure 3.7). Thus, with one exception, all the "new" buildings occur in the suburbs, while the "old" buildings occur widely throughout the town but constitute the vast majority of the age-designated buildings in the medieval core. Similarly, the relatively small number of cabins recorded by Scalé (see table 3.2) were limited either to the suburbs or to a single large plot lying between the town wall and Bow Street, suggesting the same structuration of social space as elsewhere on the duke's urban estate. By 1776 the actual condition of the duke's houses showed no such ordered variation. In the suburbs and walled nucleus alike, poor, middling, and good houses stood adjacent to each other, confirming the impression of extreme housing variability given by contemporary writers.[51]

The Administration of the Estate

The widespread distribution of the duke of Devonshire's estates throughout the British Isles placed a premium on careful management, but at the same time made this difficult to achieve. Prior to 1748 the estates had been managed by means of a network of regional agencies, and these were easily extended to accommodate the acquisition of the Burlington property. By the 1790s these regional agencies had evolved into a highly stratified functional hierarchy, in which individual respon-

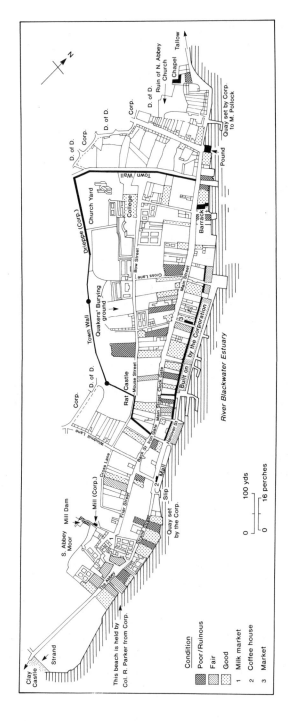

FIGURE 3.7   Housing Quality on the Devonshire Estate in Youghal in 1776

sibilities were carefully demarcated in geographical and operational terms (see figure 3.8).

The Auditor

The senior figure in the hierarchy was the London-based auditor, who was invariably a lawyer. Such supervisory "lawyer-auditors" were relatively rare at this time, even on the largest estates. They became much more common during the first half of the nineteenth century, before the rise of land agency as a profession led to a decline in the numbers of barristers and solicitors acting as land agents.[52] Overall authority for the Devonshire estates throughout the British Isles was finally concentrated into the hands of the London auditor in 1791, when John Heaton, the then-incumbent, was also appointed to the same office on the Irish estate. Previously, different parts of the Devonshire estates had been audited separately. Heaton's immediate predecessor as Irish auditor, Sir Beaumont Hotham, had been responsible for only two of the English estates, as had his predecessor, Sir Anthony Abdy. By the time of Hotham's appointment, the remaining English estates were already Heaton's responsibility. The centralization of overall authority into Heaton's hands marked a significant step in the drive for increased managerial efficiency on the Devonshire estates. This culminated in 1827 with the appointment of Benjamin Currey as auditor. In the late eighteenth century the various auditors had frequently had extensive professional and personal property interests in addition to their immediate responsibility for the Devonshire estates. Sir Beaumont Hotham, for example, had been a baron at the English Court of Exchequer.[53] The duke's affairs appear to have dominated Currey's professional life as a lawyer to a far greater extent than had been the case with his eighteenth-century predecessors. His appointment epitomized the new professionalism being brought to the management of the Devonshire estates, as the duke in common with other landowners sought to improve the profitability of his land in the wake of the Napoleonic agricultural crisis.[54]

While the relationship between successive dukes and auditors appears to have been generally harmonious, there were occasions when it became strained either through differences in personality or policy. Heaton's auditorship provides a case in point. His efficiency and loy-

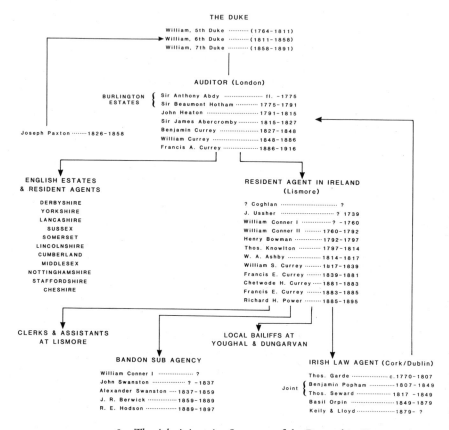

FIGURE 3.8   The Administrative Structure of the Devonshire Estate

alty in managing the estates throughout the greater part of the fifth duke's lifetime appears to have been largely unregarded both by the duke and his first wife, Georgiana.[55] The duke's indifference may have stemmed from his natural indolence and general disinclination to concern himself more than was absolutely necessary with his business affairs. Georgiana's attitude was founded on personal antagonism toward Heaton—whom she called the "Corkscrew"—which may have resulted from his generally unsympathetic attitude toward her enormous gambling debts. For example, in 1783 Georgiana confided to her mother that not only was she suspicious that Heaton had been gossiping to the duke about her relationship with the Prince of Wales, but that she also suspected him of defrauding the duke. Four years later, when Heaton seemed to be successfully resolving the duke's financial problems, Georgiana's attitude toward him softened, although she still thought him "insolent." Subsequently, as her own debts mounted, Georgiana's antagonism surfaced once again, and in 1801 she accused Heaton of prejudicing the duke against her and openly declaring himself her enemy.[56]

Georgiana's attitude toward Heaton cannot have helped his relationship with the fifth duke. Nevertheless, this relationship seems to have been tempered by a surprising degree of realism on the latter's part. His reply to Georgiana's accusation of Heaton's fraudulence indicates an acute awareness of the extent to which he relied on Heaton's expertise: "If I found out that Heaton was ever so great a rascal I should be mad to quarrel with him for it would quite ruin us."[57] Even Georgiana was occasionally prepared to admit that beneath Heaton's "tiresomeness" and "insolence" lay "a comprehensive, laborious, active mind, and a spirit of order and regularity in the arrangement of business, very pleasing."[58] These qualities appealed to the sixth duke when he inherited the title in 1811. By then, Heaton was receiving a salary of £1,000, which although large, was not unheard of. In the same year earl Fitzwilliam's agent received £1,200. The sixth duke proposed to increase Heaton's salary still further, and to give him an additional douceur of £2,000.[59] Three years later, all this had changed. Heaton's "tiresomeness" and "insolence" had given way to imbecility, and he had been replaced by Sir James Abercrombie, who "did but keep the job until the estates were put in order."[60]

The vicissitudes of Heaton's relationship with the fifth duke and his first wife were mirrored in later years by those between the sixth duke and *his* auditors. In this instance, the cause lay not in the antagonistic attitude of a hostile spouse but in the introduction onto the estate of Joseph Paxton. Initially employed in 1826 as head gardener at Chatsworth, Paxton very rapidly came to enjoy a degree of friendship and influence with the duke that entirely belied the difference in their respective social ranks, and which lasted for the rest of the sixth duke's life. The duke seems actively to have sought out Paxton's companionship, and as their relationship grew, so he increasingly sought Paxton's advice on matters which were, strictly speaking, the preserve of the auditor. The deepening financial crisis facing the duke in 1844–1845 illustrates the point. The auditor, Benjamin Currey, suggested a general retraction in spending together with the sale of outlying portions of the English estates. Paxton proposed a more radical scheme that included the sale of the entire Irish property, a move that was opposed both by Benjamin Currey and his nephew, Francis Currey, the agent at Lismore.[61] Although Paxton's suggestion regarding an Irish sale was ultimately abandoned, the general principles of his plan were accepted, and this appears to have led to a further enhancement in his status at Benjamin Currey's expense. By August 1844 Paxton was in an exultant mood. In a letter to his wife, he records the completeness of his triumph: "The victory is gained all the debt is to be paid off. . . . the Duke told Mr. Currey in my presence that there was nothing in his affairs which he might not communicate with me and advise upon in all other matters as well as this. Thus you see your own darling love is made assistant auditor . . . this is the grandest triumph your fond love has ever achieved in his many large and grand undertakings."[62] Although the Curreys' subsequent correspondence with Paxton and the duke betrays no obvious sign of irritation at this encroachment on the auditor's authority, the reality of the situation is clear enough. Not only did Paxton continue to accompany the sixth duke on his periodic visits to Lismore, as indeed he had done since these had been resumed in 1840, but when he arrived there he actively involved himself in the various improvement schemes that were in hand. Thus in 1852 it was to Paxton rather than the auditor, William Currey, that Francis Currey wrote seeking advice and approval about the intended rebuilding of the castle offices and siting of the new gasometer at Lismore.[63] The auditor might retain overall responsibility for the day-to-day running of the estates, but Paxton, it seems, had the duke's ear.

Paradoxically, the clearest evidence of the extent of Paxton's influence occurred after the sixth duke's death in January 1858. By the end of the month Paxton had offered his resignation, seemingly conscious of his responsibility for at least some of the late duke's overspending, and doubtless aware that the seventh duke would probably in any case dispense with his services.[64] Although his resignation was accepted, Paxton continued to offer advice concerning the best method of reducing the debt of nearly £1 million that the seventh duke had inherited.[65] Once again, Paxton favored the sale of the entire Irish property, and once again the move was opposed by Francis and William Currey. Given Paxton's situation following the sixth duke's death, his advice appears to have carried a surprising amount of weight. Nevertheless, after an increasingly acrimonious debate, a compromise was reached. Youghal and Dungarvan, the two most expensive and contentious parts of the Irish estate to manage, were to be sold and the remainder retained. The bulk of the money was to be raised by sales in England.[66]

With Paxton's departure from the scene, the relationship between the seventh duke and his auditor regained something of the immediacy that had characterized it under the fifth duke. Paxton's elevation had extended rather than destroyed the earlier, relatively straightforward chain of command, and this was easily reinstated after his resignation. The decisions of high policy which might be expected to have profound effects upon farming, industry, and urban development on the estate were again being taken by the duke and his auditor, usually on the basis of the specialist advice sought and received from the agents in the localities concerned.[67] This easy interchange of advice and information was greatly aided by the seventh duke's character. An austere man of evangelical persuasion, he regarded his estates as a responsibility to be discharged rather than as a possession to be enjoyed. Accordingly, the duke took a much more active interest in the day-to-day running of estate affairs than had his predecessors, and quickly familiarized himself with their managerial structures.[68] Predictably enough, the seventh duke's personal diaries and correspondence are characterized not by references to the same munificence as his predecessor's, but by comments on more mundane problems such as the cost of farm improvement and the varying fortunes of his industrial investments at Barrow-in-Furness.[69]

The Lismore Agent

Immediately responsible to the auditor were the resident agents in various parts of the country, including, in Ireland, Lismore (see figure

3.8). Conventional wisdom suggests that Irish land agents tended to be of a higher social class than their English counterparts,[70] and this seems to have been the case on the Devonshire estates prior to 1792. Until then the agency had been entrusted to various members of a local Irish family, the Conners, who had held the position under the earl of Burlington and were related to the Bernard family, later ennobled as Lords Bandon.[71] But in that year, following a period of gross mismanagement by William Conner II, the post was filled by Henry Bowman, the first English agent to be sent to the Irish estate. As a matter of policy, the Lismore agency was never again filled by an Irishman.[72] Bowman's period of office was relatively short. In 1797 he resigned, disillusioned by the social isolation he had met with at Lismore, by his new wife's refusal to join him in Ireland, but above all by the continuing hostility he had encountered not only from the middlemen on the estate, but also from the Devonshires' law agent, Thomas Garde. The few biographical details that are known about Bowman suggest that his social origins were typical of English land agents of the period, and that he was from a more humble background than Conner. Writing to the sixth duke in 1812, Heaton claimed that he "had brought Bowman up to agency," and that "his marriage to a lady of some fortune" was a significant factor in his decision to resign, implying perhaps that this marriage represented considerable social advancement for Bowman.[73]

Bowman's successor, Thomas Knowlton, remained Irish agent for twenty years, but later his responsibilities were extended to include Derbyshire, where he was to act as "general agent" at Chatsworth. Knowlton came from a family that had served the Devonshires for three generations. In Heaton's opinion, "[H]e was equal to Mr. Bowman in all that he knew in the management of land and property, and far superior to him in point of education and powers of writing, and managing the Business of an Estate requiring a system of managing, not only for property but for power. . . ."[74] His ultimate dismissal in disgrace in 1814 therefore seems all the more surprising. To modern eyes, the immediate reasons given for this dismissal seem trivial, and the reliance placed on witnesses with manifest vested interests positively unjust. Initially, on the word of his own clerk, Knowlton was accused of a series of paltry misappropriations of the duke's property, including curtain material and lamp oil, and the unauthorized use of the duke's horses. When Knowlton justified this on the grounds that, as a "general agent," the fifth duke desired that he "should be accommodated in everything that he wanted," a list of more serious charges was produced. These alleged that Knowlton had "countenanced immorality among the Duke's people," that he had lost their respect and was too severe with them, and that he was "quite unable" to manage the duke's affairs.[75] Despite Knowlton's protestations of innocence, and some unease on the sixth duke's part about the affair, Abercrombie's decision to dismiss Knowlton stood. Knowlton himself felt that as well as being made a scapegoat for the inadequacies of Heaton's final years as auditor, he was also being made to suffer from the enmity of the duke's Irish relatives, whose political machinations he had successfully exposed. Whether or not this was so, Abercrombie certainly felt that no improvements could be made in the administration of the duke's affairs while Knowlton remained.[76]

Knowlton's dismissal and the brief tenure of his immediate replacement, W. A. Ashby, mark the end of a period when the Irish agency was effectively run on an "absentee" basis. Whatever William Conner's faults—and they were numerous—he had at least been resident on the estate, and able, in however limited and self-seeking a fashion, to perform the agents' surrogate role of representing his absentee employer. Despite their greater professionalism and, in the case of Bowman at least, personal integrity, both Bowman and Knowlton were frequently absent in England.[77] Consequently, although their general mode of business may have been superior to Conner's, the benefits of this appear to have been vitiated by the inevitable inefficiencies consequent on their absence—as Garde was quick to point out. For example, in 1803—admittedly as part of a continuing policy of obstructionism toward the English agents appointed to Lismore, Garde wrote to the fifth duke alleging that Knowlton's maladministration of the Irish estate had cost him over £20,000.[78] Whatever the truth in this particular instance, and it should be noted that the duke took no immediate action, an absentee agent was unlikely to be as effective as his resident counterpart. Hence, when in 1817 Colonel William Currey was appointed agent at Lismore and became permanently resident there, the prospect was undoubtedly for an improvement in the day-to-day running of the Irish estate.

Colonel Currey was the first of three generations of the same family who filled the Irish agency until 1885. Their varied professional background reflected the changes that occurred in land agency during this period, and supports English's contention that despite the growth in the numbers of professional land agents in England by the end of the century, land agency continued to be characterized by the disparate nature of its practitioners' training.[79] On his retirement from the army, Colonel Currey had acquired practical experience managing his own farm in Yorkshire. His appointment to the Lismore agency owed much to the fact that his brother Benjamin was already satisfactorily employed on the Devonshires' legal affairs, although not yet in the capacity of auditor.[80] Colonel Currey's credentials were those of family connection and personal experience rather than professional training. Those of his successor, his son Francis, were rather different. In recommending Francis Currey as his father's replacement in 1839, the auditor stressed not only his nephew's experience helping his father in the Lismore agency, and his "plain, common sense," but also his formal qualifications as a Cambridge-trained lawyer.[81] This emphasis on a professional legal qualification was typical of land agency in England in the middle years of the century, and reflected the widespread assumption that a legal background was one of the most appropriate a land agent could have. With the exception of the two years between 1881 and 1883, when his son, Chetwynd H. Currey held the post, Francis Currey remained agent at Lismore until 1885, when he was replaced by Robert Power.

The Curreys' monopoly of the Irish agency throughout the greater part of the nineteenth century was less unusual than might be supposed. Richards notes the frequency of similar agent "dynasties" on English estates, and quotes Hughes: "Like the civil servants they [the land agents] not infrequently died in harness, and in the hope that the mantle would eventually fall on their sons or relatives."[82] In Ireland, the earls of Cork and Orrery and the earls of Bantry were served, respectively, by three generations of the Leahys and the Paynes, while two generations of the Gallweys served the earl of Kenmare, and two of the Leslie family served the earl of Shannon and the Falkiners.[83] What was unusual about the Curreys was the longevity of the legal interest which they represented. The later nineteenth century witnessed the progressive replacement of lawyers and solicitors by *professional* land agents, with Irish firms such as Hussey and Townsend offering landowners a complete agency service.[84]

During the nineteenth century the degree of independence enjoyed by the resident agent at Lismore was more limited than many contemporaries supposed. Although responsible for the routine administration of estate affairs—collecting rents, valuing property, receiving lease proposals, negotiating tenancies, enforcing lease covenants, and overseeing improvements—the agents were expected to conduct this business strictly in accordance with the broad principles of management laid down by the duke and the auditor, and applied wherever possible throughout the English and Irish estates. In Ireland these principles had been established in 1792 when, following Conner's mismanagement, Bowman was instructed to devise a plan whereby the estate could be managed "for power and profit" after the English fashion.[85] The resulting strategy was still being followed in the 1840s. As on other estates at this time, it involved reducing the numbers of leaseholders and middlemen, letting wherever possible to occupying tenants, and increasingly turning to the use of annual tenancies.[86] The agent was also expected to act as an election agent in support of the duke's preferred candidates in those constituencies where he retained a political interest, although after the 1832 Reform Act and the sixth duke's increasing disillusion with Irish politics this became a progressively less important part of his role.[87] All the most important Irish business was transmitted for the duke's attention via the auditor, and it was to the auditor that the duke normally turned in the first instance for advice on Irish affairs.[88] Direct communication between the duke and his Irish agent was relatively infrequent, particularly under the fifth and sixth dukes, although it became more common with the revival of the latter's interest in his Irish property after his visit to Ireland in 1841.

In a very real sense, therefore, the executive nature of the Lismore agent's duties gave him responsibility without power. Nevertheless, this reality did not diminish his high social profile and potential vulnerability as the resident representative of an absentee English landlord. This was a hazard for many agents in Ireland which their counterparts in England did not have to contend with. It was partly the result of the more fundamental issues of nationalism and cultural pluralism that underlay the question of land ownership in Ireland at this time. For the greater part of the nineteenth century, the social eminence that accrued from the Curreys' role as surrogate landlord seems to have outweighed the disadvantages they incurred for the part they played in representing an increasingly isolated, and for some sections of Irish society, discredited social elite. In particular, Francis Currey's role as local magistrate and Poor Law guardian, and more profitably, his directorships and shareholdings in the railway companies and other local enterprises that the duke helped to finance, not only stemmed from his position as agent but also helped to reinforce it.[89]

Against this must be set the periodic attacks suffered by the Lismore agent. Normally these were political rather than physical, and took the form of criticism in local newspapers about the supposedly sectarian nature of the management policies pursued on the estate.[90] Occasionally, however, these attacks were physically violent. During the 1857 election, for example, Francis Currey was assaulted at Dungarvan while canvassing in support of the duke's preferred candidate, the locally hugely unpopular Liberal Conservative, Sir Nugent Humble.[91] Some years later, in 1868, an attempt was made to burn down Lismore Castle itself.[92] Equally serious from the agent's point of view was the support given locally in Lismore and Tallow to the Fenian Rising of the previous year, and the more general decline in landlord-tenant relations on the estate during the Land War. Both fostered a climate in which the effective exercise of the agent's mediatory representative role became increasingly difficult. By 1884 tenant dissatisfaction on the estate had reached such a pitch and their demands for rent abatements had become so frequent that the seventh duke concluded that "we must not expect at present a return to the friendly relations which formerly existed."[93] Six months later he was still "much disappointed by the ungracious reception of the Ballynoe tenants of [his] offer of a twenty percent rebate" and he could not think of agreeing to their [much more extensive] demands.[94]

In return for these numerous and occasionally arduous duties, the Lismore agent received a generous salary that placed him in the same income bracket as many minor landowners. In 1765 William Conner II received a basic salary of £560 as well as free accommodation at the castle and a farm (subject to rent). This compared well, for example, with the £100 paid to Joseph Taylor in 1775, when he was appointed agent to the extensive Shelburne estate in County Kerry.[95] Henry Bowman and, initially, Thomas Knowlton, both received the same salary as Conner, but in 1805 it was increased to £866 when it represented over 58 percent of the total salaries paid on the Irish estate that year.[96] Ten years later the agent's salary had risen to £1,000, rather less than the £1,200 received by the chief agent on the vast Fitzwilliam estates in Britain and Ireland but still considerably more than the £600 paid to the agent on the Downshire estates.[97] Such payments by salary were unusual among Irish agents at this time. The more normal practice was to pay them a commission of about 5 percent on the rents they collected. Accordingly, the steady rise in the gross incomes of many Irish landowners until 1815 greatly benefited Irish land agents in general. Thus the rise in the agent's income at Lismore during this time was not unusual. Twenty-five years later, in 1841, the total salaries on the estate had risen to £2,855, and that of the agent to £1,400.[98]

The Bandon Subagency

Responsible to the resident agent at Lismore were the subagent at Bandon and the local bailiffs at Youghal and Dungarvan (see figure 3.8). At Bandon, the local estate was run as a semiautonomous unit under the overall direction of the Lismore agent. A picture of the duties of the Bandon agent is given in a letter written by Francis Currey in 1858 concerning the possible appointment of John Berwick. Currey wrote:

The agency at Bandon is subordinate to that here and the agent thus responsible to me and under my direction and control. He has to reside at Bandon and devote himself entirely to the business of that estate and of a small property of the Duke's near Cork and not to be concerned with any other agencies. At the same time in any cases of emergency his services should be available for any other part of the Duke's property. . . . As the management of the property involves a great deal more than the mere receipt of rents, the agent should be familiar with the business of country life, accustomed to value lands for letting and have some knowledge of agricultural pursuits. He should also have some familiarity with accounts as he would have to keep the Bandon rentals and accounts. I would attend myself during the receipt of rents . . . but much obviously depends upon the local agent for the chief superintendence of the property. . . . The condition of the Bandon property is such that an active intelligent person having once made himself acquainted with it, though he would find plenty to occupy him would not find the management very hard work. The town property in looking after houses and repairs is for the extent of it perhaps as troublesome as any part.

The salary is £350 a year with £31.10.0 allowance for the keep of a horse, a house lawn and garden rent free, and some land subject to rent. . . . it is very essential to me who am [sic] rather overworked than underworked to get a thoroughly qualified person at Bandon."[99]

Berwick was appointed, although on condition that he was allowed to retain such other agencies as he already had.[100] The circumstances of his appointment are of interest because they highlight the quite severe restrictions placed on the personal conduct of even relatively senior members of the estate's local hierarchy. Alexander Swanston, Berwick's predecessor, had resigned in some bitterness because the estate had refused to allow him to act as a trustee for his brother's affairs while remaining agent at Bandon. Writing to Francis Currey in March 1858, Swanston explained his refusal to agree to the new duke's request that he remain at Bandon for another year on the grounds that he would have to go to London whenever his trusteeship required it. He concluded that "if thirty-three years connection with the Irish estate did not entitle [him] to any consideration, another year was unlikely to make [his] chance better."[101] This was not the first time that Swanston's ambitions had come into conflict with estate policy. Fourteen months previously he had scandalized both Francis and William Currey by offering himself as a potential parliamentary candidate for Bandon. Although Swanston was not selected, the auditor still made his feelings quite clear: "I am surprised and disappointed at [Swanston] having entertained the idea of standing for the borough without ascertaining the feelings of the Duke or consulting . . . me. If it had resulted in his coming forward as a candidate I think the Duke would have been seriously displeased. . . . I think it would have shown great want of taste, to say the least of it, for Swanston to have become a candidate without having previously consulted the Duke; and I think his being member for the borough would be quite incompatible with his duties as Agent."[102] Subsequent subagents at Bandon do not seem to have entertained this sort of personal ambition, and although their professional abilities occasionally gave grounds for concern, they never again gave cause for this sort of admonition.[103]

The Law Agent.

The position of the law agent was more anomalous. Not a full-time estate employee as such, he was invariably a solicitor retained by the estate to undertake all legal transactions, including the preparation of leases for the duke's signature, notices to quit, and the frequent court cases brought to defend the duke's property interests.[104] Involvement with sensitive matters such as these afforded the law agent the opportunity, should he so choose, of trying to increase his personal influence in estate matters at the expense of the agent. Between 1792 and 1807 the then law agent, Thomas Garde, attempted to do precisely this in a bid to discredit Bowman and Knowlton and gain the resident agency for himself.[105] Garde first offered his services as resident agent at Lismore in January 1792, eight months before William Conner was forced to resign. Neither Heaton's refusal of this offer nor Garde's subsequent appointment as Irish auditor seem to have dampened his ambition. After Bowman's appointment in August 1792, Garde attempted to establish a de facto seniority over him at Lismore that would have effectively limited his role to that of assistant. It required Bowman's direct appeal to Heaton to secure his independence as resident agent.[106]

Six years later Knowlton faced the same problem, and was convinced that Garde was making yet another attempt to take over the Irish agency. In a letter to Heaton in April 1798, Knowlton defended himself against Garde's charges of lack of cooperation: "I have given him no offence, and wish to maintain an inoffensive conduct with all men, but seeing that this unjust attack cannot be accommodated on that principle, it must be ascribed to a desire for obtaining the agency for himself. To accomplish this, he will harass every English agent you can send here, no matter what his abilities are, in every way he can devise." In an illuminating passage, Knowlton continued by describing what he conceived the respective roles of agent and law agent or auditor to be: "I understand the two things are distinct departments and are intended to be kept so by you, but that they should cordially co-operate for the good of their employer; and from Mr Garde's long acquaintance with the Duke's affairs, it becomes right to commune with him on many things, where the agent wants information, that are not connected with matters of law."[107] Like Bowman before him, Knowlton was clearly prepared to cooperate with Garde on a professional basis. It was Garde's personal ambition that soured the relationship between them. The fundamental problem from Garde's point of view was that his appointment as Irish auditor did not give him the overall responsibility for the day-to-day running of the estate which he craved. Instead, it merely confirmed his existing legal responsibilities while at the same time charging him with the onerous task of winding up Conner's affairs as agent.

Garde continued his litany of complaint and innuendo against Knowlton in later correspondence with both Heaton and the fifth duke, but his attempt to usurp the Lismore agency had been recognized for what it was and had failed.[108] Although Garde's successors occasionally gave cause for concern on other grounds, none of them ever again tried to extend their personal authority on the estate in this way. Garde was replaced by Mr. Popham, who acted as law agent for all the Devonshires' Irish estates until circa 1817, when Abercrombie introduced Thomas Seward as an additional law agent to take charge of business emanating from the estates in County Waterford. Mr. Popham retained responsibility for legal affairs in Cork and the Bandon districts, but surrendered his papers concerning the duke's tithe suits to Seward, on the understanding that Seward would pay him half of any profits arising from these suits. The informal nature of this unwritten agreement was always likely to give grounds for disagreement between the duke's lawyers over the tithe issue, and in 1839 this was precisely what happened.[109] The dispute continued until 1849, when in an attempt to settle the matter, the sixth duke offered to reimburse each party the amount of their claims on each other. The Irish accounts for this and subsequent years give no indication of any such sum being paid, which suggests that if the duke's offer was accepted, it took the form of a personal payment made by him on his own behalf.[110]

Seward's long-running battle with Popham was not his only cause of embarrassment for the estate. Whether by accident or design, Seward nearly sabotaged the candidacy of Frederick Howard, scion of the House of Cavendish, as prospective Whig member for Youghal in the General Election of 1837. During the electoral registration, Seward had a prominent local Repealer, Dominick Ronayne, arrested, ostensibly for nonpayment of £270 damages awarded against him to Seward two years previously.[111] The curious timing of the arrest, and in particular the length of time that had elapsed since the original verdict, led to allegations that Seward was attempting to sabotage Howard's campaign by alienating moderate Catholic voters.[112] Although Seward was apparently able to convince Colonel Currey of the honesty of his intentions, the affair became a cause célèbre and undoubtedly hindered Howard's return. The consequences might have been far worse had not the Catholic priest in Dungarvan, Dr. Patrick Fogarty, stepped in to release Ronayne on his own surety, thereby publically placing the duke's candidate in his debt.[113] Whatever the notional degree of independence enjoyed by the law agent as the duke's legal representative, he was clearly expected to conduct himself both personally and professionally in a way that accorded with his employer's social and political principles.

Seward remained law agent until 1849, when responsibility for the whole of the duke's Irish legal affairs was taken over by his partner, Basil Orpin. Despite Francis Currey's misgivings, Orpin retained the law agency until 1879, when his declining health led Currey to press for his replacement.[114] Orpin was succeeded by Keily and Lloyd, a Dublin-based Roman Catholic firm. Their appointment was very much at the expense of Basil Orpin's nephews, who had followed him into legal practice and who had apparently entertained hopes of retaining the duke's business.[115] While the auditor felt sure that the seventh duke would have no objection to employing Roman Catholic lawyers, he nevertheless felt it necessary to consult him on the matter. Moreover, he was careful to ensure that the newly appointed firm were under no illusions about their subordinate status. Writing to Francis Currey in October 1879, William Currey stressed that "the Duke's Irish business will not be thrown bodily into their office but that certain portions of it may be carried out in the office of His Grace's solicitor in London."[116]

Estate Administration: Contrasts and Comparisons

The complexity of the administrative structures that had evolved on the duke of Devonshire's estates by the early nineteenth century found few parallels elsewhere in Ireland and then only on some of the largest estates. Moreover, size was not always synonymous with administrative efficiency. Thus while the marquis of Downshire's widely scattered 114,000 acres were administered by a similar network of local agents, increasingly centralized after circa 1801 under the direction of the Hillsborough-based auditor, earl Fitzwilliam's equally scattered 91,000 Irish acres enjoyed the benefits of no such centralized administration even as late as 1858.[117] Smaller estates—and Irish estates in general in the eighteenth century—invariably supported simpler managerial structures. Above the level of the smallest properties—where the owner might act as his own rent collector on a few hundred acres—the management was usually in the hands of a single agent who would be directly responsible to the owner not simply for rent collection, but also for overseeing improvements, negotiating leases, and—in theory—enforcing the owner's authority and protecting his interests. Among the numerous examples of this more usual situation were the earl of Roden's Tollymore estate in County Down, where prior to 1794 the agent, Mr. Moore, was responsible to the earl for half-yearly accounts, and the earl of Devon's estates at Newcastle West, County Limerick, at much the same period.[118]

But whether responsible for a few hundred acres or several thousand, a sufficient number of Irish land agents succumbed to the temptations of peculation to give the profession—in part at least—a reputation for dishonesty and high-handedness.[119] The latter in all probability stemmed from the relatively great social distance that separated most Irish land agents from the tenantry they supervised. Unlike their English counterparts, they were invariably drawn from army, clerical, or merchant families, and above all, from the ranks of the minor gentry. They were thus separated from the majority of the tenants by as great a social gulf as were the landlords—with whom of course they had much more in common, save in matters of income. Arguably, it was this discrepancy between the elitist social aspirations of many Irish land agents and their altogether more modest financial means, coupled with the opportunities for embezzlement provided by widespread landlord absenteeism, that may have accounted for the apparent readiness with which so many agents were prepared to defraud their employers. The most glaring examples are well documented. For example, between 1806 and 1836 the maladministration of Thomas Poole cost Lord Midleton well in excess of £70,000, while between 1846 and 1852 the earl of Mountcashel was defrauded of over £24,000 by the resident agent on his Antrim estates, the appropriately named Alfred Cleverly. Perhaps the most extreme case occurred on the heavily incumbered Egmont estates in County Cork. Here, the agent, Edward Tierney, was allowed such wide discretionary authority following his appointment in 1823, and was so frequently called upon for loans by his impecunious employer, that he and his brother Mathew were able to establish effective control over the estate long before the 1841 will that devised £250,000 of the earl's property onto Edward.[120] The duke of Devonshire's Irish estates were certainly not devoid of similar problems in the eighteenth century. What set them apart in the nineteenth century was the efficiency and integrity with which they were run as a peripheral part of a geographically discrete but administratively centralized estate network.

Secular Trends in the Estate's Income, 1764–1891

The acid test of the Irish estates' utility to the duke of Devonshire was their ability to generate remittances for his personal use. This depended on the efficiency of rent formation and other forms of income generation on the one hand, and on the level of recurrent and extraordinary expenditure authorized from year to year on the other. Despite changes in the accounting procedures adopted on the estate, particularly after Colonel Currey's appointment as agent in 1817, it is possible to identify the pattern of Irish income and expenditure with some precision throughout the lifetimes of the fifth, sixth, and seventh dukes (1764–1891). Compared to those submitted by later agents, William Conner's accounts (1760–1792) were straightforward, and reflected the relative simplicity of the managerial structures on the estate at the time. In theory, the accounts were presented annually and should have been closed at Ladyday (March 25th) each year. The first part of each account comprised a list of the tenants holding directly under the duke in each district on the estate, together with the amount they owed for the current year's rent (listed separately for the Ladyday and Michaelmas half-years), the size of any arrears, and the sum that had been paid in respect of both. This was followed by a list of expenditures, classified under the heads of schoolmasters' salaries, pensions,

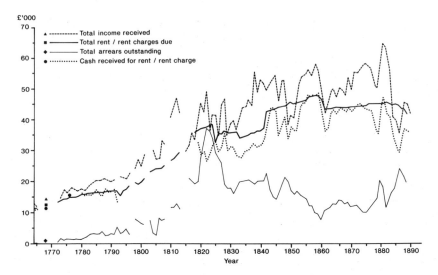

FIGURE 3.9   Income, Rent, and Arrears, 1764–1890

and almsmen; quit rents and chiefries; accountant's salary and law costs; and remittances.[121]

By the 1820s total annual income was considered to include not simply money paid in respect of rent and arrears, but also any incidental receipts together with the closing balance in hand at the end of the previous accounting year. The incidental receipts included every conceivable form of payment. In 1828, to take a random example, they included the proceeds from the sales of livestock and crops from the demesne farm and the farms in hand, money from the sale of timber from the estate woods, fines paid by people for cutting turf or extending leases, lockage payments on the Lismore canal, and legal costs paid by unsuccessful litigants against the duke. The heads of expenditure were equally varied. The remittances sent to the duke represented only one of some twenty categories of expenditure balanced in the annual accounts against the total income received, and which included remittances, works, salaries, subscriptions, compensation, schools and charities, incidental disbursements, tithe rent charge, and management.[122]

Figure 3.9 depicts the secular trend in four separate indices of income formation on the estate between 1764 and 1890: total income received, rent and rent charges due (the rent roll), money received for the rent and rent charge, and the arrears that remained unpaid at the end of each accounting year. Each highlights a different aspect of the estate's financial performance. The pronounced fluctuations in the total income reflect the inclusion of nonrecurrent payments which individually could be very large. Thus although these totals were used to balance the accounts, a better measure of the long-term performance of the estate is provided by the relationship between the rent roll and the rents actually received. The trend in the arrears supplements this, and highlights any periods of economic difficulty for the tenants on the estate. Particular care is needed in interpreting the data relating to the period of Conner's agency. Prior to 1792 the accounts that were finally passed represented a "tidied-up" version of the true state of the estate's finances, and concealed many of the consequences of Conner's erratic performance as agent. It is therefore important to remember that before 1792 much of the income depicted as accruing to the duke on an annual basis was not in fact made available to him until significantly later.

Total Income

Despite periodic downturns, the total income showed an unmistakably upward trend throughout the period. Moreover, although undoubtedly partially masked by the inclusion of nonagricultural elements such as urban rents as well as the previous year's closing balance in hand, the fluctuations in total income reveal a recognizable synchronization with contemporary agricultural cycles. The price-led agricultural expansion in Irish farming between the 1770s and the end of the Napoleonic Wars in 1815 was reflected in the accelerated growth in total income, which rose from £16,000–17,000 in the late 1770s to a peak of over £48,000 in 1812. Thereafter, the post-Napoleonic agricultural depression, the later Famine years, and the poor harvests of 1860–1861 and 1879–1880 together with the more widespread difficulties after 1883 all more or less coincided with significant downturns in estate income. By 1816 total income had fallen to £32,000; thereafter the continuing impact of the immediate depression was masked by the substantial closing balance remaining on hand at the end of successive financial years. Between 1821 and 1823 this amounted to over £11,000, and the effect of the agricultural downturn was more clearly reflected in the rent roll. The impact of the Famine was equally pronounced but short-lived: between 1845 and 1849 total income fell from £54,000 to £38,000, but then rose sharply to exceed £54,000 by 1854. Although also partly agri-cultural in origin, the downturn in the early 1860s also reflected the sale of Youghal and Dungarvan in 1859–1860 and the subsequent loss of rents. In the intervening periods, particularly 1839–1841, 1852–1860, and 1871–1878, the total income showed less variation, and fluctuated broadly between £45,000 and 55,000, reaching a peak of over £65,000 in 1882 with the payment of substantial litigation costs to the duke.

The Rent Roll

Analysis of the rent roll is instructive insofar as it illuminates the changing perception of successive dukes and their agents of the Irish estate as a potential source of income. Broadly speaking, the rent roll recorded gradual albeit sustained growth until 1840, followed by a sharp rise in 1841–1842 and relative stability thereafter—save for the fall in 1860–1861 caused by the sales at Youghal and Dungarvan. Saving this, the annual variation in the final sum demanded by the rent roll normally represented the net difference between the rents that had been reduced, usually because the incoming tenant was prepared to accept the financial responsibility for rebuilding or repairing the prop-erty, and those that had been raised, generally when middlemen's leases fell in and the property was relet to occupying tenants.[123] The steady rise in the rent roll after 1795 reflected this sort of general upward re-valuation as new leases were set at higher rents.[124] During the previous thirty years the rent roll had risen from £11,000 to £16,000; over the next thirty years it doubled to £32,000. Although the markedly slower growth under Conner (1764–1792) stands in sharp contrast to this later rise, it would be premature to conclude that this was solely due to his failure to maximize rents. The numerous tenants holding reversionary leases for lives during Conner's agency[125] would have paid head rents very much below the market value of land in the 1770s and 1780s. Consequently, the rise in rents after 1795 undoubtedly reflected oppor-tunities for rent revision that Conner did not have, as many of these leases did not fall in until after his resignation. It is a moot point how far a more zealous agent than Conner would have been able to im-prove the rent roll at a time when much of the estate was tied up in this way, although it must be stressed that, for his own reasons, Conner did not always take full advantage of those opportunities that did occur.[126]

Despite the sustained rise in rents under Bowman and Knowlton, the overall financial performance of the duke's estate in the late eighteenth century was not on a par with the average growth in rents in the region. Dickson estimates that between the mid-1770s and the end of the "French War," rents in Munster rose by on average 300 percent. Over the same period, roughly 1775 to 1815, the gross rental on the duke's estate rose by 105 percent from £14,343 to £29,411.[127] Obviously, figures such as these provide only an approximate guide to the relative order of magnitude of the rent increase on the estate, since they can be materially affected by the choice of the years used for comparison. Nevertheless, it is significant that even by the most generous estimate, at no time did the growth in the duke's rents approach the average figure suggested by Dickson. During Conner's agency they rose by barely 54 percent; between the start of his agency and the end of the "French War" they rose by 167 percent; while between 1744 and 1815, when by Dickson's calculation the average rent rise would have been considerably in excess of his overall estimate of 300 percent, the duke's rental rose by "only" 268 percent.[128]

Irrespective therefore of the particular problems caused by Conner's lax accounting, it appears that both during his agency and during the period of the reforms that came after, the duke's estate did not generate the proportionate growth in rent income enjoyed by other Munster proprietors. Nevertheless, the size of the duke's Irish income had already placed him firmly in the upper echelons of landed proprietors in late-eighteenth-century Ireland, and helped secure his similar overall position in England. Accurate analysis is hindered by the relative dearth of rental information for Ireland at this time, but it seems that comparatively few Irish landlords had incomes that were significantly in excess of the duke's. Magnates such as Earl Fitzwilliam (£21,941), Lord Donegall (£36,000), or the earl of Kingston (£20,000) may have enjoyed larger rent rolls by the 1790s, but a much more typical figure is likely to have lain somewhere between the £9,500 received by the earl of Wicklow from his Donegal and Wicklow estates in 1781, and the £3,000 received six years later by the Heathcote family from their

estate at Cappoquin.[129] In England, too, Mingay estimates that by the
1790s the rent income received by the four hundred leading landed
families varied between £5,000 and £50,000, with an average of around
£10,000. Within this group, the duke of Devonshire would have
figured prominently. In 1764 his total current income was already
£35,000, rising to an (estimated) £70,000 by 1790.[130] Significantly, the
Irish contribution to this total income declined in importance, falling
from 37 percent of the total in 1764 to under 28 percent in 1790.

The sustained growth that characterized the rent roll in the early
1820s continued into the 1830s, albeit in a more variable fashion. The
roll increased from £34,000 in 1833 to over £35,000 in 1840, and more
sharply from £36,951 to £42,671 between 1841 and 1842, a rise of nearly
15.5 percent. Donnelly has previously identified this as the only instance of a significant aggregate rent increase on the estate, a consequence he supposed of a general revaluation by the agent. In fact, this
increase was more apparent than real, and was the result of a change in
the method of accounting the impropriate tithes due to the duke. Until
1832 the tithe rent charges were included with the rents. Between 1833
and 1841 tithe agitation led to their nonpayment, and it was these arrears, paid by the government in 1842 and returned in the estate accounts as an incidental rent receipt, that comprised Donnelly's "rent
increase" of that year. The real aggregate rent increase between 1841 and
1842 was £815 or 2.2 percent of the amount due in 1841, but this figure
masks enormous variations in the increase demanded on individual
farms. This ranged from 2 to 315 percent.[131] Following rectification of
the tithe rent anomaly in 1842, the rent roll increased, albeit slowly, to
a maximum of £47,894 in 1859, a rise of 12 percent since 1842. Between
1859 and 1862 the sale of the Dungarvan and Youghal property reduced
the rent roll by £4,547 or 8 percent. Subsequently it displayed remarkable stability, increasing only marginally to £45,036 in 1883, before falling to £41,384 in 1890 as the early land sales and the imposition of
judicial rents began to have their effect.[132]

In general terms, therefore, the aggregate variation in the Devonshires' rent roll suggests that the estate was not rack-rented, and
confirms the impression given both by the agents and by other contemporary commentators that rents were designed to be moderate
and to preserve the tenants' interest in their holdings.[133] Nevertheless,

the extreme variation in the rent increases demanded for different farms in the same year—and the variation in 1842 was by no means unique—indicates that the Devonshire estate was not altogether immune from a potential source of tenant dissatisfaction which Vaughan identifies as a prime cause of rent agitation in the post-Famine period.[134] In the final analysis, however, the general lack of complaints about individual rent increases suggests that for whatever reason, most renewing or incoming tenants were prepared to tolerate them as reasonable. When serious rent agitation occurred on the estate, it was episodic and prior to 1880 short-lived. It invariably coincided with agrarian crises such as that of 1852–1853, and was directed toward a reduction in existing rents rather than the withdrawal of any proposed increase.[135]

Rents Received and Arrears

If the rent roll reflected the landlord and his agent's perception of the income that the estate might potentially provide, the cash received for rents provided a measure of the extent to which that expectation was realized. With the notable exception of the period 1818 to 1824, the total amount actually received for the rents and rent charge on the duke of Devonshire's estate usually fell below the rent roll demand. In only twenty of the eighty-six years for which data for both the rent roll and rents received survives did the total paid exceed the total due, and in each case the excess reflected the payment of arrears outstanding from previous years. These arrears were cumulative and fluctuated from year to year depending on the immediate economic circumstances. Prior to 1792 Conner tolerated a steady increase in the size of these arrears to around £5,000. Under Bowman and Knowlton they subsequently increased much more rapidly, reaching a peak of some £13,000 in 1813. This increase is deceptive. Bowman's more accurate (and honest) accounting undoubtedly identified arrears that had accrued under Conner but that he had failed to record, while under Knowlton they were greatly increased by the effects of the 1798 rebellion, and subsequently began to fall nearly as quickly as they had risen. Arguably, what was more significant as far as the duke's income was concerned, was the steady incremental buildup of arrears under Conner, because this represented not the immediate consequences of

short-term social disruption, but the long-term failure of the managerial structures on the estate itself.

The situation in the years 1818–1824 was more complex. Not only
did the cash received for the rent and rent charge exceed the rent roll
by up to £10,000 (in 1823), but these payments also coincided with a
renewed peak in the arrears of £23,000. Conceivably this reflected the
payment by some tenants of arrears generated at the depth of the
post–Napoleonic recession in 1816–1817 and, conversely, the subsequent failure of others to meet their obligations in later years. Thereafter the peaks and troughs in both the rents received and the arrears
closely reflected the periodic crises in the agrarian economy. The 1830s
were generally a decade of agricultural recovery, and this situation was
reflected on the estate by a rise in rents received (to £32,324 in 1838)
and by continuing high levels of arrears and abatements.[136] The latter
were exacerbated by the renewed bad harvests of 1839–1842, but fell
over the next three years while the amount received for rents rose substantially to £43,700.[137]

This improvement was short-lived. Between 1846 and 1853 the effects
of the potato blight led to a sharp fall in cash receipts, an equally pronounced rise in arrears (which peaked at over £21,000 in 1848), and a
marked rise in the levels of abatement. The auditor had intended to
offer relief in proportion to each farmer's potato ground and not as a
simple percentage of the entire rent, but the difficulties in acquiring
the necessary information rendered this method of relief impracticable.
Accordingly, in 1846 relief was offered that varied according to the
value of the holding and was highest for holdings worth less than £10
a year, since it was assumed that in these the loss of the potato harvest
would have had the most serious consequences for the tenants. The
total amount abated was £5,255, and although this undoubtedly was
the result of a genuine humanitarian feeling on the part of the duke
and his auditor, it was also the product of the latter's careful calculation. When recommending the abatement to the duke in October
1846, Currey concluded, "[Y]ou will have been considered to have
acted most nobly, and yet I will venture to say you will not lose one
shilling by having done so, for you would never have got paid what
you have given away."[138] The virtual absence of the blight on the estate
in 1847 resulted in the suspension of the abatement in that year, but as

the effects of the renewed outbreak in 1848 began to be felt, a more generous abatement of 25 percent was offered to all agricultural tenants, and this remained in force until 1853. By this time, the relief was no longer designed simply to alleviate the effects of crop failure, but was intended instead to encourage tenants to stay on the land.[139]

In the mid-1850s receipts rose sharply to reach £47,000–£48,000 between 1856 and 1859, their highest level ever, before falling to a low of £35,951 in 1862 under the combined effect of the sale of Youghal and Dungarvan and the agricultural depression of 1859–1864. This crisis was also mirrored by the renewed upward trend in arrears in 1860 and by the reintroduction of a 15 percent rent abatement in 1862–1863, but these proved to be temporary. The later 1860s and early 1870s were characterized on the estate by high and stable receipts (averaging over £43,000), and by relatively low arrears, suggesting that the duke's tenant farmers shared in the general prosperity that Cullen identifies as being characteristic of their class at this time.[140] Over much of Ireland the disastrous harvests of 1877–1879 ended this prosperity, and with it the uneasy neutrality that had existed between landlords and their tenants. Vaughan and more recently Hoppen have argued that the situation was exacerbated by low levels of rent increase and a lack of investment, which Vaughan argues precipitated the political mobilization of the tenantry over the land issue.[141]

The evidence from the Devonshire estate for the period between 1877 and 1891 bears witness both to the initial harvest failures and the politicization of the tenantry. During the "Land War" of 1879–1882, when under Land League direction the tenants offered to pay no more than the amount at which their holdings had been valued thirty years earlier for the assessment of the Poor Rate (the Griffith Valuation), the rent receipts fell to just under £35,000 while the arrears rose to over £19,000.[142] This was followed by an immediate and rapid increase in receipts which peaked at over £47,200 at Ladyday 1882, and by a fall in arrears to a low of £11,373 in the same year. Over the next five years receipts fell rapidly to £28,000 (in 1887), as a result of the renewed agitation under the Plan of Campaign and the increasing number of successful applications by tenants to have their rents reduced under the provisions of the 1881 Land Act. At the same time, the arrears rose to £23,745. In the closing years of the seventh duke's life the rent roll on the Irish estate began to show signs of recovery as receipts once again increased and arrears fell, trends which presaged the more general economic recovery of the 1890s.

The recitation of financial trends such as these provide a very incomplete picture of the extent of the tenant agitation that faced the duke and his Irish agents in the period after 1877. Surviving estate correspondence makes it clear that there was a rapid deterioration in the relationship between the duke and his tenantry. By this time, the duke was already in dire financial straits as a result of the decline of his industrial investments in his estate at Barrow-in-Furness. This would have limited his options in dealing with tenant demands for rent rebates, irrespective of whether he was personally inclined to accede to them. In the event, the reductions that were offered were nearly as generous as those made during the Famine, but in the heightened political climate of the 1880s they were not always sufficient to satisfy the tenants. The first allowance of between 10 and 20 percent was made in 1879, and was followed by a more modest one of 10 percent for the following year and for the first half year's receipt in 1881. The duke had already had to make allowances on his English estates, and felt encouraged to continue to do so in Ireland by the apparent lack of animosity created by the Land League meetings held at Lismore in the autumn of 1879.[143]

The duke's optimism was premature. By December 1880 Land League tenants on the Lismore estate were refusing to pay their rents, and in March the following year the Land League made its customary offer of payment of the Griffith Valuation—some 19 percent less than the rents— "on account," but this was an offer the duke could hardly accept.[144] The duke's refusal was followed not only by the predictable series of petitions from tenants requesting a reduction, but also by rather more aggressive—and effective—action. In August 1881 fifty tenants from Tallow met "to decide whether they would pay their rents," while the following month a series of "outrages" perpetrated by the Land League were reported at Millstreet, near Lismore.[145] More significantly, by the end of the following year over eighty tenants had applied to have their arrears reduced under the provisions of the new Land Act, as a result of which nearly £1,500 was written off from the arrears that year.[146]

Despite the agitation that followed Parnell's arrest and the proscription of the Land League, levels of agrarian agitation—both on the estate and elsewhere—lessened between 1881 and 1884. This may have been the result of the steadying agricultural prices of the time and the perceived effectiveness of the rent tribunals set up under the 1881 act.[147] With the renewed fall in agricultural prices in 1884, however, various sections of the farming community again found their economic position eroding, and were once more susceptible to radical political agitation. By 1886–1887 this was orchestrated through the Plan of Campaign, but the protests were much more episodic and regionally specific than in the earlier phase of the Land War, and were aimed in particular at estates that were already nearly bankrupt.[148]

Although the Devonshire estate was not a target for this type of coordinated action, tenant demands for rent reductions remained numerous and aggressive, and were made well before the formal institution of the campaign. Commenting on the earliest demands in December 1884, the duke conceded that the proceedings of the tenants at Lismore and Tallow had been "a great disappointment."[149] Six months later he agreed to an allowance of 20 percent on the current half year's rents, but this was not well received by the Lismore tenants, whose demands were evidently considerably higher. The duke was adamant: "I have been much disappointed by the ungracious reception by the Ballynoe tenants of my offer of [a] 20 percent rebatement and I cannot think of agreeing to their demands."[150] In the event, as the depression worsened, the duke adopted a more flexible attitude and sanctioned a variety of rebates of between 17 and 27 percent on the Irish rents during the remaining years of his life.[151]

The Aggregate Urban Income

In aggregate, the five estate towns provided a variable but generally minor proportion of the overall Irish income. Their financial performance prior to 1826 is hard to estimate. During Conner's agency the returns for Dungarvan, Lismore, and Tallow were included among those for the Waterford estate at large, while between 1792 and 1826 none of those for any of the towns were separately identified.[152] The urban returns that do survive before 1826 relate to Bandon and Youghal during Conner's agency. Although the duke's rents showed some increase there, this was less than on the estate at large. At Youghal, the rent roll rose by 13 percent between 1764 and 1792 from £935 to £1,060, but fell in proportionate terms from 8.8 percent to 6.0 percent of the estate total. At Bandon, the much larger roll rose by some 28 percent from £2,358 to £3,017, but again declined from over 21 percent to barely 18 percent of the overall total. In both towns the duke's income was clearly not keeping pace with even the relatively modest growth experienced on the estate at large. Furthermore, these urban rents were not always well paid. At Bandon, in particular, the late 1760s and early 1780s saw a rapid growth in the arrears. Between 1768 and 1770 these rose from over £500 to nearly £900, when they represented between 50 and 60 percent of the total arrears from the entire estate. In the early 1780s their growth was less spectacular but still pronounced. Between 1782 and 1784 they rose from £400 to £600, when they represented approximately 16 percent of the estate total. At Youghal the urban arrears remained at minimal levels throughout Conner's agency.

The slow growth of the Bandon and Youghal rents, together with the relatively great fluctuation shown by the Bandon arrears, hint at the nature of the duke's financial relationship with these towns. Although Bandon and Youghal declined in relative economic importance in the later eighteenth century as many of the most important components of trade and industry in the area relocated in Cork city, both towns nevertheless retained a variety of functions that helped bolster their respective economies.[153] At Youghal, the eclipse of the butter and beef provisions trade that had been important earlier in the century was partly compensated for by the growth in grain exports, particularly oats, to England between the 1770s and 1790s. Bandon remained an important center of woolen yarn production prior to the 1770s, and of woolen and linen cloth production afterward.[154] Moreover, both towns also witnessed the growth of a specialist retail sector as their population grew and the living standards of many social groups rose. Between 16 and 19 percent of the occupations recorded in the towns by Lucas's *Cork Directory* were retail-based, and included booksellers, grocers, ironmongers, haberdashers, and tobacconists. Predictably, the recorded occupational pattern also reflected the major functional difference between the two towns. Over 43 percent of the Bandon entries related directly to the textile industry, compared to 19 percent in Youghal, where the range of manufacturing and merchant occupations appears to have been more broadly based and consonant with the town's status as a port. The Bandon textile trades were varied, and suggest a high degree of specialization. The majority of entries were stated simply as woolen, cotton, or linen manufacturers, but a minority specified their products more precisely as dimities, thicksets, calicoes, or corduroys. The further distinction between linen manufacturers and linen drapers may reflect the town's earlier importance as a "putting-out" center, while the inclusion of several "dyers and pressers" betokened further specialization in the cloth-finishing trades.[155]

For the duke of Devonshire, these trades constituted part of a relatively sophisticated industrial complex to which he had only limited financial access. The duke's rent roll was relatively stable in these towns because, just as on the estate at large, most of his urban tenants held long and favorable leases for years or lives, which gave them the benefit of any improvement in the local economy. During periods of economic growth, these tenures effectively limited the extent of the duke's financial interest in the towns. Upward revaluation of property only occurred fortuitously as and when leases fell in. Conversely, during periods of economic difficulty, these tenures did not safeguard the duke against losses consequent upon the tenants' insolvency. Low though the duke's rents may have been, they were still liable to nonpayment if trading conditions worsened sufficiently. Hence the reason why so little of the periodic prosperity at Bandon and Youghal was apparently reflected in the duke's rent roll, which at the same time nevertheless proved to be vulnerable to periodic downturns in the local urban economy.

Figures 3.10 and 3.11 depict the financial performance of the entire urban estate between 1826 and 1890 in absolute terms and as a component within the overall rental. The absence of the full Bandon rentals for the period between 1835 and 1887 required the use of estimates, and these clearly introduce a degree of imprecision into the analysis.[156] However, it is important not to overemphasize this imprecision. The Dungarvan, Lismore, Tallow, and Youghal rental series survive virtually intact, and the probable margin of error introduced by estimation is likely to have been of the order of £300 or 5.0 percent of the rental at most.[157] It is therefore reasonable to assume that the trends depicted in

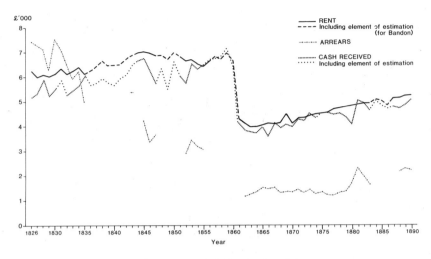

FIGURE 3.10   Urban Rents, Cash Received, and Arrears, 1826–1890

figures 3.10 and 3.11 provide an acceptable representation of the secular variation in the urban rent income. This being so, several conclusions seem justifiable. First, that prior to the sale of Youghal and Dungarvan, the urban rent demand showed some fluctuation, but afterward distinct growth; second, that the aggregate cash receipts were not unduly distorted by successive agrarian crises; and third, the aggregate urban arrears recorded a marked improvement, even though they continued to form a disproportionately large part of the overall sums owed on the estate.

The sale of Youghal and Dungarvan in 1859–1861 radically altered the pattern of urban rent demand. Between 1826 and 1859 the rental in the five estate towns fluctuated between £6,000 and £7,000, and reached its maximum in 1845. By 1863 the sales had reduced the aggregate rent demand to just under £4,000. Thereafter, the rent roll for the three remaining towns rose gradually but progressively to reach £5,250 by 1890 (see figure 3.10). In fact, the urban rent roll had been most important—in relative terms—during the late 1820s and late 1830s, when it constituted between 17 and 18 percent of the total roll (see figure 3.11). Thereafter, despite increasing slightly in absolute terms during the 1840s, it declined progressively to 14 percent of the total in 1860 and to 9 percent a year later, following the sale of Youghal and Dun-

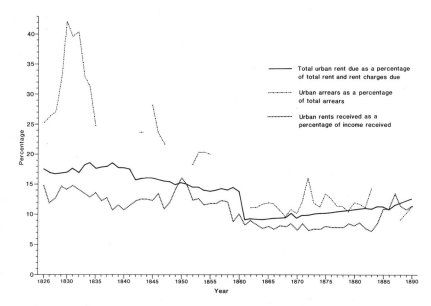

FIGURE 3.11   Urban Rents, Cash Received, and Arrears as a Percentage of
Total Rents Due, Cash Received, and Arrears, 1826–1890

garvan. The subsequent slow growth in the absolute value of the remaining urban rents (to £5,200 in 1890) was mirrored by the progressive increase in their relative value to 13 percent of the total Irish
income by the same year.

    This growth in the aggregate urban rent roll after 1861 suggests that
the estate's remaining urban property was increasingly coming to be regarded as a relatively secure source of income. This perceptual rehabilitation, if such it was, may have begun somewhat earlier. In 1852, for
example, the sixth duke rejected a series of requests for a reduction in
the urban rents at Bandon. This implies that both the duke and his
agents, if not his tenants, considered that the local urban economy had
suffered less from the Famine than had the agrarian sector.[158] There are
grounds to believe that this may have been so. The immediate effect
on the urban rents of the agrarian crises of 1848–1851, 1859–1864, and
1884–1890 was very limited. The Famine was marked by a drop in
urban income that was temporary and much less pronounced than the
decline in the overall receipts (see figure 3.11). The agrarian crisis of
1859–1864 left no imprint on the urban receipts whatsoever, while the

Land War, which had a major impact on the estate finances overall, coincided with no more than a slight dip in urban income in 1880 and a commensurate peak in the arrears of about £2,300 the following year, a value which was equalled again in 1888–1890.

The pattern of aggregate urban arrears supports the general interpretation of a reliable and strengthening urban rent roll in the later nineteenth century. Although partly obscured by the missing Bandon data, the overall trend is clear enough. From a peak of nearly £8,000 in the late 1820s and early 1830s, the total urban arrears dropped to half that amount in 1845 and to just under £1,500 between 1862 and 1879, before rising to £2,250 in 1881 and 1889 (see figure 3.10). The difference between the pre- and postsale arrears, incomplete though they are, suggests that in disposing of Youghal and Dungarvan, the duke was ridding himself of two of the more difficult parts of his urban estate, a view that was certainly held by Francis Currey.[159] The improvement in the arrears was even more pronounced in relative terms. The high urban arrears between 1826 and 1832 coincided with a pronounced fall in the estate arrears, and accordingly the urban share increased to between 40–42 percent of the total in 1830–1832. Thereafter, it seems clear that as the century progressed, and despite considerable short-term fluctuation, the urban arrears became a progressively less important part of the overall estate arrears. Between 1862 and 1890 they varied for the most part at between 10 and 14 percent of the total. The one slightly contradictory feature in this pattern is that despite their pronounced decline, the aggregate urban arrears continued to form a disproportionately large part of the total. In other words, the towns continued to generate a marginally larger share of the arrears than the relative importance of the aggregate urban rental would have suggested.

Rent Formation in the Individual Towns

Within this overall pattern, the relative importance of the different Devonshire towns as a source of income remained remarkably stable. Table 3.3 lists the average annual rental and receipts in each town in rank order for the years before and after the urban sales. Prior to these, Youghal generated the largest average rent roll (£2,252) and the highest average receipts (£2,044). Bandon came next with an average rent demand of £1,761—some 22 percent lower than in Youghal—and average receipts of £1,687—18 percent less. At Tallow the rent roll and receipts averaged just over half those at Youghal (£1,107–£1,227), while those at Dungarvan and Lismore were lower still (£552–£710). Following the urban sales, the three remaining estate towns retained their earlier rank order, although the differential between them altered as the rent roll and receipts at Bandon and Lismore increased in value while those at Tallow stagnated.

The trends in the comparative urban rent rolls, receipts, and arrears for each town indicate that the strengthening suggested by the aggregate figures was highly selective. Thus although the Youghal and Dungarvan rentals grew from £2,000 to £2,700 and from £600 to £900, respectively, as the benefits of falling leases and improved management began to be felt prior to the towns' sale, the receipts—particularly at Youghal—fluctuated widely and the arrears—again at Youghal—were among the highest on the estate. The Youghal receipts varied from £1,600 in 1826 to £2,600 in 1844, while the town's arrears fell from £2,600 in 1831 to £300 in 1860. The Dungarvan receipts fluctuated less widely around a rising trend (from around £500 in the late 1820s to a peak of £1,100 in 1859). The Dungarvan arrears remained relatively static at around £1,200–£1,300 until the 1840s, before falling dramatically to nearly £300 during the 1850s as tenants sought to clear their arrears and thus render themselves eligible to purchase their own

TABLE 3.3
Average Urban Rent Formation: Rank Order

Town	*1826–1860*		*1861–1890*	
	Roll £	*Receipt £*	*Roll £*	*Receipt £*
Youghal	2252	2044		
Bandon	1761	1687	2248	2196*
Tallow	1227	1107	1296	1182
Dungarvan	710	659		
Lismore	591	552	989	947

*Original data only.
Source: N.L.I. L.P. Estate Rentals.

property. Even so, the financial performance of both towns tends to support the agent's contention that they were the most difficult and expensive parts of the estate to manage.[160]

This implies in turn that the rather lower rents generated within the three towns that were retained by the estate—Bandon, Lismore, and Tallow—were perceived to be more productive of net income. In fact, a marked differential existed in the financial performance of these towns. Bandon, and at a lower level, Lismore, both succeeded in generating a steadily rising rental that was consistently well paid. They both witnessed a steady drop in arrears that was most pronounced at Lismore. At Bandon, both the rental and receipts increased significantly between 1860 and 1890 from around £1,900 to about £2,700. At Lismore, the rent demand grew steadily throughout the century, rising from £400 in 1826, to over £700 in 1860, and to £1,200 by 1890. The Lismore receipts also grew from around £400 in the late 1820s to between £1,000 and £1,100 by the 1880s, but showed rather more variation particularly before 1860. By 1890, the arrears owed in the town were the lowest of all, about £500, having fallen progressively from their peak of between £800 and £900 during the 1830s and early 1840s. At Tallow, on the other hand, the rent roll fell from over £1,200 in the 1830s to just over £1,000 by 1850, and barely succeeded in regaining its earlier level by 1890. The Tallow receipts followed the same pattern. Although the relatively high Tallow arrears of around £2,000 in the 1820s and 1830s were progressively reduced to barely one-quarter of that figure by 1860, this simply presaged a renewed rise that took them to £1,000 in 1890—when they were the highest in both absolute and relative terms of all. Clearly, the strengthening financial performance of the estate towns in the later nineteenth century owed much more to Bandon and Lismore than to Tallow.

Summary

The magnate status and complex geography of the duke of Devonshire's Irish estates required managerial structures that were correspondingly complex and which did not evolve into their final form until circa 1817. Prior to this, the division of responsibility between different departments had become increasingly confused as the law agent sought to capitalize on the fifth duke's lack of interest and the frequent absences of the resident agent to extend his own authority within the estate hierarchy. The changes initiated by Abercrombie among estate personnel clarified rather than altered the existing system of management, and this was never again seriously distorted by personal disputes. The intrusion of Sir Joseph Paxton into the estate hierarchy did not materially alter the day-to-day running of the Irish property, since Paxton's rise was largely at the expense of the auditor rather than the local agents.

For the most part, successive agents at Lismore were given executive responsibility without cabinet power, and this placed limitations on their freedom of action which their contemporaries did not always appreciate. Moreover, they were still required to pursue management strategies that would accommodate the consequences of the periodic agricultural crises of the day without too much disruption to the estate or loss of income, while at the same time ensuring that the duke's property rights were safeguarded. For the greater part of the nineteenth century this policy worked well enough. Nevertheless, it was vulnerable to periodic demands from Chatsworth or London for increased remittances or reduced expenditure, required to shore up the ailing finances of the English estates. Such demands reflected the very real constraints imposed upon the managerial policy of the Irish estate by its peripheral location and subordinate status within the overall Devonshire patrimony. Moreover, as the nineteenth century progressed, the Irish estate became progressively less important in relative terms as a source of income. The spectacular initial success of the seventh duke's industrial investments on his Barrow-in-Furness estates between 1863 and 1879 meant that the Irish remittances progressively fell as a percentage of total income. From a maximum value of 30 percent in 1855, they fell to 27 percent in 1861–1862, and to a low of 8 percent in 1872–1873, when total current income reached £320,000. Subsequently, the progressive decline in the return from the Barrow investments meant that the percentage of total income represented by the Irish remittances rose slightly, but to no more than 15 percent (in 1878) at best.

Within this overall pattern, the aggregate urban rents formed a varying though generally relatively minor component, which was further reduced in size by the sale of Youghal and Dungarvan in the early 1860s. Paradoxically, the remaining towns on the estate appear subsequently to have strengthened their rental performance, seemingly not being adversely affected by the deteriorating conditions on the agricultural estate. The question remains, however, of why, if the estate towns were of such limited significance financially, the fifth and sixth dukes were prepared to invest so heavily in them during the first quarter of the nineteenth century?

CHAPTER 4

Mismanagement and Neglect, 1764–1792

Bernard Scalé's survey of the Devonshire estates was typical of the sort of managerial steps being taken by many late-eighteenth-century landlords in an attempt to improve the profitability of their properties. Efficient management required a detailed knowledge of an estate and its tenants, and in turn generated a wide variety of records concerning every aspect of land ownership. On the best-run estates these might be expected to provide a continuous assessment of the efficiency gains being made and hence of the success with which the landlord's property interests were being safeguarded. Thus the annual rentals and accounts that were being kept ever more meticulously on many estates were, in effect, a summary statement of the estate bureaucracy's ability to control the complex nexus of relationships that linked them to the other actors in the local economy. This control was not absolute. Externally induced change, whether political or economic, could radically alter the local circumstances in which the land agent and his subordinates had to operate. Even in relatively difficult circumstances, however, it was possible for the quality of the agent's managerial performance to determine the extent to which such change affected his employer's interests. Thus on the Shelbourne estate in County Kerry, for example, the agent's refusal to seize the tenants' cattle for rent arrears was thought to account for the property's tranquillity during the 1798 rebellion.[1]

In a plural society such as that in eighteenth-century south Munster, the relationship between an agent and his employer's tenantry could be difficult even where management was efficient. When an agent was dishonest or ineffectual, these difficulties became acute. If tenants perceived themselves to be disadvantaged—whether by accident or design—they were liable to become increasingly vocal in their protests.

The impact of such complaints depended on the tenants' access either to the landlord or to some other senior figure in the estate hierarchy. Many agents were the subject of occasional complaints from aggrieved tenants.[2] The difficulty for the landlord lay in distinguishing between predictable petty recriminations and more serious and substantial allegations of malpractice.[3] Where the estate was managed for an absentee landlord, the problem was further compounded by the inevitable enhancement in the agent's authority. The lines of communication to the landlord would be correspondingly lengthened and in some cases maintained solely via the object of criticism, the agent himself.[4]

The surviving late-eighteenth-century records from the Devonshire estate make it abundantly clear that under William Conner II's agency (1764–1792) the duke's financial and political interests in Ireland suffered from all of these problems and more. Throughout his agency Conner pursued a consistent policy of nepotism, financial sharp practice, and political self-aggrandizement at the duke's expense. It is difficult to understand why successive auditors, particularly Sir Anthony Abdy and Baron Hotham, tolerated this state of affairs since they clearly recognized it to be unsatisfactory. Nevertheless, tolerate it they did, and in consequence they acquiesced in a relationship with Conner that was conducted with great irregularity and at long distance. In turn this acquiescence allowed the agent every opportunity to disguise his attempts to further his own or his relatives' interests.[5] Moreover, Conner's attitude mirrored that of the duke's Irish relatives, Lord Shannon and the Ponsonbys. Offered the management and representation of the Burlington (latterly Devonshire) political interest, both families fully exploited this opportunity in pursuit of their own political ambitions.

In all of this the estate towns figured little, save as the stage for Conner's personal political ambition (Bandon) and as an example of his mendacity and procrastination (Lismore). As a measure of the changing importance of the estate towns in the management of the duke's Irish estates this is entirely apposite. From a position in the late eighteenth century when, with the exception of Bandon, they were effectively disregarded by the resident agent, the towns emerged as a key element in the reassertion of the duke's authority on the estate in the early nineteenth century, and as a valuable asset in the crisis management of the duke's financial affairs from circa 1850. The following discussion appraises Conner's role as agent in these towns and beyond, and pays particular attention to the three aspects of agency where his corruption was most evident and his duplicity most profound: leasing policy, income management, and politics.[6]

Leases and Tenures

The overall managerial policy formulated by Abdy in the 1770s was designed to increase the fifth duke's income and tighten his control over the Irish estate, without involving him in undue expenditure. One of the most effective means of achieving this purpose was by shortening the leases offered to tenants. As on other estates, the type of lease being offered had long been determined by political as well as economic considerations. Under the Popery Act of 1704 and its subsequent amendment in 1709, Catholics were prevented from buying land or leasing it for more than thirty-one years, and from paying a rent that was less than two-thirds of its annual value. Although doubt has been expressed as to the real severity of these provisions, it is clear that by the 1770s the duke's Catholic tenants were still formally disadvantaged by these Penal Laws.[7] Admittedly, the process of amelioration had already begun. The "Bogland" Act of 1772 permitted Catholics to take sixty-one-year reclaiming leases of marginal land, but a substantial improvement in their position only came with the passage of the Catholic Relief Act in 1778.[8] For a numerically significant portion of the duke's Irish tenantry, therefore, the opportunity to participate in the tenurial process was artificially limited by purely political legislation for much of the eighteenth century.

Even for those members of the community unaffected by the Penal Laws, the types of lease commonly offered by landlords changed radically during the course of the eighteenth century for economic reasons. Every lease represented a compromise between the interests of the landlord and those of his tenant. Most landlords presumably wished either to optimize or maximize the net income they derived from their estates. The tenants, on the other hand, presumably hoped to balance considerations such as security and length of tenure against the level of rent and type of contractual obligations demanded and the amount of income the property could generate. In short, each lease had to provide for the interests of both parties, and it was entirely open to question whether subsequent developments in the economy favored one party more than the other.

Conventional wisdom suggests that for much of the eighteenth century the system worked in favor of the tenant rather than the landlord. The troubled conditions of the early 1690s led to low rents being set for leases which, when they expired in the 1720s, were reset at higher rents more in line with the rising agricultural prices and land values of the time. These increases were relatively substantial and initially caused some distress to the tenant community.[9] As the century progressed, however, the steady rise in agricultural prices made these rents progressively more affordable. Most of the leases set in the 1720s were for twenty-one or thirty-one years or for three lives, and did not fall in until the 1750s or later. Accordingly, most of the added value that accrued to Irish agriculture during the boom years of the 1740s and after was appropriated by the major tenants rather than by their landlords.

The tendency to grant long leases during the earlier part of the century was encouraged by the desire for "good" solvent tenants, a scarce commodity in Munster, and by the general perception that such leases were intrinsically beneficial, insofar as they were thought to encourage farm improvement by the tenants.[10] There is little evidence to suggest that this occurred in practice, but this perception may explain why at a time when land values were generally rising, many landlords responded by "tying up" their interest in their estates for relatively long periods, an apparently perverse reaction that was ultimately to prove inimical to their financial well-being. By the last quarter of the century there was an increasing general awareness of the deleterious effect long leases had on the landlords' interest in their estates, and growing concern too at what were perceived to be the adverse social consequences of the "middleman" system that was associated with them.[11] By this time, however, the middlemen were already of declining economic importance in the countryside. Representatives of an archaic social order in which they played an important financial role mediating between landlord and occupying subtenant, middlemen had always been most numerous in stock-rearing counties such as Cork, Kerry, and Waterford. Their willingness to act as brokers between the cattle merchants and the subtenants in these regions had done much to hasten the cattle trade's spread there in the 1720s and 1730s. But by the 1770s the economic position of the middlemen was being undermined both by the growing solvency of many small tenant farmers and by the increasing desire of many landlords to appropriate a larger share of the agricultural wealth of their estates for their own use. Although their final demise did not come until after the 1815 agricultural price collapse, as a socioeconomic group middlemen had already become anachronistic fifty years earlier.

On the Devonshire estate eighteenth-century leasing policy followed the general movement toward reducing the head tenants' interests in favor of the landlord's. Some 342 datable leases have been identified from this period, and they record a consistent decline in average length as the century progressed.[12] While nearly two-thirds of the total were for the relatively long and favorable term of three lives, such leases declined as a proportion of the total number of leases being set during each successive decade, falling from over 70 percent in the period 1711–1720 to under 54 percent in the period 1741–1750 (see table 4.1). Given that the twenty-one year reversionary term attached to many of these leases only came into effect after the expiry of the last life, their real length was likely to have been considerable.[13] Similarly, although a large proportion of the 124 leases set for a specific number of years were for the unusually long term of forty-one years, most of these (64 percent) were set before 1730. In contrast, over 97 percent of the shorter leases for years (thirty-one years or less) were set after 1730.

TABLE 4.1
Decennial Distribution of Sample Leases for Lives and
Years on the Devonshire Estate

	Lives	(%)	Years	(%)	Total
1711–1720	60	70.6	25	29.4	85
1721–1730	39	66.1	20	33.9	59
1731–1740	26	55.3	21	44.7	47
1741–1750	29	53.7	25	46.3	54
1751–1760	45	88.2	6	11.8	51
1761–1770	10	66.7	5	33.3	15
1771–1780	2	66.7	1	33.3	3
1781–1790	2	50.0	2	50.0	4
1791–1800	3	75.0	1	25.0	4

The Urban Leaseholds

In common with other landowners, the duke favored three-life leases with a twenty-one year reversionary term for his urban property, for such long-term leases were thought to provide the necessary incentive for tenants to undertake capital improvements.[14] One consequence of the use of this kind of lease, however, was that the landlord's opportunity to intervene directly in the management of his town was correspondingly limited. Thus in 1794 Henry Bowman concluded that the opportunities for immediate improvement in the duke's towns were severely constrained by the survival of residual lives or the reversionary term on various urban leases. For example, he found that in Dungarvan "the leases of several town holdings, as well as some of the farms, depend on the life of one Roberts, who went to America many years ago, and has not been lately heard of. There is a reversionary term of 21 years after Roberts' death; which from the best account I can get, must be nearly expired."[15] In short, although the quality and age of the building stock was the most highly visible and frequently remarked-upon index of the general condition of the urban estate, it was the leasehold pattern that determined the extent to which the duke through his agents could interfere to modify this.

Thus if the leaseholds provided the legal framework by which tenants gained access to urban space, the same was equally true for the duke. In the 1770s the urban estate was just as completely tied up with middlemen's leases as were the farms. Consequently the duke's opportunities either for raising rents or for undertaking wholesale remodeling and refurbishment of his urban property only came about on the expiry of existing and, as we have seen, frequently extremely lengthy leases. In effect the pattern of urban head tenancies operated as a matrix through which the duke's opportunity for future intervention in his urban property was very finely controlled. Moreover, although each head tenancy also represented a source of income, it was income that might, depending on when the lease was last renewed, be seriously deficient in terms of the current value of the property. Consequently in the 1770s there was every reason for the duke's advisers to try and reduce the leasehold interests on the urban estate and to tighten their fiscal and managerial control over it. That these reforms were not begun until 1792 was a consequence of the fifth duke's ambivalence and his Irish agent's corruption, and was not a true reflection of the real condition of the duke's urban estate in Ireland. O'Connor has argued that this situation was typical of towns where an absentee landlord interest was supplemented by numerous middlemen tenancies. In his study of Killmallock, County Limerick, he also argues that another frequent corollary was the decayed state of the town fabric, as head rents that could have been used for reconstructing buildings were syphoned off and occupying tenants were left with no incentive to improve. The frequency of this relationship is debatable. On the duke's estate there was certainly a correlation between attenuated tenurial chains and the decayed urban fabric at Dungarvan, Lismore, and Youghal, but at Bandon, where the tenurial linkages were equally extended, there is no evidence that the fabric was equally decayed. It would therefore seem more reasonable to look as much to the specific economic circumstances of individual towns to explain their physical condition, rather than to attempt to explain this solely in terms of tenurial structures.[16]

Table 4.2 lists selected indices of the comparative leasehold structure in the estate towns as recorded by Scalé between 1773 and 1776. The data is derived from the tenurial lists Scalé compiled to accompany the estate maps, and save for Youghal, is directly comparable for each town.[17] The head tenant and subtenant categories are self-explanatory. They designate the lessees holding directly from the duke, who were not necessarily themselves resident in the town, and their own immediate tenants. The subtenancies refer to the tenurial units that this latter group held from the head tenants and which therefore comprised part of the head tenants' overall leasehold property. The subtenancies were not necessarily synonymous with individual buildings or plots, but might contain a number of these or alternatively orchard or garden property within the town bounds. Subtenants could (and did) hold more than one subtenancy under more than one head tenant.

Table 4.2 demonstrates that the leasehold structure varied substantially between towns, not only in terms of the absolute numbers of tenants, but also in terms of the average size of their holdings, the extent of nonresidence, and the strength with which tenurial links persisted between town and country. The most important measures are

TABLE 4.2
Comparative Leasehold Structure in the Estate Towns, 1773–1776

	Bandon	Dungarvan	Lismore	Tallow	Youghal
Head tenants (HT)	101	8	17	31	80
Subtenants (ST)	396	188	139	235	n/c
Subtenancies (STc)	505	221	219	289	264
% Headtenants resident	30	0	53	19	38
Average size of HT holdings*	5	14	12	8	2
Average ST per HT	4	24	8	8	n/c
Average STc per HT	5	28	13	9	3
Average size of ST holdings*	1.3	0.6	1.5	1.0	n/c
% HTs with land in town parks	4	13	12	65	14
% HTs also STs	25	0	41	16	n/c
% STs with land in town parks	5	0.5	5	0.4	n/c
% STs with multiple subtenancies	15	17	24	12	n/c
Total town park HTs	6	5	4	26	38
Total town parks STs	30	26	12	0	43

*: in roods
n/c = not calculated

those provided by the ratios between head tenants, subtenants, and subtenancies. Together with the average size of the head tenant and subtenant holdings, these give some indication of the relative difference in economic status between the various tenurial groups. The assumption is that there will have been a basic congruity between the number and size of the properties leased by individual tenants and their socioeconomic standing. Accordingly, the greater the ratio value, the greater the assumed difference in status. Where high ratio values are combined with high levels of head tenant nonresidence, this status difference is likely to have been reflected in relatively low levels of social interchange between the two groups. Using this approach, Dungarvan stands out as the town where the status difference between the duke's tenants was apparently most pronounced, and Bandon and Youghal as the towns where for some of the tenantry it was likely to have been least.

At Bandon, the head tenants and subtenants formed the largest groups in their respective categories, but the ratio between them was the smallest by a considerable margin. Similarly, while the average size of the head tenants' holdings in the town was relatively small (the second smallest after Youghal), that of the subtenants was relatively large and was only exceeded at Lismore. The recorded size differential between them was correspondingly low, and in fact for most of the tenancies may have been even lower, since the average size of the head tenancies has been inflated by the inclusion of several disproportionately large holdings. These included the properties held by Francis Bernard, Epey Cross, George Conner, John Harris, and John Lapp. All save Harris owned between twenty-six and fifty-six subtenancies. These head tenancies lay on the northern periphery of the town where they consisted of both agricultural plots and linear residential development along the roads leading into the town. These head tenancies were of a different size order to the remainder, and remind us that as in most preindustrial towns, Bandon was likely to have had at least a small nucleus of magnate figures whose wealth would have been significantly greater than that common in the rest of the community.[18] Certainly, Francis Bernard was one of the duke's most substantial tenants-in-chief and bitterest political opponents. In addition to his urban property, he held over 60 percent of the Bandon town parks as well as substantial farms at Laragh. This concentration of property gave the Bernard family immense local influence which they wielded with sufficient panache to deny the duke the political patronage of Bandon for much of the later eighteenth century.[19] For the rest, the low differential between the average size of head tenant and subtenant holdings, the relatively low average number of subtenants renting from head tenants, and the relatively high proportion of head tenants who themselves rented from other tenants, all suggest that whatever their precise tenurial status, the majority of the duke's other tenants in Bandon belonged to the same broad economic and, as O'Flanagan has demonstrated, religious spectrum. Presumably, this was based on the specialized woolen and cloth manufacturing and mercantile activities identified by Lucas in 1787.[20]

At Youghal the tenurial structure was also characterized by a relatively low status differential between the head tenants and the subtenants, and was thus comparable with Bandon. The total number of head tenancies on the duke's estate was second only to Bandon, but on average each head tenant held fewer subtenancies and these, moreover, were of smaller average size than their Bandon counterparts. In fact, none of the Youghal head tenantry were of the same status as Francis Bernard or Epey Cross. Only four held more than ten subtenancies and none more than nineteen. The relatively few head tenants who held land in the town parks between them accounted for no more than one-fifth of its total area. The overall impression is that the duke's head tenants were men of more modest property than their fellow head tenants in Bandon, and that accordingly they were even less clearly distinguished from their own subtenants in economic terms. O'Flanagan's research suggests that this economic homogeneity was mirrored by an equally pronounced confessional homogeneity.[21]

The duke's estate in Dungarvan did not possess a magnate family like the Bernards, but otherwise the evidence suggests that socially it was more polarized than either Bandon or Youghal. The tenurial indices listed in table 4.2 amply bear out later descriptions of the town as being largely inhabited by impoverished fishermen. Nevertheless, the relatively few head tenants held (on average) the largest holdings and received rent from the greatest number of subtenants. Significantly, none of the head tenants were themselves resident on the duke's urban estate. This suggests the sort of minimal social interaction with their subtenants that one would expect from eighteenth-century descriptions of the town. The largest holdings were those of Michael Green and George Markham, who between them rented well over half of the duke's urban estate and were immediate landlords to more than 66 percent of its subtenancies. Green was also the only head tenant to possess land in the town parks, but this amounted to no more than twenty-one acres or 1.6 percent of the total.

The other side of this particular coin, of course, was that the subtenants' buildings were generally ramshackle cabins and their rents correspondingly low,[22] but this reality simply emphasizes the social polarity involved. At six-tenths of a rood, the average size of the subtenants' holdings was the smallest in any of the towns. Significantly, none of the head tenants in Dungarvan were subtenants on any other property, that is, held from another tenant rather than the duke, and only one subtenant held land in the town parks. Seemingly, in 1775 the social ligaments in the community were relatively well defined. If the majority of the urban head tenants did not possess an interest in the lands traditionally set aside for the community's use, then neither did they engage in anything other than a clearly demarcated—and superior—tenurial relationship with the mass of the tenantry on the duke's estate. There was no blurring of the distinction between the two groups of the sort that occurred at Youghal or Bandon. On the other hand, some sort of economic differentiation was quite clearly occurring within the ranks of the subtenants themselves. Over thirty of them (17 percent, the second highest total) leased multiple subtenancies and were obviously engaged on their own account in the property market. The names of these people mean little at this distance, but it is interesting to note that as a group, two-thirds of them held only one other cabin besides their own, and that of the remainder the average holding was five and the largest, the vicar's, twelve. Similar sorts of process are observable in the other estate towns, where they were combined with a more flexible relationship between head tenant and subtenant status.

Lismore and Tallow displayed less extreme variations in their tenurial structure save in two respects. Tallow stands out as the one town where the tenurial linkages between the urban head tenants and the town parks remained overwhelmingly strong and broadly based. Lismore, on the other hand, displayed a relatively complex tenurial structure, characterized by a comparatively high incidence of multiple leasing by subtenants and subleasing by head tenants. In Tallow nearly two-thirds of the head tenants held land in the town parks, and this group also tended to be the largest leaseholders in the town. The only exception was Charles Seward. His eight-acre holding on Tallowbridge Street supported thirty subtenants and was one of the largest in the town, but he did not hold land in the town parks. The strength of the tenurial links between the town and town parks would seem to be a function of time. The immediate comparison is with Bandon, which like Tallow dated from the Munster Plantation. In both places the town parks were laid out coevally with the towns and were intended to supplement the urban economy. Compared with the medieval settlements at Dungarvan, Lismore, and Youghal, insufficient time had elapsed at Bandon and Tallow to weaken the tenurial links between each town and its parks, although by the 1770s these had taken different forms.

At Bandon, they were characterized by a concentration of both urban and town park property in the hands of the leading magnate family, the Bernards, which explains why the percentage of head tenants holding town park lands was so low. At Tallow, where such social primacy had not evolved, these linkages were characterized by the more evenhanded survival of linked property rights over a numerically larger group of joint urban-rural tenancies. Both cases represented significant instances of the survival of originally more important and widespread tenurial linkages between urban and rural property. In the three towns of medieval origin, in contrast, this was no longer true. Not only was the proportion of head tenants with land in the town parks much smaller than in Tallow, but in each case they held collectively only a small portion of the land that was available.[23]

The relatively low proportion of resident head tenants reinforces the impression of strong and continuing rural linkages in Tallow, since in this case the "absentees" will almost certainly have been rural residents. At Bandon and Youghal, on the other hand, one cannot discount the possibility that the nonresident head tenants may have resided in parts of the town not owned by the duke. In all other respects, the remaining values for Tallow suggest that the town's tenurial structure was unremarkable, and stood midway between the extreme status polarization at Dungarvan and the broader-based structures at Bandon and Youghal. At Lismore, the tenurial structure was more complex, and was characterized by seemingly contradictory trends. The relatively large ratio values recorded for subtenants and subtenancies per head tenant suggest a clearly demarcated status differential between the two tenurial groups. This is belied, however, by the high incidence of head tenants who leased subtenancies from fellow tenants (41 percent). This apparent contradiction can be explained by the existence of another small group of magnate head tenants: Henry Jervais, Jeremiah Coughlan, Thomas Tuckey, and Andrew Crotty. Between them, they held 61 percent of the subtenancies in the town. As at Bandon, their holdings would have had the effect of raising the average values recorded in table 4.2 for the subtenants and subtenancies per head tenant in a way that would have inflated the holdings for the majority of the head tenants. The contradiction between these seemingly high per capita holdings and the high incidence of subleasing by head tenants is therefore more apparent than real. If most of the head tenants were less extensive property holders than table 4.2 suggests, it is easier to understand why they may have been willing to lease property from other tenants. Nearly one-quarter of the subtenants themselves leased multiple subtenancies, indicating that, as at Dungarvan, processes of economic differentiation were taking place within the tenant population that were not consonant with simple tenurial status.

The Implementation of Leasing Policy

The normal method of setting a lease involved a lengthy process of competitive tendering by interested tenants and consultation between the Irish agent and the auditor before the duke of Devonshire finally signed the perfected document. The initial stages appear to have been quite informal. As an existing lease neared expiry, the property might be advertised ("canted") but it is quite clear that this was not done on every occasion.[24] Interested parties submitted a written proposal to the agent stating the rent they were prepared to pay, what sums (if any) they were prepared to expend on improvement, and the type of lease they would prefer. Frequently, these proposals were accompanied by some special pleading as to the justice of their case. The proposals were then forwarded by the agent to the auditor, together with the agent's comments on the suitability of each applicant in terms of his solvency, experience, religious affiliation, and—most importantly—past loyalty to the duke's political nominees.[25] If any applicant sent a proposal directly to the auditor, this was invariably returned to the agent for his comments, thereby reinforcing the crucial role the agent played in determining which proposal was most likely to be accepted. The informality and competitive nature of these proceedings frequently led to complaints, as unsuccessful applicants found either that their status as sitting tenants did not automatically ensure success, or else that their proposal had not received the attention they felt it merited.[26] The system was also open to manipulation by both applicants and agent alike. For example, in supporting a proposal for the farm at Bally-moodranagh in 1783, Richard Musgrave successfully argued that the previous rent for the property had borne no relation to the true value of the land since it had been pushed up by "the rancorous competition between two brothers." His complaint reflected a widespread feeling that canting made tenants overvalue the land and thereby reduced their subsequent ability to improve it.[27] In the later eighteenth century lease renewals were invariably the occasion for a significant increase in rent, as property was revalued upward in line with the rise in land values and agricultural prices. Consequently, one of the most frequent reasons why a proposal failed was that the rent offer was too low. When this happened, the auditor was normally reluctant to accept a second, higher bid from the unsuccessful applicant on the grounds that to do so was unfair to the other applicants who had initially made higher offers.[28]

Once a proposal had been accepted by the duke and the tenant declared, the lease was drawn up in a form that was fundamentally the same whatever the term involved. Each lease normally specified the lessee, the entry date and fine (if any), the conditions of entry and the denomination of the property, the length of the term in lives or years, the annual rent and when this was payable, any payments to be made for taxes or in lieu of heriot and capons, and the designated mill at which the lessee was to grind corn and the manorial court at which he was to do suit. Additional clauses sometimes required the service of an armed horseman, but were more normally concerned with specifying the circumstances in which the duke could distrain the tenant (usually for nonpayment of rent) or in which the tenant could sell his residual interest in the lease (only under license).[29] The payments in lieu of heriots and capons were nominal, and clearly harked back to an earlier age when the tenurial relationship between landlord and tenant was overtly feudal. So too did the entry fine. For landlords, fining represented a way of increasing immediate income by mortgaging part of the future income from the estate, the quid pro quo for the tenants being the offer of favorable leases, usually in perpetuity. The earl of Cork and Burlington favored this method in the 1720s and 1730s, and until the 1750s, at least, these fines could be very substantial, particularly for agricultural holdings.[30] For urban property, the fine appears to have been standardized at about five shillings for each tenement, although for more substantial property it could be as high as £30. For the larger farms it was frequently in excess of £100, and among the sample leases reached a maximum of £700 for Laragh in 1719 and again for Scanavidogue in 1726.[31]

These fines commonly represented between four and seven years' purchase at the agreed rent, but no consistent relationship is discernible between the size of the rent and the size of the fine, although in theory the latter should have been reduced in proportion to the former. In the second half of the century entry fines became the exception rather than the rule; where additional capital payments were required from incoming tenants, these increasingly took the form of an undertaking to expend an agreed sum on capital improvements. No evidence exists to suggest that attempts were made by the duke's agent to influence the choice of lives inserted in the three-life leases, although this was attempted on other estates.[32] On the Devonshire estate the lives were usually those of the lessee together with two of his immediate relatives, perhaps his wife or son or daughter. Nearly as common were the names of other, now equally anonymous people, who were perhaps locally prominent at the time. None of the sample leases used as lives the sort of national figures advocated by Grieg for the Gosford estates in 1821, who had the advantage that their demise would be well publicized.[33]

As existing leases fell in, farms and town holdings alike were subdivided and, increasingly, let only to tenants who would occupy and improve rather than to absentee middlemen. Sitting tenants were only favored for renewal if they intended to reside.[34] Dickson suggests that such moves were common on Munster estates at this time, and for similar reasons. By letting directly to occupying tenants, the landlord could hope not merely to obtain a larger proportion of the increasing market value of the property, but also to influence the tenants' voting behavior in a more immediate fashion.[35] Although advertising vacant farms carried the risk that the competition between tenants might encourage the offer of uneconomic rents, both Conner and the fifth duke were aware of this problem. Writing to Abdy in 1774, Conner concluded: "I think his Grace adjudges right in not letting for a very advanced price but preferring a moderate rise by which the tenant will be well able to pay his rent, improve the land and have a reasonable profit for his labour."[36] What constituted a "moderate rise" and a "reasonable profit" were of course open to question, but certainly Conner showed some awareness of the level of rent individual farms could bear. In 1780, for example, he advised Hotham to refuse Francis McCarthy's offer of £110 rent for Killmoyleran precisely because "it was more than could be made from the land."[37]

Conner's role in the implementation of the overall management policy was important, if not entirely honest. Of local origin, he was sensitive to circumstances about which the auditor might not be fully aware. In his recommendations to Hotham about lease proposals, he was alert both to sectarian and political considerations, as well as to the relative merits of each proposal. This advisory role placed agents such as Conner in a very strong position in the local community and rendered them susceptible to bribery.[38] In the case of the Devonshire estate, it was a system that seems to have favored Protestant tenants who were either personally known to Conner or who had a long connection with the estate, and who had a record of political allegiance to the duke. For example, of the six applicants for Lower Mogeely in August 1785, three were refused because they were "Papists" and a fourth because of his relative lack of farming experience. The choice Conner favored was between Robert Welsh, "a gentleman of good character and substance," even though he only offered £180, marginally less than the existing rent of £197.18.10, and Messrs. Bowles and Boyce, who offered the same rent but who were described as "the real friends of the Duke's Interest."[39] Similarly, a year later, in June 1786, two of the four proposers for Macromore were excluded because Conner knew nothing of their circumstances, while the ultimately successful applicant, John Wren, was described as "a very industrious honest man and a punctual good tenant of good substance."[40]

Where the property gave the tenants the right to vote in borough elections, political considerations were equally important. In these circumstances the past and probable future political allegiance of the prospective tenants received particularly close scrutiny. When the lease of Knockroe fell vacant in 1778, the choice of tenant was dictated by the fact that the farm was within one and a half miles of Tallow church, which gave its inhabitants, if Protestant, the right to vote in the town's elections. Accordingly, one applicant was refused because he intended to leave the farm to the son of avowed political opponents of the duke, a second on the grounds of religion, and a third because he was an apothecary and not a farmer. Significantly, the sitting tenants were also refused a renewal because they already held two of the six farms within the charter bounds of the borough. Conner thought that a third farm would constitute an unwise concentration of politically important property in their hands. The successful candidate, George Teape, was a Tallow resident and "a man of substance, worth £1,000."[41]

Conner was equally alive to the more general political advantages of Abdy's direct letting policy. Where occupying tenants held from a middleman or head lessee, it was they rather than the duke whom the tenants favored with their votes. At Bandon, where in 1786 Conner estimated the ratio between occupying tenants and head lessees to be between 30:1 and 50:1, he found that if he applied to the sitting tenants (who were mostly freemen) "to vote for the person the Duke recommends, the answer I get is, they do not know the Duke, they are not tenants to him, and they must oblige their landlord." To remedy this problem, Conner advised Hotham "to let to the real occupiers as fast as the leases fall in, by which means the inhabitants or the most of them would . . . know the Duke twice a year at least, this mode and this only, can make the Duke of consequence with the inhabitants."[42] Two years later Garde advocated a similar policy for Lismore, where large tracts of ground, then out of lease, posed a threat to the duke's political interest. Should these be let to "gentlemen of fortune," Garde argued, these men could create their own political interest in opposition to the duke's by subletting to numerous undertenants who, by reason of residence, would have votes in the borough. Garde suggested that the duke should let these lands directly, enforcing residence by clauses inserted in the leases, and political loyalty by the strict enforcement of these clauses.[43]

In theory, the consequence of Abdy's policy of subdivision and direct letting should have been a progressive rise in the number of tenants on the estate. As table 4.3 demonstrates, this did occur, but to nothing like the extent the rapid implementation of Abdy's policy would have entailed. Between 1764 and 1791 the overall number of recorded tenants on the estate rose by 17 percent from 329 to 386, but most of this rise was accounted for by the Lismore district, where the number of tenants holding directly from the duke rose from 93 to 132. The other districts either recorded a very marginal change, as at Bandon where the total rose by 11 percent from 91 to 101, or like Youghal remained virtually static. This low and selective rate of increase in the number

TABLE 4.3
Tenants Holding Directly under the Duke

Year	1764	1768	1777	1780	1781	1782	1783	1784
Lismore	93	93	103	122	122	125	124	125
Chief rents	22	22	21	21	21	21	20	21
Jointure	19	18	17	18	18	18	18	18
Youghal	79	79	79	79	79	79	79	79
Bandon	91	92	94	97	100	100	100	104
Western estate	15	15	13	11	11	11	12	12
Western Jointure estate	10	10	10	10	9	9	9	9
Gillabbey			5	5	5	5	5	5
Ballyrafter			7	7	7	7	7	7
Ballygalane			5	4	4	4	3	3
Total	329	329	354	374	376	379	377	383

Year	1785	1786	1787	1788	1789	1790	1791
Lismore	130	131	132	134	132	132	132*
Chief rents	21	21	21	21	21	21	21
Jointure	18	19	19	19	19	19	19
Youghal	79	79	79	80	80	80	79
Bandon	104	102	102	101	101	101*	101
Western estate	10	10	10	11	11	11	11
Western Jointure	9	9	9	9	9	9	9
Gillabbey estate	5	5	5	5	5	5	5
Ballyrafter	8	7	7	7	7	7	7
Ballygalane	3	2	2	2	2	2	2
Total	387	385	386	389	387	387	386

* Estimate. Account defective.
Source: Estate accounts.

of tenants was a function of the relatively stable leasehold structure already identified as characteristic of the estate under Conner, and which was also responsible for the slow overall growth in rents at this time. Abdy may have identified the means whereby the duke's effective control over his estate might be improved, but the existing tenurial structure dictated that the implementation of his plan would be delayed.

Implicit within the managerial policies devised by Abdy and Hotham was the defense of the duke's property rights. During Conner's agency, and apart from the effects of his own predation, these were threatened in a variety of ways: internally, by the increasing disinclination of tenants to comply with the clauses in their leases stipulating suit at mill; and externally by widespread salmon poaching on the Blackwater, the growing revolt against tithes, and Lord Cahir's attempt to claim title to 1,600 acres of mountain land near Lismore at Ballyin and Ballyrafter. With the exception of the mill dispute, these issues affected the agricultural rather than the urban estate. Poaching on the Blackwater had plagued Richard Musgrave's tenancy of the fishery ever since he had first leased it in 1738, but such was the value of the fishery that the duke subsidized the legal costs his tenant periodically incurred in its defense.[44] The tithe agitation was particularly serious on the Waterford part of the estate between 1784 and 1787, when it was associated with "Whiteboy" disturbances and successfully prevented tithe farmers from bidding for the tithes.[45] Although the duke sought compensation under the provisions of the "Tumultuous Risings Act" of 1787,[46] Garde suggested that a more permanent solution lay in letting the tithes to immediate representatives of the parish. They would hold the tithes in the interests of the parish and apportion the rent on a mutually agreed basis.[47] It is not known whether Garde's suggestion was acted upon, but by the early 1790s tithes were again a live issue on the estate.[48] Lord Cahir's attack on Ballyin and Ballyrafter was more successfully dealt with, although his litigious zeal prolonged the contest for six years. It began in 1773, when Lord Cahir prevented "the Duke's surveyor," presumably Bernard Scalé, from surveying the disputed property on the border between Counties Tipperary and Waterford.[49] In Garde's phrase, what "gave colour" to Cahir's claim was the duke's tenants' habit of permitting the undertenants on Cahir's adjoining property to build booley huts—temporary shelters used by herdsmen on upland pastures—on the duke's land, a practice that presumably reflected the contemporary growth in population pressure in marginal areas. An initial attempt by the duke to prove title by a processionary bill was dismissed in 1777 on a legal technicality without prejudice to his claim. Two years later, despite Cahir's success in appealing for a retrial, a Cork jury found in favor of the duke for a second time and the land was returned to the estate.[50]

In common with the practice on other estates, the duke's tenants were obliged by the covenants in their leases to grind their corn at one or other of the manorial mills on the estate.[51] These covenants were potentially of increasing value as corn growing spread in the region during the 1770s and 1780s. In theory, tenants of the duke's mills should have enjoyed a virtual monopoly of this trade among his other tenants. In practice, however, widespread defaulting by tenants at Bandon and Tallow led to the bankruptcy of the mill tenants there by the late 1770s.[52] At Tallow, Conner exploited the situation to his own benefit. At Bandon, the case was complicated by Conner's previous inability to prove the tenants' obligation to grind at the mill, which necessitated legal action by the duke in 1774 in an attempt to establish this right.[53] How successful the action was is not clear. A year later an ejectment was brought against the mill tenant, John Harris, for nonpayment of arrears amounting to £402. When the bill of ejectment was finally enforced in 1776, the tenant's brother, Michael Harris, paid both the arrears and the current year's rent of £100 and assumed responsibility for the tenancy. This regularized the situation but did not solve the problem of the defaulting tenants. In 1777 Conner engaged with Harris in cooperative action against the defaulting tenants, but this too seems to have failed. Four years later Michael Harris was ejected for nonpayment of £250 arrears, and, despite pressure from Lord Shannon, was replaced by relatives of Conner's, Jacob and Thomas Biggs.[54] Given the increasing penetration of the money economy through all levels of Irish rural society at this time, the estate's continuing inability to enforce the covenants requiring suit at mill was almost inevitable. These covenants were anachronistic, and really only made sense in a localized manorial economy characterized by limited monetary exchange. In late-eighteenth-century Munster they were rendered superfluous by the growing pace and extent of the commercially based intra regional and international exchanges which, among other things, underpinned the prosperity of Bandon and Youghal.

Nepotism and Alienation

The evidence presented so far has related to the managerial policies instituted by the duke's auditors and intended by them to be implemented by the Irish agent. The full extent of Conner's manipulation of these policies to further his own interests only became apparent after Heaton's appointment as auditor in 1791. The opportunities for concealment provided by Hotham's habit of referring all Irish correspondence back to Conner for advice and comment ended, and once again the way was open for tenants to voice their grievances with some prospect of a fair hearing. Conner was no longer able to present an idealized and unrealistic version of estate affairs to an auditor who, for whatever reason, was willing to accept this fantasy as truth. Not surprisingly, therefore, the complaints that survive from the early years of Heaton's auditorship portray a picture of Conner's management that is somewhat at variance with that offered in his previous correspondence with Hotham.

The main complaints against Conner were recited in a series of letters to Lord Frederick Cavendish and John Heaton written independently by Thomas Garde and Sir Richard Musgrave between 1790 and 1792. Musgrave had been M.P. for Lismore in the duke's interest, and was a close friend and political ally of George Ponsonby. His family had been tenants of the Deer Park and other land near Lismore for at least two generations, but on the expiry of their existing lease in 1786 they had been dispossessed of the Deer Park by Conner.[55] Accordingly, one might question the objectivity of Musgrave's testimony, were it not corroborated by Garde. The list of complaints is impressive: that Conner had for many years favored his friends and relatives with leases at gross undervaluations; that in order to do so he had suppressed proposals and discouraged competition; that he had allowed relatives to remain in possession of property at Bandon and Dungarvan even though their leases had expired; and that he had created his own financial interest at Bandon, Tallow, and Youghal by setting up trusts for different properties under various nominees. To these specific complaints were added the more general charges of drunkeness, insolence, and "a contemptuous sullen indifference to the tenants' interests" which had effectively lost the duke much of his remaining political influence.[56]

Conner's nepotism was most recently and flagrantly demonstrated in the case of Sir Richard Musgrave's lease of the Lismore Deer Park, but it had been exercised in principle for many years prior to this. The main beneficiaries were his immediate relatives and associates, including the Gumbletons and the Coughlans at Lismore, the Keilys at Dungarvan, and the Splanes and the Biggs at Bandon.[57] In some instances farms were announced as having been relet to one of Conner's relatives before the existing lease had expired. In other instances, farms were not advertised at all but were let privately at rents that gave the new tenants a highly inflated profit. At Kilcalf, for example, Robert Gumbleton was reputed to be clearing £300 a year in 1792.[58] In all such cases the effect was to reduce open competition. Conner's habit of letting it be known that certain existing tenants (including the Musgraves) would not get a renewal had the same effect, and together these tactics minimized the rents Conner's intended recipients had to pay, a point that was made by Musgrave to Hotham as early as 1786. Where alternative proposals were received for favored farms, Musgrave alleged, Conner informed his relatives of the size of the competing offers, so that by increasing their offer by a few pence per acre they could be sure of the preference.[59] In the case of the Lismore Deer Park, the Musgraves were not even informed that the farm was to be relet, and consequently could only make a late offer. This was refused, initially on the grounds that the land, being within the charter bounds of Lismore borough, was to be subdivided and let directly to occupying tenants. Later, after Conner claimed that suitable tenants could not be found for these smaller farms, Hotham agreed that both the Deer Park and the neighboring six hundred acres of Kilnecarrigy should be let to Counselor Gumbleton.[60] Two years later, in 1792, Garde voiced the strong suspicion that this arrangement concealed one of Conner's personal trusts, Counselor Gumbleton having been ill and resident in Bath for some years.[61]

The readiness with which Hotham acquiesced in Conner's recommendation concerning the Deer Park and Kilnecarrigy caused Musgrave to suspect that he had actively connived with Conner in the matter.[62] Whatever the truth in this instance, and it must be stressed that there is no other evidence to support Musgrave's view, it is clear that Conner's other financial trusts were concealed from the auditor. These included two farms at Youghal, nominally held by two of the duke's "common drivers"; various unspecified properties at Bandon alluded to by Garde in 1792; and the mills and quay at Tallow. The Tallow property is the best documented. In 1792 anonymous "Friends"

of the duke made a variety of allegations against Conner concerning
his activities in the town. He was accused of misappropriating part of
the £500 the duke had given for the reconstruction of the market
house, preventing its use by others, and engaging in a cartel that had
engrossed the quay and charged exorbitant tolls for its use. The same
group also charged Conner with possessing a concealed partnership in
the town mills, something which Garde already suspected.[63] Conner's
involvement in this concern began some time after 1788, when Bowles
and Boyce, the tenants he was alleged to have combined with, took
over the tenancy from Robert Hallaghan. As at Bandon, the profitability of the Tallow mills had been greatly reduced by the tenants'
non-compliance with their leasehold covenants, and by 1777 Hallaghan was in financial difficulties. After a protracted lawsuit, he was finally evicted for nonpayment of £432.10.0 arrears in May 1788.[64]
Throughout these proceedings Conner's correspondence with Hotham
betrayed no sign of his intended financial involvement, but it did express his continuing concern over the interests of Bowles and Boyce as
prospective tenants. Given the problem of noncompliance, Conner
urged the enforcement of existing leasehold covenants requiring tenants to grind at the duke's mills. Furthermore, Conner took pains to
denigrate competing offers, while at the same time stressing the merits
of Bowles and Boyce. As men of substance with a record of political
loyalty to the duke, he argued, they were the ideal candidates for what
was an expensive and politically important tenancy. The new rent was
set at £85, considerably more than the £45 Hallaghan had paid, with
an agreement that the new tenants should spend an additional £600
on rebuilding the rundown mills, although Conner estimated that it
was likely to cost them considerably more. Four years later Conner
and his associates were able to let the concern for £236.10.0 a year.[65]

Conner's willingness to enhance his income by these devious means
was entirely in character, and mirrored his other attempts at self-
aggrandizement. These varied from his persistent efforts to have his
son nominated as one of the duke's common councilmen at Bandon
and his cousin appointed to one of the duke's vacant livings, to more
ludicrous attempts at personal social advancement. In 1788, for example, Conner offered to lend his employer £8,000, but Hotham declined to mention the suggestion to the duke.[66] The most lasting

monument to Conner's ambition was Lismore Castle, part of which was repaired at the duke's expense but under Conner's direction during the late 1780s. Despite Hotham's strictures, the cost rose from an estimated £470 in 1787 to over £770 in 1789. Conner's enthusiasm for the project interfered with his other duties. The apparent need for his personal supervision of the building operations was a frequently cited excuse for his continued absence from England at this time.[67] When the Conners surrendered the castle in 1792, Garde described it as "a very convenient house, two parlours, hall, seven bedrooms etc plus two good gardens and 40 acres of land worth two guineas per acre, for which Mr Conner only charged himself £10 per year."[68] Clearly, Conner had been as willing to enhance his domestic circumstances at the duke's expense as he had his financial status and local prestige.

Income Disbursement

On first inspection, Conner's accounts reveal little obvious sign of any irregularity. They survive in a complete form for only sixteen of his twenty-eight years as agent, but ancillary records make good some of the missing data for the deficient years after 1772.[69] Table 4.4 summarizes the relative importance of each expenditure category recorded by these accounts as a proportion of the total recorded spending cost between 1764 and 1791. Obviously, the figures underrepresent the real totals for the entire period, but there is no reason to suppose that a complete enumeration of the spending pattern would have resulted in proportions that were significantly different. The overwhelming impression is that the estate was intended to be run at the least cost consonant with efficient management, and that the prime objective was to produce as large a remittance as possible for the duke's use. Between 1764 and 1791 over 89 percent of the total disbursements took the form of remittances. Little consideration appears to have been given to the possibility of financing either infrastructural improvements in the local economy or agricultural improvements on individual farms as a means of improving the estate's financial performance. Instead, the management policy was reactive, and relied in the main on "the rise of the times" to ensure that rent income rose, without actively attempting to create circumstances in which this rise might be encouraged.

TABLE 4.4
Total Recorded Management Costs and Remittances,
1764–1791 (Sixteen-Year Sample)

	(£)	(%)
Schoolmasters' salaries, etc.	4,256	1.73
Quit rents, etc.	8,188	3.34
Accountant's salary, etc.	8,424	3.42
Remittances	219,940	89.59
Law costs	2,303	0.94
Improvements	2,397	0.98
Total	245,508	100.00

The largest components in the management cost were the quit rents and the accountant's and other salaries, but in each case these represented less than 4 percent of the total expenditure. The quit rents were paid to the Crown for lands that were originally leased by Raleigh as part of the Munster Plantation.[70] The chief rents were paid to a variety of individuals for properties that the duke held as leasehold. At Youghal these included seven tenements in the town, for which the mayor received £6.8.8, and Magner's Hill, held from the Ronayne family for £5 a year. At Bandon the quit rents totaled £97.12.8 a year, and on the Lismore estate, £83.17.6.[71] The existence of these rents, together with the chief rents paid to the duke, provides an apt reminder of the complexity of the duke's title to his Irish estate. The incremental processes of acquisition and disposal over two centuries had ensured that by no means all of his land was held in fee simple. Conner's salary accounted for the bulk of the annual wages bill. He was paid £480 as agent for the Waterford estates and £80 for Bandon. The separate identification of these salaries reflects the fact that the two agencies had originally been distinct, and were only amalgamated when Conner succeeded his father at Lismore.[72] Most of the legal costs were paid to Thomas Garde and fluctuated considerably, reaching a peak of £455 in 1791.[73] Of the remaining spending heads, the schoolmasters' salaries and pensions represented a charge on the estate that arose from the first earl of Cork's endowment of a school at Bandon, and schools and almshouses at Lismore and Youghal. The schoolmasters each received a salary of £30, while the six almsmen at Lismore received annual pensions totaling £33 and the six almswomen at Youghal pensions worth £30. Also included under this head was the cost of repairs not only to these schools and the almshouses, but also to Tallow market and Lismore Castle itself, as well as the cost of maintaining the monument to the first earl of Cork in the Youghal parish church.[74]

The relative scarcity of accessible eighteenth-century Irish estate accounts of any duration makes it difficult to determine whether this expenditure pattern was normal. Research by David Large suggests it was entirely consonant with spending on the Fitzwilliam and Charlemont estates at least. His more general conclusion, that expenditure on administration and improvement on many late-eighteenth-century Irish estates was usually minor compared to the remittances, finds support in Beckett's more recent study of English estates. Beckett concludes that although improvement expenditure undoubtedly increased as time progressed, in the 1790s it was rarely more than 5 percent of the gross rental on even the largest estates. Exceptions such as the 18 percent spent by Coke on his Holkham estate in Norfolk were the result of the landlord's particular inclination toward agricultural improvement and of the impoverished state of his land.[75] Moreover, although the late eighteenth century was a period of widespread landlord involvement in infrastructural and settlement improvement in Ireland, it is not axiomatic that this absorbed a disproportionately large part of landlord income. In many instances, landlords contented themselves with creating or improving the infrastructural base for settlements, but stopped short of further investment in the building stock itself.[76] Conceivably, therefore, on estates where there was a more active involvement in improvement than on the Devonshire's property, the proportionate cost need not have been significantly greater than that sanctioned by the duke.

Examination of Conner's accounts in the light of his correspondence with Sir Beaumont Hotham reveals a number of deficiencies in his financial management that are not immediately apparent from superficial inspection. These range from the periodic omission of parts of the estate from the annual rental to gross delays in remitting rents, and, in the case of some years, not submitting accounts at all. Conner's carelessness in collecting rents was quickly recognized by Garde when he examined the accounts in 1792, but it also extended to the payments due from the estate for quit rents and chiefries. Sums due to the archbishop of Cashel and the dean of Lismore were allowed to fall heavily into arrears in the 1780s, and were not finally paid until 1790.[77] Unprofessional although these errors were, they were minor compared to Conner's seeming inability either to close his accounts on time or to remit the rents as fast as the duke and the auditor wished. Complaints, demands, and exhortations about these delays occur with increasing frequency throughout the correspondence between auditor and agent.[78]

Figure 4.1 summarizes the periodicity of Conner's remittances compared with those of his two English successors, Henry Bowman and Thomas Knowlton. The percentage figures represent the proportion of the total recorded remittances that were made in a given month. The difference between Conner's agency and those of his successors is marked. Bowman and Knowlton remitted over 40 percent of the total amount sent each year within six months of the close of the account, and over 73 percent by the end of the same calendar year. Conner's total for each period was, respectively, 16 percent and 40 percent, much of which was only paid after Hotham's attempt in 1786 to enforce rent payment within the "hanging gale."[79] Moreover, although Knowlton's remittances were affected by the 1798 rebellion (which explains the anomalous secondary peak sixteen months after the close of account), Conner habitually made a significant proportion of his remittances between one and two years after each account was supposed to have been closed. By any standard, the efficiency of the remittance procedure improved significantly after Conner's resignation.

The fundamental reason for these delays appears to have been Conner's inability or unwillingness to force the tenants to pay their rents on time. In his letters to Abdy and Hotham, Conner makes frequent reference to the problems he experienced in collecting rents, but gives no indication that he felt in any way responsible for the situation he was allowing to develop. While acknowledging that the auditor had a right to complain about the late and erratic remittances,[80] Conner regarded the tenant's nonpayment of rent as a de facto problem about which he could do very little. For example, in explaining to Hotham his failure to close the Ladyday 1774 account as soon as he intended, Conner wrote: "I was greatly disappointed by many of the tenants, who gave me the strongest assurances that they would clear off all rent and arrears, for which I have since made many applications, to no pur-

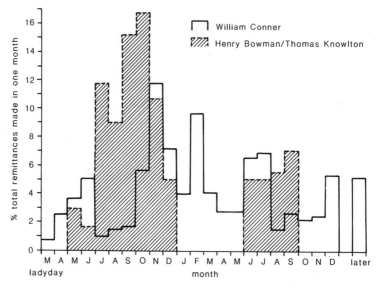

FIGURE 4.1   Average Proportionate Periodicity of Remittances from
Ladyday, 1764–1813

pose. Those tenants in arrears have votes in the Boroughs, and were
they to be pushed by legal means, they would instantly declare against
the Gentleman recommended by the Duke."[81] Political considerations
such as these may well have been valid, but they do not explain
Conner's apparent readiness to accept the tenants' explanations for
nonpayment in other cases. In 1781 and again in 1788 these explanations were economic, claiming a dearth of specie until after stock had
been sold at forthcoming fairs.[82] In 1784, while assuring Hotham of his
continuing best efforts to collect the outstanding arrears, Conner
gloomily confided to him: "[I]ndeed you can't form an idea of some of
the people I have to deal with or of the difficulty attending the receipt
and recovery of the Rents of this Estate."[83]

It is difficult to judge from this distance how far these delays were
externally induced and the consequence of problems in the local economy. On several occasions between 1776 and 1778 Conner wrote com-
plaining about the difficulty of obtaining bills of exchange,[84] and
certainly the decade was a difficult one for agriculture. Nevertheless, it
is noteworthy that the delays in accounting and remitting continued
throughout the agricultural upturn of the 1780s. Moreover, as Garde

pointed out in a caustic comment in 1792, Conner certainly did not avail himself of the opportunity for legal action to reduce the arrears. Writing to Heaton, Garde expressed surprise that Conner "should be backward in his accounts, since there are not better paid rents in Ireland than the Duke of Devonshire's. This I must suppose to be the case where for some years I have not been applied to for any proceedings at Law to be carried out for the recovery of such."[85] Whether through inefficiency or for some other more deliberate reason, it seems clear that Conner was willing to let arrears mount beyond the level considered acceptable by the auditor, and that he failed to use all necessary means to have these reduced.

The habitual delays in Conner's remittances were a constant cause of complaint throughout his agency. On three occasions, however, his financial management was so dilatory that it gave rise to a crisis of confidence. This occurred in 1775, when Conner was suspected of withholding money for his own use; between 1781 and 1784, when Conner failed to submit accounts and at one time admitted to having £12,000 of the duke's money in his own hand; and between 1788 and 1791, when he again failed to submit accounts and was finally calculated to owe the duke over £15,000 in arrears. This last crisis was terminal, and led directly to Conner's enforced resignation in 1792.

The evidence for the growing concern about Conner's management in 1775 comes from the letters he wrote defending his own actions. Writing to Sir Beaumont Hotham in December of that year, Conner acknowledged that from "the great rent roll" of the estate in his care, Hotham and the duke might have reasonably expected to receive larger and more regular remittances. Conner explained his inability to do so as the consequence of the unusually large nonrecurrent payments made that year for the Cavendish bridge at Lismore (£4,300) and Scalé's survey (£1,100); the large arrears still outstanding from the Michaelmas 1774 and Ladyday 1775 rent rolls; and the loss of £2,000 when the duke's Irish banker, Francis Carleton, went bankrupt the previous year. Consequently, Conner continued: "[N]othing could hurt me so much as his Grace having thought that I should delay [the remittances] to answer any purpose of my own . . . in the whole time of about ten years that I have had the honor of being employed by his Grace, I never converted nor used any of his Grace's money to any purpose but his own, except the salary he allows me, and not even that until it became due."[86]

While subsequent events might suggest a healthy skepticism about Conner's protestations of personal probity, Carleton's failure, like that ten years later of Sir Robert Warren & Co., his successor as the duke's Irish banker, represented a hazard no agent could have foreseen.[87] What was in question was the relationship between Carleton and Conner and the extent of the agent's liability to the fifth duke for the lost rents. In an apparently successful defense against the duke's claims, Richard Lawton, Carleton's partner, alleged that through friendship the Conners had permitted Carleton to retain the duke's rents and use them for his own business purposes. Despite this charge, and despite legal advice that he was personally liable for the sums lost by Carleton, Conner retained the agency.[88]

Nine years later his management was again under rigorous scrutiny, when Mr. Downs was sent from England to investigate the Irish accounts. The situation on this occasion was much more complex. Not only had Conner once again failed to make adequate remittances, but he had also failed to submit his accounts for 1782–1784. Furthermore, the collapse of Warren's bank had left some £16,000 of the duke's rents in jeopardy. Initially, Conner was sanguine. He admitted to holding £12,000 of the rents, not for his own use, but because of the high interest rates then current. At 11–12 percent, they would result in a loss of £30 to £40 on every £1,000 remitted.[89] In reality, Conner was more indebted to the duke than he realized. A rough draft of "the supposed state of Mr Conner's accounts" compiled at Chatsworth in October 1784 calculated that he owed £18,174 for the balance of rents due between Ladyday 1781 and Ladyday 1783, and that Warren & Co. still owed £9,050 of the original £16,000 in their hands at the time of their stoppage. Downs's more careful calculation reduced the total slightly, but he still concluded that the tenants were over £11,851 in arrears and that Conner owed £14,751.[90]

Once again, despite the size of these debts, no action was taken against Conner. In February 1785, after a silence of four months, he wrote to Hotham stressing the efforts he was making to collect the arrears, but at the same time admitting that he had not been entirely successful. Subsequent letters continue in the same vein, but very soon

Conner's old self-confidence and concern with his own affairs reasserted themselves.[91] The missing accounts were not finally submitted until 1786, while those for 1785–1787 were delayed until 1788.[92] Remarkably, in these circumstances, Conner chose to ignore Hotham's instruction to attend a general meeting of all the Devonshire agents in London in October 1785, excusing himself on the grounds of ill-health and the demands made on his time by his duties as provost of Bandon. Eventually this meeting did take place. Writing to Hotham in April the following year, Conner once again apologized for his lack of activity, this time over "the plan agreed" with Hotham in London. The excuses on this occasion were again Conner's ill-health, as well as the necessity of his appearing as a juror in the Cork and Waterford assizes.[93]

The contents of this letter set the tone for much of the correspondence between Conner and Hotham during the remaining years of his agency. Conner had always been quick to excuse his shortcomings or the delay in passing his accounts on the grounds of illness or pressure of work, but in the final years of his employment he did so with increasing frequency. On seven occasions between 1786 and 1791 Conner postponed meetings with Hotham, who in turn became increasingly concerned over Conner's continuing failure to close his annual accounts and the slowness of his remittances.[94] Despite his instruction in 1785 that no rents were to remain unremitted in Conner's hands, Hotham was again having to press for these a year later.[95] Matters finally came to a head in 1791, when Hotham was replaced on health grounds by the meticulous Heaton, but it is clear that prior to this change even Hotham's patience had been exhausted. In June 1790 Hotham wrote two letters of "severe censure" to Conner for neglecting estate business, particularly during the general election of that year. Conner's reply was characteristic: in concentrating on the Cork and Waterford elections he thought he had the duke's concurrence, and regretfully, illness prevented him from complying with Hotham's request to come to England to close his accounts.[96]

The speed with which Conner's agency was terminated after Heaton's appointment indicates more clearly then anything else the degree to which Hotham's lax control was ultimately responsible for the disorder on the Irish estate. Hotham's failure to visit the estate regularly and his refusal to deal directly with any of the Irish tenants made Conner's po-

sition virtually unassailable.[97] By contrast, Heaton's pressure on Conner
was immediate. Within weeks of his appointment as auditor, and possibly prompted by the private complaints he and Lord Frederick
Cavendish had already received about Conner's misconduct under
Hotham, Heaton wrote demanding that Conner pass his outstanding
accounts from 1788 onward. By Heaton's estimation, over £15,125 remained unaccounted for.[98] Conner's reply was evasive and, as events
subsequently demonstrated, untrue. Acknowledging that (once again) a
large arrear remained in tenants' hands, he nevertheless claimed that
"the three years accounts you desire of the estate in my collection
ending Ladyday 1790 are made out long since," and that Garde's request for his presence at the Waterford assize had prevented him from
attending on Heaton with these.[99] Unlike Hotham, Heaton was not to
be fobbed off. By February 1792 the decision appears to have been
taken to remove Conner, although care was taken not to alert him to
this fact.[100] In July of that year, with evidence mounting against him of
nepotism, mismanagement, and financial irregularity, Conner agreed to
resign, although not without one last attempt to retain some measure
of de facto control over the estate finances.[101] After his resignation
Conner was paid an honorarium of £300 a year on the understanding
that he give what help he could to his successor. But so great was the
state of disarray of his accounts that even with Conner's help, Garde
could make little headway in closing them. In his initial report to
Heaton, Garde described the accounts as being worse then he imag-
ined: "I was not able to get through half the first year's account, that of
1788, no rental produced, and many leaves missing necessary to ascertain the rents in his account . . . I could not close any one of them for
want of vouchers to ascertain the rents." In fact Conner's accounts were
not finally closed until two years before his death in 1799.[102]

Urban Expenditure

With the exception of the Cavendish bridge, built over the Blackwater at Lismore between 1773 and 1779, virtually no urban improvement
expenditure of any kind is recorded in Conner's surviving accounts.
The payments that are listed either financed necessary repairs to
schools and other urban institutions for which the estate was responsible, or else contributed to alleviating distress among the urban poor,

or helped to meet unexpected costs, such as those for the repair of the flood-damaged town walls at Bandon in 1789.[103] Urban tenants, on the other hand, were occasionally encouraged to make capital improvements to their property by the offer of commensurately reduced rents, although in these instances Conner was under strict instructions not to commit the duke to capital expenditure of any kind.[104] This was entirely in accord with the reactive and remittance-maximizing strategies that characterized the estate's management under Abdy and Hotham, but it makes the fifth duke's expenditure of over £8,400 on the Lismore bridge appear anomalous. However, since the bridge's final cost bore so little relationship to the initial estimate, the duke can hardly have conceived that it would eventually cost him so much.

It is not clear where the idea for the bridge originated. The later eighteenth century was a period of widespread landlord investment in communications, and to judge from his early association with the project, it is possible that Sir Henry Cavendish, a locally resident relative of the duke's, may have been involved in promoting the scheme.[105] In any case it would be wrong to assume that the fifth duke was totally uninterested in projects of this sort. In the early 1780s he financed the replanning of Buxton in Derbyshire as a spa town.[106] The earliest surviving reference to the proposed bridge dates from August 1771, when John Morrison, an architect living in Midleton, County Cork, who had worked for Lord Shannon, submitted the first of a series of designs and estimates. Morrison's designs appear to have been favored by Conner, but eventually it was Thomas Ivory, a Dublin architect recommended by Sir Henry Cavendish, who was appointed.[107]

It was recognized from the outset that the project was inherently difficult. The Blackwater was prone to violent flooding which was made worse from the contractor's point of view by the river's confluence with the Ounishade at the site of the proposed bridge.[108] Problems dogged the construction of the bridge from the beginning, and led to a number of revisions of Ivory's original plans which eventually added more than £3,000 to the original estimate of £5,300.[109] Inevitably, the magnitude of this cost overrun created further problems of a different kind. As the demands for funds increased, so the auditor became increasingly suspicious of both architect and contractors alike. Initially, the extra sums required were quickly paid, following Ivory's explanatory letters on the subject. Later, however, Hotham became much more cautious, especially when the additional money was required to pay for further alterations to Ivory's already modified designs, and to help the contractor's make good their earlier defective workmanship. Despite these problems, work continued on a regular although seasonal basis, and the bridge was finally completed in March 1779. It collapsed in 1853.[110]

For no immediately apparent reason, Conner's attitude toward Ivory appears to have been deliberately obstructive. In July 1772, a year before Ivory was appointed, Conner queried whether he intended to supervise the project personally, and suggested that his quotation for materials was inflated. From the outset, Conner refused Ivory's request to implement the normal system of stage payments to the contractors. Consequently, within a month of his appointment, Ivory was obliged to write to Abdy requesting that he instruct Conner to comply.[111] Over the next six years Conner continued his allegations of dishonesty, adding for good measure his view that Ivory deliberately inflated his claim for traveling expenses, and that he had no right to expect his fee (of 5 percent of the construction cost) to be paid on account as the stage payments were made.[112] Hotham fully acquiesced in this last point, although in fact Ivory was perfectly correct in his assertion not only that this was the normal method of paying architects in Ireland, but also that this was what his original agreement with Abdy entitled him to. After an increasingly acrimonious correspondence with Hotham, Ivory gave way, and from November 1776 onward refrained from requesting that his fees be paid in this way.[113]

With the completion of the bridge in March 1779, Ivory submitted a request to Conner for payment of the balance of his fees. Three years later, as a direct result of Conner's procrastination and Hotham's failure to force him to close the bridge accounts, these fees, amounting to over £238, had still not been paid.[114] Ivory was in no doubt as to the cause of the delay. Writing to Hotham in December 1780, he described Conner's continuing lack of action, and concluded: "[I]f you do not interfere and order me to be paid, I have little expectation from the tender mercies of Mr Conner." Ten months later he again pressed Hotham to take him "out of Mr Conner's hands and order me to be paid." Ultimately, Ivory appears to have been successful. Conner's accounts for 1781 list a payment of "£800 to Darley & Stokes to complete their demands and £260.19.3 to Thomas Ivory to complete his."[115] Unusually for sums of this size, the entries were not dated. Moreover, their timing was curious, since in his last recorded letter to Hotham in May 1782 Ivory was still pressing for payment. Although it was normal practice for the accounts to balance one year's income against the next year's expenditure, the latter was normally only accounted until the following Ladyday, March 25th. Either Conner mistakenly included the payments to the contractors and architect in the year previous to the one in which they should have appeared, or else this was one more instance of his calculated dishonesty.[116]

Political Management

One of the allegations that led to Conner's resignation was that he had attempted to create his own political interest in Bandon at the duke's expense.[117] In fact, Conner's attempt at usurping what little political influence the duke retained in that borough was insignificant compared to the more general political control exercised over much of the duke's urban estate by the earl of Shannon and John Ponsonby. The difference between them was that whereas Ponsonby and Shannon exercised their influence by agreement with the duke, Conner was engaged in a premeditated and entirely hostile attack on his employer's political interest. The political connection between Henry Boyle, first earl of Shannon, and the Burlington estates predated the Devonshires' acquisition of the property in 1748. From the early 1720s Boyle had been head agent for the Burlington property, and had been given the disposal of its political patronage by the third earl of Burlington. Boyle's second marriage to Lord Burlington's youngest sister in 1726 cemented this already close relationship. But in 1748 Lady Henrietta Boyle's marriage to Lord Hartington not only dashed Boyle's hopes of inheriting the Burlington property, but also raised the specter of his main political rivals, the Ponsonbys, exerting an increasing political influence over it. The Devonshire-Ponsonby connection had begun while the third duke was lord lieutenant of Ireland between 1737 and 1744. In 1739 William Ponsonby, Viscount Duncannon, and later second earl of Bessborough, had married one of the duke's daughters, and in 1743 John Ponsonby, Duncannon's younger brother, had married another.[118]

The political ambitions of these various protagonists were played out in an urban arena characterized by constitutional diversity and electoral variation. Bandon and Youghal were both corporate boroughs, where voting was restricted to a relatively small section of the corporation. Dungarvan, Lismore, and Tallow were "potwalloper" boroughs, where residence within the towns was the major voting qualification. In the two corporate boroughs municipal elections were of special importance since, as Conner recognized, they provided the main means whereby a political interest could be established.[119] At Bandon, parliamentary votes were limited to the provost and the twelve free burgesses, who with the commonality comprised the corporation. The provost was elected annually by the free burgesses from among themselves, and they in turn were elected from a twelve-strong common council chosen by the freemen. At Youghal the electorate was considerably larger. The corporation consisted of the mayor (who was also an alderman), the recorder, another nine aldermen, two bailiffs, and the burgesses and freemen. The burgesses were those who had served as bailiff, while the freemen were admitted by favor of the mayor and aldermen, and were not necessarily required to reside in the borough. Although Youghal's charters granted no right to send M.P.'s to Parliament, members had in fact been sent by the corporation on a prescriptive basis since 1370.[120]

In both corporate boroughs, therefore, the key to parliamentary control lay in influencing a relatively small minority within the corporation. At Bandon the key figures were the provost and the burgesses, while at Youghal the crucial group were the aldermen, since it was they who admitted the freemen who were entitled to vote. Although it would be inaccurate to say that property ownership was unimportant for this purpose in these boroughs, it is probably true to say that it was less important than in the three "potwalloper" boroughs. In these, the right to vote was conditional upon residence and the possession of a minimal property qualification. Consequently, it was a relatively simple matter for the duke's head tenants to subdivide the properties they held within the charter bounds of the borough and create large numbers of forty-shillings freeholders, each with the right to vote and loyal only to their immediate landlord. To meet this threat, Garde urged Hotham in 1788 to let vacant holdings in Lismore directly to occupying tenants whom the duke could influence, rather than to middlemen who would create their own interest.[121] At Lismore and Tallow voting was limited to those Protestant freeholders living within a mile and a half of the town church.[122] At Dungarvan the electorate consisted of the 1,700 or so householders in the borough, together with the 150 freeholders in the manor of Dungarvan. In 1832 the Parliamentary Commission on Borough Representation found no grounds in the charter to support this practice. It seems simply to have been a customary usage, similar to the one that developed at Tallow prior to 1778, when legal proceedings reinstated the more limited franchise described above.[123]

By the time of Conner's agency, these variations in the electorate were paralleled by an equal diversity in the boroughs' political status and representation. In none of them, however, can there be said to have been an active Devonshire interest between 1760 and 1791. The representation was either in the hands of influential local gentlemen who could not be removed, or else was vested in the earl of Shannon and, increasingly, Speaker Ponsonby. Lord Shannon's interest was at least partly legitimized by his family's long managerial association with the Burlington boroughs, which the fifth duke seemed happy to continue. The Ponsonby influence, on the other hand, was altogether more opportunistic, and although essentially hostile to that of Shannon, seems also to have been sanctioned by the duke, particularly after 1783, when the earl of Shannon declined the further management of the duke's boroughs. From as early as 1757, Speaker Ponsonby had been contemplating the wholesale takeover of Lord Shannon's interest. By 1778 he was clearly regarded as the formal guardian of the "Devonshire interest" in some of the boroughs at least.[124]

Shannon's influence was greatest at Youghal, which was effectively a "close" borough under his control. In later years, Knowlton alleged that this was the result of deliberate predation by Lord Shannon and Sir Robert Boyle "during the long minority of the fifth Duke" (1764–1769).[125] In fact, the earl of Burlington had lost control of this borough long before it passed into the Devonshires' patrimony in 1748. Consequently, although Shannon certainly made a successful attack on Youghal at the General Election of 1761, this was at the expense of the

Hyde family and not the duke of Devonshire. It is inconceivable that the duke would have asked the earl to manage his electoral interests at this and the two successive elections of 1776 and 1783 if he had thought Shannon guilty of such a hostile act.[126]

At Bandon the situation was different. In 1761 the town was nominally in Devonshire hands, and was represented by William Conner I (the duke's agent and father to William Conner II) and Thomas Adderley, a Derbyshire friend of the duke's. Adderley was later listed as a member of the Shannon faction.[127] On Conner's death in 1766, his seat was lost to James Bernard, father of the first Lord Bandon. Bernard was a major tenant of the duke's and an influential figure in his own right. His election signaled the culmination of the Bernards' attack on the borough. They were only prevented from usurping Bandon in its entirety by the earl of Shannon. By successfully delaying the Cork assizes, where James Bernard had hoped to challenge the election of the provost of Bandon, Shannon forced Bernard into a situation where he had either to accept enormously inflated and open-ended legal costs or else to come to terms over the representation of the borough and the corporation. In September 1767 Shannon signed an agreement with Bernard on behalf of the duke of Devonshire's interest, which effectively divided the corporation and the representation of the borough between them. Replacement burgesses were to be nominated by the leaders of the party in which the vacancy had occurred, and the casting burgess was to be nominated only after consultation between both parties. After a transitional period, in which the Bernard family were to fill the first pair of vacancies for Parliament and the duke's representatives the second, each party was to have the alternate nomination for the borough.[128] Hewitt argues that both parties continued to honor the agreement until after the Union, despite the continuing ties of political affiliation and consanguinity that might have encouraged Shannon to acquiesce in the Bernard family's designs on the borough. In 1768 Francis Bernard and Thomas Adderley were again returned, while between 1776 and 1791 a Ponsonby nominee, Lodge Morres, held one seat ostensibly in the Devonshire interest.[129] The remaining seat was held successively by William Brabazon Ponsonby in 1776, Francis Bernard in 1783, and Broderick Chinnery in 1791, in the Shannon interest.

Although not a close borough in the conventional sense, Bandon was not truly open either, since the 1767 agreement ensured that other interests were unlikely to succeed. By contrast, the duke's three "potwalloper" boroughs—Dungarvan, Lismore, and Tallow—were open. They were thus politically more prestigious than either Bandon or Youghal.[130] Like Bandon, they provided an arena in which the continuing political rivalry between Lord Shannon and the Ponsonbys was played out, both prior to Lord Townshend's viceroyalty, when these men were at the height of their power as borough magnates and "undertakers," and afterward when their national prestige was declining.[131] At Dungarvan, Lord Shannon retained a precarious foothold until 1776, when his candidate, John Bennett, was ousted on appeal by Godfrey Greene, and his interest extinguished. Even before this, Shannon's interest had looked vulnerable. In 1768, for example, Robert Carew, ostensibly a Shannon nominee, had been returned as much thanks to Speaker Ponsonby's influence as to Lord Shannon's.[132] A nominal Devonshire interest was not reestablished in the borough until the election of C. B. Ponsonby in 1791. During the intervening period the town was represented, first, by the maverick independent, Sir William Osborne, and then by Godfrey Greene and Marcus Beresford.[133]

The Ponsonbys' eventual success in replacing the Shannon interest in Dungarvan was matched at Lismore, where their nominees represented the borough nearly continuously between 1761 and 1797. Throughout this period one seat was held by Sir Henry Cavendish and his son, nominally in the Devonshire interest but in reality as firm allies of the Ponsonbys.[134] The other seat was held in 1761 by another Ponsonby ally, S. Moore, and thereafter by Colonel (later General) Gisborne and by Sir Richard Musgrave—yet another Ponsonby friend.[135] Significantly, Musgrave's election for Lismore in 1790 was jeopardized by the antagonism that Conner had engendered among the electorate, and which he tried unsuccessfully to attribute to Musgrave.[136] At Tallow, Lord Shannon continued to exercise a dominant influence until at least 1783 and possibly a little later. Prior to 1776, he returned Nicholas Lysaght, third son of Lord Lisle, and afterward Richard O'Brien Boyle (Shannon's nephew) and John Hobson. The second seat was held by Colonel Hugh Cane between 1768 and his

death in 1793. Although some parliamentary lists refer to him as a pro-
tégé of Lord Shannon's, he appears to have been an independent
member, elected at his own expense although professing a general at-
tachment to the duke's interest.[137]

Colonel Cane's fidelity to the Devonshire interest was exceptional.
Why the fifth duke showed so little interest in the political disposition
of his Irish boroughs, and why he was seemingly so content to let the
earl of Shannon and the Ponsonbys vie with each other over them, is
hard to explain. Hewitt suggests that it resulted from the generally
low value accorded to political patronage in Ireland before the Union,
combined with the duke's notorious disinclination to involve himself
in the management of his own affairs.[138] Given the duke's apparent
perception of his Irish estates as a source of revenue rather than as a
cause for expenditure, this argument appears reasonable. It does not,
however, explain why the duke was not alerted to the advantages of a
more active political management of his estate by the value Shannon
and his rivals clearly placed on the Irish boroughs. Moreover, both
Garde and Conner were aware of the political dimension that underlay the normal practice of estate management, and in particular of
the problems that could occur when the tenants' economic interests
and political loyalties diverged.[139] For this reason alone, it would seem
reasonable for the duke to have authorized a more active political
management of the "Burlington" boroughs in his own name. As it
was, his studied noninterference provided not merely the Ponsonbys
and to a lesser extent Lord Shannon with a significant part of their
political power base, but also created the circumstances in which, at a
less exalted level, Conner too could hope to indulge his political ambitions.

In common with many of Conner's other managerial and financial
malpractices, the evidence for his attempt at political self-aggrandizement is provided in the first instance by retrospective comments in
the correspondence between Garde and Musgrave and Heaton in 1792,
and second by the corroboration provided by Conner's own earlier
correspondence with Hotham. The substance of Garde and Musgrave's
allegations was that Conner endeavored to have his son and other
relatives nominated in the duke's interest at municipal elections in
Bandon. By establishing his kinsmen first as common councilmen and

then as burgesses, Conner apparently hoped to subvert the duke's interest in the corporation and thereby usurp the alternate nomination for the borough's M.P. Conner's own correspondence certainly lends credence to this view. In 1778, when Conner was elected provost of Bandon in his own right, he repeatedly pressed Hotham to agree to the nomination of his cousin, Thomas Biggs as a common council-man, although in the event he had to accede to Sir Henry Cavendish's nomination instead. Five years later, when Cavendish was elected to the vacant post of burgess, Conner at last got his way and Biggs was nominated to the common council. In the same year Conner made the first of several requests that his son Roger be nominated to the common council.[140] In 1786 Conner successfully proposed Thomas Biggs for a vacant burgess post, and two other relatives, James Splaine and Jacob Biggs, for the common council. In each case, Conner omit-ted to mention to Hotham that these men were his relatives, but stressed instead their past fidelity to the duke's interest and their local standing as men of property.[141]

Conner's tactics at Bandon reflected the nature of the borough and were of course made easier for him by his family's long association with that part of County Cork. His father had been an M.P. for Bandon in 1761, and was in fact accused of betraying one of the duke's seats there to Francis Bernard in 1768.[142] Bandon provided Conner with his greatest chance of political success. Since residence was not the primary parliamentary voting qualification, the limited electoral franchise meant that Conner did not have to engage in the expensive business of bribing or coercing large numbers of venal free-holders to vote for his candidate, as would have been the case in the duke's "potwalloper" boroughs. In fact, as Conner's political attack on Lismore demonstrated, there were ways round this problem, but these depended on placing compliant relatives as head tenants on a signifi-cant amount of property within the charter bounds of the borough. Conner showed no interest in the other boroughs, presumably be-cause of the likely expense at Dungarvan and the dearth of support for the duke's interest there, and because of the strength of the Shan-non influence at Tallow and Youghal. At Lismore, Conner's attack never seems to have progressed beyond the initial insertion of the Gumbletons as head tenants for the Deer Park and Kilnecarrigy in

1790.[143] A year later Garde remained convinced that Conner's intention had been to subdivide these properties and create numerous freehold votes in precisely the manner he had warned Hotham against in 1788.[144] Clearly, Conner's enforced resignation in 1792 was not merely long overdue in terms of the managerial efficiency of the duke's estate, but was also singularly fortuitous for the future of his political interest as well.

Summary

By 1792, and indeed for much of the preceding three decades, the duke of Devonshire's income, influence, and interest in Ireland were at their lowest ebb. His estate did not seem capable of responding to the spectacular economic growth of the period in the way that some other Munster properties managed to do; his patronal relations were exercised at second hand with a tenantry whom he had never actually met; and the considerable political influence that had been attached to the Burlington property was either dissipated or else exercised through and on behalf of his Irish relatives by marriage, the earl of Shannon and John Ponsonby. Many of these problems had in fact been inherited with the estate in 1748. Shannon was by then already well entrenched in the boroughs, where he was soon to be challenged by Ponsonby, and most of the estate was tied up in leases of characteristically long duration. Not only did this inevitably limit the duke's opportunities to engage in long-term strategic planning, but it also severely limited the financial benefit he might derive from this planning. The existence of such long leases was almost certainly a major factor in explaining why the duke's income failed to rise at a rate that was commensurate with the average regional increase in rents in Munster after 1760.

That being said, it is nevertheless also clear that the duke's estate was the scene of quite spectacular maladministration by the Lismore agent between 1760 and 1792. In itself this was not unusual: agents quite frequently took advantage of the opportunities offered by their role as surrogate landlords to advance themselves in financial and other ways. What was unusual in Conner's case was the grand scale of his malpractice, and the lengthy period over which it was tolerated by successive auditors. Conner was first suspected of gross financial mal-administration some twenty years before his resignation, and grounds for similar suspicions occurred regularly thereafter. Moreover, Conner appears to have made little attempt to maintain reasonable relations with the duke's tenants on a personal level. Instead, he seems to have engaged on a consistent policy of nepotism and placement without the slightest regard for its effect on the relations between the duke and his tenantry.

The fifth duke of Devonshire has been recorded for posterity as a man who was personally lethargic and who was content to let others take charge of his affairs, with the exception of the menage à trois with Georgiana, his first wife, and Lady Elizabeth Foster, who was to become his second, which so entertained London society in the 1780s and 1790s. Accordingly, it would be tempting to conclude that much of the blame for the disastrous situation that developed on his Irish estate should be laid at the duke's door. In one sense, such a conclusion is inescapable. After all, if the duke had taken a more active interest in the management of his property, he would presumably have been quickly alerted to the way in which his various Irish interests were being abused. On the other hand, both the Irish agent and the London auditor had, in their differing capacities, a responsibility to the duke to ensure the sound management of his estate, whatever their employer's personal inclinations in the matter. At this level it seems that both agent and auditor were culpable: the agent because of his deliberate dishonesty and manipulation of his employer's interests for personal gain; and the auditor for permitting a lax and irregular system of ad-ministration to develop which encouraged the agent's malpractices. Indeed, William Conner's agency demonstrates above everything else the importance of close and effective central control for estates that were as geographically widespread and economically diverse as those of the duke of Devonshire. Where such control was lax or impeded, the responsibilities upon the local agents were all the greater and their op-portunities for self-aggrandizement commensurately more numerous. It was the future fourth duke's misfortune that when he inherited the Burlington estate in Ireland in 1748, he also inherited the services of a

family who were utterly ruthless in their exploitation of the opportunities for personal advancement which their authority as his agents
gave them. The fifth duke of Devonshire was doubly unfortunate in
having London auditors who, prior to 1792, were seemingly incapable
of doing anything about it.

CHAPTER 5

"For Power and Profit"

The Reorganization of the Urban Estate, 1792–1832

William Conner's resignation in July 1792 ushered in a period of managerial interventionism on the duke's urban estate that stood in complete contrast to the neglect of earlier years. Over the next forty years, until the Great Reform Act of 1832 ended the sixth duke's active borough-mongering, successive agents pursued policies that were designed to tighten the duke's economic control over his tenantry, increase his annual income, and reestablish the political authority he had lost thanks to the duplicity of his servants and the self-interest of his relatives. These policies were pursued with varying degrees of success and emphasis by Conner's English successors. Thus whereas Henry Bowman was primarily concerned with securing the duke's urban and rural property interests, Thomas Knowlton's appointment led to a programme of politically inspired urban improvement and management. Although Knowlton was forced to resign in 1814, the improvements were continued under W. A. Ashby and W. S. Currey and culminated in the recapture of the borough at Youghal in 1822. Thereafter, although the sixth duke was content for a time to enjoy the fruits of his political success at Youghal and Dungarvan, any further urban improvements he sanctioned in his estate towns were undertaken as much for aesthetic and social reasons as for any other purpose.

This chapter discusses the urban improvements that were carried out on the estate between 1792 and 1832, together with the motivations that lay behind them and their financial and political impact. The first main section examines the changing policy objectives themselves, and explores the urban development programmes that were put in train to achieve these. The second main section considers whether, ultimately, these policy objectives can be said to have been achieved and at what cost. Since the estate was in no sense a closed social or economic system, the success or failure of the urban improvement policy was determined as much by developments in the community at large as by the managerial efficiency and tenant attitudes on the estate itself. As chapter 2 demonstrates, early-nineteenth-century Ireland was characterized by the intensification of existing regional and social contrasts, and these changes affected towns in different ways.

The population growth experienced by the duke's towns provides a case in point. Although it is generally agreed that population growth played a major if still controversial part in promoting regional disparities in pre-Famine Ireland, the evidence indicates that on the Devonshire estate the tenantry were largely insulated from the worst effects of any imbalance between population growth and resources by the commercial nature of the regional economy. Table 5.1 suggests that in Bandon, Tallow, and Youghal growth may have been similar to or rather more than the 68 percent growth rate recorded for Ireland as a whole between 1800 and 1841, when the country's population rose from about 5 million to 8.4 million.[1] Dungarvan probably experienced population growth that was only marginally below the national aver-

TABLE 5.1
The Estate Towns: Estimated Population Growth, 1800–1841

	Bandon	Dungarvan	Lismore	Tallow	Youghal
1800	4,784–	5,508–	940–	1,716–	4,892–
	6,578	7,574	1,293	2,360	6,727
1813	–	4,930	1,569	2,258	–
1821	10,179	5,105	2,330	2,329	8,969
1831	9,917	6,527	2,894	2,998	9,608
1841	9,049	8,625	3,007	2,969	9,939

Percentage change, 1800–1841 (all positive)

	51–107	14–56	132–219	26–73	43–103

Source: Table 3.1, and Vaughan & Fitzpatrick, Irish Historical Statistics. Population 1821–1971.

age, while at Lismore, where the estate-funded expansion of the housing stock was relatively extensive, the population grew by at least twice this average.

There is little evidence to suggest that the Devonshire tenants' conditions of existence became more marginalized as a result of this population growth. Ó Gráda identifies the localities containing the estate as areas where the population grew by less than 30 percent between 1821 and 1841; higher, certainly, than in many parts of east Leinster, but far less than in many of the coastal districts of Connacht and west Munster.[2] Admittedly, the Lismore agent's correspondence does speak of dearth among the poorer urban tenantry after the harvest failures of 1800–1801, but the crisis seems to have passed quickly without an unduly prolonged effect.[3] Where evidence does exist to show a periodic deterioration in the condition of the urban tenantry, it relates either to the effects of political crises such as the 1798 rebellion, or to the impact of technological changes on one-time staples such as the linen industry, or to a perceived worsening in the terms of trade after the Union.

Bandon exemplifies these causal relationships. In the later eighteenth century the town had been an important center of first the woolen and then the linen industry. Despite periodic downturns in these staples, they had been resilient enough to ensure the continued existence of industrial employment in the locality, at least until the 1790s. However, the 1798 rebellion so disrupted the flow of credit that these industries were brought to an effective standstill. As early as January 1797 there was widespread unemployment and destitution among the weavers and laborers in the town.[4] Subsequently, trade revived, but the depression of the mid-1820s drove both the town's linen and woolen industries into terminal decline. Contemporary writers estimated that whereas these industries had employed between 1,000 and 1,500 weavers in 1825–1826, this total had fallen to less than one hundred by 1836–1837.[5]

The decline in the textile industries at Bandon demonstrates the potential effect exogenous economic change could have on the fortunes of the duke's estate towns, but it should be remembered that the potential effect of political change was equally far-reaching. The Act of Union resulted in the abolition of two hundred of the three hundred Irish parliamentary seats, including those for Tallow and Lismore.[6] This placed a premium on Irish seats and made urban improvement

for political purposes much more worthwhile, at least in the short
term. It is one of the ironies of the period that the other major political change, Roman Catholic Emancipation, contained the seeds that
were to destroy forever the sort of landlord borough-mongering that so
motivated Thomas Knowlton after the Union. The enfranchisement
and growing politicization of the duke's Catholic tenantry constituted
the single most important social change on the urban estate in the
forty years prior to 1832, and led ultimately to the duke's withdrawal
from precisely the sort of political activity that had given rise to most
of the improvements in the estate towns between 1800 and 1822.

Managerial Policies: Changing Objectives

Preparations for the rehabilitation of the estate were already underway even before Conner finally resigned in July 1792. Bowman and
Garde had already been directed by the auditor to devise a plan for the
estate's future management over a month previously. Their joint appraisal of what was required survives as a series of memoranda from
that and a subsequent meeting in January 1793, and in the form of the
Annual Reports that Bowman submitted to Heaton between 1794 and
1797.[7] The plan they proposed was both remedial and strategic. They
had two remedial concerns: first, to secure those of the duke's papers
that had been maliciously withheld by Conner and that were needed
to prove the duke's title to his property,[8] and second, to rectify as much
as possible of the damage caused by Conner's corruption and neglect.
To this end, rangers were appointed to preserve the woods from further depredation, while evidence was sought concerning the overhold-
ing and nonpayment of rent and tolls condoned by Conner. Finally,
the leases that Conner had executed for his various friends and relatives
in and around Tallow and Lismore were held in abeyance for legal investigation. Eventually, some at least of these were found to be perfectly in order and were finally ratified by the duke in 1804.[9]

The strategic importance of the new plan was apparent from the
start. At their first meeting with Heaton, Bowman and Garde were informed that their plan had "to promote the double end of power as
well as profit," particularly in and around Bandon, Dungarvan, Lismore, and Tallow, the four boroughs where the duke was thought to

retain some chance of regaining political control. Youghal was considered to be beyond all hope of recapture.[10] Heaton believed that it was possible to achieve these political and economic goals in tandem without prejudicing either. In fact, as James Abercrombie subsequently recognized, Heaton's objectives were inherently contradictory.[11] Political power could only be bought—and retained—at the expense of property, whether in the form of capital investment in the elections themselves or in politically judicious improvements, or by agreeing to particularly favorable leases or by tolerating large arrears. Moreover, as events were to demonstrate, even with this type of outlay there was no guarantee of the tenants' continuing political fidelity. Property, in contrast, provided a generally much more reliable form of investment. As matters turned out, the improvement policies pursued on the estate never achieved the equable duality of purpose envisaged by Heaton. The accelerating pace of social and political change, together with the differing personal inclinations of the agents themselves and the varying commitment of the duke to his Irish affairs, always ensured the preeminence of one or other of the policy goals.

Planning for Profit: 1792–1797

Although Bowman made little apparent progress toward the recapture of the duke's boroughs, it would be misleading to assume that he disregarded the political responsibilities that attached to his duties as agent. Rather, he appears to have been convinced that the only way to secure the duke's political rights was to first increase his economic control over his property. In order to achieve this goal Bowman proposed a gradual but fundamental change in leasing policy. As existing leases fell in, the properties would be subdivided and relet to suitable occupying tenants rather than to nonresident middlemen. As a group, these middlemen had benefited greatly at the duke's expense from the general upswing in agriculture during the last quarter of the century. This "English" system had long been common practice on the duke's estates in Britain, and although it had been previously recommended to Hotham and Conner for use in Ireland, they had made no attempt to introduce it there.[12] Bowman was well aware of the difficulties involved. Writing to Heaton in December 1792, he described the general condition of many farmers on the estate:

[They have] labored under such Acts of tyranny from that honorable set called "middlemen" that they have in a general way very little property, and, what is more to be lamented, less confidence. Their mode of husbandry is also bad, their implements worse; and if possible, their buildings and conveniences still worse. They are filthy, which is a natural consequence on indolence [sic]. . . .They must in a great measure be furnished with new methods to do their work, new implements to execute them, and buildings and conveniences to manufacture their produce when brought to maturity.[13]

In order to remedy these problems, Bowman proposed a careful matching of tenants and tenancies. The size of each subdivision would vary according to the tenant's ability, and the length of lease (which would be for years only) would depend on the degree of expenditure and effort required to bring the land into profitability. Bowman also suggested that the duke should bear the capital cost of improving the existing farm buildings, and that for a temporary period only the occupying tenants should have the right to sublet up to one-third of their farms as small holdings for "poor people." This latter suggestion was far from the carte blanche to create a new class of minor middlemen that it appeared to be. Bowman was aware of the existence on the estate of a significant number of impoverished peasants, who in his own words "were by no means qualified to be good tenants." By permitting the occupying tenants to sublet to this group in a strictly controlled fashion, Bowman hoped to provide the poorest families with a means of livelihood, and the more able individuals among them with an opportunity to demonstrate their suitability to be accepted as tenants in their own right.[14] This strategy allowed the occupying tenants to husband such resources as they did have while at the same time permitting them an additional source of income. Moreover, by offering shorter leases than before, the duke could exercise much more effective political control over his tenantry, and might in this way hope to reassert his political authority over his estate.[15] Equally favorable building leases would be offered to urban tenants willing to make good the widespread decay that was the ubiquitous consequence of Conner's neglect of the duke's towns. Ultimately, Bowman envisaged a situation in which the tenants' confidence in their landlord would grow sufficiently to encourage them to forgo leases altogether and accept tenancies at will, although he conceded that this would only be possible by "liberal and steady treatment."[16]

This tenurial ideal was never completely achieved. Although tenancies at will became increasingly widespread on the urban estate during the early nineteenth century, leasehold tenures remained a significant part of the property transactions between the duke and his tenants both before and after the Famine. For example, at Tallow approximately 44 percent of the tenancies in 1837 were leasehold.[17] Between 1820 and 1837 forty leases had been executed for property in the town, all of them for between one and three lives with a concurrent term of up to ninety-nine years. At Dungarvan leasehold tenures constituted over 52 percent of the 210 nonfreehold tenancies in the town in 1860.[18] Once again the majority of these were for between one and three lives, with terms of up to ninety-nine years running concurrently. Of the remaining ninety-nine nonfreehold tenancies, eighty-two were for one year only, while the rest were for terms of between seven and twenty-one years but held on an annual demise. As table 5.2 demonstrates, there were pronounced decennial differences displayed by the two different categories of tenure. The majority of the annual and annually demisable tenancies occur in the later decades after 1840. While the incidence of leases for lives is more even, the potentially longer three life leases with a concurrent ninety-nine-year term were most frequent in the 1820s, while two- or three-life leases with a shorter sixty-one-year term tended to predominate in the 1830s and 1840s.

These examples confirm that Bowman's proposed phasing out of leasehold tenures only achieved a delayed and partial success. There were two reasons why this should have been so. In the first place, Bowman's immediate opportunity to modify the existing tenurial structure and begin the process of urban improvement was severely limited by the survival of numerous leases for lives with extensive terms still to run. Although a small number of houses were out of lease by 1794 in Bandon, Dungarvan, and Youghal, the only real opportunity for early improvement was at Lismore, where one-quarter of the town was held at will. Even here, the leases on the remainder of the urban property were not due to expire completely for the next twenty-one years, while Tallow was "so tied up with leases that the prospect of advantageous improvements [was] at a great distance."[19] At Youghal, the situation was exacerbated by the existence of a number of perpetuity leases. These effectively deprived the estate of any further influence over the management of the property in question.

TABLE 5.2
Dungarvan: Decennial Lease Distribution by Tenure

	Annual/Annually Demisable	Leases for Lives
Pre-1820	0	15
1821–1830	1	25
1831–1840	16	25
1841–1850	49	28
1851–1860	35	16
Total	101	109

Source: N.L.I. L.P. Ms 6170.

Even where the estate regained possession of important urban property, there was no certainty that new tenants could be found willing to
take it on the type of short leases Bowman contemplated. Thus the
second reason why his plan was never completely adopted was simply
that tenancies at will and other tenures of short duration were not appropriate to all types of urban property. For example, in 1802 some of
the duke's major manufacturing tenants at Bandon refused to accept
twenty-one-year building leases on the grounds that the term was too
short to allow them to recoup the capital outlay they were required to
make on new buildings. The Reverend Richard Lloyd, one of the
duke's political friends in the town, tried to alert Knowlton to the dangers inherent in the situation. In November of that year he wrote: "I
can sincerely assure you that many of the tenantry at Bandon are dis-
satisfied and some of the more wealthy are turning their thoughts to
other places where they can get permanent establishments. They say
(and there is some truth in it) that by staying in Bandon they lose the
best parts of their lives in uncertainty when they should be forming a
settlement for their children."[20]

A month later Lloyd expressed his fears in broader terms:

In general in Ireland the plan of the proprietor has been and is, to establish
whenever he can persons of trade and capital who will circulate their industry
and property for the benefit of his estate and he never hesitates to give men a
lease in perpetuity at a moderate rent for the quantity necessary for their accommodation. This has been done by the late Lord Kingsborough at Mitchelstown, and by Sir John Craven Carden at Templemore. . . . [I] venture to

say that it will not be in your power to establish manufacturers of capital on the terms you suppose, that the terms are equitable I have no doubt, but they are not fitted to Ireland.[21]

Although Bowman's opportunities to undertake urban improvements were severely constrained by the existing leases, he quickly took advantage of those that were available. At Bandon he was responsible for the construction of the new quay along the Bridewell River, and for laying out thirty tenements on its southern side. His opportunity to do so came with the expiration in 1794 of a lease held by John Stammers, one of Lord Bandon's political allies. Stammers had sublet to Henry Beamish, Lord Bandon's agent. It was Bowman's refusal to grant a renewal to Beamish that led Lord Bandon subsequently to allege that this was an act of deliberate discrimination against his friends. As the Reverend Lloyd later pointed out to Knowlton, this was unlikely. Beamish was alone among a number of Lord Bandon's friends in not receiving a renewal, and a more probable reason for his failure was the valuable location of the site and the decrepit and rack-rented nature of the cabins he had allowed to be built there. In contrast, tenants leasing the new tenements were required to build substantial two-story houses of stone and lime. By 1798 few of these had been built, a circumstance Lloyd ascribed to the rebellion.[22]

Lismore: The Delayed New Town   Bowman's main activities were concentrated at Lismore, where his plans for the town were ambitious. He proposed an integrated rural-urban development scheme that would enhance Lismore's status to that of a regional market center. Bowman clearly recognized the interdependent nature of the urban and rural sectors in the economy, and the importance of local and regional trade in sustaining towns like Lismore. Accordingly, his plan placed particular emphasis on improving communications. It proposed the construction of a canal linking Lismore and Youghal via the River Blackwater; the completion of a new road over the Knockmealdown mountains, making Lismore more accessible from County Tipperary; an extension to the mail road from Waterford to link Lismore directly with Cork; and the construction of a new inn at Lismore together with the progressive reconstruction of the town's entire housing stock.[23]

Bowman outlined the advantages of his plan to Heaton in January 1793:

The great advantage to be derived to the Estate near Lismore, will be that of having coal brought to the Bridge to burn limestone, which abounds on the southern side of the river, to improve the uncultivated parts of the mountain through the middle of which the above mentioned road must go, and by the same means the grain and other produce of the estate may be sent to the best Market, at a small expense. Another advantage will be derived from the situation of Lismore; it will in all probability command the trade of the adjoining country for several miles north and west of it, there being no other navigable river near on these points, and thereby it may become a kind of inland port of considerable trade. There will in all probability be a reasonable return for the money laid out on the Canal, by a Toll or Tonnage on the vessels traveling thereon, independent of the advantage above mentioned, and the duke will be amply compensated for any subscription he may be pleased to make, towards first making the Road, by having an easy means of getting lime to the uncultivated part for its improvement. The prospect of these improvements will point out the necessity for a good inn, both for accommodation and as an inducement for the general public to resort thither.[24]

A year later, in his first Annual Report, Bowman was more specific about the advantages accruing to the town from its improved communications with Tipperary: "Lismore will become a kind of inland port to which corn of every kind, beef, mutton etc. with which the County of Tipperary abounds will be brought, and in return the carriers will take back timber, coal etc. to Tipperary, being articles much wanted there and with which at present that county is but indifferently supplied."[25]

The success of Bowman's intended reconstruction of Lismore depended upon the extent to which this investment in communications succeeded in improving the local economy. Bowman argued that given the probable rise in the value of property as the various improvements began to take effect, the duke would be better advised to bear the cost of the rebuilding himself, and thus reap the immediate benefit of any rise in rents, rather than to let the ground on building leases and allow the added value to accrue to his tenants. Bowman proposed that the existing houses and cabins be replaced by a variety of different house types, costing from between £30 to £500 each to build. The better houses costing between £200 and £500 were to be constructed in the center of the town, and were to be reserved for tradesmen, retail shop-keepers, and private families. "People of a lower description, such as la-bourers and mechanics" were to be accommodated in cheaper housing on the town's outskirts.

Clearly, the existing sociospatial status patterns were not merely to be perpetuated but positively reinforced. Bowman estimated the total cost of the building program to be £60,000, but argued that this could be spread over several years at an annual cost of between £1,000 and £3,000, the equivalent of between 5 and 15 percent of received annual income.[26] Each of the tenants was to be allocated a plot of between two and ten acres in the town lands, but here Bowman admitted the ex-istence of a problem. The ideal lands for this purpose were Ballymoo-dranagh and the Deer Park, both of which were leased by William Conner Gumbleton, who was reluctant to sell his interest.[27] While this issue was never effectively resolved, the question of ensuring the politi-cal fidelity of the new urban tenants was very soon overtaken by events. Bowman's original intention had been to achieve this by letting the newly built houses at will, but with Lismore's disenfranchisement under the Act of Union in 1801 the issue of the borough's represen-tation became a dead letter.[28]

Subsequent events were also to affect the overall implementation of the plan. The only projects that were completed before Bowman's res-ignation in 1797 and the outbreak of rebellion a year later were the inn, the canal, and the road to Clogheen in County Tipperary. Work on all three commenced during the spring and summer of 1793, but only after Bowman had experienced great difficulty in obtaining reasonable estimates from local contractors. In May of that year he complained to Heaton: "[T]he fact is, they are totally unacquainted with taking any sort of work by the piece or the measure, and are afraid of deceiving themselves, to guard against which they ask an ex-orbitant price."[29] In the event, he made his own estimate of £2,397 for the canal, but accepted the contractor Samuel Ward's estimate of £1,747 for the inn, preferring this to his competitors' bids on the grounds of the contractor's apparent competence.

This was illusory. After two years, during which the project was dogged by the workmen's inefficiency—which demanded Bowman's close personal supervision—and by periodic shortages of labor caused by the more urgent demands of the potato harvest, work came to a complete halt in June 1795 when Ward was arrested for bankruptcy. In August of that year, following Ward's failure to come to terms with his creditors, Bowman determined to finish the building and sue Ward for the cost.[30] The start of the inn's trading was delayed by the 1798 rebellion, when the building was occupied by part of the militia garrison defending the town. Surprisingly, the inn is not separately identified in the Lismore rental, and so it is not clear when it opened. What is known, however, is that by 1810 the innkeeper was in financial difficulties. Despite a substantial subsidy in the form of a heavily reduced rent, he was obliged to petition the duke to forgive his arrears, citing lack of trade as their cause.[31]

The inn survives today as a prominent form-element in the townscape. A substantial four-story Georgian building, it stands in the center of the town as a highly visible reminder of past patronal investment in Lismore's functional base. The canal basin and warehouse complex also survive, but are more peripherally located on the banks of the Blackwater below the bridge rebuilt in 1858 (see figure 5.1). The canal's construction was also disrupted: by flooding, by the accidental collapse of the foundations of one of the locks, and by the periodic shortage of labor. Bowman's original plan provided for a single-width canal one and a half miles long, which would enter the Blackwater just above Cappoquin and accommodate the largest vessels then plying the river between Youghal and Cappoquin. By extending the head of navigation to Lismore, Bowman ensured that the town's intended growth as the major transshipment point for agricultural produce in the lower Blackwater valley would be at Cappoquin's expense.

The initial phases of the work were rapidly completed. By late August 1793 three-quarters of the canal had been dug and the main warehouse raised to roof level. Work continued intermittently throughout Bowman's absence in England during the following winter, and in April 1794 he was able to report that work on the lock had begun and that he hoped to have the canal filled by the end of June. Thereafter the project began to falter. In May work stopped completely for two weeks because of the absence of labor during the potato planting season, while July saw the first occurrence of the flooding that was to hamper work on the canal until its completion. Building continued on

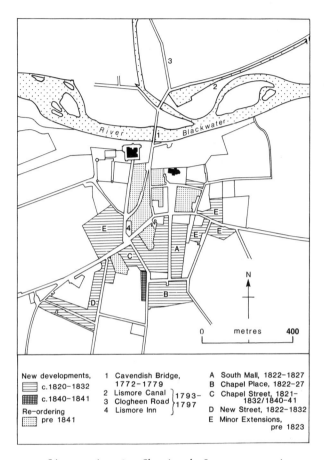

FIGURE 5.1   Lismore, circa 1841, Showing the Improvements circa 1772–1832

a seasonal basis thereafter, and the canal finally became fully operational in 1796.[32]

It is difficult to assess the extent of the canal's success. Separate lockage accounts only survive from the 1850s, and during Bowman and
Knowlton's agencies at least any income generated by the canal was not
included in the annual accounts.[33] What is clear is that despite the
completion of the crucial road link with southern Tipperary in 1797,
the canal's opening did not lead to any significant commercial or industrial development at Lismore. Whatever the role played by the
canal in rearticulating local trading patterns between southern Tipperary and the Blackwater valley, it did not engender a major transfor-

mation of Lismore's economy. It is not difficult to see why. In common
with most Irish canals at this time, the Lismore Canal lacked a significant source or market for industrial raw materials, and had to rely on a
highly seasonal trade in agricultural produce. By itself this trade was
insufficient to make any canal immensely profitable. The only Irish
canals with a realistic chance of success were those which, like the
Lagan and Newry Canals, either served an increasingly industrialized
region or aided the extraction of Ireland's only important mineral resource, coal; or which like the Grand Canal, served a population center
that was of sufficient size to generate an assured and extensive aggregate trade.[34]

The Lismore Canal was also too short to offer any significant economies of operation over existing local trade routes. The one advantage
barge traffic could offer was that of the slow uninterrupted movement
of large quantities of heavy or bulky goods over considerable distances.[35]
The Lismore Canal formed part of a waterway that was less than
twenty miles long, and which inevitably involved heavy "breakpoint"
transshipment costs at either end. Finally, the success of Bowman's
scheme depended on the canal's ability to attract a significant volume of
trade from the Clonmel and Carrick-on-Suir hinterlands across the
Knockmealdown mountains via the improved but still nevertheless relatively arduous road. However, the Suir was navigable as far as Carrick,
and these localities were already well served by this river-borne trade as
part of Waterford's extensive hinterland. Moreover, there was nothing
that Youghal could offer as an outlet port that Waterford could not
surpass.[36]

With hindsight, the likely limitations to Bowman's ambitious plans
for Lismore are all too apparent, but from the perspective of 1793 there
was no reason why they should not succeed. The underlying thrust of
the economy was still toward expansion, and the estate itself was manifestly underdeveloped in terms of its agricultural potential. Moreover,
Bowman was doing no more than propose the type of project that had
been widely adopted, particularly in east Ulster, north Leinster, and
southeast Munster, by other landlords eager to "improve" their property.[37] Within twenty miles of Lismore, for example, the King family
was engaged in rebuilding Mitchelstown and John Anderson was beginning his new town at Fermoy. Elsewhere in the region, Dunman-

way, Kenmare, Killarney, and Portlaw were also redeveloped from the late eighteenth century onward by their respective landlords, while in County Limerick, Adare, Bruff, Glin, Kilfinnane, and Newcastle were all rebuilt by their owners in what O'Connor describes as the faithful landscape replication of the landlord's ordered and hierarchical view of society.[38]

Bowman's proposals for Lismore were therefore entirely consonant with the spirit of improvement that prevailed among many Irish land-owners in the early 1790s. But his plans for the estate were to be dis-rupted by the tensions and economic difficulties that attended the 1798 rebellion. Bowman had notified his intention of resigning in January 1796 and handed over responsibility to his successor, Thomas Knowl-ton, in the summer of 1797, a year before the outbreak of fighting in May 1798. However, by then it was already clear that Bowman's policy of shortening leases was running into difficulties, particularly on the Bandon estate. The problems had been compounded by Bowman's long and frequent absences in England. Four large farms had fallen out of lease on the Bandon estate at Ladyday 1795, and in July of that year Bowman estimated that when relet, their total rent could be advanced by £500. Six months later he had to report that nothing had been done to subdivide the 2,500 acres in question, and that although all the ten-ants were under notice to quit at Ladyday, few had tried to find alter-native accommodation since almost all expected to be continued as tenants. With the growing local disorders and Bowman's continuing absence in England, thirteen of the subtenants on these farms took the opportunity to overhold. They refused to give up possession either to Bowman when he returned to Ireland in August, or to his brother William, who acted as his deputy during the transitional period prior to Knowlton's arrival, or indeed to Knowlton's deputy, John Panton, who collected the rents in Ireland during the worst of the rebellion.[39]

The defiance shown by these tenants in the face of their landlord's delegated authority was not universal on the Devonshire estate, but was certainly symptomatic of the growing unrest and lawlessness in parts of Munster in the months prior to the outbreak of the rebellion. In Febru-ary 1797, with the imminent threat of a French invasion and the collapse of local credit, Heaton suspended all further attempts to imple-ment the new system of management begun under Bowman. No further leases were to be executed under the new system, and tenants who had recently agreed with the duke on this basis were to be offered the opportunity to sublet their farms at will in return for their agreement to absolve the duke from his building obligations.[40] During the remainder of the year, to judge from Knowlton's increasingly alarmist reports, the situation in and around Lismore steadily worsened. Knowlton's letters to Heaton contain a growing litany describing maimed cattle, burnt crops, and assassination threats and attempts. More seriously from the duke's point of view, they also list a growing number of rent defaulters, usually middlemen whose own subtenants had refused to pay their rents either through fear or conviction.[41] On October 20 Knowlton wrote to Heaton:

I see not the least probability of my being of further service to his Grace by remaining in Ireland any longer at this time, otherwise I would not retire. The disturbances and disorders of this wicked people though very disagreeable do not frighten me from my duty, but as it is quite clear that no more rents will be paid until the disorders are quite settled, I believe my services are not required and that I may beat a retreat without injury to his Grace's Interest.[42]

Knowlton returned to England shortly afterward, and for the next eighteen months the Irish estate was run on a "care and maintenance" basis by his deputy.[43] The initial attempt at urban improvement was over.

Planning for Power: 1800–1822

When Knowlton returned to Ireland in June 1799 the prospects for urban improvement had been transformed. The rebellion had been suppressed, and although a minority of the duke's tenants had taken advantage of the disorder to break their leases and to "graff" (burn) their land, there had in fact been singularly few direct attacks on the duke's property.[44] The growing confidence that followed the restoration of an admittedly uneasy peace was signaled on the estate by the rapid fall in the outstanding arrears and by the continued rise in rent income. But the greatest prospect for change lay in the political arena. Talk of Union was in the air. Although Pitt's initial proposals had already been defeated in the Irish Parliament in January 1799 by an unlikely combination of Whiggish patriots and "orange" and commercial interests, Pitt's commissioners were again at work producing the revised proposals that were ultimately to be accepted by both Houses of Parliament the following year.[45] Of the various legal, constitutional, financial, and economic clauses that were embodied in the act when it finally became law on January 1, 1801, it was the provision for a reduced Irish parliamentary representation—at Westminster—that most affected the duke. With the abolition of the Irish Parliament in Dublin, two hundred of the existing three hundred Irish seats disappeared. One hundred and sixty-eight were lost when 84 of the 117 Irish parliamentary boroughs were disenfranchised on the grounds of insufficient population or wealth, and a further 33 when the representation in each of the surviving boroughs was reduced to a single seat. County representation remained as before, with each of the thirty-two counties returning two members. An earlier proposal to reduce this to one seat apiece had been rejected on the grounds that it would exclude independent and secondary interests.[46]

Of the five Burlington boroughs nominally controlled by the duke prior to the Union, only three retained a seat in 1801. Dungarvan was one of five post-Union Irish boroughs in which the franchise was based on a property qualification: householders in the borough with property worth more than £5 per year and freeholders in the manor worth more than forty shillings a year were entitled to register as voters. Bandon was one of the thirteen so-called burgess boroughs, where the right to vote was limited to the corporation, while at Youghal the franchise included the freemen as well as the corporation.[47] Lismore and Tallow had both been disenfranchised. Consequently, once the duke had established his claim to their parliamentary representation as a beneficiary under the terms of the earl of Cork and Burlington's will, he was entitled under the provisions of the act to receive £15,000 compensation for each. Despite an attempt by the "independent electors" of Tallow to stake a rival claim, the duke eventually received £20,000 by 1803; the remaining £10,000 was held in trust in government securities for his heir, the marquis of Hartington.[48]

The drastic reduction in the number of Irish boroughs after the Union, together with the fact that they were now represented in the imperial rather than the national parliament, meant that the question of their control was of much greater political consequence than before. Heaton was well aware of this reality. After obtaining Bowman's assessment of the state of the duke's electoral interest in Ireland, Heaton wrote to Knowlton in July 1801, directing him to consider with Thomas Garde how best the duke might regain his political power not only in Counties Cork and Waterford but also in Bandon, Dungarvan, and Youghal.[49] Their report was not particularly optimistic. In County Cork the duke's interest was so low he was "far from having it in his power to nominate a member," and in County Waterford it was doubtful whether he would succeed in naming one member at the next election. At Bandon and Youghal "nothing could be done" in the foreseeable future. Only at Dungarvan was there thought to be any prospect of early success, and even then only after careful and expensive attention to the management of the borough. In fact, as events turned out, the duke was able to regain control not only of Dungarvan, but also eventually of Youghal. In addition, it proved possible for the duke to reinstate the earlier agreement of 1767 whereby he shared the alternate parliamentary nomination at Bandon with the Bernard family. At Dungarvan these management strategies involved the entire reconstruction of the duke's property by 1820. At Bandon and Youghal the political management was largely tenurial in character, and concerned only a minority of the duke's tenants.

Dungarvan   The problems facing Knowlton at Dungarvan were complex. The duke was only one of several landowners in the town, and his property there was fragmented and lay outside the town's original medieval core. The other landlords were politically fickle, and were as willing to combine against him as to ally themselves with him. Moreover, the duke's tenants were not only themselves extremely impoverished, and generally ineligible under existing property qualifications to vote, but they were also susceptible to the influence of the Catholic clergy and to the appeal of more vigorous "nationalist" politics than the duke was himself prepared to espouse. Their political fidelity was therefore by no means assured, irrespective of the expenditure sanctioned on their behalf.

Knowlton's solution was to try to neutralize the opposing political interests as far as he could, while at the same time strengthening the duke's interest by creating as many freehold votes as possible and by implementing a politically judicious program of urban renewal. By providing employment, improving local urban amenities, and bolstering the local urban economy, he intended to raise the tenants' expectations of the duke and attach them more firmly to his politics. At the time of the Union Dungarvan provided an arena for five competing political interests. The most important were those of the duke, the marquis of Waterford, and the Greenes and Keilys. Sir Thomas Osborne and Thomas Carew also retained some minor influence in the town arising out of their property ownership, but following Carew's decision to ally himself with the duke rather than with Osborne against him, these interests had declined in importance.[50]

Knowlton's first attempt to neutralize the duke's political opponents was hampered by the relative weakness of the duke's own power, and very soon ended in defeat at the General Election of 1802. Knowlton had concluded that in the circumstances, the best course of action was to attempt to continue the duke's existing loose alliance with Lord Waterford. The Waterford interest was based on the Revenue, and was, in Knowlton's estimation, less stable and therefore politically less dangerous than the property-based interest of the Greenes and Keilys.[51] This unlikely alliance between the Tory marquis and the Whig duke, or more correctly, Ponsonbys, had begun in 1789, when both had come under attack in the borough and county from a coalition between Lord Grandison and the Greenes and Keilys.[52]

The alliance survived throughout the 1790s largely on the basis of each party's mutual opposition to the impending Union, and certainly with no illusions on the part of the duke's servants. In July 1795, for example, Garde expressed his candid opinion that the Waterford interest was more important both politically and financially to the duke than the duke's interest was to the marquis. Not only was it impossible for the duke to unseat the Waterford interest in the eponymous county, even if allied with a third party, but the marquis's support was positively beneficial insofar as his personal popularity aided the acquisition of grand jury funding for the duke's improvements at Lismore.[53] Two years later Bowman was more cautious. In advising Heaton how to deal with a request from one of Lord Waterford's allies for a lease renewal in Dungarvan, he concluded:

Mr Dalton is a steady friend of the marquess of Waterford, and I doubt not will be so of Mr Ponsonby, whilst the two interests are united in the county of Waterford. But whenever they are separated, I have as little doubt of his sticking to the former and forsaking the latter. . . . I will take the liberty to observe that all possible prudent care should be taken [that] Lord Waterford's friends do not get into possession of too much of the duke's property within that borough.[54]

In 1802, in a coup de main that was perhaps inevitable rather than extraordinary, but which nevertheless amply demonstrated the pragmatic and tactical nature of Dungarvan politics, Lord Waterford severed all political connection with W. B. Ponsonby, and ended Knowlton's hopes of a political alliance in the post-Union borough. Allying himself instead with his natural allies, the conservative Greenes, Lord Waterford ensured the return of Major Greene as M.P. for Dungarvan in opposition to the Devonshire interest in the election of the same year.[55] Thus within a year of his initial appraisal of the political prospects at Dungarvan, Knowlton was faced with the collapse of the main plank in his strategy, and with the necessity of relying solely on his ability to strengthen the duke's vote from within the estate itself.

Preparations for the Dungarvan improvements seem to have been initiated very shortly after Ponsonby's defeat. Ten months later, in May 1803, Knowlton was urging Heaton not to accede to a petition from the town's Roman Catholic inhabitants for a new chapel site, largely on the grounds that "the land they want may be of great importance in our future operations for recovering command of the borough. I believe it is or will be building ground, out of which may be created many good votes, both for the borough and the county."[56] Subsequent correspondence makes it clear that Knowlton's primary concern was the possible survival of the third life on the head lease of the intended building ground. This individual, a Mr. Roberts, had gone to America some thirty years previously and had not been heard of since. Until the question of his putative existence had been satisfactorily resolved, no work could begin. Bowman had been aware of this problem in 1794 and had tried unsuccessfully to obtain information concerning Roberts's whereabouts.[57] Subsequently, Garde's advice to Knowlton had been that nothing should be done to disturb the occupying tenants until conclusive proof of Roberts's death had been obtained. In the event, Knowlton acted on the general belief that the last life together with any reversionary term had expired, and procured all the occupy-

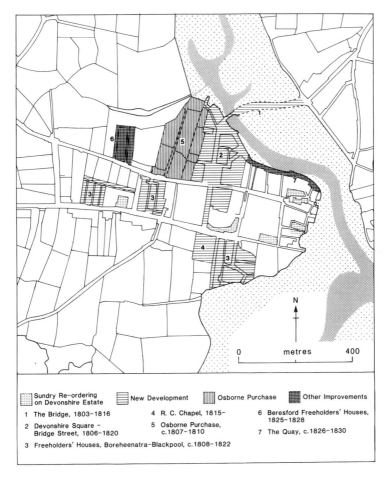

FIGURE 5.2   Dungarvan, circa 1841, Showing the Improvements Circa 1806–1830

ing tenants to attorn to the duke, thereby circumventing the issue and enabling work to commence.[58]

A comparison of figures 3.3a and 5.2 reveals the full extent of the alterations that were then carried out on the duke's estate in the town over the next seventeen years. Three major projects were begun: the Devonshire Square-Bridge Street development, the bridge, and the forty-shillings freeholders' housing at Blackpool and Boreheenatra. These were superintended by Knowlton until his dismissal circa 1814, and thereafter by his successors, James Abercrombie, W. A. Ashby, and Colonel Currey, who appear in general to have adhered to his original plan.

THE DEVONSHIRE SQUARE DEVELOPMENT   The new ensemble of streets built on the land freed by attorning the "Roberts" lease was the earliest and visually most important part of the town plan laid out at the duke's expense. As well as the Square and Bridge Street, it also included William Street and Cross Bridge Street. These streets were already marked out in 1806 to the plan of William Atkinson, a Manchester architect and pupil of James Wyatt, who three years previously had been commissioned to survey and replan Bandon and Lismore.[59] Atkinson's designs for Dungarvan epitomize the ordered structuring of urban social space already alluded to as characteristic of the ascendancy's hierarchical view of society, and symbolizes in particular O'Connor's "zone of substance."

In a letter to Heaton in October 1806, Knowlton described at length his motives in promoting the rebuilding, its progress to date, and the effect the work had already had on public opinion.

The best situations for building in this town belong to his grace. They form a sort of nucleus or core in the center of the town [sic.]. These I found covered by a parcel of mud cabins in ruins, not one of them good enough to give the occupier a vote. . . . I saw that it might be converted into the best part of the town; that it might all be made valuable building ground, and to give [the duke] a decided preponderance in the borough; and that, if he built on it himself, I presumed he might keep the command of what he created. . . .

. . . A great quantity of the best materials, of timber, Welsh slate, Yorkshire flags and Portland stone for fireplaces and hearths, have been imported from England, at a much cheaper rate than must have been given for materials of very inferior quality, had they been purchased in Ireland, and a great number of bricks have been made on his grace's estate near the town. . . . A central square and several streets have been laid out by erecting register pillars, and contracts have been made with workmen for building twelve houses of the inferior sort immediately, but which will create good votes for the borough; and these are actually begun on.

I have determined on the building houses of this description first, with a view to offer them to such of the deserving and industrious inhabitants of the old cabins as may appear to deserve them, which we must throw down to make our new streets and openings: a measure which humanity dictated, and does not appear to be impolitic. I thought I was acting consistently with the duke of Devonshire's character, and would rather raise his popularity.

To this state we have advanced in our progress, and it has created a revolution in the public sentiment in respect to his grace's power. It has convinced the people that he is in earnest. They had been accustomed to hear a great deal talked of, but to see nothing done. As they have seen nothing but paltry election tricks and subterfuges, it was difficult to convince them that his grace was serious. The collection of these materials has at last effected their conviction, and under this first impression has certainly created a powerful influence, by imposing the belief on the people that all future resistance to him will be vain. It has set men's minds a-speculating and roving. Some expect they may be favored with a good house, others that they may obtain profits by being employed or by selling something during the erection of these buildings, which their opposition would deprive them of; in short, that they may come in for something, although they may have no determinate idea of what.[60]

The overwhelming impression is of a decidedly political exercise, in which the agent determined his course of action in the light of its probable consequences for the duke's interest. The provision of new housing for tenants made homeless by the initial building operations might be humane, but it created good votes and strengthened the duke's political following. Similarly, it was thought advisable for the duke to bear the cost of building the new houses himself because in doing so, he would obviate the need for lengthy building leases that would have weakened his political authority over the town. Hence, too, Knowlton's satisfaction at the uncertainty and raised expectations created in the minds of the duke's tenants: the hope of personal gain and the fear of its loss were deemed, in the short term at least, to be powerful ties binding the townspeople to the duke.

In the event, the construction of the houses in the Devonshire Square-Bridge Street area did not go quite as Knowlton intended. The earliest houses were built as planned at the duke's expense, but the unexpectedly urgent call for freeholders' houses and the premature construction of the bridge shortly after 1808 appear to have diverted funds from the Square before it was completed. The first houses were built on Bridge Street and Cross Bridge Street in 1807. Work on the houses in the Square was underway in 1810, but these were not completed until 1822, and were built in part at least by private individuals on building leases.[61] In the absence of any subsequent reference in the accounts to ducal investment in this part of the housing project, the existence of these leases suggests that by this time the estate's original intention to pay for the entire building program had been replaced by a willingness to accept building tenants as long-term "partners" in the scheme.

There were cogent reasons why this was desirable. The whole point of the rebuilding program was to ensure that the duke regained control of the borough. In 1806 this was duly accomplished with the return of his candidate, General George Walpole.[62] At the general election of the following year, however, the seat was very nearly lost again when Walpole faced a determined challenge by the Beresford family's candidate, Colonel Richard Keane. Matters were made worse for Walpole by the faulty registration of many of the duke's freeholders. The general blamed Knowlton for this, and tried to have him replaced as election agent by Philip Splane.[63] In the event, Walpole was elected by forty-two votes, but this was less than expected and fueled the fears already expressed by Lord George Cavendish about the pace and political effectiveness of the improvements.[64] In April Knowlton had been called upon to explain why the twelve new houses he had engaged to build the previous October had not been completed. Although Knowlton explained the delay on the grounds of the unsuitability of the winter weather, he nevertheless accepted the reality that the imminent election demanded that work recommence immediately, and instructed Atkinson accordingly.

Privately, Knowlton was convinced that the Ponsonbys were behind both Lord Cavendish's complaints and General Walpole's attempt to have him replaced as election agent. Writing to Heaton on May 27, after Walpole's election, Knowlton concluded: "You also know that the Ponsonbys had the management and took everything, and now you see that the moment I have recovered Dungarvan they are impatient to seize the management again to themselves . . . if they had the management they would lose the borough again."[65] Nevertheless, the narrowness of Walpole's victory seemed to indicate that Lord Cavendish's fears were not without foundation, and that not only should the pace of improvement be speeded up, but that the money should be spent on those projects that yielded the highest immediate return in terms of votes. By this time, popular sentiment and electoral necessity dictated that these should be the proposed bridge over the River Colligan, and, following the Relief Act of 1793, the provision of freeholders' housing.

THE BRIDGE   The earliest reference to a new bridge at Dungarvan
dates from 1804, when the quarter session grand jury held in the town
sent a petition to the fifth duke, observing that "the erection of a
bridge over the River Colligan . . . would produce the most important
and permanent advantages to the town by facilitating and procuring at
all times its intercourse with the surrounding country." The memorial
continued by claiming that the project was beyond the grand jury's
means since it would inevitably involve buying out the owner and
tenant of the existing ferry, and concluded by asserting that not only
was the duke the only person able to afford it, but that a bridge would
considerably improve the value of his property in and around the
town.[66] Quite what effect this candor had is not recorded, but it accurately presaged the growing local popularity of the scheme. Writing in
1808 to congratulate General Walpole on his second return, the Reverend Jabez Henry was in no doubt as to its political value: "You have recovered the borough for his Grace, and you are the fittest person to
recommend to the family in what manner and by what means they
will be sure to keep it. . . . to the latter purpose I only beg leave to suggest the uninterrupted progress of his Grace's improvements here, but
above all the bridge, to that object all descriptions of your Electors are
most impatiently looking."[67]
    Knowlton subsequently claimed that a bridge had formed part of his
intended improvements from the outset, but nothing was in fact done
until 1808, when Lord Waterford's political maneuvering forced
Knowlton to act precipitously to forestall his rival scheme. Knowlton's
original intention had been to delay building the bridge for another
two years while the other projects within the overall scheme matured,
and until it was possible to purchase land for the purpose on the Abbeyside bank of the River Colligan. The extraordinary expenses that
the duke had had to bear in supporting General Walpole's election in
1806 and 1807, in financing the new housing, streets and square, and
in purchasing Sir Thomas Osborne's estate, had also been a factor in
Knowlton's mind militating against earlier construction of the bridge.
However, at some point soon after the 1807 election the duke's intention to finance a bridge had been made public. In Knowlton's view,
this alerted Lord Waterford to the political capital to be made out of
such a project, and set in train his attempt to promote his own scheme

and thereby upstage the duke.[68] In October 1808 Sir John Newport wrote to Lord George Cavendish warning him of Lord Waterford's intentions, but Knowlton seems already to have been aware of these and to have taken action. Prior to the Waterford Assize where Lord Waterford intended to make his presentment, Knowlton informed Henry Gumbleton, one of the grand jurors, that the duke "assuredly intended to build a bridge and would not therefore trouble the Grand Jury for any of the County's money for that purpose." At the same time, Knowlton solicited Gumbleton's help in getting a presentment for an approach road to the bridge, which enabled Gumbleton to "decidedly state the declaration he had had from the Duke's agent." This had the desired effect, and Lord Waterford's presentment was refused.[69]

Nevertheless, Knowlton recognized that as long as the bridge remained unbuilt the threat of further intervention by Lord Waterford remained real. Writing to Heaton on October 20, he concluded that "this effort of Mr Beresford's . . . precipitates us on the measure. A bridge must be immediately set about, either at the Duke's expense or by application to the Grand Jury by one of his friends for a presentment."[70] As with the houses around the Square, Knowlton's own inclination was that the duke should build the bridge at his own expense under a private act of Parliament. In so doing he would be able to retain control of the structure once it was completed, and use it to further his own political ends by offering free passage to his supporters while demanding a toll from his "enemies." Knowlton had been unaware of the deadline for obtaining an act at the next session of Parliament, and since there was now inevitably going to be a delay in achieving this, he concurred with Heaton that something should be done to signal the seriousness of the duke's intentions. To achieve this, he directed Atkinson to collect materials for stockpiling in situ, in particular, "a cargo or two" of Runcorn stone to be laid down on the spot.[71]

Work was underway on the bridge by 1810 and it was completed in 1816, at a reputed cost according to Lewis of £50,000. The accuracy of this figure is hard to judge, since only three annual accounts survive from the period between 1810 and 1816. However, during those three years the total expenditure on the bridge amounted to more than £9,000, which, if it indicates nothing else, demonstrates that Atkinson's original estimate of between £7,000–8,000 for the entire project was grossly optimistic.[72] Inaccurate financial forecasting was not Atkinson's only deficiency as an architect. His original designs for the bridge were overornate, and were, according to Samuel Ware the architect who replaced him in 1813, "suitable to a nobleman's park or a great city."[73] The precise circumstances of Atkinson's departure are not known. Seven years later, when Knowlton was trying to justify his conduct as agent, he alluded to the work of "an expensive and careless architect over whom [Heaton] allowed him no control" as one possible reason why his management might have been thought extravagant.[74] Certainly, the tone of Samuel Ware's 1813 report is very much that of a man brought in to cut costs. He found Atkinson's original design for a five arch bridge barely begun, but with a vast quantity of freestone lying on the quay, having been brought from England at a reputed cost of two shillings per cubic foot. The bridge that was finally built was simpler and cheaper, and remains to the present day as the only link across the River Colligan between Dungarvan and its suburb at Abbeyside.[75]

FREEHOLDERS' HOUSING The unexpectedly narrow margin of General Walpole's victory in 1807 bore eloquent testimony to one inescapable fact: capital investment in improvement projects did not necessarily produce lasting political benefits. As events at the General Election of 1826 were to demonstrate, even a major and seemingly popular scheme such as the Dungarvan bridge could not be relied upon to generate long-term political loyalties, even among the duke's own tenantry. Thus of the measures taken by Knowlton to remedy the deficiencies in the duke's electoral register after the 1807 election, it was his sustained house-building campaign, designed to create a large and politically obedient freeholder electorate from among the duke's tenantry, that was likely to prove the most effective.

The principles underlying the marshaling of such "political mercenaries" were widely understood in Ireland during the years immediately before and after the Union. They rested on the concept of a vote acquired by virtue of possession of freehold property, which was itself of considerable antiquity. The diagnostic characteristic of freehold property was that it was either owned outright, or else was leased for an indeterminate period. A lease for one life was a freehold, a lease for 999 years was not. Moreover, not only did a lease for years disenfranchise the lessee, but it also banned him from making leases for lives of part of the property and thereby creating votes. During the eighteenth century the commonest form of property qualification for freehold votes—available only to Protestants—was the forty-shillings franchise. As chapter 2 has shown, this was a minimum and not an absolute value. By extending this franchise to the much more numerous and, relatively speaking, impoverished Catholic community, the 1793 Catholic Relief Act not only provided landlords with an opportunity to increase their electoral strength, but also gave votes to many tenants whose holdings were only nominally worth the minimum sum. In Malcomson's phrase, "the Roman Catholic rabble" who were thereby enfranchised were objected to not because they were Roman Catholic, but because they were a rabble.[76]

Knowlton was in no doubt as to the dire consequences of the 1793 act, both for the country at large and for the duke's political interest. Writing to Heaton in 1807, he concluded:

[B]y the new mode . . . where there was one freeholder last year, there will be at least five a year hence. There was last year about 2,000 freeholders in the county of Waterford, and next year there will be 10,000 of these fictitious, fraudulent freeholders—for such I deem them. The way is this. Of half an acre of land with a mud cabin on it, they create what is called a freehold by a lease for one life. They charge a high rent for the land, and one shilling a year for the house or cabin, and the tenant, who cannot speak a word of English, who has no more knowledge than a brute beast of moral good or evil . . . is brought forward and told he must swear his holding is worth 40 shillings a year, and which is then registered accordingly. They are brought into the courts by hundreds by their landlords, and in this manner and of [sic] this literal description, and are registered altogether, swearing the oath all at once in the Irish language, without observing what they are doing, or I verily believe knowing what they are doing. The landlord afterwards keeps the lease in his possession, so that they are to all intents and purposes his hirelings.

The question, then, is whether it be wise and honorable to lock up the estate to a cotter-tenantry, and make fraudulent freeholders, which will undoubtedly retard, if not totally put an end to, the improvement of the estate for ages . . . or consent to impair the political influence at county elections for a period—perhaps only a short one, as I presume the inconveniences of the present mode will manifest themselves.[77]

Behind Knowlton's emphatic prose lay a real dilemma. If the duke's political rivals were prepared to adopt this course of action, what alternative did he have but to do likewise, even though this might well be at the expense of efficient farming and rent formation? In short, where did the duke's priorities lie in Ireland, in income maximization or in the reclamation of his political influence? In the event, the urgency of the situation after the 1807 election appears to have overcome whatever scruples Knowlton had, which in any case concerned the effect of these "fraudulent" freeholders on the management of the agricultural estate rather than on the towns. The situation was made particularly ominous by the news in April 1807 that the marquis of Waterford was negotiating to purchase Major Greene's estate, since this would give him a preponderant interest in Dungarvan.[78] The sale alerted Knowlton to the dangers of territorial aggrandizement by the duke's political rivals in the borough, and prompted him to seek to strengthen the duke's position by similar purchases. After protracted negotiations, Knowlton agreed to purchase Sir Thomas Osborne's somewhat smaller estate in the town for £7,400 in October 1807, but as a result of unexpected delays the sale was not finally completed until 1810.[79]

The pressures on the duke's electoral position in Dungarvan in 1807 were exacerbated by a renewed request from the parish priest for land at Boreheenatra for the site of a new Roman Catholic chapel. The request had originally been made in 1803, when Knowlton cited a variety of practical and social reasons why the duke should refuse it. In Knowlton's view the request was at best ill-judged, and at worst a deliberate attempt to stir up sectarian strife. Moreover, the land in question was earmarked for the intended town improvements.[80] The renewed request was evidently made during the campaign that preceded the 1806 election, timing which is unlikely to have been coincidental. Despite General Walpole's personal support for the application, Knowlton was adamant that it could only be granted at the cost of alienating the Protestant community and sabotaging the campaign to retain political control of the borough.[81] In January 1807 Knowlton stressed the openness of the borough and the overriding need to make the most of what property the duke possessed there:

His Grace's building ground is comparatively small to what it could be wished to ensure a command . . . his lands for occupation with the houses he will build or otherwise to create influence are circumscribed, not affording a desirable sufficiency to tie the people by sufficiency of accommodation. Under such circumstances it is impossible to advise His Grace to give away any of his lands to satisfy the avaricious and culpable views of the priest. . . . [All] this sacrifice would not create any permanent or indeed temporary influence of a commanding nature, but only a short lived inefficient popularity with a party.[82]

Heaton's initial reaction was to agree with Knowlton; he endorsed the letter with the note: "not to part with land in the borough for a papish chapel or anything else." Six months later, however, presumably as a result of General Walpole's declaration in the meantime that he would resign if the priest's request was not acceded to, Knowlton had once again to justify his position.[83] On this occasion he avoided any suspicion of sectarian bias and set his arguments in a broader economic context. After describing the disputed plot as one where twenty fishermen's cabins already existed and where more could be built, Knowlton outlined the economic role of these people and their probable importance to the future growth of the town.

All that these people want is a small house with a strip of land about twelve feet wide, which they throw up into a ridge . . . against the sunny side of which they dry their hake taken during the season, and they may all be made good 40/- freeholders at a small sacrifice to his Grace. For the fish they often get from £10 to £30 and even £40 and the more thrifty of them lay it up and in time accumulate enough to purchase a sloop. . . . In this way Dungarvan has grown from a fishing town into a fishing and trading town, and there are more coasting vessels built there and belonging to it at this moment, then to Youghal, Cork and Kinsale put together. They are in fact the carriers for the whole province of Munster. To give this land away which is in fact giving away power where we are weak . . . would be madness in the extreme; as it would be giving away both property and power within the borough, when there is so much reason and occasion to increase both.[84]

Knowlton's arguments must eventually have prevailed, because although the duke did ultimately give a site for the new Catholic chapel, this was delayed until 1815 and did not encroach on the land required for the freeholders' houses or impinge on the established Anglican church (see figure 5.2). Although a program of house building was clearly underway by 1808, when Knowlton was able to report that "as fast as we build houses we are able to get good tenants for them," it is not certain that these were specifically for freeholders; Knowlton may have been referring to the houses in Bridge Street and on the

Square.[85] The first unambiguous reference to completed freeholders' houses occurs three years later in 1811, when Knowlton sent twenty-seven leases for freehold property in Boreheenatra to Chatsworth for completion. The instructions that accompanied these leases provide an insight into Knowlton's intended tenurial management of this potentially unruly freeholder electorate. All the lessees were of low social status: twenty-three were fishermen, two were tanners, one was a laborer, and one was a gardener. The houses were all of a uniformly small size and each lease was to be completed for one or two old lives "but by no means for the life of the tenant." In other words, by citing elderly or "decayed" lives, the lease could be expected to expire long before the demise of the tenant, who would presumably be dependent on the duke's goodwill for a renewal. Moreover, the leases were strictly for the houses themselves; the land behind them that the fisherman required for drying their catch was reserved to the duke "as a means of control."[86] In other words, not only was the tenant's lease for his house likely to be preternaturally short, but his access to the land he needed to carry on his occupation was, tenurially, even less assured.

The total number of freeholders' houses built under the aegis of Knowlton and his immediate successors cannot be determined with certainty. The accounts for 1822–1823 contain two entries that refer separately to repairs to the slating of 284 freehold houses in Dungarvan and to repairs to the roofs of 483.[87] Two years later Henry Witham wrote to James Abercrombie concerning the registration of 101 freeholders, but like the 137 registered in 1826, these may have included some reregistrations under the eight-year rule introduced in 1795.[88] A newspaper report in 1829 estimated the total electoral register in the town to consist of 744 forty-shillings freeholders, 42 £20 freeholders, and 15 £50 freeholders, but did not specify how many of these were the duke's and how many occupied recently purpose-built freehold houses.[89] Consequently, the most accurate indication of the number of new houses built by Knowlton and his successors to create freehold votes may be that provided by a comparison of the First Edition of the Ordnance Survey Six Inch Map (see figure 5.2) with the 1:500 map of Dungarvan surveyed in 1880. A comparison of these sources with the 1853 Dungarvan freehold valuation suggests that approximately 383 freeholders' houses were built in Blackpool, Boreheenatra, and Abbey-

side by the 1840s.[90] The discrepancy between this and the larger of the
1822 figures may have been due to freehold leases being given for other,
non-purpose-built housing on the estate that had previously been
leased for lives.

These freehold cabins were characterized by low status and high density and corresponded in some ways to O'Connor's concept of a "zone
of need." Nevertheless, the political circumstances surrounding their
construction suggest that they cannot be seen as evidence of the spatial
and economic marginalization of their occupants by their landlord.[91]
On the contrary, it may be argued that although the agent had to take
reasonable precautions to ensure these tenants' political fidelity, it was
in no one's interest for the relationship to degenerate into mutual antagonism. The duke, or more precisely his candidate, required the freeholders' political allegiance, while the tenants benefited from their
landlord's goodwill. Certainly, the political expenditure recorded in the
annual accounts for Dungarvan prior to 1832 implies a continuing
readiness on the duke's part to maintain and improve the quality of the
freeholders' houses. Between 1822 and 1829 this expenditure averaged
£170 a year over and above the cost of registering freeholds and the
actual expense of the elections themselves, such as the £800 spent on
the General Election of 1826.[92]

Bandon   Although extensive improvements were carried out in
Bandon during Knowlton's agency, they were on a smaller scale than
those at Dungarvan and do not seem to have formed part of the strategy
that eventually succeeded in enforcing the duke's political rights in the
borough. Nevertheless, Knowlton was authorized to spend well over
£10,000 on improvements in the town between 1804 and 1813, while
between 1815 and 1820 his successors spent a further £5,359.[93] The most
ambitious proposal was for a canal which was put forward by the town's
merchants for the duke's support. This was designed to link the town
with the lower Bandon River, which its backers claimed would improve
Bandon's export trade by making it accessible to larger vessels. After an
investigation of the project's feasibility by Knowlton in 1801 and 1802,
the route that was finally chosen by the canal's promoters was considered
to be disadvantageous to the duke's estate and his support was withdrawn, whereupon the project collapsed.[94]

The estate-funded improvements overseen by Knowlton and his successors were more successful, and cast some doubt on O'Flanagan's suggestion that the duke did not take an active interest in Bandon's economy at this time. Between 1804 and 1820 the estate built new quays along both the Bridewell and Bandon Rivers, reordered and extended the street network, and erected new housing. While admittedly none of this represented direct investment in commercial or manufacturing premises, it nevertheless facilitated the expansion of manufacturing activity, particularly on the south side of the town.[95] In 1806 the construction of Burlington Quay was begun along the south side of the River Bandon, and this eventually linked Weir Street to Wesley Quay and the bridge. By 1813, Cavendish Row, Devonshire Square, and the new extension to Bridge Street (the old Bridewell Lane) had been laid out and leveled, and a total of twenty-six houses together with a new sessions house constructed. Between 1815 and 1820 Knowlton's successors carried further sundry improvements. These included additions to the houses in Cavendish Square and Cavendish Street, the widespread flagging of streets, and the construction of a new shambles, inn, and market house. In addition, the Market Quay was built, while Bridewell Street was realigned and rebuilt and renamed Cavendish Quay (see figure 5.3). The construction of the sessions house was prompted by Lord Shannon's decision in 1802 to build a rival courthouse on his peripheral suburban estate at Irishtown. This would have had the double effect of increasing the earl's prestige in the town and the value of his property there, all to the duke's detriment. In the event, Knowlton's action forestalled the earl, although not before he had made a further attempt to have the sessions removed from Bandon altogether to his own town at Clonakilty.[96]

Knowlton's improvements represented the first material benefits to accrue to Bandon under the revised managerial strategy of 1801. The absence of a coherent management policy had caused much uncertainty and dissatisfaction among the Bandon tenantry immediately after the Union. Consequently, while it is reasonable to assume that this capital investment may well have engendered the same sort of public gratitude to the duke which was one of Knowlton's primary aims at Dungarvan, it is important to stress that the reassertion of the duke's parliamentary authority in Bandon owed very little to such

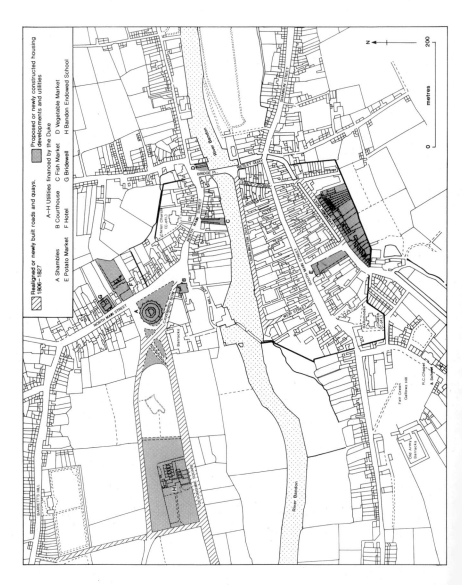

Legend (within map):

⬛ Realigned or newly built roads and quays. ▨ Proposed or newly constructed housing developments and utilities 1806–1827

A–H Utilities financed by the Duke

A Shambles   B Courthouse   C Fish Market   D Vegetable Market

E Potato Market   F Hotel   G Bridewell   H Bandon Endowed School

0   200 metres

N

Map labels: BARRETT'S HILL, NORTH MAIN STREET, CASTLE HILL, River Bandon, BRIDGE PL., WELEY QUAY, Christ Church (prot.), SOUTH MAIN STREET, MILL STREET, UNDERGROWN QUAY, SHANNON STREET, Barracks, WEIR STREET, UNDERGROWN SCHEME, River Bandon, Fair Green, Gallows Hill, R.C.Chapel, R.C.Chapel, Old Army Barracks, St.Finnbarr's Church (prot.)

public sentiment. Instead, it was achieved by the tenurial pressure that the duke's advisers were able to bring to bear on the Bernard family as a result of the fortuitous falling out of their leases for land adjacent to the town. The Bernards were leaders of the Tory faction in Cork politics, and were the most politically powerful of the duke's middleman tenants.[97] As rentiers of substantial parts of the duke's estate around Bandon, they had long exercised a virtual monopoly on the political representation of the borough without actually owning any property within it.

The origins of this political struggle have already been outlined in chapter 4. The 1767 agreement signed between the earl of Shannon on behalf of the duke and James Bernard was honored by both parties until James Bernard's death in 1790. Thereupon his son, Francis Bernard, who had been ennobled under the earl of Shannon's patronage as the first earl of Bandon, began a systematic campaign to extend his influence within the corporation at the duke's expense.[98] Writing to the fifth duke in 1801, Lord Bandon explained that although he did not regard the 1767 agreement between the duke and his father as binding upon him, he had nevertheless acquiesced in it as far as the nomination of M.P.'s was concerned. He had only deviated from it in corporation matters insofar as he had thought it necessary to nominate his own friends to the Common Council in order to prevent William Conner from establishing an interest there.[99] Three years earlier the Reverend Lloyd had put matters in a rather different light. Writing to Garde in a general rebuttal of Lord Bandon's allegations concerning the loyalty of the duke's Bandon tenantry, Lloyd commented:

[As] to the borough of Bandon, when my Lord Bandon talks of the duke's interest in it, he should tell what interest he has left him in it, for in my opinion he has left him none, except he can call the expense of supporting the Corporation an interest of the duke. The tolls and customs of the town are the property of the duke and they are given to the Corporation without lease from year to year for twenty guineas. The Corporation let them for two hundred or more. This profit goes to pay the provost £100 and the remainder to pay the expenses of the Corporation.[100]

Lord Bandon's letter of 1801 was prompted by his growing concern over the duke's failure to renew his leases for various denominations of Coolfaddo, and in particular for the 602 acres of Laragh and Shinagh

that were partly enclosed within his Deer Park.[101] The leases had expired in 1799, but well before then, in 1787, the Bernard family had
sought an assurance from the then-auditor, Baron Hotham, that they
would be renewed. Hotham's reply was ambiguous. Although he refused the request on the grounds that it would set an unacceptable
precedent, he nevertheless assured Bernard "that when a proper time
comes for renewal, his pretensions certainly will not be forgotten, if
he should then be inclined to offer the fair value for the holdings."[102]
Despite its ambiguity, Hotham's reply apparently satisfied the Bernards. But in 1797, when the leases were nearing expiry, Bowman had
refused to renew them to Lord Bandon, and had instead let the bulk of
the land directly to twenty-three of his erstwhile tenants, reserving only
sixty-two acres to the Bernard family on a twenty-one-year lease.[103]

Bowman's actions were entirely in accordance with the new leasing
policy formulated as part of the 1793 management plan, and were also
dictated by the economic uncertainties surrounding the prospective
Union.[104] Moreover, it was a decision which, in Knowlton's view, was
unavoidable if there was to be any realistic prospect of urban improvement at Bandon. Writing to Heaton in April 1798, Knowlton concluded:

I am confident, from the situation of the farm at Coolfaddo, that the Duke
cannot be advised to let it in any way but from year to year, consistent with
the system of improvement you have adopted. . . . The lands in question will
no doubt become of great value, and will be indispensable for the purpose of
improving the Duke's town and estates, and ought to be kept within his reach
until a favorable time comes for distributing them properly. In every political
light . . . I believe it is equally indispensable, for by dividing this and letting it
to the town at short leases [sic], he will be able easily to manage them [sic];
but by renewing Lord Bandon's lease, he will put it into his lordship's power
to do whatever he pleases.[105]

Lord Bandon had already received a rebuff from the fifth duke when
he had first broached the matter of his leases in 1799. In his letter of
September 1801 he was therefore quite candid in linking his desire for a
renewal of his leases with the question of the new arrangements made
necessary by the reduced parliamentary representation at Bandon. Lord
Bandon suggested that he and the duke should have the alternate nomination of the M.P. for the borough, with the proviso that he be permit-

ted the first return in deference to a long-standing pledge to a friend that he should have the seat for Bandon. Despite Knowlton's misgivings, the duke accepted the offer, although with the additional stipulation that the renewal of Lord Bandon's leases should be conditional on his surrendering control of the corporation as well. This condition proved unacceptable. After further inconclusive discussions with Knowlton, which convinced the agent that Lord Bandon's real intention was to obtain his leases and then renege on the agreement for an alternate return, matters were left where they were. Each side honored the alternate parliamentary nomination, but the issue of control of the corporation, and with it the question of Lord Bandon's leases, was left unresolved.[106]

These concerns were too important for the respective parties to permit them to remain in abeyance for long. Four years later Knowlton's success in regaining legal possession of the market tolls at Bandon from the corporation and Lord Bandon's discovery of Hotham's letter of 1787 purporting to contain the promise of a renewal, combined to ensure that the question of the representation at Bandon and the Bernards' leases there was once again at the forefront of the managerial problems on the Irish estate.[107] Lord Bandon's discovery of Hotham's letter in 1805 encouraged him to engage in a protracted and ultimately fruitless correspondence with the fifth duke, in which he endeavored to convince him that Hotham's "promise" constituted the strongest of moral grounds for the renewal of his leases. The duke refused, partly on the grounds of impracticability but largely because he considered that no auditor of his had the right to promise a renewal in this way.[108] Knowlton's success in obtaining possession of the market tolls the following year prompted a more immediate reaction from Lord Bandon. He declared himself absolved from his 1801 agreement with the duke, and refused to nominate the duke's candidate for the 1807 election until some progress had been made over his leases.[109] This stalemate led to a further series of meetings between Knowlton and Lord Bandon which lasted from August 1806 to October 1807, and which were characterized by Lord Bandon's equivocation. At various points in the negotiations he intimated his readiness to sell his half of the borough representation to the duke for £4,000, but then very quickly withdrew and instead offered the duke the alternate nomination in return for a renewal of the tolls and a lease in perpetuity for the lands in his park then out of lease.[110]

At some point in these proceedings Lord Bandon evidently agreed to reinstate the alternate parliamentary nomination. In the by-election of August 1807 occasioned by Viscount Boyle's succession as earl of Shannon, it was the duke's candidate, George Tierney, who was elected.[111] Lord Bandon's reinstatement of this agreement was certainly not as a quid pro quo for obtaining a perpetuity lease for his lands, nor was it as part of an agreement whereby he relinquished control of the borough. In 1811 he wrote to the fifth duke assuring him of his continued fidelity to the spirit of the 1767 agreement, "whatever the result of my application for a lease may be."[112] Two years later Lord Bandon brought the whole question to the attention of the sixth duke. Despite protracted negotiations between Knowlton and Sampson Stawell, Lord Bandon's agent, concerning the possible sale of the latter's interest in the borough to the duke, no agreement was reached. Consequently, the corporation remained in the hands of Lord Bandon, who supported it financially throughout the pre-Reform period, while the parliamentary nomination alternated between him and the duke.[113]

At first sight the duke of Devonshire's political success at Bandon might appear less than clear-cut, but it was in fact a remarkable achievement. In 1801 Knowlton and Garde had concluded that "nothing could be done" about the borough. The duke's power was at such a low ebb that no realistic means were apparently available to prevent the total eclipse of the duke's residual interest by Lord Bandon's encroachments.[114] Six years later the principle of an alternate return had been established and was to last for more than a quarter of a century. Writing to the sixth duke in 1813, Heaton was in no doubt as to the magnitude of this success nor indeed of that at Dungarvan, and of the importance of Knowlton's role in achieving both: "A member for Dungarvan was obtained and an alternate return for Bandon established, both of which would have been completely lost under the old management of Irish agents, under the influence of your relatives in Ireland."[115] Two days later he added, "Mr Knowlton has the merit of securing the election of Mr Tierney for Bandon, which I think nobody but himself could have managed. The bringing back to your family of the borough of Dungarvan is to be entirely attributed to his talent and management. The measure was a child of his own, and cannot I conceive be supported without him."[116]

The reasons for the variation in Knowlton's tactics at Bandon and Dungarvan are readily apparent. At Dungarvan, Knowlton had to create and then placate a property-based electorate that was as numerous as it was impoverished. At Bandon, where the parliamentary franchise was still restricted to the provost and twelve free burgesses, the electoral body was small enough to allow for the effective exertion of economic pressure either on individuals within it or on its patron. Consequently, Knowlton could hope to achieve as much at Bandon by the relatively cheap business of manipulating individuals as he could at Dungarvan by the much more expensive process of creating and then manipulating an entire electorate by capital investment in housing and infrastructural improvement. In strictly political terms, therefore, Knowlton's £10,000 expenditure on urban improvements at Bandon was not absolutely necessary. Presumably, it was justified on the grounds that it enhanced the value of the duke's estate in the town, and would help create goodwill toward him as landlord. In any case, it was entirely consonant with the spirit of improvement that informed the estate's management following Conner's dismissal.

Youghal   The political opposition that the fifth and, after 1811, the sixth duke encountered at Youghal stemmed from the earl of Shannon's long management of the borough. In the arduous and protracted contest that ensued between 1807 and 1822, however, it was Shannon's placemen in the corporation as much as the earl himself who were to be the duke's main protagonists. As at Bandon, the duke was ultimately successful because of the limited nature of the borough's parliamentary franchise, which allowed his auditor to exert effective economic pressure on key individuals in the corporation. Even more than at Bandon, this strategy was entirely separate from the issue of urban improvement. In fact the "improvement expenditure" in Youghal during this period amounted to a politically negligible £662, made up of the occasional sums required to maintain the college, free school, and almshouses.[117] The absence of significant improvement expenditure at Youghal seems to have been a question of lack of opportunity. In contrast to Bandon, where in 1806 Knowlton wrote of "a general falling out of leases" which had given the duke "the command of the entire town," much of the duke's property in Youghal remained tied up in perpetuities and other extensive leases. Twenty-four years later, in 1830, over 70 percent of the recorded leases were either for three lives with a concurrent term of years or were renewable forever.[118]

The Devonshires' renewed interest in regaining control of the borough at Youghal predated by at least nine years the accession of the "politically conscious" sixth duke who is conventionally supposed to have instigated the move. As at Bandon and Dungarvan, the idea emanated from within the senior levels of the estate administration rather than from the duke himself, and seems to have been prompted by the corporation's continuing encroachments on the duke's property rights in and around the town. These included ownership of the foreshore and "bed and soil" of the River Blackwater, which had been granted by patent to the earl of Cork and Burlington.[119] The estate had long recognized that encroachments had been made onto the foreshore both by the corporation and by individuals. Scalé's map of 1776 (see figure 3.6a), for example, depicts the corporation's recently built quays as standing on land claimed by the duke. Twenty years later, in 1796, Henry Bowman took action to restrain the unauthorized reclamation of the tidal marsh to the north of the town, which under the terms of the same patent rightfully belonged to the duke.[120]

Knowlton began to investigate the extent of the corporation's encroachments on the duke's estate in 1802, presumably in the light of the management plan of the previous year, and with a view to taking legal action to regain the land that had already been lost and to prevent further depredations.[121] In the event, little was achieved other than to demonstrate the extent of Garde's duplicity in the affairs at Youghal. For the past thirty years he had acted as the corporation's law agent under Lord Shannon and, Knowlton suspected, had turned a blind eye to their attacks on the duke's property. In response to Knowlton's request that he prepare a case for council's opinion on the encroachments, Garde wrote to Heaton claiming that he had "discovered" that the corporation intended to make great inroads onto the duke's estate, and promised to investigate the matter fully.[122]

There matters rested until 1807, when the hiatus in the management of the Shannon interest following the death of the second earl

prompted George Giles, one of the duke's tenants at Youghal, to suggest to Knowlton the possibility of a coup against the third earl before
he had time to consolidate his authority in the borough. The opportunity arose from the reduction in the number of Shannon adherents
among the corporation freemen by reason of death or disqualification,
a situation the second earl had tolerated in his declining years. The
third earl intended to rectify this problem by calling a court d'oyer
hundred, the corporation body that formally ratified candidates for
freedom, at which the requisite number of freemen-at-large would be
nominated by the mayor, who was a Shannon appointee. Since the
mayor also possessed a right of veto over any proposed meeting of
the court d'oyer, he had a virtual veto over the entire proceedings.[123]
Giles's suggested that since many of the existing freemen were nonresident, they were unlikely to attend the court d'oyer, particularly if there
was no expectation of opposition. In these circumstances, he proposed
to exercise his right as an alderman and nominate an alternative surprise list of freemen in the duke's interest, hoping that insufficient of
Lord Shannon's followers would be there to vote them down.[124]

Giles's proposal was taken sufficiently seriously to warrant consideration by both the duke and Lord George Cavendish. While clearly
recognizing the danger that Giles might be playing his own game, in-
tending to establish his own interest in the borough, and recognizing
too the difficulty of maintaining an interest should the duke succeed,
the decision was taken to proceed. The attempt failed. In a move of
doubtful legality, the mayor refused to call the Devonshire nominees,
and repeatedly postponed a succession of courts d'oyer in August 1808
until a majority of freemen candidates in the Shannon interest could
be mustered. Eventually, these numbered 109, of whom only 10 were
resident. Although the duke contemplated legal action, it is not clear
whether this was actually undertaken. In any case, by September 1808
Knowlton was in no doubt as to the pressure the Ponsonbys in particular would try to exert to prevent further attempts on the duke's part to
recapture the borough. In a letter to Heaton, Knowlton candidly acknowledged that another attempt to capture Youghal might well
damage the Ponsonbys' hopes of future electoral success in County
Cork, as it would undoubtedly destroy their existing pact with the earl
of Shannon in that county. But, Knowlton, argued, the pact was

already a dead letter, the pressure on the earl from his own political allies had seen to that; and in any case surely the Ponsonbys owed enough to the duke, from whose property their own interest derived, to support him at Youghal? Events suggested otherwise. By the end of the same letter, Knowlton was able to report precisely the sort of dissembling approach by the Ponsonbys to Shannon which he had feared, in which they disassociated themselves entirely from the duke's renewed attack on Youghal.[125]

Despite Knowlton's confidential declaration in December 1809 to John Hudson, the Youghal bailiff, that it had been decided to "take measures for the recovering of the duke's lost interest in the borough of Youghal," nothing further of any significance was done until the accession of the sixth duke in 1811 precipitated the series of events that were ultimately to lead to the recapture of the borough.[126] Whether the sixth duke was convinced by Knowlton's lengthy account of the malign political intent of his Irish relatives is not known, but it is clear that the duke very quickly decided to take a more active political role in Ireland than his father had done.[127] Early in 1812 he wrote to the Earl of Shannon claiming the patronage of Youghal. Shannon's reply was unequivocal: "I confess I am at a loss to know where your Grace has found any proof that the representation of the Borough of Youghal had ever been in the possession of that branch of the Boyle family from which you are descended. . . . Your Grace seems to consider the borough of Youghal as property belonging to you. In this opinion I am sorry that I can never agree."[128]

The sixth duke was not deterred. In the General Election of October 1812 William Ponsonby stood at Youghal as the Whig candidate in the Devonshire interest against the earl of Shannon's candidate, Sir John Keane. He was defeated by eighty-nine votes. Although not so crushing a defeat as that suffered by the Hon. George Ponsonby in the same election in County Cork, where he came in a poor third with 1,031 votes after the two Tory candidates, Viscount Bernard with 2,195 and the Hon. Richard Hare with 1,724, William Ponsonby's failure nevertheless still contributed to the eclipse of the Ponsonby leadership of the Whig faction in Cork politics.[129] More importantly, it signaled the absolute necessity for remedial action in Youghal if the duke was ever to succeed in regaining the borough.

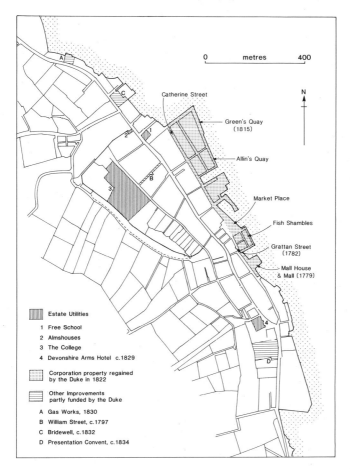

FIGURE 5.4   The Duke's Improvements at Youghal, circa 1841

That this action was forthcoming is witnessed by a letter to the sixth duke, written by the auditor in 1822 at the end of "the Youghal affair." Describing the successful conclusion of negotiations with the mayor and the corporation, the auditor, James Abercrombie, outlined the strategy pursued on the duke's behalf. Following Ponsonby's defeat in 1812, the duke's claim to the land that had been reclaimed from the Blackwater was reasserted, in the expectation that the individuals who had built upon this, many of whom were Shannon's friends in the corporation, "would be so much at the duke's mercy that they would desert from Lord Shannon to him."[130] Many of the buildings in question were held by the corporation for public use, and included the assembly rooms, quays, and market (see figure 5.4). Accordingly, evidence had been sought concerning the circumstances of their construction, any alterations that had been made to the existing boundaries of the duke's property, and whether the corporation had consistently exercised the rights it claimed over the newly reclaimed foreshore.[131]

Abercrombie was extremely critical of the agent—presumably Conner—who had originally allowed these encroachments to take place, but he was critical too of the narrow political view which (the by now dismissed) Knowlton had taken of the problem. He continued:

Political views were those alone which were originally taken of the question, and when I took it up in 1814 no real progress had been made and the case was very imperfectly conducted. You were however committed and nothing remained but to prosecute it with industry and prudence. I have always endeavored to make it quite as much a question of property as of politics. The former is durable and valuable, the latter doubtful and expensive. But in compliance with the opinion of others and with your sentiments, when care is taken not to give too much for influence, I have endeavored in the present management to unite both objects.[132]

Abercrombie's attempt to widen the managerial objectives in dealing with Youghal represented a radical departure from Knowlton's politically motivated strategy, but the political success he ultimately achieved was nevertheless real enough. Eviction orders had been served on the corporation tenants from 1815 onward, and although the corporation had taken defense against these, the duke was ultimately able to prove his title to the land. The corporation appealed to the House of Lords, but this appeal was still pending in 1822 and was preempted by the agreement of that year.[133] A major factor in Abercrombie's success were the generous terms which he as auditor was able to offer, but which Knowlton, as agent, would not by himself have been able to sanction. It seemed to Abercrombie

to be very hard to take without compensation the property of others which had been extended under the eyes of your agents, and who had made no apparent remonstrance on your part. It is also to be remembered that but for a bad law which allows the heir of a person who had never been in Ireland to reclaim his property at a greater distance of time than would have been allowed to him if a resident proprietor you would not have succeeded. Your father was never in Ireland and by his absence you have in this matter been a gainer, but that circumstance would have ensured the odium and injustice of taking the property of these people without compensation.[134]

The details of the agreement were straightforward. The corporation would admit liability in the impending appeal, agree to the immediate introduction of a specified number of freemen-at-large in the duke's interest, and admit his exclusive right to nominate all future corporation officers. In return, the duke would waive his claim for the costs of the current action, and would compensate all those corporation tenants who had lost the title to their property to him with half its current market value. In addition, those tenants who had not adopted an unnecessarily obstructionist attitude would receive a twenty-one-year lease at a sufficiently reduced rent to reimburse them for the remainder of the value. The cost of the immediate compensation alone amounted to over £22,000, but in return for this the duke finally obtained effective control of the borough. On May 16, 1822, his takeover was formalized when he and fifty of his supporters were elected as freemen.[135]

With the freemen electorate packed with the duke's supporters in this way, and with the future control of the politically vital post of mayor also secured by the duke, the earl of Shannon was obliged to surrender his control of the parliamentary borough. Shannon was the only person not to gain something from this agreement, but he had in fact already rejected an earlier offer from Abercrombie of the alternate representation of the borough either for a fixed term of years or for his life.[136] Abercrombie correctly guessed that Shannon's "friends, irritability and want of prudence" would make him reject the offer, and took great care that once he had done so, he was not given an opportunity to reconsider. Whatever the magnitude of the duke's immediate victory, Abercrombie's private opinion was that he would have great difficulty in keeping Youghal, and might at best hope only for a preponderant interest in a borough that was less completely closed than before.[137]

Planning for Prestige, 1811–1832

The continued pursuit of political goals at Dungarvan, and in a modified form at Youghal, after 1811 represented only part of the overall urban management strategy pursued at that time. The accession of the sixth duke brought to the ownership of the estate a man who, although initially ambivalent about his Irish property, quickly came to regard it with great affection, and who in consequence sanctioned considerable expenditure on its general improvement quite apart from the cost of these specifically political objectives. This additional expenditure appears to have been predicated on a benevolent paternalism toward his tenants, together with a desire for the sort of ostentatious display that was later made manifest in his massive extension to his ancestral home at Chatsworth, Derbyshire.[138]

Although he had visited Lismore in 1810 as the marquis of Hartington, to celebrate his coming of age, the sixth duke's first visit as title holder was in 1812.[139] During this visit the duke displayed early evidence of what has been described as his "compulsive mania for building" by sanctioning the reconstruction of the habitable part of Lismore Castle and proposing the foundation of a new village on the periphery of his estate in the Knockmealdown mountains. The castle was completed over the next two years at a total cost to the estate of more than £23,500; the projected village was, perhaps fortunately, never begun.[140] In a letter to the anonymous "G. M." written from Lismore Castle in September 1812, the sixth duke outlined his plans for the new settlement, and amply demonstrated the essentially romantic and unrealistic nature of his vision.

If it were not for the glare and racket that surrounds me I would tell you of an enchanting plan I have formed which is to be put into immediate execution—in a barren spot in the middle of the mountains where my estate begins and forms the boundary of this county, dangerous from robbers, neglected by man and ungrateful to heaven, is to rise a group of forty neat wholesome cottages with sufficient land to each and means of defense from the outlaws who are expected to attack this colony, which will in time protect my property and change the face of the mountain into cultivated happy land—then you must fancy farms parceled out and freeholds and gardens and inhabitants placed there chosen from the best in conduct as well as in valor, and then you must know that this creation is to be distinguished by the name of Spencerstown.[141]

No more is heard of Spencerstown, and on the duke's next visit to Lismore in 1814 his concern was entirely with Abercrombie's plans for the development of the estate, and with his satisfaction with the newly completed castle, which was "perfection itself only they have painted the outside light blue in my absence." In a telling phrase the duke also described his satisfaction with Abercrombie's style of management: "[H]is views of this country and plans for improving are everything I could wish. He makes me feel quite sanguine about it and no longer in the dark which was Knowlton's way to keep me."[142]

Abercrombie's improvements were quickly implemented. Although they included the infrastructural and housing improvements already described at Bandon, they were very much concentrated in and around Lismore, where Abercrombie's primary concern with the enhancement of property value rapidly became apparent. Work was initially concentrated on the further refurbishment of the castle and its grounds, on farm improvement, and on extensive replanting of the ornamental woodlands around the town. Over £19,159 was spent in this way between 1815 and 1820.[143] By the time of the duke's next visit to Ireland in 1822, these improvements had begun to mature and reap distinct social benefits. The entries in the duke's diary recording his visits to Bandon, Lismore, and Youghal bear witness not merely to his satisfaction at the progress of the work, but also to the civic enthusiasm which they had engendered and which his personal appearance mobilized. The entry for August 31, for example, described the duke's arrival at Lismore. "My reception by the yeomanry and tenantry at the borders of the county was . . . touching and a flattering tribute to the good which has been done here. The face of the valley is wonderfully changed, the plantations are extensive and flourishing, the house very comfortable and the luxuriance of the gardens astonishing."[144]

The duke's reception at Bandon was equally enthusiastic, and mirrored his own approval of the recent improvements there. After being drawn into the town for two miles, the duke addressed the townspeople outside the new inn. He described the town as "a new creation" since he was last there ten years previously.[145] Even at Youghal, where the recent political contest might have been expected to leave a legacy of bitterness among the defeated members of the corporation, the tone was warm and conciliatory. The duke was met by the corporation and townspeople en masse, driven round the town, and given the freedom of Youghal in a gold box. In return, the duke assured the townspeople of his particular interest in the fortunes of their town, and resolved to persevere in his efforts to promote them. His diary concluded: "The poor old members of the corporation suffered a little but behaved very well, there was not a word which could wound Lord Shannon. They drank the House of Cavendish. I said with thanks I should be proud to follow the steps of those who had always been the steady and consistent friends of the people and constitution."[146] Superficially, at least, the generosity of the 1822 settlement had been sufficient to defuse any potential resentment.

The success of the duke's visit in 1822 appears to have reinforced his willingness to invest heavily in the improvement of his Irish estates. Between 1821 and 1832 a total of £48,975 was spent on improvement projects of all kinds. Of this an estimated £30,195 was spent on specifically urban improvements at Bandon, Dungarvan, and Youghal, but above all at Lismore, where the town was substantially replanned between 1820 and 1824.[147] During his visit to Lismore in 1822 the duke referred to the "surprisingly altered and improved" appearance of the town,[148] presumably as a result of the extensive rebuilding that had begun in the previous two years, when the Green, the North and South Malls, New Street and West Street were laid out (see figure 5.1).

Remodeling on this scale inevitably involved some social dislocation. The accounts for 1821–1822 refer to the demolition of sundry "poor peoples'" houses on Gallow's Hill and the rehousing of their occupants in purpose-built accommodation in West Street.[149] Further major alterations followed. In 1822–1823, a new road was cut from the bridge to the town, necessitating substantial alterations to the existing castle grounds; sewers were laid along the new roads; the new shambles and meat market were begun; and the existing cabins along Chapel Lane were demolished prior to the road's realignment. In 1823–1824, Chapel Place was constructed to connect Chapel Lane with the South Mall, the boundaries of the Catholic churchyard were laid out, and the new police house was built.

Chapel Place was the last major addition to the street plan in Lismore during the 1820s building campaign. Thereafter, estate-financed construction was directed toward making minor infrastructural improvements and to extending the stock of artisans' housing. The infrastructural improvements were largely complete by 1829, and had consisted of laying footpaths and curbstones, building walls, and making numerous minor additions and repairs to existing institutional property. The new artisans' housing was built in a peripheral location along New Street. Identical new houses were also built at the north end of Chapel Lane, but the estate rentals indicate that these were let at a higher premium, possibly because of their more central location.

This new housing was begun as soon as the streets were laid out, but the work was initially slow and the completion rate varied. Only sixteen of the New Street houses had been completed by 1826, although the remainder of the seventy-five depicted in the Ordnance Survey map of 1841 (see figure 5.1) were finished by 1832. The housing in Chapel Lane was even slower to reach completion. Again only seventeen were finished by 1826, and although this number had doubled by 1832 the remainder of the fifty-five houses depicted in 1841 were not completed until circa 1840.[150] The house building in New Street and Chapel Lane was financed completely by the estate, and the rate of completion therefore presumably reflected the project's priority in the light of the other demands on estate funds at this time. The housing in Chapel Place and on the South Mall, on the other hand, like that along Main Street, was erected by the tenants themselves on building leases, and was completed at a rate that reflected the resources that were available to the individuals concerned. Significantly, virtually all of the housing depicted in these streets in 1841 had been completed by 1827.[151]

The use of building leases during the 1820s was in complete contrast to Bowman's original proposal in the late 1790s, when he envisaged the duke funding the entire program but thereby also gaining the full and immediate benefit of the resulting capital enhancement. By the 1820s the economic situation had changed. The agrarian expansion of the 1790s and after had been dramatically halted by the 1815 agricultural crisis, and the slump that followed showed little sign of ending by the early 1820s. Moreover, during the intervening period there had been little evidence that the Lismore Canal would promote the looked-for growth in the town's trade. Accordingly, there was every reason for the duke to try and spread the cost of reconstructing the town as widely as possible, particularly given the other major items of expenditure at Dungarvan, Youghal, and elsewhere to which he was already committed. The use of such building leases was feasible at Lismore because the

duke was cooperating with an urban clientele who were of a more substantial economic status than those at Dungarvan.

By 1832 this combination of direct estate involvement and tenant
participation had given rise to sociospatial patterns that were much
more irregular than the centripetal pattern of 1773 (see figure 3.4b). In
particular, an attempt had been made to realign the major high-status
axis in the town away from its original east-west orientation along
Main Street, to run north-south along the North and South Malls between the Anglican church and the Catholic chapel. Later tenurial surveys and the contemporary rentals identify this axis as the one with the
highest average rents (over £6.0.0 compared to £2.19.0 in Main Street),
and as sharing the most secure forms of tenure with Main Street. In
both streets properties were held for leases of between sixty-one and
ninety-nine years with two or three lives concurrent. In the remaining
parts of the town tenancies were either annual, or, in the case of the
freeholders, were normally held for a maximum of twenty-one years or
one life.[152]

By contrast, the estate-funded improvements carried out during the
1820s at Bandon, Dungarvan, and Youghal concentrated on rebuilding
market facilities and other public utilities, rather than on erecting further housing. At Bandon, approximately £5,983 was spent between 1820
and 1832 on a variety of projects which included extending the meat
market and building the fish and potato markets in 1823–1824 (£922),
reordering Cavendish Square in 1826–1827 (£860), and building a new
school on the Bridewell Quay in 1831–1832 (£130). The remainder was
spent on further repairs or additions to public buildings erected earlier
at the duke's expense, such as the inn, the market house, and the shambles, and in leveling and paving the streets and in laying sewers.[153] This
concern with marketing reflected the contemporary transformation of
Bandon's functional base. Following the decline of the traditional textile staples, Bandon's economy had come to depend much more on
trades and services than on manufacturing.[154]

During the same period over £3,700 was spent at Dungarvan, mainly
on repairs to freeholders' houses. This expenditure was over and above
the other ad hoc payments the duke was expected to make to aid
the general improvement of the town, such as the £600 he gave toward
the cost of the new Roman Catholic chapel, but was just as political in

character.[155] Indeed, such was the liberality with which these political demands were met, that Colonel Currey began to suspect that it tended "rather to injure than to benefit those on whom it is conferred, in as much as it lessened their exertions in support of themselves."[156] Following the 1822 agreement and the payment of the compensation which this entailed, the expenditure at Youghal during the remainder of the pre-Reform period was less overtly political. Some £7,233 was spent on improvements between 1822 and 1832, of which £2,286 was spent improving the wharfage and warehousing facilities, and £2,390 on building a new inn, the appropriately named "Devonshire Arms Hotel," in 1830.[157]

These relatively limited improvements were very much more characteristic of the expenditure that was to be sanctioned on the urban estate during the remainder of the nineteenth century, than were the major transformative campaigns pursued at Dungarvan and Lismore between 1806 and 1832. The main urban management tasks in the future were to be the refurbishment of the existing housing stock—involving a variable degree of tenant participation—and the provision of an increasingly wide range of urban services and amenities. These were frequently established in cooperation with one or another of the agencies of local government set up by parliamentary legislation as the century progressed. Significantly, none of these later improvements were either to require or indeed be offered the level of capital support that had been available to the estate towns between 1793 and 1832. The question remains, however, of whether, in the light of the managerial objectives identified in 1793 and 1801, this earlier investment was money well spent.

The Costs and Consequences of Improvement

The extensive improvements described in this chapter had financial and political consequences that affected the estate in different and sometimes unforeseen ways. The mounting cost of the urban improvements far outweighed any increase in urban rent income they generated and which could compensate for them (see chapter 3). Accordingly, any assessment of the economic impact of the urban improvements has to consider the effect their cost had on the income-generating capacity of the Irish estate at large prior to 1832. Politically, the hard-won gains at Dungarvan and Youghal were relatively short-lived. Successive elections in the 1820s demonstrated with increasing clarity the real limits of the duke's political influence in Ireland, and created a situation that facilitated his rapid withdrawal from borough-mongering in the years following the Reform Act. Arguably, therefore, the politically led urban investment was even less successful in the long term than the socially and economically motivated transformations attempted by Bowman and Currey.

The Financial Costs

In economic terms, the acid test of the utility of the Irish estate to the duke was its ability to generate remittances. These, however, constituted but one of the twenty categories of recurrent expenditure incurred by the estate in the 1820s.[158] Previous assessments of expenditure on nineteenth-century Irish estates have frequently had to rely on attempts at categorization that are themselves liable to ambiguity. The original accounts do not necessarily lend themselves to modern concepts of productive and nonproductive expenditure, and it can be difficult to desegregate spending in these terms. This issue is discussed elsewhere. Our concern here is with the impact the capital expenditure on improvement had on the Irish estate's ability to generate remittances between circa 1793 and 1832.

Figures 5.5 and 5.6 depict the remittance and improvement expenditure on the Devonshire estate between 1764 and 1830 in monetary terms and as a percentage of received income. Interestingly, the real contrast in improvement expenditure emerges not between Conner's and Bowman's agencies, but between Knowlton's and those of his two immediate predecessors. Save for the £4,700 spent in 1794 on the Lismore Canal and inn, Bowman's actual expenditure on capital improvements did not amount to very much. When it did occur, it was clearly to the detriment of the remittances. This correlative effect is seen more clearly in the much higher levels of improvement expenditure sanctioned during Knowlton's agency and that of his immediate successors. Between 1800 and 1820, and particularly after the sixth duke's accession in 1811, high levels of improvement expenditure inevitably led to low remittances (see figure 5.5).

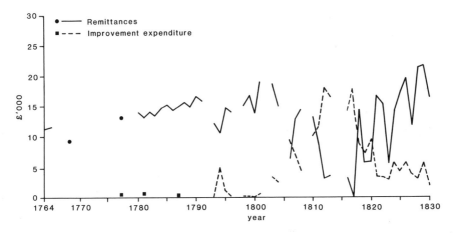

FIGURE 5.5   Remittances and Improvement Expenditure on the Duke of
Devonshire's Irish Estate, 1764–1830

The first major trough in remittances coincided with the first peak
in improvement expenditure (over £3,400) in 1806, while a similar but
more pronounced pattern occurred in 1811–1813, when the remittances
fell to a minimum of £3,000 and improvement expenditure peaked at
£17,926. Major troughs in the remittances recurred in 1816 and 1817,
and again in 1819 and 1820, when they barely averaged £3,000. Indeed,
save for 1818, the period between 1811 and 1820 was one in which the
Irish estate can hardly be said to have been productive of remittances at
all (see figure 5.5). This pattern was inevitable. Both the remittances
and the capital expenditure on improvement were, in effect, competing
for the same free balance that remained once the irreducible costs of
running the estate had been met. The more significant question is
which type of expenditure was given priority and why, and this depended on the attitude of the duke and on the managerial and financial exigencies of the estate at large.

The surviving evidence suggests that the higher levels of capital expenditure on improvement after 1811 were sanctioned much more
readily by the sixth duke than the much smaller earlier sums had been
under his father. Despite the apparent willingness in 1801 to invest
heavily in the recovery of both profit and power, Knowlton was subsequently called upon on more than one occasion to explain why the remittances were correspondingly low. The problem was exacerbated by

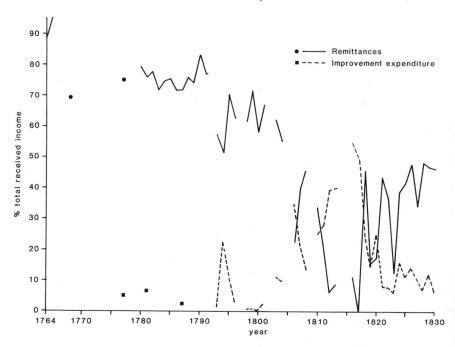

FIGURE 5.6   Remittances and Improvement Expenditure on the Duke of
Devonshire's Irish Estate as a Percentage of Total Received Income, 1764–1830

the irregularity already alluded to in the payments made by the duke's
Irish bankers. Matters came to a head in August 1806, when in an epi-
sode reminiscent of Conner's agency, Knowlton was accused of misappropriating the duke's money and of lax management. His reply
stressed that none of this money ever remained in his hands for a
"moment longer than could be avoided and that none beyond the
customary usage has been allowed to remain in the hands of the tenants." This alluded to the custom whereby tithe payers were allowed a
year's grace before payment was finally demanded. More significantly,
Knowlton also explained that lower than usual remittances had been
made that year because of the extraordinarily large payments he had
been obliged to make for building materials at Dungarvan.[159]

During the fifth duke's lifetime the remittances and improvement expenditure together used up approximately 80 percent of the total
income received in Ireland. Prior to 1794 the remittances accounted for
virtually all of this percentage; between 1806 and 1820 each category ac-

counted for about half (see figure 5.6). Thereafter the general rise in received income combined with the gradual although fluctuating fall in the sums spent on improvement meant that together these two spending heads absorbed a declining proportion of the total Irish income (see figure 5.6). The remittances absorbed a more widely varying proportion of received income, and although they were always less in proportionate terms than they had been prior to 1805, they nevertheless displayed the beginnings of a renewed upward trend after 1806. Annual spending on improvement averaged just over £4,700 in the 1820s, while the remittances averaged £17,260 save in 1822–1823, when the extraordinary payment of over £22,000 in compensation at Youghal reduced them to £5,690.

The growth in annual income undoubtedly widened the options open to the sixth duke in his use of his Irish income, and accommodated him in his desire, recorded at the end of his life, "that although an absentee proprietor, [he] should stand well in the country as a liberal employer of labour."[160] This attitude presumably ensured an acceptance of the inevitably detrimental effect that the large improvement expenditure had had on the remittances after 1811. Certainly, although Abercrombie expressed growing concern over the expenditure at Chatsworth in 1817, and Benjamin Currey expressed similar fears about the general financial situation ten years later, the contemporary correspondence between auditor and agent betrays no concern at the continuing capital expenditure in Ireland prior to 1832.[161] Admittedly, the growing ability of the estate to generate increasingly large remittances while at the same time sustaining the improvement spending must have abetted this lack of concern to some degree. But this spending was always a matter of choice. Accordingly, it is reasonable to conclude that the openhanded and sympathetic interest in the Irish estate that the sixth duke displayed during his early visits to Lismore gave rise to a willingness on his part to accept a reduction in his Irish income as the price to be paid for socially beneficial capital investment in his Irish property.

So far, the improvement expenditure has been discussed in global terms, but of course a significant although variable proportion of this expenditure was spent on agricultural rather than urban projects, primarily the reconstruction of tenants' farmhouses and the replanting of

woodland. Figure 5.7 attempts to identify the specifically urban component in this spending both in monetary terms and as a percentage of
the annual spending on all improvements. Because of their accounting
methods, Bowman's and Currey's figures have to be regarded as estimates rather than precise totals. Although these agents usually costed
the urban materials separately, their accounts returned monthly aggregate labor costs that included work on both urban and agricultural improvements. In the early 1820s these labor costs were running at
between 20 and 30 percent of the total annual improvement cost. They
have been apportioned for this calculation according to the relative size
of the urban and rural materials costs.[162] During Knowlton's agency the
total urban labor and materials costs were specified more exactly.

Figure 5.7 is rendered regrettably incomplete by the absence of accounts for 1802–1803, 1809, and 1814–1815, but the overall picture is
nevertheless reasonably clear. During Bowman's last years and the first
years under Knowlton, urban improvement expenditure was negligible,
other than for the canal project in 1794–1795. Between 1804 and 1813
urban improvement spending reached an annual peak of £11,500 and
an annual average of over £6,300, when it accounted for up to 98 percent of all improvement spending. Both urban figures fell substantially
in 1812 and 1813 as a result of the massive expenditure sanctioned by
the sixth duke on Lismore Castle during these years. By the time the
accounts resume in 1816–1817, urban spending had reached its recorded
peak of over £13,600 (85 percent of the year's total improvement costs)
with the culmination of the Dungarvan works. Thereafter it fell to between £1,600 and £5,600 in the 1820s as the Lismore building programme and the projects at Bandon, Dungarvan, and Youghal were
completed. Nevertheless, these sums still represented the greater part of
total improvement expenditure, and reflected the continuing priority
given to urban renewal on the estate prior to the Reform Act. They
thus emphasize once again the importance placed on the urban property as a key element in regaining and maintaining effective political,
social, and economic control of the estate at large.

The question remains, however, of whether this was money well
spent. Table 5.3 provides an estimate of urban improvement expenditure between 1793 and 1830, together with the average urban rental between 1826 and 1832 and an estimate of the number of years' purchase

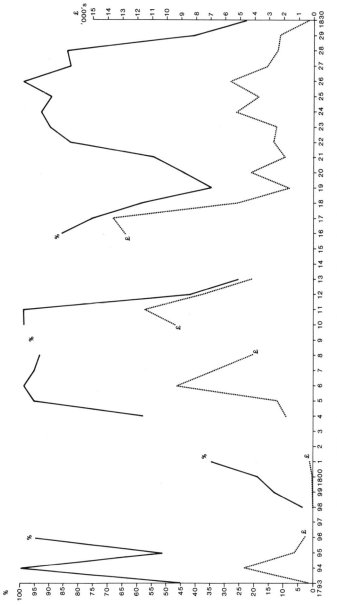

FIGURE 5.7   Estimated Urban Improvement Expenditure on the Duke of Devonshire's Irish Estate, 1793–1830

TABLE 5.3
The Urban Estate, 1793–1830:
Improvement Outlay, Rentals and Years' Purchase

Bandon	Dungarvan	Lismore	Tallow	Youghal	Total
		Improvement Outlay £			
22,407	71,277	29,079	892	28,073	151,728
14.8%	47.0%	19.2%	0.6%	18.4%	100.0%
		Average Rental £			
1,811	564	450	1,277	2,027	6,121
		Number of Years' Purchase			
12.4	126.5	64.6	0.7	13.8	24.8*

* Average

required at these rents to recoup the urban capital outlay. The rentals represent the first period when specifically urban rents can be desegregated from the division totals with any accuracy.[163] The figures for improvement outlay are minima, as are the number of years' purchase, since these are calculated on the basis of the number of annual rentals required to recover the initial investment, and take no account of the capital value of the estate before improvement nor of any shortfall in the rents themselves. The figures also exclude the expenditure on Lismore Castle from 1812 onward but do include the £22,000 spent on political compensation at Youghal in 1822–1823, since this was an integral part of the urban management policy in that town.

The table demonstrates the clear primacy of the Dungarvan expenditure within the overall outlay, together with the seemingly anomalous lack of capital investment at Tallow. This is particularly striking given the fact that Tallow produced a rental that was over twice as large as that at Dungarvan and nearly three times the size of that at Lismore. This lack of investment may have reflected the relative modernity of Tallow's plan and fabric. Certainly, it cannot be explained solely in terms of the survival of an inhibitive leasehold structure in the town, since the leases at Youghal were similarly inimical to ducal intervention and yet that town was the recipient of over thirty times as much investment. Conceivably, Tallow's disenfranchisement in 1801 and its close proximity to Lismore may have acted as more important bars to the free use of the ducal purse. Disenfranchisement meant that there was no political capital to be gained from major transformative investment, while the presence of the ducal seat at neighboring Lismore may in any case have had the effect of concentrating ducal spending there instead.

Table 5.3 also sheds light on the relative importance of economic considerations within the complex array of motivations behind these urban improvements. It has already been argued that after circa 1797 in no town was the motivation purely economic. At Dungarvan it was entirely political, although Knowlton's strategy involved the use of economic incentives to manipulate the electorate. At Bandon and Youghal the initial motivation was political, but subsequent investment in the 1820s was directed toward commercial ends. At Lismore, where Bowman's earlier motives were avowedly profit-oriented, the later work under the sixth duke was much more an exercise in socially benevolent paternalism. Given this varied motivation and the economically nonproductive expenditure it encouraged, there is little cause for surprise at the gross disproportionality that emerged by 1830 between the importance of the towns as sources of income and the capital invested in them. This discordance was particularly acute at Dungarvan and Lismore, where the urban estate would have had to be sold for, respectively, 126 and 64 years' purchase in order to regain the initial outlay alone. At Bandon and Youghal the higher rents and marginally lower levels of investment offered the more realistic prospect of recouping the investment within twelve to fourteen years.

In short, despite the equal emphasis on "profit" and "power" in the management strategies of 1793 and 1801, the subsequent management of the urban estate evolved toward the realization of a series of essentially noneconomic goals. The eventual cost of these precluded any possibility of recouping the capital outlay in those towns where this outlay had been highest. This was due in large measure to the fact that the towns that were the most susceptible to the political and social goals that underlay this noneconomic planning, Dungarvan and Lismore, were also those that generated the lowest rent income. In these two towns, therefore, the success of the improvements has to be judged in noneconomic terms. At Bandon and Youghal, where political success was ultimately achieved by essentially nonfinancial strategies, and where capital investment correspondingly played a supportive rather than a primary role, the extent of this investment was much more in accord with the income-generating potential of the duke's urban estate.

It is difficult to avoid the conclusion that as an exercise in fixed-capital enhancement, the urban improvements on the Devonshire estate were a very mixed success indeed. But this of course was not the way they were viewed, either initially by Heaton, Knowlton, or the fifth duke, nor later by the sixth duke. Of all the people involved in the business, only Abercrombie appears to have been at all doubtful about the wisdom of spending large sums for political gains that by their nature were uncertain. But as Abercrombie himself realized, the duke was already committed to this sort of expenditure. All he could do as auditor was attempt to ensure that some benefit in property also accrued to the estate from this political outlay. Insofar as the later expenditure at Bandon and Youghal in the 1820s does appear to have had a more overtly commercial purpose, he would seem to have succeeded. But if this is so, it is also true that large sums were expended for political reasons in the estate towns. The debatable success of this expenditure has already been alluded to. Why was this so?

The Political Consequences

Table 5.4 lists the election results in the three remaining Burlington boroughs together with those for County Waterford for the period 1801–1831. The relative success of the duke's candidates seems to suggest that the calculation on which the political expenditure had been based was justified. Dungarvan was retained successively by General Walpole, Captain Clifford, and George Lamb from 1807 onward; at Bandon the alternate return worked acceptably—save for the rebellion by the ultra-Protestants in 1831; and George Ponsonby retained Youghal from the General Election of 1826—the first after the 1822 agreement—until 1832. In County Waterford, where politics were intimately bound up with those at Dungarvan, Richard Power was returned in the Devonshire interest between 1806 and 1826.

Seemingly, therefore, the political goals set by Heaton under the fifth duke and subsequently ratified by the sixth duke were achieved—at least in the short term. But as chapter 2 has demonstrated, Irish politics were rapidly changing in ways that increasingly undermined the type of patronal manipulation that had reasserted the duke's political

TABLE 5.4
The Devonshire Interest: Election Results 1801–1831

	Bandon	Dungarvan	Youghal	Co. Waterford
Gen. Election 1801	Broderick Chinnery	Edward Lee	Sir John Keane	John Beresford / Richard Power
Gen. Election 1802	Broderick Chinnery	William Green	Sir John Keane	John Beresford / Edward Lee
By-Election				J. C. Beresford (1806)
Gen. Election 1806	Capt. Courtney Boyle	General H. Walpole*	Viscount Bernard	J. C. Beresford / Richard Power*
Gen. Election 1807	Viscount Boyle	General H. Walpole*	Sir John Keane	Richard Power* / W. C. Beresford
By-Election	Wm. S. Bourne (1815)			Lord G. T. Beresford (1814)
Gen. Election 1818	Capt. A. W. J. Clifford*	General H. Walpole*	Viscount Bernard	Richard Power* / Lord G. T. Beresford
Gen. Election 1820	Viscount Bernard	Capt. A. W. J. Clifford*	John Hyde	Richard Power* / Lord G. T. Beresford
By-Election		George Lamb (1822)*		
Gen. Election 1826	Viscount Duncannon*	George Lamb*	George Ponsonby*	Richard Power* / Henry Villiers Stuart
By-Election	Lord John Russell (1826)			Lord G. T. Beresford (1830)
Gen. Election 1830	Viscount Bernard	George Lamb*	George Ponsonby*	Lord G. T. Beresford / Daniel O'Connell
By-Election	Viscount Bernard (1831)		George Ponsonby (1830)*	Sir Richard Musgrave / Robert Power
Gen. Election 1831	Viscount Bernard	George Lamb*	George Ponsonby*	
By-Election	Capt. A. J. W. Clifford (1831)			

*signify Devonshire candidates. Dates in parentheses indicate year of By-elections.

interest in his boroughs. These changing political realities first im-
pinged directly on the duke's electoral interest in 1826, when his political authority was directly challenged by Daniel O'Connell's Catholic
Association. Arguably, the General Election of 1826 represented a challenge to the Catholic Association to demonstrate the extent of popular
support for Emancipation. If this was so, then it was a challenge that
the Catholic Association was ill-prepared to meet nationally after the
internal dissension that had riven the organization in the wake of the
defeat of the 1825 Relief Bill.[164] Consequently, it was left very much up
to the county branches of the Catholic Association, such as that in Waterford, to organize local electoral revolts.

The object of the Catholic challenge in County Waterford was Lord
Waterford's family—the Beresfords—who epitomized the Protestant
Ascendancy and landed political interest in Ireland. Lord George
Thomas Beresford held one of the two parliamentary seats for the
county which were shared with the duke of Devonshire, and which the
Beresford family had long regarded with a proprietorial air. Paradoxically, the opportunity to challenge the Beresford hegemony, and with it
inevitably that of the duke, came in the person of another, but this
time liberal, Protestant landlord, Henry Villiers Stuart. Villiers Stuart
had settled at the family seat of Dromana in the summer of 1824, and
had quickly established a reputation as a generous improving landlord
with an interest in Catholic affairs. By August 1825 he had accepted the
position of the Catholic Association's candidate for County Waterford
at the forthcoming general election, and had been recognized by the
Beresfords as their prime opponent.[165]

The duke's attitude to the contest was crucial. With some four hundred freehold voters at his command in the county, his support was
necessary to ensure success for Villiers Stuart and had at least to be
neutralized if Lord Beresford was to win. The duke himself favored
Catholic Emancipation. He was also aware of the moral obligation he
was under to continue his "acquiescence" with Lord Beresford, and of
the danger to peace and stability in Ireland if the "rancorous clamour"
of contending sectarian ideologies was allowed full rein.[166] Accordingly,
from at least August 1825, Colonel Currey was instructed to inform the
duke's freehold tenants that they were to vote solely for Richard Power,
the sitting Whig M.P., and to observe "a strict neutrality" between Lord

Beresford and Villiers Stuart.[167] It says much for the residual authority
of the duke that despite Power's unexpected and unauthorized coalition
with Villiers Stuart on the 25th of that month, this injunction was
generally accepted by most of his tenants until O'Connell's personal
intervention ten months later helped "to put an end to the absurd
notion of neutrality."[168] The contest in the meantime had developed
uniquely into one in which the major point at issue was whether holders of the franchise had the right to exercise this freely. The duke's attitude on this subject was proprietorial and entirely normal for a
member of the landed aristocracy: his tenants were expected to vote as
he directed, his "political friends" were left to their own discretion.[169]

The deferral of the election from October 1825 to July 1826 undoubtedly provided the Beresfords with the breathing space they required to
regain some of the ground lost to Villiers Stuart in the initial registry.
Their indiscriminate proselytization of the freehold tenantry on numerous estates at this time is echoed in the Lismore agent's correspondence
by frequent complaints alleging the unauthorized canvassing and bribery of the duke's freeholders by all parties.[170] As the struggle for the freehold votes became more urgent, so too did the criticism of the duke's
neutrality. As early as September 1825 Lord George Hill urged Abercrombie to concede that Power's coalition with Villiers Stuart rendered
the duke's "neutrality" particularly damaging to Lord Beresford.[171] The
appeal went unheeded, and by May 1826 the Beresford camp had
adopted sterner measures, and were reported to be building fifty freeholders' houses in Dungarvan for the express purpose of opposing the
duke in the borough should he not support them in the current county
election (see figure 5.2).[172]

In the event, both the duke and Lord Beresford were outmaneuvered
by the Roman Catholic clergy's participation in Villiers Stuart's campaign. Although the precise nature of the leadership provided by the
clergy in the Catholic Association is debatable, it is clear that the priests
played an important role in the Stuart campaign by utilizing the organi-
zational structure of the Catholic Church and its spiritual authority to
rally support.[173] The local Catholic clergy were made honorary members
of the Catholic Association's barony committees which monitored the
registration of the Catholic vote, and were charged with the responsibility for personally canvassing every freeholder in their parishes.[174]

As the election approached the debate became increasingly sectarian, and the priests' spiritual authority was more frequently used to reinforce the appeals of the lay agitators. The Beresfords alleged that this pressure extended to the bishop declaring it a "mortal sin" to vote against Stuart and the parish priests suspending the celebration of mass if parishioners did not agree to vote for him. These allegations are not proven, but it is nevertheless still clear that the priests' moral authority was of great influence in persuading the Catholic freeholders to vote for Stuart against their landlord's wishes, and therefore possibly against their own immediate economic interests as well. The "sheet anchor" of the Tory campaign, as Thomas Wyse described it, had always been the economic pressure landlords were able to bring to bear on their freeholder tenants in the event of their disaffection. To counter this, the Catholic Association had been obliged to raise additional funds in the form of a new "Catholic Rent" in order to support freeholders made homeless or unemployed because of their support for Stuart.[175]

On the Devonshire estate the pressure exerted by the Catholic clergy and Catholic Association activists like Wyse was successful in persuading the majority of the duke's Catholic freeholders in Dungarvan, Lismore, and elsewhere to give their second votes to Villiers Stuart in direct contravention of their landlord's wishes. Early in June 1826, in the closing weeks of the campaign, Colonel Currey acknowledged the inevitability of the Catholic freeholders voting for both Power and Villiers Stuart and his inability in the face of clerical pressure and O'Connell's rhetoric to prevent them from doing so.[176] Accordingly, when Lord Beresford's election agent, John Keily, complained to Currey about the extent of this clerical canvassing, Currey conceded that since he could not prevent it, neither would he any longer seek to prevent those of the duke's freeholders who wished to register in support of Lord Beresford from doing so.[177]

The duke's "strict neutrality" may have been at an end, but the clerical influence continued. During the actual poll the local Catholic clergy succeeded in preempting Currey's plan to marshall the duke's freeholders to vote in an orderly and controlled fashion by providing alternative means of transport to the hustings in Villiers Stuart's name. Colonel Currey's clerk at Lismore was powerless to prevent this happening, and could only complain about the ingratitude of various tenants whom he had thought loyal to the duke's wishes.[178] The local parish priests were entirely candid about their intentions, and in a series of interviews with Currey acknowledged that their purpose was to ensure their continuing influence over the duke's freeholders until the last possible moment.[179]

Lord Beresford's defeat by Villiers Stuart signaled the very real limitations that now existed to the duke's political influence over his freehold tenantry. The tenants' actions demonstrated that whatever the liberal views of their landlord toward "the Catholic Question" and Ireland generally, and whatever the sums he had expended in capital improvement on the estate as much for their benefit as his own over the previous twenty years, this was insufficient to outweigh the direct appeal of sectarian politics, particularly when these had the sanction of their Church. This was a lesson that was not lost on the duke's advisers. During the run-up to the by-election for County Waterford in March 1830, which had been occasioned by Villiers Stuart's premature resignation, both Colonel Currey and his brother, the auditor, quickly recognized the inevitability of the duke having to concede to his freehold tenants the right to vote as they wished. The duke's initial view was rather different. His overriding concern given the heightened political feeling that accompanied the passage of the Catholic Relief Bill, was to preempt a contest in County Waterford by insisting that his tenants comply with his own avowed neutrality and abstain from voting altogether.[180] By his own calculation, this would have left Lord George Beresford as the only candidate with a realistic chance of success. But as both Abercrombie and Benjamin Currey pointed out, this decision would appear to the Catholic community not only as tacit support for the Beresfords, but also as a political volte-face that would undermine the duke's previously declared support for Emancipation.[181] Moreover, it was a stance that only made sense when there was no prospect of an alternative candidate offering himself for election, whereas in reality it was made apparent to the duke from at least June 1829 that John Barron intended to oppose Beresford in the Catholic interest.[182]

In the event, Benjamin Currey's view prevailed. In a list of instructions to Colonel Currey dated October 7, 1829, the duke's acceptance of the new political reality was made plain. Currey was instructed to inform the tenants that the duke himself remains neuter, leaving the election to the free and unbiased choice of the freeholders, including in the number his own tenants, *but he will not withhold from them the knowledge and expression of his own neutrality.* . . . That as [the Duke] takes no positive part in the election, he does not wish to press his tenants to be neuter against their inclination, but hopes to diminish the evil of the contest by acting as much as possible in conformity to the spirit and object of the law as altered in regard to the elective franchise. . . . The great object of the duke is not to identify himself with either party, and to interfere with the election in no way whatsoever" (emphasis in original).[183]

Colonel Currey was to announce the duke's decision once an acceptable Catholic candidate had come forward. In the auditor's view, the timing of this announcement was absolutely crucial. If the duke conceded to his tenants the right to vote as they wished before a respectable candidate was announced, which was what Barron's initial approach to the duke in June 1829 had been intended to achieve, it would appear that he had given in to the bullying tone of the early election meetings, and in particular to O'Connell's veiled threat that he would be thrown out of Dungarvan. Moreover, the Catholic interest might take advantage of the situation to declare a radical as candidate, whom the duke would then perforce be obliged to support in opposition to his own moderate liberal views. On the other hand, as Colonel Currey pointed out, whenever the announcement was made, the Beresfords were likely to interpret the duke's decision as a hostile act, and were still more than capable of opposing him in Dugarvan in consequence.[184] Benjamin Currey's view was that above everything else, even the retention of Dungarvan, the duke had to be shown to have acted in an honorable manner consistent with his reformist politics, but that it had also to be demonstrated that he was not susceptible to threats either from the ultra-Protestants or from O'Connell and the Catholic clergy.[185] Barron announced his candidacy in January 1830, and two months later was beaten by Lord George Beresford by a margin of 143 votes. Beresford retained his seat at the General Election of August 1830, but a year later the Protestant interest in the county was eclipsed when both seats were won by liberal candidates.[186]

The threat posed to the duke's candidate in Dungarvan by the radicals was potentially very real, but George Lamb did succeed in retaining his seat for the borough in 1830 and again in 1831. In 1830 rumors that Daniel O'Connell was to contest the seat proved unfounded. Al-

though O'Connell supported Lamb's opponent, the radical Dominick
Ronayne, Lamb's record of support for Catholic issues, combined perhaps with the liberal and judiciously timed relief that Colonel Currey
provided to alleviate local distress, ensured his return.[187] Nevertheless,
the political writing was on the wall. By 1830 the duke's authority
within the Catholic-dominated constituencies really existed only on
sufferance. It was not simply a question of the duke's influence being
dependent upon his candidates' continuing support for Catholic
causes, although this was obviously important. Indeed, when any apparent deviation occurred, he and his advisers were quickly criticized.[188]
Rather, as events in the 1826 and 1830 elections had shown, the Devonshire interest was increasingly vulnerable to the appeal of more radical
nationalist sentiments than the duke, as a Whig, was prepared to support. The Devonshire interest had barely survived the issue of Emancipation despite the duke's avowed support for it; it was not to survive
the issue of Repeal, which he opposed.

     In the "Protestant" boroughs of Bandon and Youghal the shared or
newly regained Devonshire interest was also under renewed threat by
the early 1830s, but for different although related reasons. Whereas the
duke's influence in Dungarvan and County Waterford was vulnerable
because he was thought to be insufficiently wholehearted in his support of Catholic rights, the opposition at Bandon and Youghal arose
precisely because the duke was seen to be too supportive of these issues
and of reform generally. Matters came to a head in the immediate
post-Reform period, but in the closing years of the unreformed corporations the signs of ultra-Protestant restiveness were already apparent.
At Youghal, Colonel Currey only succeeded in implementing the
duke's wish to introduce Catholic freemen-at-trade into the corporation against sustained Protestant opposition led by the Greenes.
Currey's surviving notes on the matter make it clear that although he
paid scrupulous attention to the economic bona fides of the potential
Catholic candidates, his real concern was the fundamental political
calculation of how many freemen would vote for the sitting Whig M.P.
for the town, George Ponsonby.[189]

     At Bandon the Protestant revolt in 1831 took an altogether more seri-
ous turn. In May of that year, at the height of the parliamentary
reform crisis, the burgesses refused to vote for the duke's candidate,

Captain A. W. Clifford, on the grounds that since he was an advocate of reform, to do so would be contrary to the oaths they had taken to maintain the "franchises, rights, customs and privaleges [*sic*] of the corporation." Instead, the burgesses proposed and elected Lord Bandon's son, Lord Bernard.[190] The revolt appears to have been a genuine grass-roots affair, and although Colonel Currey subsequently expressed disquiet over the unexpected delay in Viscount Bernard applying for the Chiltern Hundreds, the matter was finally resolved in June when, "after some management" by Lord Bandon's agent, John Swete, Captain Clifford was finally elected to the by-now vacant seat.[191] But once started, the revolt continued, and two years later, finding himself once again unable to fulfill his electoral obligations to the duke, Lord Bandon terminated his financial support for the corporation and resigned his influence within it.[192]

For the duke of Devonshire the revolt at Bandon signaled once again the growing limitations to his political authority as an absentee patron and as such mirrored the changing political climate of the times. The older paternalist structures of the Ascendancy period were fast breaking down in the face of the assertion of an aggressively sectarian radicalism that was increasingly and stridently nationalist in tone. This, in turn, generated an equally sectarian defensive response on the part of Protestants, who in the south of Ireland at least were ever conscious of their growing demographic and cultural marginality. Increasingly, the traditional sources of authority were being challenged and replaced by others thought to be more closely aligned with the political aspirations of each community. It was the sixth duke of Devonshire's particular misfortune that he had presided over massive capital expenditure on his Irish estate for partly political reasons, at precisely the moment when the political structures that could justify this expenditure were in the process of dissolution.

Summary

The partial reconstruction and general refurbishment of the duke of Devonshire's Irish estate towns between 1792 and 1832 constituted one of the high points of interventionist management on the estate. Thereafter, particularly following the financial crisis of 1845 and with the striking exception of the seventh duke's investment in Irish railways in the 1860s and 1870s, the managerial ethos was one of containment and contraction rather than innovation. Consequently, the early decades of the nineteenth century stand out as a period when the Irish estate was perceived by the London-based administration as offering positive opportunities that could be exploited for the duke's benefit, rather than as a problem that offered nothing but negative prospects for the patrimony at large. Nevertheless, it is debatable whether the opportunities as they were perceived in 1793 and 1801 had been properly exploited by 1832, at least as far as the urban estate was concerned. It has been shown, for example, that the levels of urban investment far outweighed any possible economic return they were likely to generate. Even at Lismore, where Bowman produced a coherent economic plan for the town and its region rather than simply the series of ad hoc infrastructural improvements that characterized the later work at Bandon and Youghal, this was not enough to generate the looked-for economic growth. Paradoxically, it was only at Bandon and Youghal, where the improvements were relatively less extensive (and less expensive) than those at Lismore and where the rent base was much higher, that there was any realistic prospect of a return on the investment.

Even where the urban investment can be shown to have had a primarily political purpose, and where straightforward economic considerations were correspondingly less important (although not entirely neglected), the spending can be argued to have had limited long-term success. The reasons for this, however, were exogenous to the estate and reflected the accelerating pace of change in Irish political life, something that could not possibly have been foreseen from the perspective of 1793. The duke's political expenditure in the three remaining post-Union boroughs amounted to over £115,000, but only succeeded in securing the representation of Dungarvan and Youghal, and alternately, at Bandon, for the relatively limited period of time remaining before the Reform Act of 1832. Moreover, it was political power that was being increasingly and acrimoniously challenged from a variety of quarters long before the 1832 act was passed. In short, it can be argued that if not in 1793, then certainly by 1814 when Abercrombie took his decision to continue with the program of political investment, it was already fast becoming too late to achieve the desired political goals in this fashion, as the transformation of Irish politics eclipsed the opportunities for the exercise of such traditional urban patronal authority.

In the long term, therefore, the major legacy of the duke of Devonshire's capital investment in his Irish estate towns prior to 1832 was the creation of an improved urban environment within which subsequent tenurial relations between the duke and his tenantry were played out. This relationship was itself far from static, and mirrored not simply the major demographic, economic, social, and political trends in nineteenth-century Ireland, but also the changing fortunes of the Devonshire estates in England as well. Chief among these were the successive financial crises that dogged the sixth and seventh dukes between 1845 and the late 1880s, and which invariably gave rise to a call to liquidate the Irish property in support of the English estate. By 1832, therefore, the stage had been set for a continuing social discourse between the duke and his urban tenants, which was to explore and reflect the changing and indeed narrowing parameters within which residual patronal authority could be exercised in nineteenth-century Ireland.

CHAPTER 6

Changing Attitudes

Estate Management and the Estate Towns, 1832–1891

The passage of the Irish Reform Act in 1832 signaled both the beginning of the duke of Devonshire's withdrawal from active interference in the politics of his Irish estate towns, and the end of his leading involvement in their physical transformation. Thereafter the relationship between the duke and his urban tenants was characterized by evenhanded but ultimately limited financial patronage under the sixth duke and by increasing economy under the seventh duke. The 1830s therefore constituted a major turning point in the relationship between the duke of Devonshire and his Irish urban tenantry. Although the sixth duke subsequently occasionally sanctioned a large capital outlay on his Irish estates, particularly during times of distress such as the Famine, this expenditure was generally directed toward agricultural improvement, where it was used for reproductive purposes such as improving drainage or farm buildings.[1] Very little was spent on the towns, where in place of the lavish improvement expenditure of earlier decades, spending was limited to minor repairs to housing or occasional investments in public buildings such as schools or markets. There were two reasons for this reduced urban spending: the active pursuit of politics no longer provided a raison d'être for improvement, while earlier commercially led developments such as that at Lismore had failed to prove profitable. Under the seventh duke even this limited urban expenditure was curtailed, while conspicuous nonproductive expenditure such as that on Lismore Castle was abruptly stopped.

In fact, the accession of the seventh duke in 1858 instigated a process of patronal disengagement that ultimately led to the eclipse of the

Devonshires' importance as Irish landlords. Successive stages in this process were marked in the towns by the sale of the duke's property at Youghal and Dungarvan in 1859–1861 and at Bandon in 1894.[2] These sales were not prompted solely or even mainly by events in Ireland or on the Irish estate, but by the worsening finances of the Devonshire patrimony within the British Isles at large. They thus bear witness to the growing subordination of the Irish estate throughout the nineteenth century to the interests of the duke's English property. As time progressed, the Irish property increasingly came to be regarded as a potential source of capital, to be liquidated if necessary in order to shore up the Devonshires' proprietorial status in England. In the event, the decision to sell in Ireland was delayed for considerably longer than at one time seemed likely. Even so, the fact that such sales were under consideration from at least the 1840s reflected the early—and growing—vulnerability of the Irish estate.[3]

These themes of minimalist investment, patronal disengagement, and the subordination of the Irish periphery to the English core provide the leitmotif for any exploration of the urban management policies pursued in Ireland in the duke's name after 1832. Accordingly, they form the nucleus of this chapter. The first section establishes the local contexts for the post-Reform urban management policies by exploring the changing size and functional base of the duke's towns from the 1830s onward. This section is followed by an analysis of the overall pattern of expenditure on the Irish estate after circa 1832 which relates this pattern to the successive—and worsening—financial crises that came to dominate the running of the Devonshire estates at large. The declining urban expenditure within this overall pattern and the parallel process of political disengagement are both accounted for in terms of "crisis management." This was reactive in character and required either the minimization or extinction of the duke's existing patronal commitments in Ireland.

As in the pre-Reform period, the context for these later changes in the management of the Devonshire estates continued to be provided by the broader secular trends in the economy and society at large. These included the demographic adjustments during and after the Famine together with the consequent agrarian restructuring, and the growing politicization of the land question, as farmers in particular sought to defend the gains they had made in the aftermath of the Famine.[4] In the towns, the duke's patronal role was increasingly affected by the accelerating pace of municipal reform and the growing number of administrative institutions that this reform spawned. In theory, these provided rival sources of urban patronage and authority. In practice, the duke was careful wherever possible to cooperate with these bodies, and indeed was increasingly anxious to shed some of the financial burden of urban patronage on to them. The relationship between the duke and groups such as the Gas Commissioners or the Town Commissioners was therefore not generally competitive or rancorous, but rather was characterized by the duke's willingness to accommodate municipal decision making as long as this did not impinge upon his remaining property rights. The commissioners, on the other hand, persisted in regarding the duke as a potential benefactor long after he had made it clear that he wished to minimize his role in this regard.

The Size and Functions of the Urban Estate, 1831–1891

Population

Table 6.1 lists the total population, estimated Devonshire tenant population, and the overall average houseful occupancy rates for each of the estate towns for an intercensal sample between 1831 and 1891.[5] The pre-Famine trends recorded by each town were broadly similar save at Bandon, where in contrast to the growth elsewhere the population was already falling by 1831. After the Famine the population of all five towns fell, albeit at different rates. By 1891 Lismore and Tallow may both have lost 47–48 percent of their immediate pre-Famine population. The incomplete nature of the post-1870 figures for Bandon make it impossible to calculate an equivalent figure, but certainly at Dungarvan the population as a whole fell by nearly one-third between 1841 and 1861. The average occupancy rates mirror these trends. In all the towns save Youghal they increased prior to 1841, and in all save Tallow they fell progressively thereafter.

Between 1831 and 1841 Bandon and Dungarvan both recorded an increase in the estimated number of the duke's tenants. In the three remaining towns the best estimate suggests that the number of the duke's tenants fell. Between 1841 and 1845 all five towns recorded a decline, and

TABLE 6.1
The Estate Towns: Population Estimates and Occupancy Rates, 1831–1891

	Bandon	Dungarvan	Lismore	Tallow	Youghal
1831					
Total pop.	9,917	6,527	2,894	2,998	9,608
Tenant pop.	1,569	2,972	2,670	2,376	1,550
Occupancy	7.3	5.6	8.1	6.6	7.9
1841					
Total pop.	9,049	8,625	3,007	2,969	9.939
Tenant pop.	2,262	3,548	2,534	2,123	1,336
Occupancy	8.8	7.3	8.8	7.1	7.3
1845					
Total pop.	n.d	n.d.	n.d.	n.d.	n.d.
Tenant pop.	1,596	3,402	1,871	2,032	1,112
Occupancy	7.7	7.0	8.1	8.0	6.9
1851					
Total pop.	6,909	6,865	2,319	1,986	7,372
Tenant pop.	1,481	3,337	1,792	2,047	1,208
Occupancy	6.7	6.7	7.5	8.9	6.6
1855					
Total pop.	n.d.	n.d.	n.d.	n.d.	n.d.
Tenant pop.	1,796	3,181	1,652	1,534	871(?)
Occupancy	6.7	6.4	7.1	7.7	6.5
1861					
Total pop.	6,243	5,886	2,085	1,629	6,514
Tenant pop.	1,521	sold	1,394	1,274	sold
Occupancy	6.7	6.1	6.8	6.6	6.4
1865					
Total pop.	n.d.		n.d.	n.d.	
Tenant pop.	6.4		1,599	1,419	
Occupancy	1,591		6.6	5.7	
1870					
Total pop.	n.d.		n.d.	n.d.	
Tenant pop.	1,815		1,631	1,248	
Occupancy	6.6		6.4	4.8	
1871					
Total pop.*	6,131		1,946	1,332	
1875					
Total pop.			n.d.	n.d.	
Tenant pop.			1,500	1,207	
Occupancy			5.9	4.7	

	Bandon	Dungarvan	Lismore	Tallow	Youghal
1880					
Total pop.			n.d.	n.d.	
Tenant pop.			1,461	1,260	
Occupancy			5.6	4.7	
1881					
Total pop.*	3,997		1,860	1,232	
1885					
Total pop.			n.d.	n.d.	
Tenant pop.			1,396	1,177	
Occupancy			5.3	4.4	
1890					
Total pop.			n.d.	n.d.	
Tenant pop.			1,315	1,112	
Occupancy			5.1	4.1	
1891					
Total pop.	3,488		1,632	1,088	

Pop: Population. Occupancy: number of persons per domestic house.
* Township populations.
n.d = no data.
Sources: 1841–1891 Census, N.L.I. L.P. Estate Rentals.

this decline continued at Bandon, Dungarvan, Lismore, and Tallow (marginally) up to 1851. Youghal recorded an increase in the duke's tenants by this time, but this figure is rendered uncertain by the considerable variation in the number of domestic houses recorded in successive rentals. With the exception of Bandon, where the admittedly incomplete record suggests some growth in the tenant population between 1851–1855 and again after 1865, the duke's urban estate experienced a generally progressive decline in tenant numbers in the post-Famine period. At Lismore and Tallow, this decline was sustained throughout save for the years 1861–1865 (at Tallow) and 1861–1871 (at Lismore). At Dungarvan and Youghal the decline was consistent prior to the sale of the urban estate in 1859–1860. The higher township populations recorded for Lismore and Tallow in the censuses of 1871, 1881, and 1891 reflected the enlarged enumeration unit these censuses used, and as Mason has shown, overestimated the true urban population.[6] Given the monopolistic nature of the duke's ownership of these towns, the estimated tenant populations provide a better guide to their size.

In general, these trends accord with the conventional view of post-Famine Irish urban demography. Mason, for example, concludes that smaller towns lost a disproportionately greater share of their population than larger centers, as the latter retained or improved their functional base, a view reiterated by Forster.[7] Clarkson has emphasized the same point in relation to Ulster. Most of the towns in the province that experienced absolute growth between 1841 and 1911 were located in the eastern counties, where a more diversified economy created an urban sector that benefited from high levels of industrial employment, early integration within an effective transport network, and generally higher levels of affluence.[8] Cullen stresses the regional character of urban population loss immediately after the Famine. Prior to 1861 it was concentrated in Munster and Connacht, largely because of the loss of the impoverished families who had crowded into the peripheral cabins of the poorer towns in the pre-Famine period, and who had been engaged in agriculture. In Munster the urban population fell by over 11 percent from 386,941 in 1841 to 343,263 in 1851, and by a further 7 percent to 319,748 in 1861. Thereafter provincial urban population loss was more widespread and was driven by economic rather than demographic factors. If we exclude the exceptional case of Belfast, provincial urban growth in the 1870s and 1880s was "virtually negative," and was the result of the demise of much small-scale urban industry in the face of increasing competition from larger English and Irish firms.[9]

Urban Functions, Family Occupations, and Rent Formation

Table 6.2 lists the correlation coefficients derived for the relationship between the total tenant population and the rent demand in the estate towns, calculated for the sample years used in table 6.1. This relationship varied significantly between different parts of the urban estate, but in no case was the growth in rent demand a straightforward function of an increase in the size of the urban tenant community. At Lismore and Tallow the strong inverse relationship implies that the loss of population may actually have aided the rent-forming ability of the remaining tenants. At Youghal no correlation whatsoever existed between rent demand and the number of Devonshire tenants. At Bandon and Dungarvan an inverse relationship existed, but was so weak as to suggest that other factors were more important in determining rent demand.

One possible explanation for these different relationships lies in the

TABLE 6.2
The Estate Towns: Population Size and Rent Demand

	Bandon	Dungarvan	Lismore	Tallow	Youghal
Coefficient	−0.49	−0.37	−0.89	−0.69	+0.03
Signif.	no	no	99%	95%	no
Sample	8	6	12	12	6

composition of the nineteenth-century rent roll in each town. At Bandon and Youghal, where the duke's property was concentrated in the center of the town, his rent roll retained a relatively large manufacturing and trading element. For example, of the 440 professional, trading, and manufacturing entries listed for Bandon in *Slater's Commercial Directory* of 1846, over 80 percent were located on the duke's property.[10] Accordingly, in these towns the demand for the duke's property in the mid-nineteenth century continued to be as much commercially as residentially derived. Hence variations in the size of the total tenant population on the urban estate would not necessarily have outweighed competitive commercial pressures in determining the rentable value of property. At Dungarvan much the same argument applied, at least to the duke's property in the town center. The effect of the 383 freeholders' houses in Blackpool, Boreheenatra, and Abbeyside on the relationship between rent demand and the size of the tenant community is likely to have been disproportionately small because of the low fixed rents they paid, varying between 13/4d and £1.10s per year. Moreover, as table 6.3 indicates, although these three towns shared in the general decline in occupation levels that characterized many provincial towns in post-Famine Ireland, they nevertheless succeeded in retaining a relatively extensive and complex occupation base.[11] While the sectoral composition of this employment was not significantly different from that in Lismore and Tallow, other than in the existence of shipping trades at Dungarvan and Youghal, each of the sectors in the three largest towns contained approximately twice the number of trades and professions as those in Lismore and Tallow.

Arguably, the competition for commercial property in Bandon, Dungarvan, and Youghal may have been further enhanced by the arrival of the railway in these towns between 1851 and 1870.[12] Conventional wisdom suggests that the growth of Ireland's railways helped

TABLE 6.3
The Estate Towns: Nonagricultural Employment by Sector, 1824–1870

Economic Sector		Bandon				Dungarvan			Lismore				Tallow				Youghal		
		1824	1846	1856	1870	1824	1846	1856	1824	1846	1856	1870	1824	1846	1856	1870	1824	1846	1856
Gentry	%	21.7	13.4	16.9	14.7	20.4	10.7	08.5	45.3	20.3	19.6	18.6	36.5	11.6	10.8	09.6	21.3	16.1	13.2
	N	54	68	76	63	32	39	35	29	29	29	21	31	19	18	15	49	95	69
Professional	%	08.0	09.1	08.1	10.5	08.3	06.3	06.3	04.7	11.9	08.8	10.6	14.1	06.2	05.4	03.2	11.3	12.0	10.9
	N	20	46	39	45	13	23	26	03	17	13	12	12	10	09	05	26	71	95
Craft Industry*	%	36.5	37.2	27.1	29.5	39.5	37.8	30.5	06.2	27.2	25.0	23.8	16.5	47.2	54.2	40.3	32.6	34.8	32.3
	N	91	188	122	126	62	115	125	04	39	37	25	14	77	90	63	85	206	165
Food & Drink	%	30.1	32.0	36.4	36.1	21.7	29.0	35.6	40.6	32.9	35.1	38.9	25.9	27.0	21.1	41.7	28.3	23.3	29.8
	N	75	162	164	154	34	106	146	26	47	52	44	22	44	35	65	65	138	151
Transport	%	-	-	-	-	05.1	04.9	06.3	-	-	-	-	-	-	-	-	01.3	05.6	05.3
	N	-	-	-	-	08	18	26	-	-	-	-	-	-	-	-	03	33	27
Building	%	01.2	02.0	04.4	02.3	02.5	08.8	01.0	01.6	01.4	02.0	02.6	01.2	-	-	01.9	01.3	01.9	02.6
	N	03	10	20	10	04	03	02	01	02	03	03	01	-	-	03	03	11	13
Other	%	02.4	06.3	06.4	06.8	02.5	10.4	12.0	01.6	06.3	09.5	05.3	07.1	08.0	08.4	03.2	03.9	06.2	05.1
	N	06	32	29	29	04	38	49	01	09	14	06	06	13	14	05	09	37	26
Total sep. entries		249	506	450	427	157	365	410	64	143	148	113	85	163	166	156	230	591	506
Total sep. trades/professions		30	82	72	67	32	68	74	14	37	42	31	17	36	39	28	50	89	82

*Textiles, wood, metal, leather, earthenware, glue and wax. N: Number
Source: Slater, Commercial Directory of Ireland 1846–70 & Pigot, Hibernian Provincial Directory 1824.

TABLE 6.4
The Estate Towns: Family Employment by Sector, 1831–1851

	Bandon		Dungarvan		Lismore		Tallow		Youghal	
	N	%	N	%	N	%	N	%	N	%
1831										
Agriculture	191	14.12	82	5.21	66	11.83	11	1.83	58	3.09
Manufactures/Trade/Craft	818	60.50	645	41.00	193	34.59	298	49.58	815	43.54
Other	343	25.37	846	53.78	299	53.58	292	48.58	999	53.56
TOTAL	1352		1573		558		601		1872	
1841										
Agriculture	308	25.35	413	22.47	220	40.89	147	25.88	516	24.36
Manufactures/Trade/Craft	647	53.25	1010	54.94	202	37.54	299	52.64	1010	47.69
Other	260	21.40	415	22.58	116	21.56	122	21.48	592	27.95
TOTAL	1215		1838		538		568		2118	
1851										
Agriculture	207	21.10	24	1.75	149	32.67	69	15.78	338	19.81
Manufactures/Trade/Craft	496	50.56	895	65.32	162	35.53	252	57.66	717	44.37
Other	278	28.30	451	32.92	145	31.80	116	26.54	651	38.16
TOTAL	987		1370		456		437		1706	

Source: 1831, 1841 and 1851 Census
N: Number of families   %: Percentage

TABLE 6.5
The Estate Towns: Family Occupancy Rates, 1821–1851

	Bandon	Dungarvan	Lismore	Tallow	Youghal
1821	1.54	1.31	1.35	1.17	1.92
1831	1.43	1.35	1.55	1.33	1.55
1841	1.62	1.56	1.58	1.36	1.65
1851	1.56	1.42	1.48	1.46	1.58

Sources: 1821, 1831, 1841, and 1851 Census.

reorder the country's provincial urban network, as well-located towns began to prosper at the expense of their more peripheral neighbors in what was an increasingly well-integrated national economy.[13] Thus the economic performance of individual towns may have been increasingly determined by their relative location within the adjusting national space-economy, as well as by their ability to provide specialist or redistributive services. Table 6.3 suggests that despite the growing competition from Cork and Waterford, the duke's largest towns—Bandon, Dungarvan, and Youghal—all survived this reordering process. It is therefore reasonable to conclude that long after the Famine the level of competition for commercial property in these towns continued to obscure any direct relationship between the number of the duke's urban tenants and the size of his urban rent demand.

At Lismore and Tallow, where the duke owned the entire town, the commercial component in the mid-nineteenth-century rent roll was relatively small and the residential element correspondingly large. Consequently, the rent roll is likely to have been much more sensitive to variations in the size of the tenant community than in the other towns. Moreover, as table 6.2 shows, this was an inverse relationship: as the tenant population fell, so the rent demand rose. Tables 6.4 and 6.5 suggest why. Table 6.4 lists family employment by sector in the estate towns between 1831 and 1851, and provides evidence to support Cullen's suggestion that much of the pre-Famine urban population growth was agriculturally based. All the estate towns recorded both an absolute and a relative increase in the number of farming families between 1831 and 1841. This increase was most pronounced in Tallow, but gave rise to the highest proportion of "farming" tenants at Lismore, where over 40 percent of the total population was supported by agriculture in 1841.

Ten years later this form of employment had declined significantly in all five towns. Table 6.5 lists the average family occupancy rates for the estate towns between 1821 and 1851, and demonstrates that the high average occupancy rates recorded in table 6.1 were not necessarily synonymous with large family units. They were also a function of that other index of poverty, multiple occupancy. All the estate towns record an increase in family occupancy rates prior to 1841 and a decline thereafter.

This evidence suggests that in the pre-Famine period the duke's urban estate received precisely the sort of marginalized and impoverished excess population identified by Donnelly and Connell in Munster and Navan, and which Cullen considers to have been characteristic of provincial town life in Ireland at this time.[14] Their impact on the duke's urban estate depended on the character of each town and on the size of its occupational base. The commercial character of the duke's estate at Bandon, Dungarvan, and Youghal limited the negative financial impact of this pauper community in these places. At Lismore and Tallow, however, these pauperized immigrants were relatively numerous. Their arrival would have done little to improve the rentable value of the residential property in these towns, or the likely prospects of successful rent collection there. They may, in effect, have acted as a drag on the successful financial management of this part of the urban estate, creating a negative impact that would have been disproportionately greater there than in the larger and functionally more diverse towns.

By the same token, however, the removal of this excess population through mortality or migration would have had a relatively great beneficial impact on the management of Lismore and Tallow. Once again, some consonance would be established between the size of the tenant population in these towns and the functional base available to support them. While this is not to suggest that these towns' economic future was thereby automatically assured—their marketing and trading base remained too small and reliant on processing agricultural raw materials for that—there is some evidence to suggest that they succeeded in at least weathering subsequent economic crises. Table 6.6, for example, indicates that even during the height of the agrarian crisis of the early 1860s and 1880s the majority of the tenants at Lismore and Tallow were

TABLE 6.6
The Estate Towns: Average Arrears Per Tenancy

	Bandon	Dungarvan	Lismore	Youghal	Tallow
1841	n.d.	2.32	n.d.	n.d.	4.87
1845	2.79	2.44	2.97	2.53	3.75
1851	n.d.	0.38	2.18	3.54	2.71
1855	1.93	0.60	3.04	4.83	n.d.
1861	n.d.	sold	1.53	2.35	sold
1865	1.80		1.67	2.53	
1870	1.40		1.22	2.22	
1875	n.d.		1.16	1.59	
1880	n.d.		1.71	2.13	
1885	n.d.		1.43	2.62	
1890	n.d.		1.97	3.67	

All figures in £.
n.d. = no data.
Source: N.L.I. L.P. Estate Rentals.

placed under less financial strain than during the Famine years. In short, if these arrears are taken as a measure of the tenants' inability to meet their basic financial obligations, then it is clear that in the short term the crisis induced by the Famine had a more immediate and serious effect on the urban economy at Lismore and Tallow than anything that came later. Indeed, the general fall in average arrears over most of the urban estate during the middle years of the century suggests that for most of the duke's urban tenantry, this was a period of increasing personal prosperity, when they were better able to maintain their economic stake in the community.

Estate Expenditure and Urban Management

Estate Expenditure

The secular trends in the overall estate and urban income were discussed in chapter 3. The remittances received by the duke out of this income constituted only one among a series of payments that this revenue had to support. As before during Knowlton's agency, these remittances remained sensitive to the fluctuations in the other spending heads. Table 6.7 attempts to distinguish between productive and nonproductive expenditure on the estate at this time by consolidating the original expenditure categories under the following heads: remittances, capital improvements, estate enterprises, extraordinary expenditure, management, and patronage. The remittances are self-explanatory. As with all outgoings, they were accounted in retrospect as part of a balance drawn with the previous year's income, and were normally sent by banker's draft via Cork to the auditor in London. The expenditure on capital improvements included drainage and new buildings on farms, urban rebuilding, and roads. This has been distinguished from the management and estate enterprise costs on the grounds that, unlike these, it might in the long term be expected to enhance income through the improvement of capital stock.

By contrast, the management expenses involved a wide variety of nonproductive payments, including chief rents, tithe rent charges, taxes, insurance, law charges, political costs, salaries and pensions, as well as the day-to-day running costs of Lismore Castle and its gardens. The estate-enterprise expenses comprised the net cost of running the demesne farm and woodlands, together with any farms that happened to be in hand. Arguably, the expenditure on patronage could be included with the other management costs, but it is instructive to identify this item separately, since it provides a useful index of ducal liberality. The sums involved were paid as donations or subscriptions to a wide variety of churches and chapels of all dominations, as well as to nonsectarian charities and in the form of salaries to the staff of the national and endowed schools on the estate. Extraordinary expenditure displayed the greatest variation, and included most notably the £48,000 spent by the sixth duke between 1851 and 1858 on his visits to Lismore and rebuilding the castle there. As Ó Gráda observes, this can only be regarded as a form of conspicuous consumption, and cannot readily be aligned with any other form of expenditure on the estate.[15]

The remittances and aggregate expenditure costs recorded linear trends that were broadly similar (see figure 6.1). Both were positive, and were characterized by relatively low growth rates of 0.37 and 0.46 percent per annum. Analysis of the fluctuations around these trends, together with a comparison of the average expenditure sanctioned by each duke, indicates that variations occurred in the pattern of expenditure and remittances that coincided with the known changes in each duke's attitude to the Irish estate (see table 6.7). Nowhere was this in-

TABLE 6.7

Average Expenditure in Ireland by the Sixth and Seventh Dukes of Devonshire, 1816–1891

| | Sixth duke | | | | | | Seventh duke | | | |
| | 1816–1858 | | 1816–1891 | | | | 1858–1891 | | | |
	Mean	Std*	% income	Mean	Std*	% income		Mean	Std*	% income
Remittances	£16434	£6143	36.0	£18130	£5946	37.7		£20340	£4862	39.9
Capital improvements	4907	2719	11.7	5219	2274	11.4		5626	1408	10.9
Estate enterprises	1179	464	2.7	1024	403	2.2		822	146	1.6
Extraordinary expenditure	4151	3021	8.5	2832	2952	5.8		689	790	1.4
Management	13290	4659	30.5	14517	4422	31.2		16115	3498	32.0
Patronage	1844	484	4.2	2014	601	4.4		2390	618	4.7

Std* = Standard deviation

dicated more clearly than by the remittances. Overall, these averaged more than £18,000 or just under 38 percent of received income, but under the seventh duke they rose to an average of £20,340 (39.9 percent) from the £16,434 (36 percent) received on average each year by his predecessor.[16] The standard deviations indicate considerably less variation around the higher figure received by the seventh duke. These suggest that a reasonably successful attempt was made to maintain the remittances at a higher level during his lifetime.

These trends were not coincidental. During the sixth duke's lifetime the remittances suffered not only from the effects of the successive agricultural depressions and crises described earlier (chapter 3), which led to reduced rents and higher relief expenditure, but also from periodically high demands for capital resulting from specific developments on the estate itself.[17] Foremost among these demands were the politically motivated improvements at Dungarvan prior to 1820 and the compensation payments at Youghal in 1823 (see chapter 5), as well as the rebuilding of Lismore Castle.[18] All of these took priority over the remittances in the apportionment of income (see figure 6.1). The changing nature of this "priority" expenditure reflected the sixth duke's increasingly ambivalent attitude towards his political influence in Ireland. This topic is dealt with at length below, but it may be noted here that while the sixth duke acquiesced in active although proxy borough-mongering prior to the 1832 Reform Act, thereafter the growing violence and cost of Irish politics led him increasingly to a position of virtual neutrality, whereby he offered no more than what he considered to be his "legitimate" interest in support of candidates he approved of.[19] Thus by the 1840s political expenditure such as that used to regain the boroughs of Dungarvan and Youghal prior to 1823 would not have been contemplated, even if it had seemed likely to succeed. Instead the duke's renewed interest in his Irish property expressed itself in the conspicuous expenditure already noted at Lismore.

Throughout the sixth duke's lifetime the Irish estates were run in a way designed to ensure harmonious landlord-tenant relations rather than to maximize net income. In 1839 the auditor, Benjamin Currey, was able to report to the sixth duke that his property in Ireland "is well regulated and steadily progressing . . . [and] everyone is satisfied and grateful to you for your uniform kindness and consideration."[20] This paternalis-

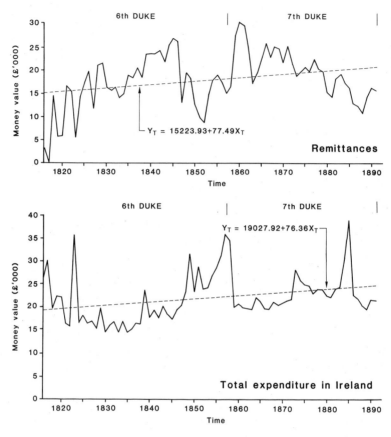

FIGURE 6.1 Remittances and Total Expenditure on the Duke of Devonshire's
Irish Estate, 1816–1891

tic concern on the duke's part for the welfare of his tenantry was also
much in evidence during the Famine, but it was tempered by the auditor's more cautious reasoning. Thus while the duke sanctioned extensive
rent reductions, in itself an act of generosity when the agricultural rents
in particular were badly paid, and approved the creation of temporary
employment, the auditor only made these proposals after satisfying himself that in the long term they would benefit the duke's interest.[21] Employment was given "as much as possible in reproduction works such as
drainage which will improve the estate," taking care at the same time
that the property did not "in too great degree find employment for
others badly managed, as such a course would swamp the estate."[22]

In fact, Currey appears to have been genuinely affected by the suffering he witnessed during his visits to Ireland in 1846 and 1847, but he was nevertheless quite clear in his own mind as to the probable long-term benefits that would accrue to the duke and other landed proprietors from the Famine.[23] Admittedly, his initial view was the most sanguine. Writing to the sixth duke from Lismore in October 1846, Currey concluded:

Deeply as everyone must lament and deplore its consequent present suffering, yet I am certainly convinced that the failure of the potato crops and the necessary measures adopted in consequence will ultimately advance the prosperity of Ireland and very greatly advance the value of property in it. The large expenditure of money advanced by the state at moderate interest and expended in drainage and other productive works, must do an immensity of good, and the landlords will not suffer, for the increase in the annual value of their property from the money expended will enable them to pay back the money.[24]

A year later Currey's tone was less bullish, but he was still convinced that the creation of employment, particularly in railway projects and by government-funded estate improvement, would provide the necessary breathing space during which the surplus population could find gainful employment.[25]

The auditor's conviction as to the value of employment in "reproductive works" was presumably one reason why the improvement expenditure on the estate was marginally higher under the sixth duke than under his successor (see table 6.7). Another reason was the sixth duke's own perception of his responsibilities as an absentee landlord. Writing in 1858 to the seventh duke, Francis Currey, the Irish agent, explained the high costs incurred on the Lismore property in particular as being partly due to the sixth duke's desire to be seen as a liberal employer of labor. Moreover, as Currey noted, so great had been the beneficial effect on the Irish estate of the lavish expenditure under the sixth duke, that he was now able to cut it in half, with an annual saving of £13,000, something that would previously have been impossible.[26]

Francis Currey's concern to demonstrate to the seventh duke his awareness of the need to reduce management costs in Ireland reflected the renewed financial crisis facing the Devonshires. In 1814 the Devonshire patrimony had been encumbered by mortgages of over £593,000, the result of the fifth duke's extensive land purchases combined with his ambitious reconstruction of Buxton in the 1790s (which alone cost more than £120,000) and, of course, Georgiana's debts. On her death in 1806 these totaled £109,315. By the time of his own death in 1858, the bachelor duke's lavish expenditure—on his embassy to Russia and on his houses in England and Ireland and their contents—had virtually doubled the size of the cumulative debt to just under £1 million. Even in an age of aristocratic indebtedness, the seventh duke's inherited debt stood out both for its size and composition.[27] The implications for the Irish estate were ominous. Despite his well-deserved reputation for profligacy, the sixth duke had in fact been anxious about his financial affairs as early as 1827, and consideration had been given to the sale of the Irish estate in 1829 and again, more seriously, in 1843–1845.[28] On this second occasion there had been a major conflict of advice, and perhaps interest, between the Curreys and the rising star of the Chatsworth establishment, Joseph Paxton.

The crisis had arisen when Benjamin Currey alerted the duke to the growing difficulty of servicing his already excessively large mortgages, and the consequently crucial need to reduce his still uncontrolled spending.[29] The auditor considered that the debt could be satisfactorily reduced by the judicious sale of outlying parts of the English estates combined with a reduction in extraordinary expenditure. Without apparently informing Currey, the duke sought Paxton's advice, which was unequivocal. By Paxton's estimation, the duke had already lost well over £1 million in compound interest, and as the cost of borrowing was likely to rise faster than any increase in the duke's income due to improvements, enough land should be sold to liquidate the entire debt at once. Paxton favored Ireland, where he thought the management costs excessive. He concluded that the duke could raise £800,000 by the sale of forty thousand acres in Cork and west Waterford, and still retain Lismore Castle and its immediate environs, which would bring in £10,000 a year.[30]

The duke's reaction was favorable. Acknowledging Paxton's letter, the duke concluded, "I have long looked to a sale of Irish property as the only possible way of paying off my mortgages. But of late years the state of Ireland has made me think it is impossible."[31] Shortly afterward, in July 1844, the duke wrote to Benjamin Currey informing him of the planned sales in Ireland. The duke recited Paxton's reasons (without attributing them to Paxton), and reiterated too Paxton's implied criticism of the auditor for his failure to inform the duke earlier of the size of the debt.[32] Currey's reply was diplomatic. After pointing out to the duke that he had presented him with a paper outlining the pros and cons of an Irish sale in 1829, the auditor stressed not only the reasons against selling in Ireland but also the reasons against making extensive sales at all. Not only was the duke's Irish estate likely to double in value, but the low differential—half a percent—between the cost of borrowing money and the interest on extensive land sales constituted a major reason militating against such a drastic diminution of the family inheritance.[33]

The duke was not convinced. It was only after George Cavendish, whose advice the duke had sought out, agreed with Currey as to the inadvisability of selling in Ireland, that the estate was reprieved—but only on the understanding that the Irish remittances were to be increased to at least £26,000.[34] Francis Currey gloomily confided to his uncle Benjamin that "in order to secure the amount of remittances required by the Duke, I must in some measure cripple the expenditure on permanent improvements."[35] Figure 6.1 indicates that however unwillingly, the necessary adjustments were made, at least in the short term. Remittances rose from £25,000 in 1844 to £27,500 in 1845 before falling marginally to £26,300 in 1846. Thereafter the fall in rents and the rise in relief expenditure occasioned by the Famine, followed by the decision in 1851 to invest in rebuilding Lismore Castle, resulted in a fall in the remittances to between £13,000 and £18,000 during the remainder of the sixth duke's lifetime.

The seventh duke shared none of his predecessor's pleasure in Irish property. The decision not to sell in Ireland in 1845 appears to have heightened the sixth duke's renewed interest in his estate there, a development subsequently witnessed by both the frequency of his later visits and by the scale of his expenditure. By contrast, the seventh duke was a remote figure, who had been made bereft by the early death of his wife, Blanche, in 1840. In 1858 he regarded the by-now alarmingly encumbered Devonshire estates as a source of concern rather then enjoyment. None of his diaries or personal correspondence indicate the same delight in Lismore which the sixth duke felt on his renewed visits there in the 1840s.[36] Instead the tone throughout is somber and businesslike, with frequent references to the poverty of much of the land and the continuing need for agricultural improvements. Attempts by the tenantry and local dignitaries to present testimonials of gratitude and welcome were discouraged.[37]

The seventh duke was not to be persuaded by sentiment, and the possibility of an Irish sale was again considered in the months following his accession. Faced with inherited debts of nearly £1 million, the duke's own inclination was to sell the entire Irish property, a view Paxton enthusiastically supported.[38] Ironically, Paxton had already resigned from the seventh duke's employment because of his feelings of responsibility for the sixth duke's debts.[39] The Curreys and Alexander Swanston, the Bandon subagent, were strongly opposed to the intended sale on much the same grounds as Benjamin Currey had been in 1845. Unlike England, estates in Ireland had yet to reach their full value, purchasers would be difficult to find for such a large amount at fair value, and the sale of the Irish estate would diminish the social and political consequence of the dukedom, a point which had already been made quite independently by the duke of Bedford.[40]

Paxton's reply was dismissive. Not only had Irish estates sold well through the Encumbered Estates Court, but the recent enormous expenditure on the Irish estate, which would aid its sale, had not given rise to increased remittances. Furthermore, if Swanston was correct, and these could be increased to £30,000 a year, then either it indicated that the estate had been mismanaged in the past or else it could only be done at the expense of the duke's popularity. This would continue, whereas a sale would be a nine days' wonder. Finally, although agreeing that any large sale would damage the status of the dukedom, Paxton argued that such damage would be even greater if the sales took place in England, and that sales of the outlying English property (which was all that the Curreys contemplated) would in any case pay off no more than half the debt.[41]

Despite Paxton's eloquence, a compromise was reached. Youghal and Dungarvan—generally perceived to be the two most expensive and contentious parts of the estate to manage—were to be sold and the remainder retained. The property at Dungarvan was sold off piecement—first to occupying tenants and then finally through the Landed Estates Court—in 1859–1861, and realized £29,500; the estate at Youghal was disposed of as one lot to a Mr. Lewis for £60,000.[42] Throughout these proceedings the estate managed to preserve the duke's reputation for liberality. Houses in Dungarvan that had been built by the tenants on forty-one, sixty-one, or ninety-nine-year building leases were sold at between eighteen and twenty-two years' purchase, while farms were sold at a valuation that deliberately discounted the value of any improvements the tenants had made. By May 1860 Francis Currey was able to report that "the course pursued by the Duke has given much satisfaction. . . . On the whole I am sure that in disposing of the Dungarvan property the Duke has acted with justice and generosity towards his tenants but not in the almost extravagant manner described in the newspaper statements."[43]

The decision to sell Youghal as one lot raised different problems, particularly in regard to the timing of the sale. By September 1860 Francis Currey was urging the futility of further delay in trying to find a purchaser. While he was confident that the existing delay had been beneficial, insofar as property prices had risen, he was by no means convinced that they would continue to rise, particularly since they were sensitive both to harvest fluctuations and variations in the cost of borrowing. He concluded, "[T]he Duke has never expressed to me any desire to hasten the sales or the contrary. I apprehend there can be no particular advantage to hurry them but on the other hand when he has made up his mind to sell there seems no adequate reason for deferring a sale unless for some nearly certain advantage."[44] In the event, the initial purchase agreement was signed with Lewis in November of that year and the deal was completed two years later.[45]

The liquidation of these parts of the Irish estate ushered in a new managerial ethos concerning the remainder. In contrast to the sixth duke, whose "weariness" with business affairs George Cavendish saw as being partly responsible for the auditor's alleged reluctance to keep him properly informed, the seventh duke took a much more active personal interest in the management of his estates.[46] In Swanston's phrase, the duke was "determined to know all his affairs minutely," and this led to more stringent control over spending on the Irish estate.[47] The work at Lismore Castle was stopped (with the great tower left unfinished), and no further extraordinary expenditure of comparable size was ever sanctioned out of the Irish receipts again. The average net cost of running the estate farm and woodland enterprises was also reduced by nearly one-third (see table 6.7). The effect on total expenditure in Ireland was immediate: it fell from over £34,000 in 1858 (63.3 percent of income) to £19,800 (36.5 percent) in 1859, and fell again in 1861, when it represented 35.2 percent of income, the lowest proportion ever in the seventh duke's lifetime.

These measures allowed the remittances to be increased to £28,000 in 1859 and then to around £30,000 in 1861–1862, when at over 53 percent of income they represented the largest proportion ever remitted. The improvement was short-lived. The worsening agricultural crisis between 1862 and 1863 led to aggregate rent reductions in each year of more than £5,500, which in turn reduced remittances to £17,500 in 1863 and to £19,500 in 1864. Thereafter strengthening agricultural prices permitted the remittances to be increased to between £22,000 and £25,000 a year until 1871, but spending also rose, despite the duke's efforts, to levels which remained well in excess of those of the 1830s (see figure 6.1). Furthermore, when the estate's income fell in 1879–1880 and began its progressive decline after 1882, expenditure remained relatively high, and even increased in 1885 to its highest recorded level (£38,000) as a result of the payment of £13,000 in law charges.[48]

The seventh duke's failure to cut spending in 1859 to the levels current in the 1830s, or even subsequently to maintain the reduction he did achieve, was a consequence of the irreducible nature of much of the estate expenditure. Conspicuous expenditure was easily cut, since the only person really affected was the duke himself. Indeed, the duke may be said to have been fortunate in having this opportunity for cost cutting. Cuts in real terms in spending on patronage or capital improvement were theoretically possible but difficult to achieve in practice. The sixth duke's policy of giving generously to institutions and charities connected with the estate had been important in ensuring harmonious landlord-community relations, and for this reason alone would have been difficult to abandon. As it was, the seventh duke continued his predecessor's policy of relatively open- and evenhanded patronage, although he was careful to decline further requests from places such as Youghal where the patronal connection had been severed.[49] Nevertheless, average expenditure on patronage increased marginally from £1,884 under the sixth duke to £2,390 under the seventh duke (see table 6.7).

It was equally difficult to cut spending on improvement, especially since this was bound up with the increasingly contentious issue of agrarian politics.[50] The 12 percent or so of income spent in this way under the sixth and seventh dukes was relatively high, and was certainly regarded by contemporary opinion as generous and conducive to good landlord-tenant relations.[51] In 1883 Chetwynd Currey, the agent, concluded that one of the main reasons why successive Land Acts had only a limited effect on the estate was the liberal management policy pursued over the previous sixty years. Only thirteen tenants had their rents reduced by the Land Court, and since 1871 only nine had been ejected for nonpayment of rent.[52] Seemingly, the vast majority of tenants had been content to live under a management system that shared improvement costs with them and that, provided they expended an equal sum, charged them no interest on the landlord's expenditure.

Currey subsequently estimated that over the previous fifty years, the duke had sanctioned the expenditure of between £6,000 and £10,000 a year on all forms of improvement.[53] Under the seventh duke, average annual improvement costs increased marginally to £5,626 from the £4,907 paid under his predecessor, but fell slightly in proportionate terms to under 11 percent of income (see table 6.7). The largest single component in the annual estate expenditure in Ireland was the aggregate management cost, and this was effectively irreducible. It comprised items which were for the most part either impossible to reduce, such as the quit rents, or, like the taxes, tended to increase. Under the sixth duke the aggregate management cost averaged £13,290 (30.2 percent of total income); under the seventh duke it increased to £16,115 (32 percent; see table 6.7). In short, throughout the lifetime of the sixth and seventh dukes nearly one-third of all the Irish estate income had to be allocated for nonproductive purposes, with, in the agent's eyes at least, little possibility of any significant reduction being made in it.[54]

Urban Improvement Expenditure

Figure 6.2 depicts the global trend in estimated capital improvement expenditure in the towns in cash terms and as a percentage of the total improvement and works costs between 1832 and 1869. Table 6.8 presents the same data as decennial averages. The figures are derived from the disbursement entries in the surviving annual accounts, but because of differences in the way these were compiled for different parts of the

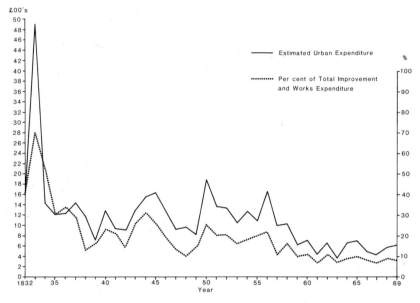

FIGURE 6.2 Estimated Urban Improvement Expenditure in Ireland by the Duke of Devonshire, 1832–1869

estate, they undoubtedly underestimate the true total cost.[55] At Bandon, Dungarvan, and Youghal the labor and materials costs of urban and agricultural improvements were specified separately, and consequently the total improvement costs in these towns can be identified with reasonable accuracy. At Lismore and Tallow this is not possible. A single return of the total labor cost involved in all projects was made every two or three weeks, with the only distinction being that maintained between laborers and craftsmen. While this accurately reflected the "direct labor" system used for building projects on the Lismore and Tallow division, it precludes any detailed estimate of the labor costs and improvements carried out in these two towns—as Francis Currey had occasion to explain to William Currey in 1860.[56]

The accompanying figures thus represent a conservative base estimate of the probable total urban improvement cost, but it is unlikely that the Lismore and Tallow urban labor costs would have significantly altered their order of magnitude. Between them, these two towns accounted for some £12,398 (28.7 percent) of the £43,1154 estimated to have been spent on urban improvements between 1832 and 1869. In

TABLE 6.8
Decennial Average Urban Improvement
Expenditure, 1832–1869

	Urban Total	Urban Average	% Total Works
1832–1839	13,601	1,700	34.3
1840–1849	11,545	1,154	18.7
1850–1859	12,296	1,230	17.7
1860–1869	5,661	566	8.9
Total	43,114		

Total and average figures in £.
Source: N.L.I. L.P. Estate Accounts.

any given year, labor costs are estimated to have constituted between 20 and 30 percent of the *total* improvement spending in the Lismore and Tallow division.[57] If the *urban* total in the division is adjusted upward by the same proportion, then a maximum urban improvement cost of just over £16,000 is indicated for these two towns during this period, raising the proportion represented by the overall urban spending from 18.3 to 19.9 percent of the global improvement figure (£235, 391).

Irrespective of these attempts at refinement, the combined urban improvement costs depicted in figure 6.2 clearly comprised a relatively small and declining proportion of the overall spending on all works and improvement. The emphasis on agricultural improvement reflected that sector's importance as the prime mover in the estate's economy. The unusually high urban expenditure in 1833 was caused by extensive politically motivated housing renovation in Dungarvan prior to the election of the following year, and represented virtually the last occasion when the estate indulged in such political manipulation.[58] Thereafter the recorded annual urban improvement cost varied between £700 and £1,900 until 1858, before falling to between £400 and £700 following the sale of Youghal and Dungarvan. In the thirty years prior to their sale, estate improvement in these two towns cost £22,187, or 60 percent of the total estimated urban improvement cost during that period, apparently confirming Francis Currey's opinion that, in gross terms at least, they were the two most expensive parts of the estate to manage. In comparison, Bandon accounted for 13 percent of the total, while Lismore and Tallow between them absorbed the remaining 27 percent.

TABLE 6.9
The Estate Towns: Rent Yield Per Unit Cost

	Bandon	Dungarvan	Lismore & Tallow	Youghal
Works:rent	1:10.1	1:2.7	1:5.1 – 1:3.9*	1:5.3

*Allowing for approximately £3,000 under-estimated labor costs.
Source: N.L.I. L.P. Rentals.

In fact, Currey's perception was slightly misplaced. The true financial worth of each division on the estate was a function of income as well as costs. If each town's rent demand is calculated as a ratio of their total works cost, then while Dungarvan certainly emerges as the least productive part of the urban estate, with a rent return of less than three times the size of the unit works cost, Youghal was at least as profitable on a unit-cost basis as Lismore and Tallow, and possibly considerably more so (see table 6.9). Bandon, on the other hand, is distinguished as by far and away the most productive urban division, with a ratio value twice as high as Youghal's. As the sale correspondence between Paxton and the sixth duke implies, however, Lismore was regarded as the core of the eponymous estate, and for that reason alone its retention was considered to be essential.

The urban expenditure depicted in figure 6.2 involved a variety of individual improvement projects, including the construction or enhancement of various public utilities and amenities. For example, between 1852 and 1889 these included the gas supply at Lismore, Bandon, and Dungarvan; the public water supply at Bandon, Lismore, and Tallow; and relaying the sewage system at Bandon and Tallow between 1861–1869 and at Lismore in 1889.[59] In addition, the duke also financed the construction of the new bridge at Lismore in 1856 to replace Thomas Ivory's eighteenth-century bridge that had collapsed, while at Bandon the street money that was collected as part of the tenants' rents was regularly expended on reflagging and maintaining the town's thoroughfares.[60]

All of this expenditure was regarded as capital improvement and was returned as such in the estate accounts. The donations that the duke made to various charitable and religious building projects in the towns, such as the construction of the Roman Catholic chapels at Dungarvan and Youghal, or the seemingly never-ending requests for money from the nuns of the Lismore convent, were over and above this, and were entered into the accounts as charitable subscriptions.[61] Finally, the urban improvement costs also included the very occasional sums spent on extending the existing housing stock, as at Tallow in 1851–1852, when thirteen new laborers' cottages were built in West Street, or the much more frequent repairs the duke was covenanted to make to the roofs and outside woodwork of houses held by various tenants.[62] As this implies, the housing stock did not have an indefinite life-span. In 1860 and again in 1867 Francis Currey explained to the duke that the relatively large sums spent on urban repairs were a consequence of the inevitably dilapidated condition of property falling out of lease, which in the case of the small residential tenements was frequently so bad as to demand their total reconstruction.[63]

Currey's explanation of the urban costs reflected his overriding concern to justify the overall level of expenditure on the estate under the more stringent managerial regime imposed by the seventh duke. As on the estate at large, so too in the towns, the seventh duke was less willing to continue his predecessor's liberality if this could be avoided. Thus whereas the sixth duke not only provided a site for the Lismore Gasworks in 1852 but also became its major shareholder and financial benefactor, the seventh duke limited his patronage of the later installations at Bandon and Dungarvan to the donation or provision of a site, and by 1877 was quite willing to sell his predecessor's shares in the company at Lismore.[64] Similarly, while the sixth duke installed the first public water supply at Lismore at his own expense, the subsequent and admittedly more ambitious scheme at Bandon was the object of much more limited patronage by his successor.[65]

By the same token, when expenditure on repairing tenants' houses in Bandon began to rise in the late 1870s and again in the 1880s, the Irish agent felt it necessary to move quickly to ensure that the local subagent was made aware of the need to reduce this spending to a more acceptable level. Writing to J. R. Berwick, the Bandon subagent, in 1883, Francis Currey identified the problem as the result of the growing use of permanent estate labor to make the repairs, rather than insisting, as previously, that tenants submit a written estimate of the likely cost, part of which would then be deducted from their rents. Currey estimated that whereas under the old system the annual works cost at Bandon had averaged £550 between 1850 and 1869, under the new system implemented by Berwick this cost had risen to an average of £1,200 between 1870 and 1882, "culminating in the altogether abnormal amount of £2,366" in the latter year. Currey was adamant: he was "decidedly of the opinion that this system should be discontinued."[66]

All of this mirrored the worsening financial situation facing the seventh duke as a result of the progressive failure of his industrial investments at Barrow-in-Furness and the unexpectedly slow rate of return on his expenditure at Eastbourne. At Barrow, the duke's indefatigable promotion of the iron and steel works, shipyard, and Furness railway prior to the business collapse of 1874, and his enforced role as their financial savior thereafter, resulted in expenditure by the mid-1880s exceeding £2,000,000. At Eastbourne, where the development was designed to be self-financing, a total investment by 1893 of £748,000 had resulted in a surplus of barely £36,000.[67] Given this state of affairs, it is hardly surprising that the seventh duke was loath to accept more than what he felt to be his legitimate responsibility toward his urban property in Ireland.

Participant Expenditure

In practice, this ducal spending constituted only one of three potential sources of improvement expenditure available to the urban estate. The others were the rate-financed spending administered by the Town Commissioners set up under the Lighting and Cleansing Act of 1828 and the Towns Improvement (Ireland) Act of 1854, and tenant expenditure carried out to fulfill leasehold obligations.[68] Arguably, the duke was aided in his attempts to minimize his direct expenditure by the existence of the Town Commissioners as a new and alternative source of patronage. The relationship between the duke and the commissioners was delicately balanced. On the one hand, it reflected the duke's willingness to continue to help fund—within reason—the improvement of the public amenities in his towns, and on the other hand, the commissioners' growing consciousness both of their own newly acquired authority and the need to maintain ducal goodwill.

The 1828 act applied to all "cities, corporate and market towns" in Ireland. It empowered the commissioners appointed under its provisions to levy a property-based rate of between six pence and one shilling in the pound in order to finance "the cleansing, lighting and paving" of streets. Youghal was the first of the duke's towns to adopt this measure when the corporation accepted the lighting and cleansing provisions in 1830. The money was used to help fund the installation of gas lighting supplied from a gasworks constructed on a site provided by the duke. Twelve years later the town adopted the remaining provisions for watering and paving.[69] Bandon adopted all the measures save that for paving in 1835; the Devonshire estate continued to fund street repairs in the town until the 1890s.[70] There is no evidence that a Commission was ever established at Tallow under the 1828 act, but those established under the provisions of the 1854 Town Improvement Act both there and at Lismore enjoyed comparable legislative powers.[71]

In each case, the relationship between the duke and the commissioners was cordial. Nevertheless, it was characterized by the commissioners' repeated attempts to pressure the duke into fulfilling what they perceived to be his responsibilities as ground landlord, and by the duke's equal determination neither to sacrifice any of his existing property rights nor to agree to anything beyond his (already limited) customary expenditure. The commissioners' determination can perhaps be explained by the discrepancy in the size of their resources compared to the duke's. Between 1831 and 1836, for example, the average rate raised from the entire town at Youghal was £440, compared with an average rent yield from the duke's estate there of £2,107. At Bandon the discrepancy was nearly as great: the average rate yield between 1836 and 1843 was £388, compared to an average rent yield on the duke's estate in the town of £1,734.[72]

The earliest dispute between the duke and the Town Commissioners was potentially the most significant, but eventually it was resolved amicably. In June 1842 the Youghal Gas Commissioners approached Francis Currey to determine whether the duke continued to claim ownership of the quays between Grattan Street and the Ferry Slip which he had regained from the corporation in 1822, and if so, to request that he put these into repair. Currey's reply was delphic. Although the duke did regard these as his property, they had been relet to tenants on repairing leases, and it was the tenants rather than the duke who had failed in their obligations. The initial meeting was inconclusive, but ended with Currey's expression of the duke's goodwill. Replying to the commissioners' notification of their intention to adopt the remaining provisions under the act to flag and water the town, Currey assured them that the duke was "inclined to aid rather than obstruct them," but added that "any particular request must be subject to consideration on its own merits."[73] It is not clear whether agreement was ever reached on the harbor issue. A year later Currey made a further offer: if the commissioners were prepared to pay a nominal rent in recognition of the duke's rights to the "bed and soil" of the docks enclosed by the quays, he would put them into repair for public use without further charge other than the existing wharfage fees.[74]

The other recorded conflicts of interest between the duke and the commissioners in his various towns were relatively minor. At Youghal an attempt was made to force the duke to repair some sewers, and two years later to give up decayed houses in Grattan Row for road improvement. Neither request was acceded to. A similar lack of success attended the Dungarvan commissioners' request for sanitary improvements in 1851, the Bandon commissioners' request in 1880 that the duke demolish some dangerous houses on his estate in North Main Street (and thereby create employment), and the Lismore commissioners' demand in 1885 that the duke cease to charge his customary fee for the use of the pens in the town's livestock market.[75] In each case the answer was either that the duke considered these requests to be unjustified economically or else that they represented an unwarranted intrusion into the management of his private affairs. However, this apparent intransigence must be set against the duke's willingness in 1859 to sell the meat, fish, and vegetable markets at Dungarvan to the Town Commissioners for less than their full commercial value, and his readiness four years later to make over the entire Lismore water supply to the Town Commissioners for a nominal rent.[76] While these actions were clearly consonant with the seventh duke's desire to minimize his urban patronal role, they were nevertheless also instrumental in ensuring the continued provision of important public utilities for these two communities at less than their real cost.

Tenant Expenditure and Leasehold Structure

The third source of improvement expenditure on the urban estate derived from the tenants' varying obligation to rebuild or maintain their rented property. This aspect of the tenurial relationship between the duke and his tenants inevitably involved a series of compromises. Each party attempted to maintain what was, from their point of view, an optimal interest in the tenancy in question given the prevailing competition for property. The tenants' decisions may be envisaged as normally having been taken within a relatively limited information field. In an environment where a history of loyalty to the estate was important, there is little evidence in the Application Books and agent's correspondence to suggest that many applicants for leases were well informed about the alternative locations available to them beyond their immediate chosen environment.[77] The decisions of the estate hierarchy, on the other hand, were necessarily more widely informed. The Lismore agent had the responsibility for maintaining a consistent scale of values in the rent levels he implemented over the entire Irish estate, while the decisions of high policy made by the duke and his auditor were determined by the prevailing conditions on the Devonshire patrimony at large.[78]

The nature of each tenant's building obligation varied with the extent to which his economic interest was preserved in his tenurial bargain with the duke. Generally speaking, the greater the tenant's potential profit, the greater his obligation. Thus the relatively few lengthy leases granted on the estate during the nineteenth century offered the tenant the possibility of gaining substantially from any increase in the property's value, but invariably required that he accept responsibility for constructing and maintaining its buildings. These building leases required that the tenant erect the buildings to an agreed plan within a specified period and to a specified minimum cost. The length of the lease varied according to the sum that the tenant was prepared to spend, and this was in effect the mechanism by which a compromise was achieved with the duke's property interests. The Building and Application Books record various applications of this principle. For example, at Youghal and Dungarvan during the 1840s and 1850s, building lots were let in the town center for between sixty-one and ninety-nine years at rents of between £5 and £10, providing the tenants agreed to spend between £200 and £300 on the buildings.[79]

Repairing leases, which by the nature of things were more frequent, involved a different kind of trade-off between the tenant's investment

[A]

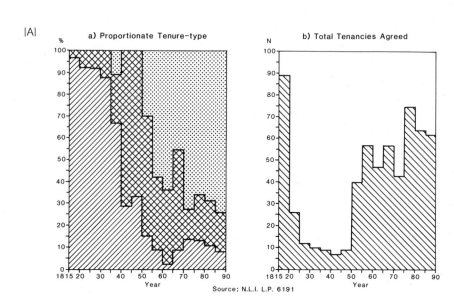

a) Proportionate Tenure-type

b) Total Tenancies Agreed

Source: N.L.I. L.P. 6191

Leases >1 year   Annual tenancies   Weekly/monthly tenancies

[B]

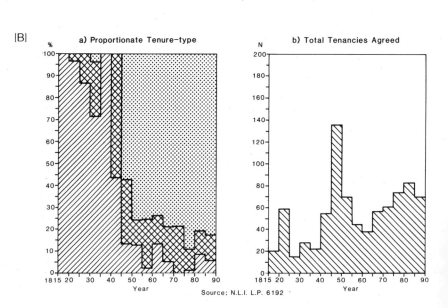

a) Proportionate Tenure-type

b) Total Tenancies Agreed

Source: N.L.I. L.P. 6192

FIGURE 6.3   A: Bandon Tenurial Structure, 1815–1890
B: Lismore Tenurial Structure, 1815–1890

and the duke's property rights. Normally, the agent reduced the first year's rent to compensate the tenant for part of the cost of any repairs that were required before he could take possession. Thereafter the tenant was responsible for the entire cost of repairs and was also required to surrender the buildings in good habitable condition.[80] As with a building lease, therefore, under these conditions the tenant shouldered most or all of the financial burden for keeping the property in repair. Where tenants made further improvements to the property over and above the stipulations in their original lease, they could normally expect to receive compensation, but only if the improvements had been carried out with the agent's prior approval.[81] With the shorter annual and weekly or monthly tenancies, the responsibility for repairing the property lay with the estate, while the cost of any improvements was shared with the tenant on a proportionate basis. The tenant either contributed a lump sum, normally less than one-third of the estimated cost, or accepted an increase in rent. The Building Books indicate that the requests for improvements made by the short-term tenants were usually relatively modest, frequently involving nothing more than the insertion of additional windows or a new floor or ceiling. Accordingly, the unit costs were also relatively low. For example, at Lismore and Tallow they averaged £10.18.0 between 1869 and 1879.[82]

Given these differences in the property obligations falling on the duke and his tenants, what effect did the nineteenth-century changes in leasing policy have on the apportionment of urban costs on the estate? Figures 6.3 and 6.4 provide a quinquennial breakdown of the type and number of tenancy agreements made in all of the towns save Dungarvan between 1815 and 1890. The proportionate tenure-type histograms indicate that the other four towns experienced a precisely similar shift from a predominantly leasehold tenurial structure prior to 1840–1850, to a situation in the second half of the century in which the vast majority of new agreements were either for weekly or monthly tenancies. This transition was most pronounced in Lismore and Tallow and least pronounced at Youghal.

The histograms of the total tenancies indicate that with the exception of Youghal, this shift was accompanied by a significant rise in the total number of tenancy agreements recorded in each five-year period. At Lismore and Tallow this rise was relatively short-lived, and the

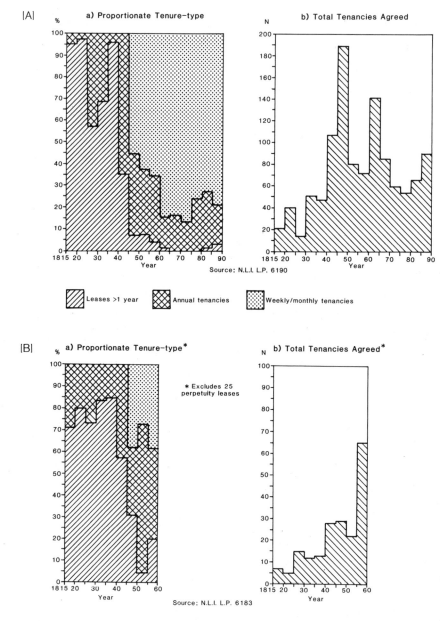

FIGURE 6.4   A: Tallow Tenurial Structure, 1815–1890
           B: Youghal Tenurial Structure, 1815–1860

number of agreements soon fell back, although to a level that remained higher than during the "leasehold" period. At Bandon the rise was sustained, but the total number of tenancy agreements never achieved the earlier peak of 1815–1820. At Youghal the first appearance of a limited number of weekly and monthly tenancies between 1845 and 1850 was accompanied by a slight increase in the quinquennial total, but the most pronounced rise in this total occurred between 1855 and 1860. This suggests that the decision to sell the estate in 1859 was locally unexpected. The rise in the number of tenancy agreements resulted from the short average tenure enjoyed by the weekly and monthly tenants, and from the increase in the number of contractual bargains made for each piece of property as a result of the policy of direct letting to occupying tenants. Previously, a single lease would have been made out to the head lessee of each property. At Lismore, over 63 percent of the monthly and weekly tenancies granted between 1840 and 1890 lasted for less than fifteen years, while during the same period at Tallow over 75 percent lasted for less than ten.[83]

These patterns reflected the continuing attempts by the agents to reduce the number of leaseholds on the estate, thereby increasing the duke's economic control over his tenantry and improving the responsiveness of rent formation to economic change. This policy had of course first been suggested by Henry Bowman, but its early implementation was only partly successful. The dramatic increase in the number of weekly and monthly tenancies in the 1840s suggests that when the duke and his agent finally succeeded in implementing this policy, they were brought face to face with an entirely new tenurial problem. As the remaining middlemen's leases continued to fall in, so the duke was brought increasingly into a direct tenurial relationship with a much more numerous and relatively impoverished socioeconomic class who were of a very different cast to the earlier head lessees.

In many instances, these people had been the under-tenants of the erstwhile middlemen,[84] while others included some of the impoverished rural-to-urban migrants who formed an increasing proportion of the population in the duke's towns at this time. Lacking the necessary resources, these people would have been incapable of funding extensive leasehold tenures even if the estate had continued to make these available. Leasehold tenure, whether for lives or for the shorter periods of

years which became increasingly common during the 1830s, represented a considerable financial commitment on the part of the tenant,
but provided a correspondingly secure and relatively prestigious tenurial status. Accordingly, in normal circumstances it appealed to men
of some property. Weekly and monthly tenancies, on the other hand,
demanded no such long-term financial commitment on the part of the
tenants, but neither did they provide the same security of tenure. They
were therefore more appropriate to the poorest social groups in the
urban community. At Lismore, for example, the average weekly rent in
the 1840s was just under eleven pence, and rose only marginally to one
shilling and six pence by the 1880s.[85] Although not significantly lower
in aggregate than the average rents paid for annual tenancies, the
weekly payment of these rents made such tenancies accessible to people
who would have found it impossible to pay even this amount on a
yearly or half-yearly basis.

The growth in the number of weekly and monthly tenancies meant
that increasingly the financial responsibility for urban maintenance
shifted away from the tenants and on to the estate. In itself this was
hardly consonant with the duke's wish to minimize management costs
in Ireland, but clearly it was only one factor in the property equation.
Balanced against it was the increased control the duke enjoyed over
his property as a result of the shorter tenancies, and his prospect, in
consequence, of a more realistic income relative to the capital value of
the building stock. Moreover, it is quite clear that this shift in financial responsibility was never total. Despite the policy of short-term
direct letting pursued from the 1840s onward, enough of the earlier
leases for lives or years survived to ensure that the previous centripetal
tenurial status patterns also survived in a recognizable fashion in most
of the duke's towns until at least the 1860s (see figures 6.5, 6.6, 6.7,
6.8, 6.9).

At Bandon and Lismore they survived until the 1890s. In both these
towns the central "leasehold" zone, where the majority of property was
held for lives or years, survived more or less intact, although with some
diminution in the proportion of leasehold tenancies. At Bandon,
rather more significant tenurial replacement occurred on the south side
of the town, where falling leases on the Burlington and Cavendish
Quays and on Castle Road and Stanton's Lane were replaced by weekly

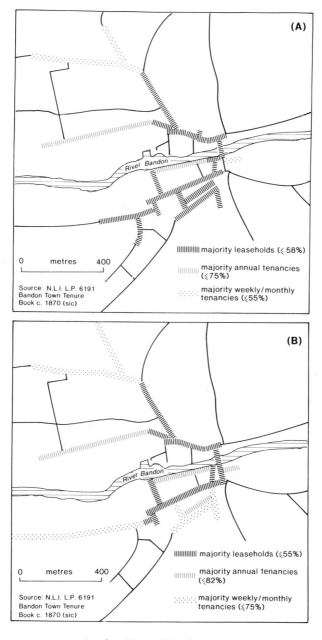

(A)

River Bandon

| 0 | metres | 400 |

Source: N.L.I. L.P. 6191
Bandon Town Tenure
Book c. 1870 (sic)

||||||||||| majority leaseholds (⩽58%)

|||||||||| majority annual tenancies (⩽75%)

majority weekly/monthly tenancies (⩽55%)

(B)

River Bandon

| 0 | metres | 400 |

Source: N.L.I. L.P. 6191
Bandon Town Tenure
Book c. 1870 (sic)

||||||||||| majority leaseholds (⩽55%)

|||||||||| majority annual tenancies (⩽82%)

majority weekly/monthly tenancies (⩽75%)

FIGURE 6.5 Bandon, Tenure Distribution in 1860 and 1890

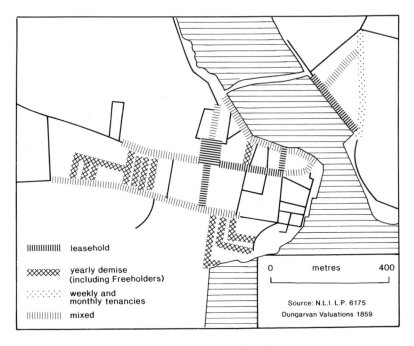

FIGURE 6.6   Dungarvan, Tenure Distribution in 1860

or monthly tenancies. Conversely, in both towns the peripheral zone dominated by weekly and monthly tenancies became even more pronounced. At Lismore such tenancies accounted for over 80 percent of the total number in this zone by 1890. Most were located on streets that had been built during the town's expansion in the 1820s and 1830s. Consequently, the town's leasehold core continued to correspond with the settlement's original medieval nucleus. At Bandon the equivalent rise in the proportion of weekly and monthly tenancies in the outer suburbs was from a minimum of 55 percent to over 75 percent. By 1890 these tenancies were characteristic of areas such as Barrett's Hill and Kilbrogan Street, which had already emerged in the 1770s as extramural suburban zones outside the plantation borough. In both towns the mixed streets recorded relatively even proportions of leasehold, annual, and monthly tenancies.

Similar patterns characterized Youghal and Dungarvan on the eve of the sale of the duke's property there. At Dungarvan the freeholders' housing remained discernible as peripheral clusters of yearly demisable

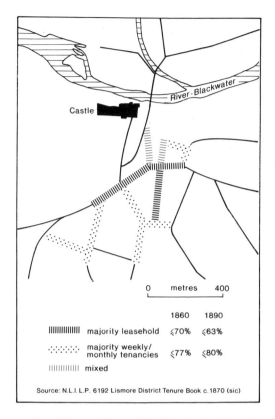

FIGURE 6.7   Lismore, Tenure Distribution in 1860 and 1890

property, standing in mutually exclusive contrast with the leasehold
core on Devonshire Square, William Street, and Main Street, itself now
dominated by building leases. The tenurial pattern on the remainder of
the estate was more mixed, save across the River Colligan in Abbeyside, where some status differentiation was evident. At Youghal a
marked tenurial contrast existed on the estate between the streets in
the original medieval core, where the majority of tenures were leasehold and included some twenty-five perpetuity leases over which the
duke had virtually no control, and the quayside area of Green's Quay,
Catherine Street, and Grattan Street. Here most of the valuable commercial properties were held on annual tenancies at rents that were two
or three times as high as those paid in the residential leasehold core.[86]
Clearly, the estate maintained close control over its prime commercial

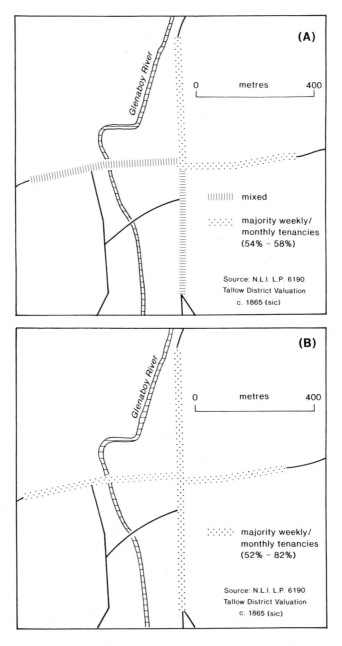

FIGURE 6.8   Tallow, Tenure Distribution in 1860 and 1890

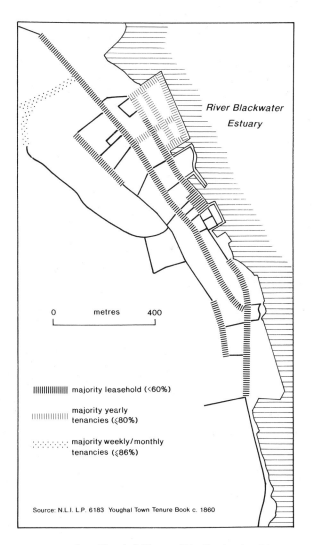

River Blackwater
Estuary

0   metres   400

||||||||||||||| majority leasehold (<60%)

|||||||||||||||| majority yearly
tenancies (≤80%)

majority weekly/monthly
tenancies (≤86%)

Source: N.L.I. L.P. 6183 Youghal Town Tenure Book c. 1860

FIGURE 6.9   Youghal, Tenure Distribution in 1860

property in this part of the town. The only areas characterized by weekly and monthly tenancies were the peripheral low-status cabin developments along Cork and Raheen Lanes. These had been erected in the early 1840s, presumably in response to the population growth of that period.[87]

Of all the duke's towns, only Tallow failed to retain a significant number of leasehold tenancies in its town center. By 1860 the leasehold structure recorded in earlier valuations had been so eroded that no street was dominated by leasehold tenure.[88] The main thoroughfares in the town—Barrack Street and West Street—were mixed, while peripheral roads such as Bog Lane and Tallow Bridge Street were dominated by weekly and monthly tenancies. Thirty years later the transition was complete. In the previously mixed streets, weekly and monthly tenancies predominated, while in Bog Lane and Tallow Bridge Street they accounted for over 82 percent of all tenancies. This relatively rapid tenurial shift had no immediately obvious proximate cause, but it may well have reflected an earlier weakening in the town's leasehold structure as a result of the fortuitous falling in of head leases.

These patterns imply that the tenants' continued to make a significant contribution to the repair of the urban core in all of the towns save Tallow throughout the sixth and seventh duke's lifetimes. Nevertheless, as earlier leases began to fall in in the various town centers, so the estate began to become involved in the repair and maintenance of an increasing proportion of the core property. At Tallow the estate was responsible for the repair of virtually all the property by 1890. The relatively few leases for years or lives granted by the seventh duke in his towns were invariably for public utilities such as schools, banks, or barracks. This implies that in common with other landowners, the duke was still willing to delegate a significant portion of his property rights in order to attract financial and other services that might enhance the overall economic viability of his urban estate at large.[89]

Political Disengagement

The income generated by the Irish estate represented one form of property that accrued to the duke in his capacity as an Irish landowner; political influence, in theory, represented another. Generally speaking, the Irish Reform Act of 1832 significantly reduced opportunities for the sort of borough-mongering that had motivated Thomas Knowlton during the first decade of the century—although, as Hoppen has recently demonstrated, in the county constituencies landlord authority enjoyed a brief revival during the 1850s.[90] In fact, as chapter 5 has shown, the duke of Devonshire was already becoming progressively disillusioned with the cost and venality of Irish politics well before the 1832 act (which he supported) accelerated the political realignment of his boroughs. The history of the sixth duke's involvement in Irish borough politics between 1832 and 1858 was characterized by his continued attempts at personal disengagement in the face of pressure from successive Whig governments to intervene fully and frequently, and despite the near-total misunderstanding and periodic hostility of both his Catholic and Protestant tenants. During the 1830s, in particular, Irish borough politics were for him a continuing source of anxiety and expense, as he sought on the one hand to maintain what he regarded as the "legitimate" interest his property gave him, and on the other to placate the Whig administration of Lords Grey and Melbourne, and restrain the radically opposed interests of Repealers and ultra-Protestants alike.

   The sixth duke never really defined what he meant by his "legitimate interest," and this imprecision gave rise to a series of misunderstandings with his Irish agents as they sought to interpret these instructions in the light of the urgent calls from various quarters for the duke's political support. The sixth duke's view appears to have been that his extensive borough property gave him the right to make public his support for a particular candidate, without necessarily actively furthering the individual's campaign. In the heady atmosphere of nineteenth-century Irish politics, such a stance was hardly calculated to please anybody. The duke's preferred candidates might very well need—and demand—more active support; the duke's tenants generally failed to understand the motives lying behind such limited involvement; and on more than one occasion the duke's agent thought it necessary to go beyond this limited commitment. In contrast, the seventh duke's opportunities for involvement were very much more limited than his predecessor's, even if he had been disposed to take advantage of them. The sale of Youghal and Dungarvan removed the two most venal boroughs from whatever remaining influence the duke possessed, while the emergence of a strong localist Protestant faction at Bandon, which had already resulted in the defeat of the pact between the sixth duke and Lord Bandon in 1831, combined with the substantial survival of leasehold property there to ensure that this borough too remained out of the seventh duke's reach.[91]

The changes wrought in the Irish elective franchise by the 1832 Reform Act and subsequently by the Irish Franchise Bill of 1850 did not favor the sixth duke's political balancing act.[92] Passed by Lord Grey's Whig government against substantial Tory opposition, the 1832 act was intended in Ireland as in England to widen the franchise and make it more representative of the new classes emerging within nineteenth-century society. It was hoped, thereby, to defuse the potential for a radical assault upon society by nonenfranchised groups, driven by despair at the seemingly intransigent nature of its increasingly nonrepresentative power structures. Thus, as Stewart notes, it was not a deliberate step toward "democracy," but rather a pragmatic attempt to secure the stability of the state.[93] Irish Whigs regarded the Irish Reform Act as the logical culmination of a process of reform that had been going on since the Act of Union. Irish Conservatives regarded it as a threat to the Protestant Ascendancy in Ireland, the position of the Anglican Church of Ireland, and to the very legislative Union itself. O'Connell's radicals welcomed it for precisely these reasons, but were quickly disillusioned as the much more limited nature of the real reforms became apparent.[94] Under the provisions of the act, the borough franchise was extended to include all householders who either occupied premises worth at least £10 or who paid at least £10 a year in rent. At the same time, provision was made to retain for life the voting rights of existing £5 and forty-shillings freeholders who happened to live within the newly revised and generally reduced borough boundaries.[95] Unlike the forty-shillings freeholders in the county constituencies, this group had not been disenfranchised as part of O'Connell's deal with the government to secure the passage of the 1829 Catholic Emancipation Act.

As in other borough constituencies, these proposals represented a significant extension of the franchise in the duke's remaining boroughs, but one that nevertheless still only incorporated a very small minority of the overall urban population. Thus, at Bandon, the commissioners inquiring into the proposed alterations in 1831 concluded that reform would increase the electoral college from thirteen (the provost and twelve free burgesses) to 240 £10 householders, an increase from 0.1 to 2.4 percent of the 1831 population. At Youghal the increase in the size of the electorate was more pronounced but still only affected a minority of the population. The unreformed franchise had been limited to the al-dermen, burgesses, and freemen of the corporation, whether resident or nonresident. In 1832 they were estimated to total 263 (2.7 percent) of the 1831 population of 9,600. After the revised borough boundary was finally agreed to, the franchise increased to 413 (4.3 percent), including 326 £10 householders who had previously had no vote. In Dungarvan the pre-1832 franchise was completely different. It included rural free-holders in the manor of Dungarvan as well as those in the town itself, together with some 200 registered householders, making a total of 871 in all. Nearly 600 of these were forty-shillings freeholders, most of whom enjoyed a precarious existence as fishermen. Under the original provisions of the 1832 act, the number of voters would have dropped to about 210, but the subsequent retention for life of the existing forty-shillings freehold voters ensured that even within its much reduced geo-graphical area, the borough electorate remained at about 700 (8.1 percent of the population).[96]

By ensuring that political representation remained in the hands of relatively small groups within the boroughs, the 1832 act also ensured that the intimidation and manipulation previously applied to the unre-formed electorate continued. Moreover, the act did not even succeed in defining these new "political" elites in a particularly consistent or pre-cise fashion. The property qualification was difficult to define—much depended on whether the "beneficial interest" or the "solvent tenant" test was used—while the continuing system of voter registration in-vited widespread personation—the fraudulent impersonation of one voter by another. Although the 1850 Franchise Act succeeded in resolv-ing some of these abuses, the incontrovertible fact was that borough electorates remained numerically small elites, vulnerable to internal community pressures at precisely the time when the sectarian composi-tion of many urban communities was undergoing significant change.[97] O'Flanagan has shown that this was certainly true of the Devonshire towns. Between the 1770s and early 1850s the Protestant "cores" of

Bandon and Youghal were substantially infiltrated by Catholic tenants, who established themselves within these central zones on a highly segregated basis. At Dungarvan and Tallow the Catholic preponderance that had already been displayed in the 1770s was further reinforced by 1851. At Lismore the relatively mixed community of the 1770s was replaced by an almost exclusively Catholic one by 1851.[98]

These changes in the sectarian composition of the community in the three boroughs had various political consequences. At Bandon the changes were not sufficiently mirrored in the reformed electorate to upset the Conservative Protestant hegemony prior to the election of William Shaw as Liberal M.P. for the town in 1868.[99] At Dungarvan the overwhelmingly Catholic electorate, dominated for a generation after 1832 by the forty-shillings freeholders, provided an arena for competition between moderate and radical Catholic political opinion. Only at Youghal was the changing sectarian composition of the community at large reflected in the electorate. Consequently, successive political contests in the town in the 1830s and after involved real sectarian rivalry rather than the reinforcement of existing sectarian dominance.[100]

This analysis is borne out by the events at successive elections in these boroughs between 1832 and 1837 (see table 6.10). The most radical political changes occurred in Youghal. In 1832 the "opening" of the borough as a result of the changes in the franchise caused the sitting Liberal member, George Ponsonby, a relative of the duke's, to decline an "unwinnable" contest with Daniel O'Connell's son, John.[101] O'Connell retained the seat in 1835, but when he withdrew in 1837 Frederick Howard, another of the duke's relatives, narrowly secured the seat for the Liberals against an outside Conservative candidate, William Nichols. At Dungarvan the violent challenge from the radicals in 1830 and 1832 gave way, following O'Connell's alliance with the Liberal party, to an uneasy truce between the Liberals and Repealers in the period after 1835.[102] Michael O'Loghlin, a Catholic associate of O'Connell, was returned as government candidate at successive elections, despite opposition from the local Repeal candidate and erstwhile O'Connellite, John Mathew Galwey. At Bandon the resurgent Protestant working-class interest not only returned Conservative candidates throughout the period, but in so doing roundly defeated William Cavendish, one of the duke's own kinsmen, in 1837.

TABLE 6.10

Election Results in Bandon, Dungarvan, and Youghal, 1832–1837

Election Year	By/Gen	Date	Bandon (I.M.P.)	By/Gen	Date	Dungarvan (I.M.P.)	By/Gen	Date	Youghal (I.M.P.)
1832	Gen	15/12/32	W. S. Bernard C 133 / Jacob Biggs L 100	Gen	17/12/32	G. Lamb L 307 (677) / J. Galwey R 270	Gen	15/12/32	J. O'Connell R 22 (297) / R. Davis C 5
1834				By	[On death of Lamb] 15/2/34	E. Jacob L 307 / P. Barron L 260 / P. Crampton L 6			
					[Petition lodged against Jacob's return]				
1834				By	16/4/34	E. Jacob L 293 / P. Barron L 269			
1835	Gen	14/1/35	J. D. Jackson C 111 / J. R. Barry L 79	Gen	12/1/35	M. O'Loghlin L (707)	Gen	16/1/35	J. O'Connell L(R) 137 (338) / T. Smith C 130
1835				By	[O'Loghlin appt. Solicitor General] 4/5/35	M. O'Loghlin L 360 (708) / J. Galwey L(R) 88			
1835				By	[O'Loghlin appt. Attorney General] 21/9/35	M. O'Loghlin L 315 (713) / J. Galwey L(R) 153			
1837				By	[O'Loghlin appt. Baron of Exchequer (Ireland)] 16/2/37	J. Power L 283 (741) / J. Galwey L(R) 164			
1837	Gen	3/8/37	J. D. Jackson C 133 / W. G. Cavendish L 81	Gen	5/8/37	C. O'Callaghan L 261 (747) / J. Galwey L(R) 157	Gen	8/8/37	F. Howard L 158 (526) / W. Nichol C 150

L = Liberal   L(R) = Liberal/Repealer (supporter of Liberal/Repealer pact, 1835–41)   R = Repealer   C = Conservative   (338) = Total registered votes   137 = Votes cast for candidate

[Source, B. M. Walker (ed), Parliamentary Election Results in Ireland 1801–1922, Dublin 1978.]

William Cavendish's candidacy highlights the dilemma that, prior to 1837, led the duke to accept more involvement in Irish borough politics than he would ideally have liked. The 1837 election coincided with a general revival in the fortunes of Irish Tories. Accordingly, the Liberal government were anxious that as many seats as possible should be contested—particularly safe Tory ones like Bandon.[103] The decision to field William Cavendish was made by his father under intense government pressure relatively late on, after the original Liberal candidate had withdrawn.[104] Both the auditor and the Irish agent realized from the outset that the venture was hopeless. Too many of the electorate had already pledged their votes to J. D. Jackson, the sitting Tory M.P., and too few funds were available.[105] The candidate's father, Charles Cavendish, was unwilling to spend more than £500 on his son's election, while the auditor had expressly forbidden any expenditure of the duke's money in his support, or indeed the expression of anything other than "the duke's legitimate interest" in his favor.[106] Despite the sixth Duke's initial optimism, Cavendish's failure was inevitable.[107] The fact that he ran at all while receiving only limited support from the duke reflected the uneasy nature of the latter's compromise between his private inclinations and his sense of political duty.

It is clear that concern over the cost and violence of Irish elections remained prominent in the sixth duke's calculations even though he was disposed to support a Liberal government. Previous experience had shown him that active interference in Irish politics could only be carried on at some expense to property (see chapter 5). In 1832 Colonel Currey estimated that recent uncontested elections had cost £400, whereas a contested return might run as high as "£1,500 besides £400 for relief."[108] Although not high by contemporary Irish standards, these sums represented an investment the duke was increasingly loath to make.[109] Not only was he becoming ever more aware of his own indebtedness, but the sums Currey mentioned would have made a noticeable difference in the £17,000 or so he received each year from his Irish estates.[110] The duke's growing unease about these costs was indicated as early as 1832, when Benjamin Currey warned him that Dungarvan could only be successfully contested at the cost of bribing the local priests, and that in the future even this device was unlikely to ensure success, "unless at an enormous sacrifice of property."[111]

Five years later, at Youghal, the duke's primary concern was again the cost of Frederick Howard's return. Initially the Liberal candidate was to have been William Cavendish. The duke had reluctantly agreed to this candidacy, provided that Charles Cavendish paid the whole expense and was satisfied with the legitimate support the duke would have given any Liberal candidate.[112] When, at the Liberal government's instigation, Howard replaced William Cavendish and the latter was dispatched to Bandon, the duke's immediate concern was Howard's probable inability to meet the whole cost of the election, rather than his modest qualities as a candidate. The instructions received by the Irish agent on this point were succinct: "The Duke is to pay nothing and there is to be no sacrifice of property at Youghal."[113] In the event, Howard's return was complicated by a Tory petition against the result on the grounds of fraudulent voting, one of the thirty-one they pursued between 1832 and 1840.[114] Although the petition ultimately failed, the additional costs it seemed likely to impose on the duke over and above the excessive amount already spent by the agents without his authority, caused them considerable anxiety. Ultimately, the failure of the petition and the auditor's appeal to Devonshire's political principles appear to have mollified the duke, although Benjamin Currey was careful to acknowledge that in his defense of those principles he may have acted overzealously.[115]

Of equal importance in explaining the duke's desire to limit his involvement in Irish elections was his disillusionment with their continuing violence. This was nothing new in Irish politics.[116] Indeed, violence was almost inevitable, given the plural nature of Irish society and the less-than-perfect political alignment between the disproportionately small electorate on the one hand and the community they purported to represent on the other. In the duke's boroughs, however, circumstances conspired to ensure that the level of violence reached new heights at the General Election of 1832. At Youghal the general agitation over Repeal and tithe abolition was given added zest by the arrest of Dominick Ronayne, a prominent local radical, on charges arising from tithe agitation.[117] When the election was finally held, the violence of the O'-Connellite mob forced the withdrawal of Roger Davies, the scratch Conservative candidate put up by the independent electors in the town after George Ponsonby had declined the contest. Davies resigned the contest after barely twenty-seven votes had been cast. As he observed to the mayor,

I commenced the Poll yesterday with an assurance from my committee of such a majority of votes, as in this our limited constituency, where the inclination of each Elector was easily ascertained, gave the fairest promise of success, and was subject seemingly to but little casualty. Large bodies of strangers from the adjoining country were assembled during the day, and have been acting on an apparently concerted system of violence. Many of my most respectable friends have been mobbed, cut with stones, savagely beat and trampled. . . . Many of my supporters yielded to their terror, and declared themselves afraid to face the dangers of the hustings, where order cannot be preserved beyond the immediate vicinity of the Court House. Yielding to the representation of my committee, unwilling to hazard the lives and limbs of my firmer friends who are still willing to come forward . . . I decline any further contest.[118]

Davies's comments undoubtedly voice the disappointment of a defeated man, but the violence he described was not only very real but also widespread. Mobs of country people regularly took control of smaller boroughs in the way he described.[119] At Dungarvan the 1832 election was only carried by the duke's preferred candidate, George Lamb, because of the "sincere co-operation of the priests . . . who would not be dictated to by O'Connell . . . , but the violence and tumult manifested was dangerous even to the peace of the country."[120] Two years later Dominick Ronayne declared that "he would bring in [to Youghal] the population of seven parishes," with manifestly similar intent.[121]

The cost, violence, and personal abuse that accompanied borough elections on the sixth duke's Irish estate rendered them personally distasteful to him, but behind this distaste lay an even more important reason for his attempted disengagement. An avowed supporter of the principles embodied in the 1832 Reform Act, the duke conceived that the spirit of the act precluded him from active political intervention in support of any candidate. Henceforth he declined to engage in any further borough-mongering, refusing either to put forward candidates in his own name or to countenance the bribery and intimidation that such active interference frequently demanded. Paradoxically, it was his own interpretation of the Reform Act that led the duke to offer only limited support to the Liberal party that was responsible for it, both when in government and, in 1835, in opposition. Thus at the Dungarvan by-election occasioned by George Lamb's death in 1834, Benjamin Currey warned Lords Grey and Duncannon that while the duke would want to do anything pleasing to Lord Grey's government, his acts had to be consistent with his principles as a reformer.[122] Accordingly, the resident agent was given very specific instructions if the government's initial candidate, Mr. Wyse, chose to stand:

Distinctly, that you and Witham are not to engage as agents as on former occasions at the risk of your lives and health. In short, if you are necessary to carry the election, it should not be engaged in. The Duke is to do no act to injur his property, incur expense beyond as stated . . . or make promise, or do any act that could be said to be inconsistent with the principles of reform as supported by him as they have been, but that all legitimate and constitutional support he would give.[123]

Daniel O'Connell's alliance with the Liberal party between 1834 and 1841 created further problems for the management of the duke's political interest in Ireland. The sixth duke supported the alliance's immediate objective, the defeat of Peel's Conservative administration of 1835, as he did the lengthy programme of municipal, judicial, and administrative reforms that followed the return of Lord Melbourne's Liberal government in April of that year.[124] But, for the duke, the political cost of these reforms was too high if they depended on an alliance with a man whose politics he detested, and whose own political ambitions had frequently been furthered at the expense of the duke's interest and the security of his property. Accordingly, the sixth duke refused to ally himself tactically in any way whatsoever with O'Connell. Writing to James Abercrombie in December 1834, in reference to O'Connell's proposal for just such a tactical alliance in Dungarvan, the duke concluded: "Differing so entirely as I have with O'Connell in political sentiments and conduct, it is impossible for me to do otherwise than to decline to connect myself in any way with him in such matters."[125] True to his word and his Liberal principles, six months later at Youghal the duke supported neither O'Connell nor his Conservative opponent, T. C. Smyth.

If the sixth duke's attitude to his Irish boroughs was not always amenable to the operational demands of Liberal party policy on Ireland, then

at least it appears to have been reasonably well understood by the leaders of that party.[126] The same could not be said of the local communities
in the boroughs. At Dungarvan the continued existence of a large body
of impoverished forty-shillings freeholders after the Reform Act created
a particular problem. At the by-election of 1834 Benjamin Currey was
under no illusions about the fickle nature of this group:

> A vast number of the voters are fishermen, poor thoughtless and inconsiderate
> and moreover discontented from the present state of their trade, and in my
> opinion under present circumstances cannot be controuled [*sic*] without as-
> sistance, presents and temptations clearly amounting to bribery. Past kind-
> nesses and relief from want are forgotten at the moment and when opposed
> by parties who care not what they do the contest is fearful and dangerous.[127]

With such an electorate to contend with, there was no certainty of
success at any election for Liberal candidates. The niceties of the duke's
support for reform, his support for Catholic Emancipation, and even
his munificence to the town twenty years earlier, were all vulnerable to
the emotional rhetoric of Repeal and tithe abolition. Moreover, when
success was achieved, it invariably had to be bought with the intervention of some third party, such as the Roman Catholic clergy, who for
their own reasons, and at a price, were prepared to pressure the duke's
forty-shillings freeholders into voting for his preferred candidate. Thus
the intervention of the local priests secured Dungarvan for Lamb in
1832, but was done to demonstrate their political independence from
O'Connell. In 1834, when it was no longer in the Catholic clergy's interest to support a government candidate, the prospect of a Liberal victory seemed remote.[128]

Paradoxically, the full extent of the Dungarvan electorate's failure to
understand the duke's political intentions was demonstrated in the
same year, at a time when their support for what they perceived to be
the Devonshire political interest was most vociferous. During the by-
election occasioned by George Lamb's death, and after Pierce Barron
had announced his Liberal candidacy and received the duke's "legitimate" support, a remarkable local campaign was mounted to try and
persuade the duke to start a candidate, preferably George Ponsonby, in
his own name.[129] The reasons behind this campaign are obscure, but
seem to have had at least as much to do with a resurgence of local support for the duke as with Barron's unpopularity. The manifest im-

probability of the duke forwarding his own candidate after giving his support to Barron did not deter the electors. In January a petition was forwarded to the duke by sixty-five electors who, "mindful of [the Duke's] past munificence to Dungarvan," called for Ponsonby to come forward while assuring the duke of the certainty of his return. Writing at about the same time to the local agent, Henry Witham, a Dungarvan resident reported that "the public manifestation of feeling for this Gentleman is beyond description. The walls of the town are blackened with the praises of his and the Duke's name and No Barron." After the duke's inevitable rebuff of this campaign, the electorate showed its fickleness, and returned another Liberal candidate, Ebenezer Jacob.[130]

The existence of a vocal and politically active Protestant community at Bandon and the reasons for its continuing hegemony have already been alluded to. At Youghal Protestants comprised some 20 percent of the town's population, but were overrepresented in the reformed electorate. Voting patterns in 1835 and after suggest that they constituted nearly half of the new electorate, and included virtually all of the existing freemen who had been allowed to retain their vote.[131] As Hoppen demonstrates, the relaxation of the duke's Whiggish control over Bandon after 1832 allowed the growth of a virulent Protestant sectarianism in the town's politics. Initially, this may have been a defensive reaction to the capture of the borough by John O'Connell and his subsequent retention of it in 1835. Later, however, this assertiveness seems to have sprung from a newfound self-confidence among local Tories. While doubtlessly stemming from their growing numbers, this self-confidence also reflected the general revival in Conservative fortunes in Ireland after 1835.[132] Already by that year Youghal Conservatives felt strong enough to attempt to dictate to W. S. Currey the terms on which they might support a friend of the duke against O'Connell, assuming no candidate of their own was forthcoming.[133] Two years later, at the General Election of 1837, Frederick Howard, scion of the House of Cavendish and heir to the Devonshire Whig tradition, only just beat the outside Tory candidate, William Nicol, by eight votes, despite the lavish and unauthorized expenditure of the duke's money.

Howard's election was characterized by extensive antagonism between the various political parties at Youghal. The violence that this antagonism engendered has been well described by Barry and Hoppen.[134]

It is ironic that it was in large measure a consequence of the sixth duke's attempt to withdraw from borough politics, a decision itself partly determined by his abhorrence of "political excitement." In fact, the 1837 election, with its mixed results for candidates standing with the duke's support, represented virtually the last occasion on which the duke allowed wider considerations of government strategy to override his personal inclination to minimize his political involvement.

Thereafter the duke was more successful, or more determined, in ensuring that his "legitimate interest" meant precisely that. Thus, at Youghal in 1852, he refused to allow any member of his family to stand, and the seat was captured for the first time by the Conservatives.[135] Five years later the Bandon subagent, Alexander Swanston, was censured for allowing himself to be nominated as a candidate for the town, after the duke had dissuaded Lord Charles Cavendish from acceding to a government request to stand.[136] Not only would Swanston's duties as agent and M.P. have been incompatible, but the public assumption would have been that he stood as the duke's candidate.[137] However, in the same year, at Dungarvan, the sixth duke's political acumen deserted him. Having promised his usual "legitimate interest" to any moderate candidate put forward by the government, the duke found himself obliged to support a Liberal Conservative, Sir Nugent Humble, after the original Liberal candidate had stood down.[138] Despite early assurances to the contrary, Humble's address was less than conciliatory to Catholic opinion, and the duke was in consequence widely held to have renegued on his Liberal principles. The Catholic vote was marshalled by the local clergy in support of the Independent candidate, J. F. Maguire, who eventually held the seat by nineteen votes.

The contest was notable for its violence and the disaffection of the duke's remaining freehold voters. So great was the feeling engendered by the duke's apparent espousal of the Liberal Conservative cause that Francis Currey was physically assaulted by the tenants.[139] In subsequent correspondence with the auditor, Currey outlined the measures he wished to see taken both against the disaffected freeholders and Dr. Halley, the parish priest who had played a major role in organizing their opposition:

Dr Halley's duplicity and ingratitude is unmasked, he is wholly unmindful of the many favours given to him by the Duke. Some future remonstrance may be necessary against those freeholders who have allowed themselves to be entrapped and voted against the Duke's wishes. They should not continue to receive the full measure of indulgence (in rent and rates relief) they have had before. . . . There are also a few persons who made themselves conspicuously obnoxious amongst the mob, who are holding small houses from the Duke and they ought to be made to pay up all the arrears or be turned out.[140]

But the political tide was running against such attempts to display patronal displeasure. The roundness of Humble's defeat was a measure of the sixth duke's declining real influence in Irish urban politics in the face both of their increasing localism and the growth in nationalist sentiment.[141] It is probable that had the seventh duke not willingly adopted an equally low political profile, it would have been forced on him. As it was, he readily conceded that with the impending sale of Youghal and Dungarvan, it was inappropriate for him to try and influence events there during the 1859 election.[142] Four years later he accepted his auditor's advice that the electorate at Bandon was effectively independent of his control, and thereafter limited his political involvement in the constituency to a relatively generous subscription to the Liberal Registry.[143] Bandon (together with Dungarvan and Youghal) lost its independent representation in 1885, and with it disappeared the last formal trace of the duke of Devonshire's urban political interest in Ireland.[144] In reality, of course, the substantive interest had been in decline for the previous fifty years. It is a curious irony that when the seventh duke's heir, Lord Hartington, split the Liberal party and defeated Gladstone's Home Rule Bill in 1886, he was almost certainly acting directly contrary to the wishes of the majority of his family's remaining urban tenants in Ireland.

Summary

This chapter has been concerned with the changing attitudes displayed by the sixth and seventh dukes of Devonshire toward the management of their urban estate in Ireland. Prior to the Great Reform Act of 1832 the estate towns were regarded as worthy objects of investment for both political and economic purposes. This resulted in a major

transformation of Dungarvan and Lismore, and in general improvements elsewhere. The sixth duke's support for and interpretation of the
Reform Act subsequently led him to attempt a unilateral withdrawal
from active intervention in borough politics, despite the pressure to do
otherwise from successive Whig administrations and the incomprehen-
sion of his tenants. At the same time, he sanctioned high levels of improvement expenditure on the agricultural sector of his estate. In
contrast, the comparatively low level of urban spending suggests that
following the massive urban expenditure of the previous decades, the
towns were no longer regarded as productive objects for major transformative investment. In the immediate pre-Famine period, therefore,
the urban estate was typically not a major beneficiary of the high levels
of improvement spending that characterized the agricultural estate, but
neither was it a major source of income. It accounted at best for approximately one-fifth of the total rent roll.

At the same time, the urban estate was proving to be responsive to
the wider dimensions of urban change that were occurring in provincial Ireland at this time. Pre-Famine population growth (in most instances) and functional diversification were followed by population
decline, by a reduction in the functional base (in some cases), and by
an increasing switch to retailing rather than craft industrial production. There is some evidence, however, that the consequences of
this contraction were not as thoroughly deleterious for the estate as
might be expected. It has been argued that in the two functionally
simplest towns, Tallow and Lismore, this contraction was accompanied by a reordering of the relationship between the size of the population and the economic base that actually strengthened these towns'
rent-generating capacity. In the other, larger, and functionally more
complex estate towns, the correspondingly higher proportion of non-
residential property on the duke's estate masked any straightforward
relationship between the size of the tenant population and the levels
of rent formation.

But if the duke's estate towns were susceptible to exogenous demographic and economic change of Irish origin, so too they were vulnerable to internal pressures emanating from other parts of the Devonshire
patrimony. One of the major and continuing themes in the overall
management history of the Devonshire estates in Britain and Ireland

during the nineteenth century was the continuing need to enhance
capital formation in order to liquidate the rapidly growing inherited
legacy of debt. Within this context, the peripherally located and expen-
sively managed Irish estate was repeatedly identified as the ideal candidate for liquidation in order, initially, to rescue the Devonshires from
the consequences of two generations of conspicuous profligacy, and
later, to shore up the seventh duke's crisis-ridden industrial investments
at Barrow-in-Furness. The curious aspect of all this is not that the Irish
estate was designated for this role, but that so little of it was actually
sold in 1859–1861.

Faced with the continuing high cost of managing the estate, the fall
in remittances after 1871, and the increasingly antagonistic landlord-
tenant relations after 1885, it would not have been surprising if the
seventh duke had made further attempts to liquidate his Irish estate. In
fact, this was an option that was only once more considered by the
duke, in 1874, when he contemplated selling Bandon, but then dismissed the idea as being unlikely to yield a realistic return. Instead, the
Lismore property was used as security to raise a mortgage of £200,000
from the Scottish Widows Fund.[145] Although forced on the seventh
duke by circumstance, this move nevertheless signaled both his belief
in the long-term security of Irish property and his intention to remain
an Irish property owner. More significantly still, the seventh duke continued to fund, albeit with increasing reluctance, various regional railway schemes in Munster, particularly the Fermoy & Lismore and the
Waterford, Dungarvan & Lismore Railways, which were completed
between 1872 and 1878. These Irish railway investments cost the duke
£200,000 of his English income, and were designed from the outset to
encourage growth in the regional economy through the improvement
of communications and marketing infrastructures.[146]

As with so many of his decisions relating to the Irish estate, the
seventh duke's decision to invest externally derived capital into Irish
railways when local investors were either unable or unwilling to do so,
can be fully understood only in the light of the course of events within
the Devonshire patrimony at large. As at Barrow-in-Furness, so too
money was poured into the Irish railway schemes in the hope that continued investment would eventually produce the means of restoring
the family's financial position. In the event, both failed, and indeed

contributed significantly to the debts of nearly £2 million that faced the eighth duke on his accession in 1891. The effect on the Irish estate was terminal. The decision that had been put off in 1830, again in 1845, and still again in 1858 was finally taken, and the progressive dismemberment of the Irish estate begun. Bandon was sold in 1894, and under the aegis of successive Land Acts between 1891 and 1909 land was sold which, together with sales in Derbyshire, realized nearly £660,000.[147] For the Devonshires it signaled one more stage in their disengagement from Ireland, and the end of their importance as absentee patrons in that country.

CHAPTER 7

Property and Social Authority

Despite the discretionary initiatives available to them, the Devonshires' position as magnate landowners in eighteenth- and nineteenth-
century Ireland was not unassailable. The social, economic, and political authority that had customarily derived from the ownership of the
estates they had inherited in 1748 on the marriage of Lady Charlotte
Boyle to the marquis of Hartington was to prove increasingly vulnerable to a variety of internal and external challenges. In the eighteenth
century it was challenged by the predatory actions of estate employees
and fellow members of the propertied classes—the duke's Irish relatives
among them. In the nineteenth century the family's authority as Irish
landowners was progressively eroded by the increasingly successful assertion of the rights and aspirations of other social groups who themselves had long been marginalized from the effective exercise of any
form of real power. Prior to the Act of Union of 1801, the Anglo-Irish
landowning elite perceived themselves to be, and indeed were, the very
embodiment of the state. Accordingly, whenever their position *as* an
authoritarian elite was challenged they could rely on—and could themselves sanction—the support of the state. This support might either be
direct, as in the suppression of the 1798 United Irishmen's rebellion, or
indirect, as in the codification of property laws that legitimized the
elite's monopolistic ownership of the land that formed the basis of Irish
wealth. After the Union, which from the start had marginalized the position of the traditional elite within the now-changed constitutional relationship between Britain and Ireland, the state's authority was
increasingly used to sanction the external challenges to the elite that

arose from the political and economic mobilization of other social classes.

Motivations for Property Improvement

The Devonshire Estate

The Devonshires' response to these challenges was conditioned by the attitude of successive dukes to the rights and responsibilities that they perceived to accrue from property ownership. The fifth duke (1764–1811) had a well-merited reputation for indifference concerning the management of his affairs. He was neither particularly paternalistically nor politically motivated in his attitude toward his Irish tenantry. Indeed, insofar as he displayed an "attitude" toward them at all, it was one of profit maximization predicated on minimum investment in town and countryside alike. The fifth duke thus epitomized the role of the absentee landlord in Ireland. Anxious to extract as large an income as possible from the country, and unwilling to inform himself about the true condition of his Irish estates and tenantry, he allowed a laissez-faire situation to develop in which his agent's corruption and maladministration flourished.

Whatever responsibility the London auditor may have also shared in permitting these malpractices, the fact remains that had the fifth duke taken a more active interest in the management of the Irish estate, these abuses could not have flourished as openly as they did. Consequently, we may conclude that the duke was a legitimate target for the sort of opprobrium that contemporary writers like Arthur Young increasingly heaped on the practice of absenteeism, precisely because it so frequently gave rise to consequences such as these.[1] Yet there was a certain perverse logic in the fifth duke's attitude, given the changed context within which the Irish estate now functioned. Whereas under the earl of Cork and Orrery it had been the major property of an admittedly largely absentee Anglo-Irish landowner, under the duke of Devonshire it was the relatively remote Irish appendage of the family's much larger and more profitable English possessions. Moreover, whatever political interest the Irish estate had once supported had long since either been delegated or usurped, whereas its present administration provided some income at least. Given the expense and disruption that would inevitably result from any attempt to improve this situation, was it not better to accept the status quo?

Other figures in the estate administration obviously thought not, and the start of the reforms in Ireland predated the accession of the sixth duke in 1811 by some nineteen years. This time discrepancy provides a salutary reminder that wherever the patronal relationship between proprietor and tenant was mediated through a bureaucracy exercising a delegated authority, the potential existed for that relationship to be redefined in ways that were inimical to the owner's intentions. Thus on more than one occasion members of the Devonshires' bureaucracy appear to have pursued or initiated policies that were either at odds with or in advance of ducal thinking. In one sense, of course, the fifth duke's lack of interest in his affairs made this sort of bureaucratic initiative almost inevitable. But in the case of the Irish estates, the initiative came as much from tenants who had suffered under the Irish agent's malpractice as from within the estate hierarchy itself. However, in seizing the opportunity provided by the appointment of a new auditor to air their grievances against the Lismore agent, the Irish tenants were in a sense merely demonstrating the importance of the agent's mediating role in determining the nature of the relationship between landlord and tenant—for good or ill.

Although now shown to have been more active politically than was once thought, the sixth duke (1811–1858) was still essentially a romantic, as much concerned with his artistic collections and obsessive mania for building as with the mundane ordering of his affairs. When he succeeded to the dukedom he was faced with a series of partially implemented reforms instigated by his father's advisers, reforms designed to achieve a variety of sometimes conflicting economic and political goals. The necessity for many of these reforms could hardly be doubted, but not all of them had yet proved successful. Henry Bowman's plans for Lismore had proved abortive and his general leasing policy difficult to implement. His successor, Thomas Knowlton, had pursued a more overtly political strategy, but this had only proved successful at Dungarvan and then only at considerable and continuing expense. Negotiations with the Devonshires' main political rivals at Bandon were stalled, while the attempt to recover the representation at Youghal was gathering momentum for a disastrously premature climax at the

General Election of 1812. The young duke was therefore presented with a situation in which, as Abercrombie later observed, he was already committed to various courses of politically inspired action. However, this does not by itself account for the enthusiasm with which the sixth duke initially sanctioned the pursuit of these and other goals. Rather, it seems that the duke was quite willing to believe Knowlton's claims concerning the alleged usurpation of the Burlington boroughs by the earl of Shannon and the Ponsonbys, because in so doing he found cause to seek to recover seemingly long-lost property and thus enhance his dukedom's status.

Political considerations were thus foremost among the motivations that first led the sixth duke to involve himself in the decisions of high policy concerning the Irish estate. As chapter 6 demonstrates, however, the appeal of this attempt to reestablish an effective Devonshire political interest in Ireland soon began to pall. By 1832 pragmatism had combined with principle to ensure that the duke now sought to minimize rather than to maximize his political involvement in his Irish towns. The endemic violence that accompanied borough elections was personally repugnant to him, while their cost could only be borne at the expense of his other property. Moreover, his interpretation of the Reform Act of 1832 led him to conclude that, as a reformer, he could no longer justifiably engage in active borough-mongering. Within twenty years of succeeding to the title, therefore, the sixth duke had accomplished a political volte-face, largely in consequence of the realities of Irish political life and the structural changes that had occurred within it. Ironically, during this period the duke had continued to sanction massive expenditure in the pursuit of urban political goals that were rapidly moving out of his reach. Moreover, this essentially noneconomic expenditure was highest in the one town, Dungarvan, where the rent roll was least able to support it, and where consequently there was no hope whatsoever of recouping this capital outlay when the political objectives themselves proved to be elusive.

If circumstances conspired to render the sixth duke's urban political investments ill-judged, the same was probably less true of his other major investments in his estate towns at this time. Certainly, the £29,000 or so spent on Lismore by 1830 was also unsupportable in economic terms, but after the duke's visit in 1822 profit enhancement was no longer its primary purpose. Rather, this later work seems to have been designed to achieve the triple goals of enhancing the aesthetic appeal of the urban environs adjoining Lismore Castle—a personal social good presumably intended primarily for the duke's benefit—and creating employment and improving the living conditions of the Lismore tenants themselves. While the duke's advisers were careful to shift as much of the financial burden for this rebuilding on to those tenants who were capable of sustaining it, the estate nevertheless continued to accept responsibility for rehousing those tenants who could not. At Bandon and Youghal the total investment prior to 1830 was much more in line with the rents derived from the duke's estate in these towns, and after 1822 was in any case largely directed toward the improvement of the markets and other public facilities.

The sixth duke's motivations for intervening so extensively in the development of his Irish towns prior to 1832 were thus primarily political, secondly paternalistic, and only marginally profit-related. Consequently, the primary explanation for this intervention lies in the duke's perception of the extent to which political opportunities still presented themselves in his Irish boroughs, combined with his own desire to be thought of as a generous if largely absentee landlord. With the advantage of hindsight, it is easy to conclude that the duke's appraisal was misconceived and overoptimistic, but from the perspective of 1811 or even 1822, there was little reason to suppose that the pace of political change would accelerate so rapidly as to nullify the kind of political influence that the duke sought. Even so, the preponderantly political character of this urban investment, combined with the duke's own downward appraisal in 1832 of his future political rights as ground landlord, go a long way to explain the subsequent decline in urban expenditure. In the future this was directed toward the maintenance of housing and public utilities and only rarely toward the construction of new capital projects.

For over a quarter of a century before the accession of the seventh duke (1858–1891), therefore, improvement expenditure on the urban estate had been curtailed and ducal involvement in borough elections restricted to the exercise of a "legitimate interest." At the same time, however, the sixth duke had continued to sanction relatively high levels of improvement expenditure on the agricultural estate, and had set in train a major reconstruction of Lismore Castle. Both these activities continued despite the deepening financial crisis facing the duke, which led in 1844–1845 to consideration of a possible sale of the Irish estate. The different treatment meted out to the urban and agricultural divisions may be explained in terms of their relative utility to the duke. The agricultural estate had always far outweighed the estate towns in importance as a source of income, and there was therefore every reason to continue to invest in agricultural improvement as a "pump-priming" exercise, quite apart from the sixth duke's additional concern to be known as a "liberal employer of labor." On the other hand, the three surviving boroughs had been important primarily as political property. With the sixth duke's political change of heart in 1832 these considerations effectively ended, and subsequent elections over the next five years saw a much lower level of political activity by the duke's representatives, as agents and candidates alike tried to adjust to the duke's concept of a "legitimate interest." With the eclipse of the political motivation for extensive urban improvement, the duke's remaining Irish towns were managed more or less on a "care and maintenance" basis. This was adequately funded by the limited spending alluded to above, particularly since it was increasingly supplemented by both tenant and Town Commission expenditure.

Accordingly, when the seventh duke succeeded to the title, the majority of the Irish income was derived from agriculture, and spending in the towns had been reduced to a level that was consonant with their diminished importance as a source of recurrent political property gains. But by this time the managerial imperatives on the estate at large had altered, and the prime concern was to raise sufficient capital to liquidate at least some of the by now enormous debt of nearly £1 million that faced the duke. Consequently, his priorities were those of income maximization and effective capital generation. Within this scheme of things the Irish estate towns once again played an important role, only this time as a potential source of capital rather than as an arena for the exercise of political authority. The sale of Youghal and Dungarvan in 1859–1860, together with outlying parts of the estate in Tipperary, represented a compromise between Paxton's advice to sell the entire Irish property and the Curreys' advocacy that it should be retained in the expectation of a future increase in value. The final choice of Youghal and Dungarvan reflected the Irish agent's somewhat misplaced belief that they were the two most expensive parts of the urban estate to manage.

Following the disposal of Youghal and Dungarvan, the remainder of the urban estate was retained throughout the seventh duke's lifetime. Although this period saw a slight growth in the urban rent roll, the towns continued to provide only a small part of the Irish income, just as the Irish estate at large provided a progressively smaller proportion of the duke's overall income. Despite this reality, the seventh duke maintained his policy of active personal intervention in the management of his Irish affairs. Indeed, until the assassination of his second son, Lord Frederick Cavendish, by the Invincibles when he was chief secretary in Dublin in 1882, the duke was as frequent a visitor to Ireland as his predecessor. The irony, of course, was that these visits were now essentially managerial inspections, in which the seventh duke took the opportunity to become fully informed by the Lismore agent about the minutiae of his Irish affairs. The duke's overriding concern was to ensure the effective management of his property in town and countryside alike.

In a sense, therefore, the pattern of motivation had come full circle, only the context had changed. The fifth duke was concerned with profit, but was unwilling to concern himself with how it was generated. The sixth duke was equally unconcerned with the mundane details of rent formation and its management, but was very much concerned with what rents could buy and with the reassertion (as he saw it) of his political authority in Ireland. By the time of the seventh duke's accession, the alterations in the franchise and the growth of Irish nationalism ensured that such political ambitions were a dead letter, while his worsening finances ensured that in any case he had other things to worry about. The consequence once again was a duke whose patronal relationship with his remaining Irish urban tenants was profit-led, only this time in a much more informed and socially conscious manner.

The managerial strategies pursued on the Devonshire estates were thus designed to achieve different objectives at different times: income maximization in the late eighteenth century, political influence and social prestige in the early nineteenth century, and finally, income maximization coupled with capital liquidation in the later nineteenth century. These goals were not always easily reconcilable, and frequently some form of prioritization was necessary. Nevertheless, when realized they were intended to strengthen the Devonshires' position as members of the landowning class both in Ireland and in England. Thus a higher income meant greater economic security, possibly involving a reduction in the family's chronic indebtedness, and consequently enhanced opportunities to indulge in further discretionary action to support their elitist position. Securing control over the parliamentary constituencies on the estate helped to ensure that the family's politics continued to be heard in the representative bodies of the state. Finally, investment in high-profile capital projects such as the rebuilding of Lismore Castle provided an opportunity for successive dukes to signal their allegiance to peer-group norms in cultural and aesthetic matters.

General Motivations

Political Motivations   It has been suggested (see chapter 2) that similar motivations may well have prompted the intervention of other landowners in the promotion of the extensive urban and village transformations that formed part of the modernizing process in Ireland during the eighteenth and early nineteenth centuries. It does not necessarily follow, however, that these motivations—if similar—received the same order of priority elsewhere as they did on the Devonshire estates. The Devonshires' magnate status has already been emphasized. Accordingly, their objectives were those of a family who were set apart from the majority of the Irish property-owning class by their wealth and status, but who were closely aligned to the centers of constitutional and political authority in both England and Ireland. Consequently, we may speculate that both their opportunities and reasons for urban improvement ran on an altogether grander scale than was possible for many of their less affluent and less eminent fellow landowners in Ireland. For example, the extensive urban improvements sanctioned by the sixth duke for essentially political purposes may be argued to have been relatively unusual, since these only made sense in terms of his vision of his political inheritance and were only made possible by the mobilization of the extraordinarily extensive means at his disposal.

As we have seen, by no means all the Anglo-Irish propertied class possessed similar resources, and of course by no means all of them controlled boroughs. Prior to the Act of Union, 234 of the 300 seats in the Irish Parliament were held for the 117 boroughs enfranchised in Ireland prior to 1692. Of these, 56 were corporation boroughs where the franchise rested with that (numerically limited) body; 36 or so were freemen boroughs; 11 were "potwalloper" boroughs where neither property nor influence returned a member but money and bribery; and 8 were county boroughs. All save the county boroughs were effectively "closed," that is, were controlled by one or two individuals or perhaps a small clique, among whom the ground landlord frequently—but by no means always—was numbered.[2]

Only a minority, therefore, of the five thousand or so landed families estimated to have owned property in Ireland at the end of the eighteenth century can be conceived of as having been directly involved in urban political management prior to the Union. The proportion involved thereafter must have been even smaller, as the Union reduced the number of Irish seats by two-thirds to 100, making them correspondingly more desirable as a means of promoting personal or party interest. Of those members of the propertied class who were politically active prior to the Union, many, like Lord Baltinglass at Baltinglass in 1768 or the Rams at Gorey and Duleek or the Ruxtons at Ardee, took a peculiarly pecuniary concern over the management of their interests.[3]

Irrespective of whether these borough patrons were also the ground landlords of these towns, they seem to have regarded control of the constituencies' representation as so much property, which might, if circumstances dictated, be traded or even sold for place or preferment.[4] Malcolmson cites evidence to suggest that both the frequency and the cost of these sales increased as the eighteenth century progressed. Prior to 1768 the uncertain length of Irish parliaments meant that only the most impecunious or unimaginative patron could be induced to sell his seat, which gives color to John Beresford's sneer that these "were poor men living by the sale of their seats."[5] Certainly, by the end of the century, the going price for a seat even for one of the less prestigious close boroughs was considerably more than the few hundred pounds asked, for example, for Dingle between 1714 and 1731.[6] In 1790, for instance, two offers of £3,000 and £2,700 were made to the financially embarrassed widow of the erstwhile patron of Inistiogue, County Kilkenny, for the borough's seats. Her reaction was telling: "Ought I not to be affronted at the offer, as it was supposed I was venal? No one I believe would have made such an offer to your father."[7]

Clearly, for some patrons at least, participation in this "parliamentary traffic" was distasteful and raised questions of honor that overrode any financial considerations. For others—probably a small minority—the whole business of borough management was something to be avoided if at all possible. In 1736, for example, Edward Southwell complained during the contest for his borough at Kinsale that he longed to "slip [his] neck out of this noose," and only continued the struggle for fear of the retribution his opponents might exact on the economically vulnerable among his supporters in the town.[8] Sixty years later Caesar Colclough, the absentee patron of Enniscorthy, County Wicklow, was being urged by his agent not only to sell his seats but to sell the borough altogether and use the money for the good of his tenantry.[9] However, there is no evidence to suggest that such views were widely held, and it seems likely that where eighteenth-century Irish landowners were able to profit either politically or financially from borough management, they generally did so.[10]

Economic Motivations   The means by which they did so is another matter. There is as yet little evidence to dispute Malcolmson's contention that where existing or would-be patrons spent money on borough management, this was normally used either to bribe the electorate or, as we have seen, to purchase the seat, rather than fund vote-catching improvements.[11] Where the motivations for urban improvement are specifically stated or can otherwise be inferred, they relate almost invariably to economic considerations and/or the desire to create an ordered and aesthetically pleasing milieu within which the landlord-tenant relationship might be suitably regulated. Of these, economic motivations appear to have been the most frequent, and were expressed both in the willingness of proprietors to fund the construction of market houses, industries, and other forms of infrastructural improvement, and more widely in their acquisition of market and fair patents. Over 500 of the 750 or so towns and villages that show evidence for modernizing transformation or extension between 1700 and 1850 were also equipped by their proprietors with one or more of these patents.[12] These patents were frequently represented in the townscape by the presence of a market house, and these represented one of the most widespread forms of urban investment by proprietors. Among numerous surviving examples are those at Kilrush, County Clare; Fermoy and Macroom, County Cork; Castlewellan and Newtownards, County Down; Strabane, County Londonderry; Edenderry, County Offaly; and Dunlavin, County Wicklow.[13]

The strategy behind this form of proprietorial improvement is exemplified at Edenderry. The initial suggestion to build a market house in the town was made in 1717 by the agent, Mr. Meredyth. He suggested that this investment was warranted because of the improvement in the town arising from the success of its existing markets and fairs, and because "he thought it advantageous to the town to encourage good buildings."[14] Despite the "wonderful spirit of improvement got up in the people to build and improve" in the ensuing period and further discussion about the plan in the 1790s, nothing was actually done until the early nineteenth century.[15] In 1810 the plan drawn up for the improvement of the town specified that "a Market House should be erected at the expense of the Marquis and Marchioness of Downshire as an encouragement of the town . . . to contain such rooms and accommodation as may be approved of by them . . . and to be placed under such regulation as they may direct."[16]

Two years later nothing had been done, and the local agent concluded that "the Market Square being laid out and a Market House having been promised, in confidence of which being built several persons have erected houses in that situation, and the market having greatly increased of late, it appears to be desirable to make a beginning as well as to keep faith with those who have built, so as to encourage and provide accommodation for those reporting to the market."[17] In short, not only did the local economy warrant this investment, but it was necessary if the Downshire's reputation for fair dealing with their tenants was to be sustained. The Downshires would in any case retain close control over the building and profit from the tolls charged for its use. In the event, the market house was not finally built until the 1830s, the reason for the delay being the marquis's desire that the extensive arrears on the Edenderry estate should be reduced before further investment of this sort went ahead.[18]

Landlord-funded industrial developments were almost as numerous
as their provision of markets, and varied from the foundation of purpose-built industrial settlements such as Stratford-on-Slaney, to the
individually more limited but geographically more widespread construction of mills at existing settlements. At Baltinglass, County Wicklow, for example, the first earl of Aldborough established a number of
"manufactures for linens, woollens and draperies" between 1784 and
1786, some years before he founded his new town of Stratford nearby.[19]
At Castle-Blayney, County Monaghan, the town's prosperity was based
on a linen market established at the end of the eighteenth century by
the then Lord Blayney, which by 1800 had a reputed turnover of £500
a week.[20] Similarly, the meteoric rise of Clifden, County Galway, in the
mid–1820s owed much to its promoter's success in attracting commercial investment to the town on the basis of the potential it offered for
future growth, given the rising population and lack of competing markets in that part of Connacht.[21] At Sion Mills, County Tyrone, the
Herdman family established a "moral system" alongside the linen factory that supported their village, and were credited in consequence by
contemporaries with employing "700 of a peasantry who would otherwise have been starving and idle."[22]

The Herdman foundation at Sion Mills was of course typical of the
growing number of specialized industrial villages established in Ulster by
nineteenth-century capitalists, including Bessbrook, County Armagh,
and Annesborough, Dunbarton, and Shrigley, County Down.[23] The
relative success and pronounced regional concentration of these villages
are a reminder that in the long term attempts by landowners elsewhere
in Ireland to promote significant forms of nonagrarian industry, or even
to develop viable specialist textile industries, generally failed. The reasons for these failures have been outlined in chapter 2. What should be
noted here is that where such industries were promoted as a means of
fostering urban or village growth, these settlements too invariably failed
or stagnated.

In County Cork, for example, Dunmanway flourished between 1715
and 1733 under the guidance of its resident landlord, Sir Richard Fox,
who had established linen and woolen industries there. By 1749, however, these manufactures were described as being in decline and "dwin-
dling away to extinction."[24] In the same county, the earl of Shannon's

town of Clonakilty experienced rapid growth between 1770 and 1821 on the basis of its linen trade. In 1790 this trade was worth about £30,000 a year and employed over six hundred people. By the late 1820s this trade too had died away—largely, contemporaries alleged, because of the abolition of the bounty on linen exports—and linen-related employment had fallen to one-quarter of what it had been at its peak.[25] At Innishannon, also in County Cork, Thomas Adderley's improvements of the 1750s, which included drapers' houses and a bleach green, had failed by the 1840s to realize their potential and had suffered in particular from the general decline in the linen trade outside Ulster.[26] By the same period, Dingle, County Kerry, was also in decline for much the same reason, and the extensive improvements and elegant houses that had been supported by the once-flourishing linen industry were "given over to filth and decay."[27]

The economies of some newly improved towns and villages also proved vulnerable to other forms of change wrought by the ongoing processes of modernization. At Castlerea, County Roscommon, the problem appears to have been one of misdirected and overambitious investment. In the 1820s speculative tenant capital was used to rebuild the town and to erect a brewery, distillery, and tannery, but by 1846 none of these gave any appearance of success, owing, it was suggested, to the original developers having "over-estimated the capabilities of the place and the industry of its inhabitants."[28] In other towns the problems were more specifically related to shifts in the pattern of regional trade as a consequence of the development of new routes or rival towns. At Bagenalstown, County Carlow, the original ambitious plans for a new town to be called "Versailles" were thwarted by the r-erouting of the main Dublin-Cork road through Leighlin-Bridge, the nearby bridging point over the River Barrow. The settlement that was eventually built by its founder, Bagenal of Dunlecky, achieved a more modest status as a formally planned village.[29] Howth's status as the foremost Irish packet-station suffered even more spectacularly from the shift in Dublin's outport trade to Kingstown (Dun Laoghaire), following the completion of the Dublin-Kingstown railway in 1834. Twelve years later the town had declined from being "a spruce and prosperous place . . . of bustle and promise" to a "half forsaken and desolate fishing village." Newport-Pratt, County Mayo, suffered a similar fate, following the shift of its export trade in corn to nearby Westport.[30]

Aesthetic Motivations   The evidence presented here for the varied consequences of landowners' attempts to promote improvements in urban and village-based production and marketing emphasizes once again the particularist nature of the urban experience during the modernization of the eighteenth- and early-nineteenth-century Irish space-economy. Although what was arguably the proprietors' fundamental economic objective—the enhancement of income—may have been the same throughout, the tactics that were employed depended on the landowners' perception of the best means to achieve this, given the nature of the existing local economy. It has been suggested that in global terms, the straightforward enhancement of agricultural marketing provided the surest and most widely adopted means of achieving these aims, since in the long term the promotion of industrial development was limited by the structural weaknesses inherent in the Irish economy.

In comparison, the aesthetic motivations that are argued to have also underlain these improvements are more difficult to specify precisely, because both they and their morphological consequences are likely to have been more varied. The formal elements in the planning repertoire adopted in many of the transformed towns and villages shared common Renaissance origins with the architectural styles used in contemporary country-house design. In the latter case it has been suggested that these had a further iconographical significance, since their adoption averred the landowners' social status by signaling their willingness to conform to a variety of rapidly changing and socially exclusive peer-group aesthetic norms. By implication, the same reasoning might also be expected to have applied to the architecture used in the improved towns and villages. It has to be admitted, however, that this thesis is speculative: the historical record is singularly uninformative as to the precise reasons why individual proprietors—and their tenants—chose to invest in particular forms of "polite" rather than vernacular architecture.

The inferential evidence suggesting the possibility of such aesthetic-led investment takes two forms: first, the widespread survival of both public and residential buildings that were designed in a more ostentatious style than mere functional efficiency demanded; and second, the

occasional references in estate papers to minimum architectural specifi-
cations required by landlords when granting building leases to tenants.
Where money was spent on nonfunctional ornamentation, the implication is that the motivations for this ornamentation were also noneconomic, since this clearly represented the expenditure of additional
capital on which there could be no possibility of an economic return.
The chronology of this urban ornamentation—neo-Palladianism in the
early eighteenth century, neoclassicism in the later eighteenth century
and after, and a variety of picturesque "cottage ornee," Tudor, and Eliza-
bethan styles in the nineteenth century—is the same as in Irish country-
house design. This suggests that as with country-house construction,
noneconomic motivations for town and village improvement were
frequently predicated on a desire to conform to contemporary changes
in architectural fashion.

Given the widespread use of building leases to encourage tenant participation in urban and village reconstruction, it is worth emphasizing
that both landlords and their tenants might share these aesthetic or
sumptuous motives, although because of the difference in the property
base of each group the ways in which these were expressed were very
different. If the intention in each case was to reaffirm peer-group
membership, then this also implied social distancing from other groups
perceived to be socially inferior. In the case of the tenants' buildings,
such ostentation might also reflect attempts to emulate the mores of
landlords and other socially superior groups. Thus we may postulate
the existence of mechanisms of downward cultural diffusion that extended the use of architectural forms that had once been socially exclusive over a progressively wider spectrum of society. The widespread
existence in many provincial towns and villages such as Blessington,
County Wicklow, or Manor Hamilton, County Leitrim, of relatively
debased versions of various neoclassical architectural forms—door
cases, pedimentation, string courses, quoining, and so forth—suggests
that this was so. It is thus important to realize that the argument concerning the *social exclusivity* of any adherence to changing architectural
fashion in towns and villages only applies to its initial adherents. With
the passage of time these styles became more widely adopted, and the
initial exclusivity together with its iconographical importance in signaling social status was progressively redefined as numerically larger and

less elitist groups adopted these idioms to project their own statements of self-identity.

Because of the generally larger and invariably more secure property base enjoyed by landlords, their opportunities for such socially driven expenditure were correspondingly more numerous and their potential abilities to transform physical and social space correspondingly greater than those of their tenants. The argument here is that accordingly, it was they rather than their tenants who were best placed to respond sufficiently quickly to changes in architectural fashion to allow them to benefit from the initially exclusive social cachet such aesthetic sensitivity might generate. At Bagenalstown, County Carlow, for example, contemporaries noted that the new eighteenth-century settlement was originally intended to possess "considerable architectural pretensions." Although the settlement that was finally built there was more modest than originally intended, it still echoed the aesthetics of the initial concept in the generosity of its formal orthogonal plan.[31] At Blarney, County Cork, the landlord's ambitions were, relatively speaking, even more grandiose. Beginning in 1765 the proprietor, Mr. Jeffereys, attempted to establish a manufacturing town on what was described by the *Parliamentary Gazetteer of Ireland* as a "thoroughly considered but novel and preposterous plan." The centerpiece was a formal square, laid out with walks and statuary, around which were ranged "embellished" houses, several linen and cotton factories, a church, and a bridge—without a river. The last was intended to be supplied by a leet drawn from the nearby River Martin. The failure of the project was due, according to the *Gazetteer*, to Mr. Jeffereys making "his town too fine for the taste of operatives, and too grotesque for the fancy of the higher classes; in short he made the place a ludicrous embodiment of frontless and unmeaning gasconade."[32]

A more considered conclusion might well take into account the general failure of the textile industries in Cork at this time, of which Blarney would appear to have been victim. By the time the district was surveyed for the first edition of the *Six Inch Ordnance Survey Map* in 1839, the settlement was barely more than a hamlet: the plan of the square was still discernible—although probably already growing the corn which the *Gazetteer* noted seven years later—most of the houses had disappeared, and only the church and one woolen factory remained.[33] The sequence of events at Blarney demonstrates quite clearly the subordinate nature of the aesthetic considerations involved in the modernizing transformation of Irish towns and villages: without the support of a viable economy, no town, however finely wrought, could expect to thrive.

Elsewhere, however, this conjunction of aesthetics and economics appears to have been more successfully established, at least during the pre-Famine period. At Pilltown, County Kilkenny, the earl of Bessborough's town and demesne were both rebuilt in the 1820s by the local agent, a man described as "being of considerable taste . . . [who] was extremely anxious to improve and beautify the spot over which he had . . . an almost absolute control," but crucially his endeavors were supported by the initially successful foundation of corn mills and other agrarian industries.[34] Similarly, at Ballinasloe, County Galway, the principle streets were described in the 1840s as being "wide, airy and spacious and replete with pretension." They were held to reflect the "tasteful, liberal and benign spirit" of the town's proprietor, the earl of Clancarty, who had everywhere "worked such reform, and impressed such decorations and asserted such ascendancy" over the town.[35]

Clancarty's investments were made all the more worthwhile by the then-flourishing state of the town's economy, which derived from its nodal location at the western end of the Grand Canal. This encouraged Ballinasloe's growth as the major transshipment point for the imports and exports generated by the agrarian economy over a large part of northeast Connacht. On a more local level of nodality, the village of Collon, County Meath, was one of several designed or refounded by their proprietors—in this case Lord Oriel—using the picturesque "cottage ornee" style that became fashionable in the early nineteenth century. Others included Ardagh, County Longford; Dromahair, County Leitrim—improved by George Lane Fox; Drumcondra, County Dublin— described in 1846 as a "picturesque and aristocratic village"; and Enniskerry, County Wicklow.[36]

The uniform application of this peculiarly ornate style to these settlements is still capable of generating a profound "sense of place" today, and this is something that is perhaps lacking in towns and villages redeveloped over a longer period using the plainer neoclassical idiom. However, it is this so-called Georgian architectural style that is by far the most widespread among the improved towns and villages of Ireland. Its extensive use reflected its continuing popularity among all social classes in the later eighteenth and early nineteenth century. The style was prevalent from the 1750s up until the Famine, but during this time its minor decorative features changed very little. Accordingly, the "visual uniformity" that it imparts to many Irish towns and villages must be regarded as being, quite possibly, the consequence of building decisions taken over a century or more by successive generations of landlords and tenants, and as such provides testimony to the inherently emulative and conservative nature of much provincial Irish architecture. Only occasionally in the public buildings erected at proprietorial expense is there evidence of real architectural sophistication rather than a willingness to indulge in mere ornamentation. One of the most striking examples of this is the extraordinarily complex baroque market house built in 1743 at Dunlavin, County Wicklow, by the local landlord, the Hon. R. Tynte, at a reputed cost of £1,200.[37] Other equally sophisticated public buildings include the courthouse at Hillsborough built by Lord Downshire between 1765 and 1790, and the market house at Newtownards built by Lord Londonderry between 1765 and 1771, both in County Down.[38]

Architecture of this sophistication stood in stark contrast to the generally much more restrained domestic buildings erected by most tenants accepting building leases. But as we have noted, even here, tenants might be concerned to apply—in however debased a form—once-fashionable ornament in order to signal their pretensions to a desired social status. Arguably, where landlords insisted on minimum standards for property, the iconographical significance of the resulting buildings is likely to have been increased. Only tenants with sufficient capital to meet these conditions could afford to take one of these leases, and they were by definition among those best able to contemplate investing in "polite" rather than vernacular architecture. Hence by insisting on minimum building requirements, landlords are likely to have encouraged the imitative use of fashionable architectural forms by tenants seeking to make status-enhancing statements about themselves. Instances of this form of landlord stipulation occurred on the Strabane estate of the earl (subsequently duke) of Abercorn from 1757 onward; on the Killarney property of Viscount Kenmare in the 1750s and 1760s;

and on the Edenderry estate of the marquis of Downshire in the 1820s and 1830s.[39]

Property and the Limitations to Landed Authority

On the basis of the evidence presented here, therefore, it seems likely that the willingness with which the sixth duke of Devonshire was prepared to sacrifice property in pursuit of political objectives was relatively unusual among Irish landowners, even in the context of their increasing political vulnerability in the post-Union period. Where other landlords sought to assert or maintain control of their boroughs, they seem generally to have found less expensive and less materially inconvenient ways of achieving this control. For many landowners, a more fundamental concern was the enhancement of their income by means of various investment strategies. Some of these strategies, such as the extension and modernization of the agricultural marketing system, were well in tune with the structural characteristics of the Irish economy. They thus tended to be more successful than other investments such as mining, which were limited in their potential by the restricted nature of Ireland's mineral and energy resources.

Common sense dictates why there should have been this emphasis on these sorts of economic enterprise. In order to provide for themselves the disposable income required to support those political, social, or cultural activities that might result in the further enhancement of their elite status, Irish landlords had first to ensure the continuing security of their economic base in property ownership. Viewed in this light, the attitude of the fifth and seventh dukes of Devonshire, with their shared concern with the income rather than the political authority that derived from their Irish estate, seems likely to have been more typical of Irish landowners' attitudes to property than the political motives that governed the interventionism of the sixth duke.

And yet even during the height of the political interventionism on the Devonshire estate during the first quarter of the nineteenth century, the auditor, Sir James Abercrombie, sounded a warning as to the likely cost in property of the duke's political goals. Clearly, some at least of the sixth duke's advisers were well aware of the contingent relationship between the assertion of political authority and the possession of economic property. To assert the former required possession of the latter, although admittedly not necessarily in the same place. In a sense therefore, Abercrombie's cautious views were an expression of the most deep-rooted, even atavistic, motivations that arose out of property ownership in Ireland. If the assertion of the elite status of the property-owning minority depended on the wealth that accrued to them from their monopolistic control of land as the means of production, then, clearly, the maintenance of that elite position required the maintenance of that economic authority. Accordingly, any challenge to this economic authority was in effect a challenge to the position of the elite itself.

It is this fundamental relationship between the elite's possession of wealth and their ability to dominate pre-Famine Irish society that accounts for the importance of their attempts to control the system of production and marketing within the country at large, either through the sorts of urban and rural investments described on the Devonshire estate or else through the exertion of their rights of property in their tenurial relationship with their tenants. The actions taken by individual landlords obviously depended on their own attitudes and objectives, but even in the case of the most complacent absentee landlords, content merely to receive at a distance *some* rents out of their Irish estates, their status as *property owners* ensured for them and their heirs a controlling position within the relations of production. In short, even the most inactive nonimproving Irish landlord played a part in the reproduction of the social authority emanating out of property ownership, because of what he *was*, not because of what he *did*.

Where landowners *were* prepared to intervene directly or indirectly in the organization of marketing and production, they were likely to enhance their beneficial interest in their property to a commensurately greater extent. It has already been noted that with the exception of the growth of industrial capitalism in east Ulster in the early nineteenth century, the pre-Famine Irish economy remained agrarian, space-extensive, and land-based. Indeed, it was to remain so throughout the rest of the island for the remainder of the nineteenth century. Accordingly, during the pre-Famine period, the value of production continued to be realized at those points of exchange—the urban and village markets—that had been established to facilitate this. Thus by first establishing and then controlling the operation of these markets, landlords might expect to ensure that their preferential property interests in the organization of the agrarian economy on their estates would continue to be protected. They would benefit, for example, from the tolls exacted for the use of the market, from the additional rents paid for any property that had been built in expectation of an increase in the size of the permanent population attracted to the market, and from any rise in the value of the lands on their estate as a result of the more efficient marketing of their tenants' produce. Moreover, in time, the continued growth of these markets would attract other, noneconomic, functions such as schools and churches, and might require the presence of representative forms of authority such as a barracks, courthouse, or jail. All of these provided the landowner with an opportunity to assert his authority still further by either funding these institutions or playing a role in their management. Where a market settlement was being newly founded on a "greenfield site," these symbols of proprietorial authority were usually provided from the start.

If, as argued here, the key to the maintenance of the elite's authority in pre-Famine Ireland was thus an economic one, and lay in their control of the conditions under which production and marketing took place, it has nevertheless also been demonstrated that the success of this strategy was vulnerable to secular economic trends over which the property-owning minority had little control. The monopolistic nature of the landownership enjoyed by the propertied elite in Ireland ensured that some form of property delegation was inevitable: not all property could be held *in demesne*. It has been suggested that the leasehold system used to operationalize this delegation represented a form of compromise between the (inevitably) conflicting property interests of the landlord and the tenant, since any gains by one party had to be at the expense of the other. Thus much of the expansion in the Irish agricultural economy in the later eighteenth century was very much at the expense of the property interests of the landowning minority, since their predecessors had previously delegated extensive property rights to a leasehold class who, sitting on relatively low rents fixed in the 1730s and 1740s, were the immediate beneficiaries of the subsequent rise in land values.

This disproportionate apportionment of the gains of the agrarian expansion of the late eighteenth century to the more substantial tenant classes gave them a vested interest in the continuation of the existing economic formation, since it validated not only their possession of their (rented) property, but also the considerable gains they had made. Thus while the benefits to these agricultural leaseholders may have been greater than landowners originally anticipated when setting leases forty years previously, they nevertheless had the advantage of securing the tenants' participation in the existing system and thus their acquiescence in the landlord's domination of it. In the towns, too, similar sorts of thinking seem to have prevailed, and landowners frequently sought to share the capital costs involved in urban and village improvement by offering their tenants building leases. As in the countryside, this had the desirable effect from the landlord's point of view of aligning his tenants' economic interest with his own, but also as in the countryside, only at the possible expense to him of a considerable loss of income. Nevertheless, in theory, each party stood to gain something from this arrangement: the landlord because he was able to reduce the cost of securing the admittedly necessarily reduced economic base on which his status rested; the tenant because in return for the initial capital outlay in constructing the property, he stood to gain, perhaps considerably, from any future increase in its value.

Thus, depending on a combination of the long-term performance of the economy and local circumstance, the property delegation made necessary by the monopolistic pattern of property ownership in pre-Famine Ireland could work to the benefit of either the landlords or the tenants. Not surprisingly, therefore, it was subject to a continual process of adjustment, as landlords and tenants alike tried to improve their beneficial interests in the agreements they struck with each other, in the light of their perception of the changing pattern of present and—probable—future economic opportunity. Within these negotiations, however, the landlords always had the controlling advantage of being able to specify the terms and conditions under which property might be delegated to the tenant, although their opportunity to do so depended on the falling in of existing leases. Where the previous delegation of property rights had been overgenerous to the tenantry, these opportunities might be delayed, perhaps indefinitely. The landlord would then remain locked out from further participation in the management of his property and unable to reinforce his economic interests in it. Something of the sort appears to have happened at Kenmare, County Kerry, where in 1846 the proprietor, Lord Kenmare, was described as "being unhappily prevented from attempting [the town's] improvement because it is held under leases for ever."[40] At Roscrea, County Tipperary, the tenurial situation was more complicated but its inimical effect on improvement was much the same. Originally the property of the Damer family, the town had been devised along with the rest of their Tipperary estates to an absentee relative, who had subsequently mortgaged the property to London bankers for £400,000. By the 1830s an increasing amount of property in the town was falling out of lease, but none of this could be improved: the mortgagees did not have the authority to undertake such improvements and the ground landlord had neither the desire nor the ability to do so.[41]

Paralleling the survival of these sorts of extensive leasehold interests in towns and villages throughout early nineteenth century Ireland were instances where landlords attempted to reduce the number and length of the leases on their estates as a means of acquiring a greater share of the increasing value of their property, particularly prior to the agricultural price collapse of 1815–1820. The evidence for this on the Devonshire estates and for Ireland generally has been recited in chapters 5 and 6. It can be argued that neither situation was particularly favorable to the reproduction of the economic authority of the landed class in the long term. Where extensive tenant leaseholds survived, these not only prevented any increase in proprietorial incomes, but also provided an economic base for the assertion of the social but particularly the political aspirations of the tenants themselves.

The significance of this lay in the fact that the major beneficiary of Ireland's pre-Famine population growth had been the Catholic community, and accordingly it was they who constituted an ever-growing majority among the tenantry. Their political aspirations were hardly consonant with those of the landed minority, yet it was they who were the major beneficiaries of the surviving leasehold tenures in virtually every part of Ireland save Ulster in the early nineteenth century.[42] Consequently, we may conclude that the property delegation made necessary by the uneven and colonial character of landownership in Ireland after 1703, and favored by eighteenth-century landlords as a means of coercing tenant economic interests, became the instrument through

which the landlords' authority as a social and political elite could increasingly be challenged in the early nineteenth century following the
rehabilitation of Catholic property rights by the repeal of the Penal
Laws.

Moreover, even where landlords succeeded in eradicating these
lengthy leasehold interests on their estates and replaced them with
shorter terms of years or, for sitting tenants in the towns, annual,
monthly, or weekly tenancies, this may not necessarily have secured
their long-term economic interests. In effect, these tenurial adjustments represented a reduction in the beneficial property interests of a
significant section of the—by now predominantly Catholic—tenant
community, and thus arguably a diminution in the extent to which
their economic interests were coaligned with those of the propertied
minority. For these groups, who were thus facing once again a form of
economic marginalization, only this time for economic rather than political reasons, there was no longer any immediately obvious advantage
to be gained in acquiescing in the power structures of the existing
socioeconomic system. Arguably, therefore, they may have become
more susceptible to the appeal of the various radical political and
agrarian redresser movements that flourished in Ireland at this time,
and which, whatever their ostensible proximate objectives, posed a
common challenge to the authority of the traditional landed elite.[43] In
short, at a time when the general process of constitutional and political
change in early-nineteenth-century Ireland favored the increasing assertion of majority political aspirations for Emancipation, Repeal, and
Reform—all of them issues inimical to landlord interests—the ongoing
processes of tenurial adjustment were either favoring Catholic domination of surviving leaseholds, and thus strengthening the economic
basis of their mobilization as a politicized community, or else were
eroding the more general linkages of mutual self-interest that secured
the tenants' participation in the reproduction of the existing economic
formation.

Quite how far and how quickly these changes would have proceeded
had the Potato Famine not intervened in 1845–1849 to impose its own
distorting pattern of crisis and disruption on Ireland's land and people
is a matter for speculation. But it is clear that the loss of over two million people in the six years prior to 1851 and the net loss of at least an-

other two million by 1911 had profound consequences both for the structure of agararian society and the provincial towns that served it.[44] Perhaps one-quarter of all productive land in Ireland changed hands by 1861 as a result of Famine-induced bankruptcies among the landlord class. These fundamental shifts in the pattern of landownership have not been systematically explored. It therefore remains an open question whether they resulted in a further but temporary concentration of land and therefore economic authority in the hands of the existing landed elite, as convention asserts, or whether they resulted in a significant widening of the social distribution of land ownership.[45] If it was the latter, then the "landlord interest" is itself likely to have changed and perhaps weakened at a time when the pace and nature of the challenge it faced from other, previously marginalized, social groups was accelerating. Alternatively, the further consolidation of landownership into the hands of a "Darwinian elite" among landlords who had successfully survived the financial rigors of the Famine may well account for Hoppen's suggested reassertion of landlord political authority in the 1850s.[46]

These possible changes in the social composition and economic authority of the post-Famine landed elite would have had a bearing on the Famine's effects elsewhere in Irish provincial society. By decimating the poorest and most vulnerable sections of rural society, the Famine not only destroyed the nationalist and emancipationist political constituency marshalled by O'Connell in the 1820s, but—arguably—replaced it with a correspondingly strengthened tenant farming class. The point is debateable and rests on who, precisely, were the major economic beneficiaries of the efficiency gains in Irish agriculture caused by the Famine's destruction of most of the marginally productive peasantry. In the standard revisionist view, most recently articulated by Vaughan, tenant farmers gained most from a situation characterized by falling real rents and labor costs and the rising value of agricultural output. On this reading, landlords, already decimated and demoralized by the Famine, failed to invest adequately in their land in the 1850s and 1860s, and were thus in no position to subsidize their tenants when these faced increasing hardship during the deepening agricultural crisis of the late 1870s.[47]

In terms of the argument pursued here, this failure effectively destroyed whatever remained of the already weakened ties of mutual self-interest between landowners and their tenants. Accordingly, the latter turned to secular, radical, and sometimes revolutionary political groups such as the Fenian Irish Republican Brotherhood and the Land League to represent their interests in what was to become an increasingly externalized *political* challenge to residual landlord authority. Arguably, it was the growing strength and effectiveness of this challenge that finally led the state to begin to dismantle the structures of monopolistic landownership through the aegis of successive Land Acts in the period after 1870.

Athough this conventional revisionist view has not gone unchallenged, there can be no doubt over the terminal character of the challenge posed by the Land Acts to the Irish landed interest. Thus while Hoppen and Turner argue for an almost precisely opposite interpretation of the apportionment of the rewards of agriculture between 1850 and 1876, they too accept the thesis that the landed class faced economic extinction sanctioned by the legislative power of the state. Consequently, if Turner's calculation—that rents and labor costs rose between 1850 and 1876 by up to 20 percent while gross farming profits remained virtually static—proves to be accurate, this represented no more than a temporary deviation in the progressive erosion of the landowners' economic and social authority.[48] The increasingly radical and secular nature of agrarian tenant politics at this time might then be seen as the politicization of members of the property-using majority in response to the further—albeit temporary—reassertion of the beneficial property interests of the property-owning minority, whose monopoly of land ownership had been reinforced as an adventitious consequence of the Famine.

Whatever the true balance of economic power between the landowners and their tenants prior to the Land War, it is clear that from the landlords' point of view, the land legislation was ultimately to prove more destructive of their residual authority and status than any previous constitutional or revolutionary challenge mounted by their tenants. The activities of the Land League, first in Mayo, and then increasingly throughout Ireland between 1879 and 1881, represented a challenge to the authority of the state in Ireland which the government could not ignore. Mobilized on the twin issues of Home Rule and agrarian reform, first under the leadership of Michael Davitt and later under Charles Parnell, the Land League provided the means whereby tenants could withdraw from further acquiescence in the inequable distribution of landed property that underpined economic and social authority in Ireland.

Viewed in this light, the destruction of the existing pattern of land-ownership, and with it the economic base of the possibly already rede-fined landowning elite, was inevitable. The 1870 Land Act attempted to adjust the balance of beneficial property rights between landlord and tenant on the basis of customary usage; subsequent Land Acts strength-ened tenant rights still further, but also began to make increasingly at-tractive financial provision for tenant land purchase. The 1881 act established a Land Commission to set "fair" or judicial rents where ten-ants made application for these, and a Land Court was created to adju-dicate disputes between landlords and their tenants. The act also made available low-cost loans to enable tenants to purchase their farms, but so generous were the rent abatements established by the Land Com-mission—commonly between 15 and 20 percent—that barely 750 tenants availed themselves of this opportunity to buy: it remained cheaper, and just as secure, to rent. However, the Ashbourne or "Land Purchase" Act of 1885 improved the balance of beneficial interest in tenant purchase by making it possible to borrow all of the purchase money at an interest rate reduced from 5 to 4 percent. Some £5 million was made available for tenant purchase under this act, and over 25,000 tenants purchased more than 940,000 acres of land under its provisions by 1888.

Subsequent Land Acts in 1887, 1888, 1891, and 1896 were either amending bills or else were flawed from the tenants' point of view by the insertion of various restrictive clauses. Thus it was not until the Wyndham Act was passed in 1903 that the next major transfer of prop-erty ownership from landlords to their tenants occurred. The Wynd-ham Act approached the problem from the landlords' perspective, and offered them an additional bonus of 12 percent of the agreed price as an incentive to sell their estates in their entirety. Moreover, they could subsequently buy their demesne lands back from the Estates Commis-sion on the same favorable terms as their erstwhile tenants. Although some nationalist opinion saw the terms of the Wyndham Act as being unduly favorable to the landed interest, the act was in fact responsible

for the single most significant transfer of landownership from the landowning minority to the tenant majority. By 1908 some £84 million had
been committed to the purchase of over seven million acres of land,
leaving barely one-seventh of that amount still to be disposed of by
successive parliamentary jurisdictions between 1909 and 1933.[49]

These rural challenges to landlord authority were paralleled in the
towns by the further erosion of their residual patronal authority by the
creation of various municipal institutions whose authority was sanctioned by the state. Moreover, the landowners' once important role as
agents of urban innovation effectively ended with the Famine. Their
formal rights to collect market tolls had been extinguished by legislation in the 1830s, and in the post-Famine period the loss of population, the reduction in the size of the domestic market, and its growing
penetration by the products of English industrial capitalism had all
combined to make redundant their previous urban-based marketing initiatives. In effect, Ireland was by now overprovided with provincial
marketing towns, and the creation of new centers no longer made economic sense. The very small number of new towns and villages that
were established were designed to fulfill functionally specific purposes
as seaside resorts (Buncrana), packet-stations (Donaghadee), or dormitory towns (Bray).

These changing post-Famine economic contexts not only militated
against further landlord promotion of the marketing system, but they
also limited the economic benefits the landowners' derived from the
towns and villages already in their possession. At best, urban rent rolls
might show some small increase, as at Tallow and Lismore, but generally their performance was weak and reflected the progressive stagnation experienced by many sectors of the provincial urban economy.
Thus not only was it no longer possible for landowners to control the
provincial urban marketing system as they had once done, but this in
any case no longer provided the key to the maintenance of their economic authority in landownership. As we have seen, this was being
challenged quite independently by the agricultural tenants' success in
engaging the sympathetic attention of institutions of state that were no
longer dominated by and representative of the landed elite.

Finale

The passage of the Land Acts signaled the beginning of the end of the propertied elite's monopoly of landownership in Ireland. Subject to increasing coercion by the state and fearful of falling land values if they continued to hold out, landowners throughout Ireland finally submitted to the dismemberment of the property basis of their class. As the present analysis makes clear, even magnate landowners of the wealth and status of the duke of Devonshire were not immune to this process. While it is undoubtedly true that some landowners, including the eighth duke, welcomed the opportunity to rid themselves of land that they found increasingly difficult and expensive to manage, the argument here is that the loss of this land on such a grand scale led to the final termination of the social and political authority of the landed class as a recognizable entity in Ireland. Moreover, this hemorrhaging away of land provided the final—if somewhat delayed—coup de grace for the landowners' involvement in urban improvement. Without the ownership of extensive acres, there was little point in landlords attempting to rearticulate the urban market network in order to enhance their control of the agrarian economy—their one-time basis in wealth.

Where economic elites continued to thrive, they did so on a socially reconstituted basis and drew their wealth and authority from industry rather than from the land. The traditional landed elite, created in large measure by the colonial transformations of the sixteenth and seventeenth centuries, and subsequently transformed by the processes of economic and social modernization and constitutional and political change that had characterized Ireland throughout the eighteenth and nineteenth centuries, effectively no longer existed as an economically important force in Irish life. The challenge posed to this elite by the political mobilization of an impoverished peasantry in the cause of Emancipation before the Famine had been replaced by an ultimately fatal one emanating from the political radicalization of significant sections of a numerically smaller, but wealthier tenant farming community afterward. Given a sufficient economic incentive in the agricultural crisis of 1876–1879, these farmers proved themselves as capable as their predecessors of teaching the government a lesson in the politics of mass activism. The lesson was not ignored, and to this extent the politically led and externally imposed destruction of the Irish landowners as an economic class can be said to have been due to the finally successful demand for enhanced property rights by the long-alienated property-using majority.

In many ways the Devonshires' wealth and influence—in particular their ownership of vast properties in England—insulated them from the more localist pressures inherent in this decline. Their magnate status clearly provided them with a range of alternative management strategies that were not available to the majority of their less wealthy fellow landowners in Ireland. In a very real sense, the latter were much more the prisoners of their immediate Irish circumstances than the Devonshires ever could be. Landlords who depended on their Irish estates for most of their income were likely to be forced into a much more rapid accommodation with the forces challenging the social system that legitimized this ownership.

But as this discussion has shown, not even the duke of Devonshire could afford to ignore the processes of economic and social modernization and political liberalization that were gathering pace throughout nineteenth-century Ireland. While it would be wrong to conclude that successive dukes were hostile to these changes, it is nevertheless true that the pace of change sometimes exceeded even their generally liberal vision, and certainly on occasion challenged their concept of the rights of property ownership. For the most part, however, the sixth and seventh dukes, in particular, tried to accommodate the increasingly rapid pace of social and political change as it affected their towns and farms in Ireland.

That the Devonshires had their own agenda is clear enough, as is the fact that this was dominated by the growing financial problems on their English estates. As the relatively inelastic Irish remittances began to be dwarfed by the massive increase in the duke's industrial and investment income after 1850, so the Irish estate lost its earlier importance in the overall scheme of things. Increasingly, it came to be regarded as a disposable asset, to be sold as and when circumstances in England demanded it and conditions in Ireland were sufficiently favorable to warrant it. Given the increasing challenge to the position of the landowning minority in Ireland and the growing ambivalence of the state's support for them, this attitude is hardly surprising. Thus when the final eclipse of landed economic authority came at the end of the nineteenth century, the eighth duke of Devonshire readily acquiesced both in this and its inevitable consequence: the rapid dissipation of whatever social and political authority remained to his fellow Irish landowners. It is ironic, therefore, that when the country was partitioned in 1921, the "rancorous ideologies" that the sixth duke had sought so long to keep apart finally triumphed, and in so doing signaled the changed realities of life in Ireland. In the newly emergent independent Irish state, the diminishing rump of one-time Irish landlords faced a hostile and uncertain future as an anachronistic legacy of a disregarded colonial past.

Notes

Abbreviations

B. L.	British Library, London.
CW.	
[Currey] Ms.	Documents lodged at Chatsworth, Derbyshire, England, by Currey & Co. (London), solicitors to the duke of Devonshire.
CW. Ms.	The Chatsworth Papers relating to the 1st – 11th dukes of Devonshire, held at Chatsworth, Derbyshire.
L.E.O.	Lismore Estate Office Papers relating to the duke of Devonshire's Irish estates, Lismore Castle Estate Office, Lismore, County Waterford, Ireland. Subsequently transferred to the Waterford County Library Service, Lismore.
L.P.	Lismore Papers held at the National Library of Ireland, Dublin.
N.L.I.	National Library of Ireland, Dublin.
P.R.O.I.	Public Record Office of Ireland, Dublin.
P.R.O.N.I.	Public Record Office for Northern Ireland, Belfast.
T.C.D.	Trinity College, Dublin.

Chapter 1. Historians, Landlords, and Irish Towns

1. This figure is based on the results of a three-year research project carried out jointly by the author and Dr. B. J. Graham, of the University of Ulster, and funded by the Leverhulme Trust.

2. F.H.A. Aalen, *Man and the Landscape in Ireland* (London, 1978), 279–284; A. R. Orme, *The World's Landscapes*, vol 4: *Ireland* (London, 1970), 138–45.

3. J. Bateman, *The Great Landowners of Great Britain and Ireland*, 5th ed. (Leicester, 1971), 168, 208; D. Cannadine, "The Landowner as Millionaire: The Finances of the Dukes of Devonshire, c. 1800–c. 1926," *Agricultural History Review* 25, no. 2 (1977): 92.

4. Cannadine, "Landowner as Millionaire," 85–87.

5. L. P. Curtis, "Incumbered Wealth: Landed Indebtedness in Post-Famine Ireland," *American Historical Review* 85, no. 1 (1980): 332–67; D. Large, "The Wealth of the Greater Irish Landowners, 1750–1815," *Irish Historical Studies* 15 (1966): 21–45.

6. E. R. Hooker, *Readjustments of Agricultural Tenure in Ireland* (Chapel Hill, N. C., 1938); N. D. Palmer, *The Irish Land League Crisis* (New Haven, Conn., 1940); J. E. Pomfret, *The Struggle for Land in Ireland, 1800–1923* (Princeton, N.J., 1930).

7. T. Jones Hughes, "The Estate System of Landholding in Nineteenth Century Ireland," in W. Nolan, ed., *The Shaping of Ireland: The Geographical Perspective* (Dublin, 1986), 137.

8. B. J. Graham and L. J. Proudfoot, "A Perspective on the Nature of Irish Historical Geography," in B. J. Graham and L. J. Proudfoot, eds., *An Historical Geography of Ireland* (London, 1993), 1–18.

9. T. Bartlett, "The Origins and Progress of the Catholic Question in Ireland, 1690–1800," in T. P. Power and K. Whelan, eds., *Endurance and Emergence: Catholics in Ireland in the Eighteenth Century* (Dublin, 1990), 1–20; W. N. Osborough, "Catholics, Land, and the Popery Acts of Anne," in T. P. Power and K. Whelan, eds., *Endurance and Emergence: Catholics in Ireland in the Eighteenth Century* (Dublin, 1990), 21–56.

10. L. M. Cullen, *An Economic History of Ireland since 1660*, 2d ed. (London, 1987), 77–83, 113–17, 138–40; J. S. Donnelly, *The Land and the People of Nineteenth-Century Cork* (London, 1975); B. L. Solow, *The Land Question and the Irish Economy, 1870–1903* (Cambridge, Mass., 1971); W. E. Vaughan, "Landlord and Tenant Relations in Ireland between the Famine and the Land War, 1850–70," in L. M. Cullen and T. C. Smout, eds., *Comparative Aspects of Scottish and Irish Economic and Social History, 1600–1900* (Edinburgh, 1977), 216–26.

11. Summarized in W. E. Vaughan, *Landlords and Tenants in Ireland, 1848–1904*, Studies in Irish Economic and Social History no. 2 (Dundalk, 1984), 3–41.

12. R. D. Crotty, *Irish Agricultural Production: Its Volume and Structure* (Cork, 1966), 84–107; C. Ó Gráda, *Ireland Before and After the Famine* (Manchester, 1988), 131–35; Solow, *Land Question*, 50–88.

13. J. V. Beckett, *The Aristocracy in England, 1600–1914* (Oxford, 1986), 171–83; C. Ó Gráda, "The Investment Behaviour of Irish Landlords 1850–1875: Some Preliminary Findings," *Agricultural History Review* 23, no. 2 (1975): 139–55; P. Roebuck, "Rent Movement, Proprietorial Incomes and Agricultural Development, 1730–1830," in P. Roebuck, ed., *Plantation to Partition* (Belfast, 1981), 82–101; W. E. Vaughan, "An Assessment of the Economic Performance of Irish Landlords, 1851–1881," in F. S. L. Lyons and R. A. J. Hawkins, eds., *Ireland under the Union: Varieties of Tension* (Oxford, 1980), 173–99; idem, "Agricultural Output, Rents and Wages in Ireland, 1850–1880," in L. M. Cullen and F. Furet, eds., *Irlande et France, XVIe–XXe siècles* (Paris, 1980), 85–93.

14. W. H. Crawford, "Ulster Landowners and the Linen Industry," in J. T. Ward and R. G. Wilson, eds., *Land and Industry: The Landed Estate and the Industrial Revolution* (Newton Abbot, 1971), 117–44; idem, "Landlord-Tenant Relations in Ulster, 1609–1820," *Irish Economic and Social History*, 2 (1975): 5–21; idem, "The Influence of the Landlord in Eighteenth-Century Ulster," in Cullen and Smout, eds., *Comparative Aspects*, 193–203.

15. W. J. Lowe, "Landlord and Tenant on the Estate of Trinity College, Dublin, 1851–1903," *Hermathena*, 120 (1976): 5–24; R. MacCarthy, *The Trinity College Estates, 1800–1923* (Dundalk, 1992), passim.

16. Large, "Wealth," 21–45; W. A. Maguire, *The Downshire Estates in Ireland, 1801–1845* (Oxford, 1972), passim.

17. M. Turner, "Rural Economies in Post-Famine Ireland, c. 1850–1914," in Graham and Proudfoot, eds., *Historical Geography of Ireland*, 293–337; K. T. Hoppen, *Ireland since 1800: Conflict and Conformity* (London, 1989), 90–94.

18. Ibid.

19. W. G. Neely, *Kilcooley: Land and People in Tipperary* (privately published, 1983), 1–90; W. Nolan, *Fassadinin: Land, Settlement and Society in South-East Ireland, 1600–1850* (Dublin, 1979), 84–216.

20. A. Horner, "Land Transactions and the Making of Carton Demesne," *Journal of the County Kildare Archaeological Society* 15 (1974): 387–96; idem, "Carton, Co. Kildare: A Case Study of the Making of an Irish Demesne," *Quarterly Bulletin of the Irish Georgian Society* 18 (1975): 45–104; W. J. Smyth, "Estate Records and the Making of the Irish Landscape: An Example from County Tipperary," *Irish Geography* 9 (1976): 29–49.

21. P. O'Flanagan, "Rural Change South of the River Bride in Counties Cork and Waterford: The Surveyors' Evidence 1716–1851," *Irish Geography* 15 (1982): 51–69.

22. T. Jones Hughes, "Landholding and Settlement in County Tipperary in the Nineteenth Century," in W. Nolan, ed., *Tipperary: History and Society* (Dublin, 1985), 339–66, idem, "Estate System," 137–50, idem, "Continuity and Change in Rural County Wexford in the Nineteenth Century," in K. Whelan, ed., *Wexford History and Society* (Dublin, 1987), 342–72.

23. Jones Hughes, "Estate System," passim.

24. T. Jones Hughes, "Society and Settlement in Nineteenth-Century Ireland," *Irish Geography* 5 (1964–1968): 79.

25. Orme, *Ireland*, 143.

26. L. M. Cullen, "The Social and Cultural Modernisation of Rural Ireland, 1600–1900," in Cullen and Furet, eds, *Irlande et France*, 198–200; M. E. Daly, "Irish Urban History: A Survey," *Urban History Yearbook* (Leicester, 1986), 64.

27. A. A. Horner, "The Scope and the Limitations of the Landlord Contribution to Changing the Irish Landscape, 1700–1850," in *Collected Papers Presented at the Permanent European Conference for the Study of the Rural Landscape, Denmark Session, 1979* (Copenhagen, 1981), 71–78.

28. D. Dickson, "The Evolution of Social Structure in Eighteenth Century South Munster," (unpublished paper), cited in Horner, "Scope," 73; J. H. Gebbie, ed., *An Introduction to the Abercorn Letters (As Relating to Ireland, 1736–1816)* (Omagh, 1972); W. E. Vaughan, *Sin, Sheep, and Scotsmen* (Belfast, 1983), 17.

29. Daly, "Irish Urban History," 61–72; idem, "An Alien Entity? Attitudes to the City in Late-Nineteenth- and Twentieth-Century Ireland," *Etudes Irlandaises*, 11 (1985): 181–94.

30. C. Doherty, "The Monastic Town in Early Medieval Ireland," in H. B. Clark and A. Simms, eds., *The Comparative History of Urban Origins in Non-Roman Europe: Ireland, Wales, Denmark, Germany, Poland, and Russia from the Ninth to the Thirteenth Centuries* (Oxford, 1985), 45–76; B. J. Graham, "Anglo-Norman Colonisation and the Size and Spread of the Colonial Town in Medieval Ireland," in Clark and Simms, eds., *Comparative History*, 361–63; idem, The Evolution of Urbanisation in Medieval Ireland," *Journal of Historical Geography* 5, no. 2 (1979): 111–25; idem, "Urban Genesis in Early Medieval Ireland," *Journal of Historical Geography* 13, no. 1, (1987): 3–16; idem, "The Definition and Classification of Medieval Irish Towns," *Irish Geography* 21, no. 1 (1988): 20–32.

31. Daly, "Irish Urban History," 65–69.

32. Summarized in R. Dennis and H. Prince, "Research in British Urban Historical Geography," in D. Denecke and G. Shaw, eds., *Urban Historical Geography: Recent Progress in Britain and Germany* (Cambridge, England, 1988), 9–23. Individual case studies include D. J. Olsen, *Town Planning in London: The Eighteenth and Nineteenth Centuries* (New Haven, Conn., 1964), and J. Springett, "Landowners and Urban Development: The Ramsden Estate and Nineteenth-Century Huddersfield," *Journal of Historical Geography* 8 (1982): 129–44.

33. D. Cannadine, *Lords and Landlords: The Aristocracy and the Towns, 1774–1967* (Leicester, 1980), passim.

34. A. Sutcliffe, review of *Lords and Landlords,* by D. Cannadine, *Economic History Review,* 2d ser., 34, no. 3 (1981): 482–83.

35. Cannadine, *Lords and Landlords,* 21–80, 147–97, 333–53, 370–430.

36. D. Cannadine, ed., *Patricians, Power and Politics in Nineteenth-Century Towns* (Leicester, 1982), 17–122.

37. R. Trainor, "Peers on an Industrial Frontier: The Earls of Dartmouth and Dudley in the Black Country, c. 1810 to 1914," in Cannadine, ed., *Patricians,* 69–122.

38. Beckett, *Aristocracy,* 262–86.

39. J. V. Beckett, *Coal and Tobacco: The Lowthers and the Economic Development of West Cumberland, 1660–1760* (Cambridge, England 1981), chap. 7; M. J. Mortimore, "Landownership and Economic Growth in Bradford and Its Environs in the West Riding Conurbation, 1850–1900," *Transactions of the Institute of British Geographers* 46 (1969): 105–19; R. S. Neale, *Bath: A Social History, 1680–1850* (London, 1981), 95–170; Springett, "Ramsden Estate," 129–44; D. Ward, "The Pre–Urban Cadaster and the Urban Pattern of Leeds," *Annals of the Association of American Geographers* 52 (1962): 151–65.

40. Beckett, *Aristocracy,* 267–72.

41. D. Lieven, *The Aristocracy in Europe, 1815–1914* (London, 1992), 109–18.

42. Beckett, *Aristocracy,* 482.

43. Ibid., 276–78; Lieven, *Aristocracy in Europe,* 112–18.

44. M. Craig, *Dublin, 1660–1850* (Dublin, 1952); C. Maxwell, *Dublin under the Georges, 1714–1850* (Dublin, 1937).

45. W. A. Maguire, "Lord Donegall and the Sale of Belfast: A Case History from the Encumbered Estates Court," *Economic History Review,* 2d ser., 24 (1976): 570–84; idem, "The 1822 Settlement of the Donegall Estates," *Irish Economic and Social History,* 3 (1976): 17–32.

46. L. A. Clarkson, "An Anatomy of an Irish Town: The Economy of Armagh in 1770," *Irish Economic and Social History* 5 (1978): 27–45; idem, "Armagh 1770: Portrait of an Urban Community," in D. Harkness and M. O'Dowd, eds., *The Town in Ireland* (Belfast, 1981), 81–103.

47. L. A. Clarkson, "The Demography of Carrick-on-Suir, 1799," *Proceedings of the Royal Irish Academy* 87, no. 2 (1987): 13–36. See also R. A. Butlin, "The Population of Dublin in the Late Seventeenth Century," *Irish Geography* 5 (1964–1968): 51–66, and A. R. Orme, "Youghal, County Cork — Growth, Decay, Resurgence," *Irish Geography* 5 (1966): 121–49.

48. P. Connell, *Changing Forces Shaping a Nineteenth-Century Irish Town: A Case Study of Navan* (Maynooth, 1978), 8–19; Cullen, *Ireland,* 121–23, 140–42.

49. P. O'Flanagan, "Urban Minorities and Majorities: Catholics and Protestants in Munster Towns c. 1659–1850," in W. J. Smyth and K. Whelan, eds., *Common Ground: Essays on the Historical Geography of Ireland Presented to T. Jones Hughes* (Cork, 1988), 124–45.

50. K. Theodore Hoppen, *Elections, Politics, and Society in Ireland, 1832–1885* (Oxford, 1984), passim; P. Jupp, *British and Irish Parliamentary Elections, 1784–1831* (Newton Abbot, 1973), idem, "Urban Politics in Ireland, 1801–31," in Harkness and O'Dowd, eds., *Town in Ireland,* 103–24; A.P.W. Malcomson, *John Forster: The Politics of the Anglo-Irish Ascendancy* (Oxford, 1978), passim; idem, "The Parliamentary Traffic of This Country," in T. Bartlett and D. W. Hayton, *Penal Era and Golden Age* (Belfast, 1979), 137–61.

51. P. O'Flanagan, "Settlement and Trading in Ireland, 1600–1800: A Preliminary Investigation," in T. M. Devine and D. Dickson, eds., *Ireland and Scotland, 1600–1850* (Edinburgh, 1983), 146–50.

52. L. M. Cullen, *The Emergence of Modern Ireland, 1600–1900* (London, 1981), 61–82.

53. L. A. Clarkson, "Population Change and Urbanisation, 1821–1911," in L. Kennedy and P. Ollerenshaw, eds., *An Economic History of Ulster, 1820–1939* (Manchester, 1985), 137–57.

54. J. S. Curl, *The Londonderry Plantation, 1609–1914* (Chichester, 1986); R. J. Hunter, "Ulster Plantation Towns, 1609–41," in Harkness and O'Dowd, eds., *Town in Ireland*, 55–80; O. Robinson, "The London Companies as Progressive Landlords in Nineteenth-Century Ireland," *Economic History Review*, 2d ser., 15, nos. 1–3 (1962–1963): 103–17; idem, "The London Companies and Tenant Right in Nineteenth-Century Ireland," *Agricultural History Review* 18 (1970): 54–63; P. Robinson, *The Plantation of Ulster: British Settlement in an Irish Landscape, 1600–1670* (Dublin, 1984).

55. P. J. O'Connor, *Exploring Limerick's Past: An Historical Geography of Urban Development in County and City* (Newcastle West, 1987).

56. J. Langton and G. Hoppe, *Town and Country in the Development of Early Modern Western Europe*, Historical Geography Research Series no. 11 (London, 1983), 40; ibid., citing P. Abrams, "Towns and Economic Growth: Some Theories and Problems," in P. Abrams and E. A. Wrigley, eds., *Towns in Societies* (Cambridge, England, 1978), 9–34.

Chapter 2. Land and Society

1. For an earlier account of some of these issues, see B. J. Graham and L. J. Proudfoot, eds., *An Historical Geography of Ireland* (London, 1993), chaps. 6 and 7.

2. R. A. Butlin, "Land and People, *c.* 1600," in T. W. Moody, F. X. Martin, and F. J. Byrne, eds., *A New History of Ireland*, vol. 3: *Early Modern Ireland, 1534–1691* (Oxford, 1976), 165–66; A. Clarke, "The Irish Economy, 1600–60," in Moody, Martin, and Byrne, eds., *Early Modern Ireland*, 181.

3. *Commons Journal Ireland*, series 2, 2 *(1776): xxxv–xxxix* (1696 Poll Tax); T. A. Larcom, ed., *The History of the Survey of Ireland Commonly called the Down Survey, by Doctor William Petty, A.D. 1655–56* (Dublin, 1851); S. Pender, ed., *A Census of Ireland circa 1659, with Supplementary Material from the Poll Money Ordinances (1660–1661)* (Dublin, 1939); R. C. Simington, ed., *The Civil Survey*, 10 vols. (Dublin, 1931–1961); idem, *Books of Survey and Distribution*, 4 vols. (Dublin, 1944–1967).

4. P. J. Corish, "The Cromwellian Regime, 1650–60," in Moody, Martin, and Byrne, eds., *Early Modern Ireland*, 357–73; J. G. Simms, "The Restoration, 1660–1685," in Moody, Martin, and Byrne, eds, *Early Modern Ireland*, 422–29; idem, "The Establishment of the Protestant Ascendancy, 1691–1714," in T. W. Moody and W. E. Vaughan, eds., *A New History of Ireland*, vol. 4: *Eighteenth-Century Ireland, 1691–1800* (Oxford, 1986), 10–13.

5. F.H.A. Aalen, *Man and the Landscape in Ireland* (London, 1978), 148; A. R. Orme, *The World's Landscapes*, vol. 4: *Ireland* (London, 1971), 130.

6. R. G. Gillespie, *Colonial Ulster: The Settlement of East Ulster, 1600–1641* (Cork, 1985), 167–94; P. Robinson, *The Plantation of Ulster: British Settlement in an Irish Landscape* (Dublin, 1984), 150–71; A. Sheehan, "Irish Towns in a Period of Change, 1558–1625," in C. Brady and R. Gillespie, eds., *Natives and Newcomers: The Making of Irish Colonial Society, 1534–1641* (Dublin, 1986), 93–119.

7. D. Dickson, "The Gap in Famines: A Useful Myth?," in E. M. Crawford, ed., *Famine: The Irish Experience, 900–1900* (Edinburgh, 1989), 97.

8. L. A. Clarkson, "Irish Population Revisited, 1687–1921," in J. M. Goldstrom and L. A. Clarkson, eds., *Irish Population, Economy, and Society* (Oxford, 1981), 27; C. Ó

Gráda, "Poverty, Population, and Agriculture, 1801–1845," in W. E. Vaughan, ed., *A New History of Ireland* vol. 5: *Ireland under the Union, Part 1, 1801–70* (Oxford, 1989), 118–22.

   9. W. E. Vaughan and A. J. Fitzpatrick, eds., *Irish Historical Statistics: Population 1821–1971* (Dublin, 1978), 3.

   10. Ó Gráda, "Poverty, Population and Agriculture," 117–18.

   11. K. H. Connell, *The Population of Ireland, 1750–1845* (Oxford, 1950), passim; L. M. Cullen, *An Economic History of Ireland since 1660* (London, 1987), 110–19.

   12. Ibid., 54; idem, *Anglo-Irish Trade, 1600–1800* (Manchester, 1968), 60.

   13. P. Ollerenshaw, "Industry, 1820–1914," in L. Kennedy and P. Ollerenshaw, eds., *An Economic History of Ulster, 1820–1939* (Manchester, 1985), 66–69.

   14. Cullen, *Ireland*, 50–134.

   15. S. H. Cousens, "The Restriction of Population Growth in Pre-Famine Ireland," *Proceedings of the Royal Irish Academy* 64C (1964): 85–99; idem, "The Regional Variation in Emigration from Ireland between 1821 and 1841," *Transactions of the Institute of British Geographers* 37 (1965): 15–30; L. J. Proudfoot, "Urban Patronage and Estate Management on the Duke of Devonshire's Irish Estates (1764–1891): A Study in Landlord-Tenant Relationships" (Ph.D. diss., Queen's University, Belfast, 1989), 388–95.

   16. Cullen, *Ireland*, 50–134.

   17. Ibid., 121–22, 141–42.

   18. D. Dickson, "The Place of Dublin in the Eighteenth-Century Irish Economy," in T. M. Devine and D. Dickson, eds., *Ireland and Scotland, 1600–1850* (Edinburgh, 1983), 177–79.

   19. See, for example, P. J. Corfield, *The Impact of English Towns, 1700–1800* (Oxford, 1982), 99–123, and Jan de Vries, *European Urbanisation, 1500–1800* (London, 1984), 175–250.

   20. Corfield, *Impact*, 102–6.

   21. Cullen, *Ireland*, 28–29; Robinson, *Plantation*, 91–128; D. McCartney, *The Dawning of Democracy: Ireland, 1800–1870* (Dublin, 1987), 3.

   22. S. Connolly, *Religion and Society in Nineteenth-Century Ireland*, Studies in Irish Economic and Social History no. 3 (Dundalk, 1985), 3; McCartney, *Dawning*, 36–37.

   23. J. Black, *Eighteenth-Century Europe, 1700–1789* (London, 1990), 171–77.

   24. Ibid., 167–72.

   25. L. J. Proudfoot, "Regionalism and Localism: Religious Change and Social Protest, c. 1700 to c. 1900," in Graham and Proudfoot, eds., *Historical Geography of Ireland*, 185–218.

   26. M. Wall, "The Penal Laws, 1691–1760," in G. O'Brien, ed., *Catholic Ireland in the Eighteenth Century* (Dublin, 1989), 10.

   27. Ibid., 17–18.

   28. D. Dickson, *New Foundations: Ireland, 1660–1800,* (Dublin, 1984), 43; Simms, "Protestant Ascendancy," 16–20.

   29. Dickson, *New Foundations*, 44; Simms, "Protestant Ascendancy," 16–20.

   30. T. W. Moody, F. X. Martin, and F. J. Byrne, eds., *A New History of Ireland*, vol. 8: *A Chronology of Irish History to 1976,* (Oxford, 1982), 265.

   31. D. Dickson, "Catholics and Trade in Eighteenth-Century Ireland: An Old Debate Revisited," in T. P. Power and K. Whelan, eds., *Endurance and Emergence: Catholics in Ireland in the Eighteenth Century* (Dublin, 1990), 85–100; Wall, "Penal Laws," 1–60; idem, "The Rise of a Catholic Middle Class in Eighteenth-Century Ireland," in O'Brien, ed., *Catholic Ireland*, 73–83.

32. T. Bartlett, "The Origins and Progress of the Catholic Question in Ireland, 1690–1800," in Power and Whelan, eds., *Endurance*, 1–3.

33. W. N. Osborough, "Catholics, Land, and the Popery Acts of Anne," in Power and Whelan, eds., *Endurance*, 21–56.

34. L. M. Cullen, "Catholic Social Classes under the Penal Laws," in Power and Whelan, eds., *Endurance*, 57–84; Wall, "Penal Laws," passim; K. Whelan, "The Regional Impact of Irish Catholicism, 1700–1850," in W. J. Smyth and K. Whelan, eds., *Common Ground: Essays on the Historical Geography of Ireland* (Cork, 1988), 253–77.

35. Bartlett, "Origins and Progress," 9; Dickson, *New Foundations*, 152–55; R. B. McDowell, "Ireland in 1800," in Moody and Vaughan, eds., *Eighteenth-Century Ireland*, 688–89.

36. E. Hewitt, ed., *Lord Shannon's Letters to His Son*, (P.R.O.N.I., 1982), 223–36; P. Jupp, "Urban Politics in Ireland, 1801–31," in D. Harkness and M. O'Dowd, eds., *The Town in Ireland* (Belfast, 1981), 103–24.

37. Dickson, *New Foundations*, 152–55, 164–65; J. McGuire, "The Act of Union," in L. de Paor, ed., *Milestones in Irish History* (Cork, 1991), 75; P. R. Newman, *Companion to Irish History . . . 1603–1921* (Oxford, 1991), 206.

38. Dickson, *New Foundations*, 173–74, 187.

39. Connolly, *Religion and Society* 32–33; L. M. Cullen, "The 1798 Rebellion in Wexford: United Irishman Organisation, Membership, Leadership," in K. Whelan, ed., *Wexford History and Society* (Dublin, 1987), 248–95; K. Whelan, "The Role of the Catholic Priest in the 1798 Rebellion in County Wexford," in Whelan, ed., *Wexford History and Society*, 296–315.

40. McGuire, "Act of Union," 75.

41. D. G. Boyce, *Nationalism in Ireland* (London, 1982), 132–49; McCartney, *Dawning*, 41–62, 110.

42. Ibid., 118; J. E. Doherty and D. J. Hickey, *A Chronology of Irish History since 1500* (Dublin, 1989), 116.

43. See, for example, I. d'Alton, *Protestant Society and Politics in Cork, 1812–1844* (Cork, 1980), 159–92.

44. C. Ó Gráda, "Poverty, Population, and Agriculture," 118.

45. D. Dickson, "An Economic History of the Cork Region in the Eighteenth Century," (Ph.D. diss., University of Dublin, 1977), 67–73, 88–98; T. P. Power, "Land, Politics and Society in Eighteenth-Century Tipperary" (Ph.D. diss., University of Dublin, 1987), 33–44, 81–86; P. O'Flanagan, "Rural Change South of the River Bride in Counties Cork and Waterford: The Surveyors' Evidence, 1716–1851," *Irish Geography* 15 (1982): 51–69.

46. J. H. Andrews, "The Struggle for Ireland's Public Commons," in P. O'Flanagan, P. Ferguson, and K. Whelan, eds., *Rural Ireland, Modernisation, and Change, 1600–1900* (Cork, 1987), 1–23; K. T. Hoppen, *Ireland since 1800: Conflict and Conformity* (London, 1989), 87; P. Travers, *Settlements and Divisions: Ireland, 1870–1922* (Dublin, 1988), 15.

47. J. S. Donnelly, "Landlords and Tenants," in Vaughan, ed., *Ireland under the Union*, 332–50.

48. Hoppen, *Ireland since 1800*, 87.

49. A.P.W. Malcomson, "Absenteeism in Eighteenth-Century Ireland," *Irish Economic and Social History Journal* 1 (1974): 15–35; Power, "Land, Politics, and Society," 67.

50. D. Spring, "Landed Elites Compared," in D. Spring, ed., *European Landed Elites in the Nineteenth Century* (Baltimore, n. d.), 4–5; R. Herr, "Spain," in Spring, ed., *European Landed Elites*, 104.

51. L. J. Proudfoot, "The Estate System in Mid-Nineteenth-Century Waterford," in T. P. Power and W. Nolan, eds., *Waterford History and Society: Interdisciplinary Essays on the History of an Irish County* (Dublin, 1992), 530–34.

52. L. J. Proudfoot, "Regionalism and Localism: Religious Change and Social Protest, c. 1700–c. 1900," in Graham and Proudfoot, eds., *Historical Geography of Ireland*, 185–211.

53. S. Daniels and S. Seymour, "Landscape Design and the Idea of Improvement, 1730–1914," in R. A. Dodgshon and R. A. Butlin, eds., *An Historical Geography of England and Wales*, 2d ed. (London, 1990), 487; S. Wilmot, *"The Business of Improvement": Agriculture and Scientific Culture in Britain, c. 1700–1870* (London, 1990), 39–46.

54. Power, "Land, Politics and Society," 54; J. Mokyr, *Why Ireland Starved*, (London, 1983), 203–13; C. Ó Gráda, "Agricultural Rents, Pre-Famine and Post Famine," *Economic and Social Review* 7 (1974): 385–92; idem., "The Investment Behaviour of Irish Landlords, 1850–1875: Some Preliminary Findings," *Agricultural History Review*, 23 (1975): 139–55; J. V. Beckett, *The Aristocracy in England, 1660–1914* (Oxford, 1986), 178–79.

55. J. S. Donnelly, *The Land and the People of Nineteenth-Century Cork* (London, 1975), 169.

56. Cullen, *Ireland*, 78–80, 114–15.

57. Arthur Young, *A Tour in Ireland . . . Made in the Years 1776, 1777, 1778, and . . . 1779* (Dublin, 1780), vol. 2, part 2, passim; J. Meenan and D. Clarke, eds., *RDS: The Royal Dublin Society, 1731–1981* (Dublin, 1981), 22; P. J. Carty, "The Historical Geography of County Roscommon" (M.A. thesis, National University of Ireland, 1970), 109–15, 139; E. McCourt. "A Study of the Management of the Farnham Estates in County Cavan during the Nineteenth Century" (M.A. thesis, University of Dublin, 1973), 25–56; A. M. Tod, "The Smiths of Baltiboys: A County Wicklow Family and Their Estate in the 1840s" (Ph.D. diss., University of Edinburgh, 1978), 153–58, 177; J. Bell and M. Watson, *Irish Farming, 1750–1900*, (Edinburgh, 1986), 1–14; J. McEvoy, *County of Tyrone, 1802: A Statistical Survey*, 2d ed. (Belfast, 1991), vi–vii.

58. Bell and Watson, *Irish Farming*, 229–39.

59. F.H.A. Aalen, "The Origin of Enclosures in Eastern Ireland," in N. Stephens and R. E. Glasscock, eds., *Irish Geographical Studies* (Belfast, 1970), 209–23; R. H. Buchanan, "Field Systems of Ireland," in A.R.H. Baker and R. A. Butlin, eds., *Studies of Field Systems in the British Isles* (Cambridge, England, 1973), 584–607; Dickson, "Cork Region," 153–68; Ms Eng. 218, Cork and Orrery Papers, vol. 3, Lease Book and Account of the Caledon Estate circa 1714–1745, Harvard University Library, Cambridge, Mass.

60. Aalen, *Man and the Landscape*, 169–92.

61. J. S. Donnelly, "Landlords and Tenants," 332–41.

62. W. Nolan, *Fassadinin: Land, Settlement, and Society in South-East Ireland, 1600–1850* (Dublin, 1979), 92–97.

63. Dickson, "Cork Region," 542–45.

64. Power, "Land, Politics, and Society," 50–51; J. H. Andrews, "Land and People," 259.

65. W. H. Crawford, "Ulster Landowners and the Linen Industry," in J. T. Ward and R. G. Wilson, eds., *Land and Industry: The Landed Estate and the Industrial Revolution* (Newton Abbot, 1971), 117–44.

66. Leases Granted by Lord Grandison to Tenants at Villierstown, 1750–1760 (P.R.O.N.I. T.3131/C/K 4, 6, 13).

67. N.L.I. Ms 18, 750 (5).

68. H. D. Gribbon, "The Irish Linen Board, 1711–1828," in L. M. Cullen and T. C. Smout, eds., *Comparative Aspects of Scottish and Irish Economic and Social History, 1600–1900* (Edinburgh, 1977), 77–87.

69. Ibid.

70. This figure is derived from the preliminary results of research currently being undertaken by the author and Dr. B. J. Graham. They wish to acknowledge the generous funding of the Leverhulme Trust which has made this possible. S. Lewis, *A Topographical Dictionary of Ireland*, vol. 1 (London, 1837), 339–40; G. Camblin, *The Town in Ulster* (Belfast, 1951), 71, 81, 98.

71. A.E.J. Morris, *History of Urban Form before the Industrial Revolution* (London, 1979), 154–88; A. Sutcliffe, *Towards the Planned City: Germany, Britain, the United States, and France, 1780–1914* (Oxford, 1981), 10–13.

72. The classic study of this phenomenon in England is D. Cannadine, *Lords and Landlords: The Aristocracy and the Towns 1774–1967* (Leicester, 1980). See also Carter, *Urban Historical Geography*, 130–42.

73. N. T. Burke, "An Early Modern Dublin Suburb: The Estate of Francis Augnier, Earl of Longford," *Irish Geography* 4 (1972): 365–83.

74. E. Walsh, "Sackville Mall: The First One Hundred Years," in D. Dickson, ed., *The Gorgeous Mask: Dublin, 1700–1850* (Dublin, 1987), 30–50.

75. E. McParland, "The Wide Streets Commissioners: Their Importance for Dublin Architecture in the Late Eighteenth and Early Nineteenth Century," *Quarterly Bulletin of the Irish Georgian Society* 15 (1972): 1–27.

76. T. Mooney and F. White, "The Gentry's Winter Season," in Dickson, ed., *Mask*, 1–16.

77. L. J. Proudfoot and B. J. Graham, "The Nature and Extent of Urban and Village Foundation and Improvement in Eighteenth- and Early-Nineteenth-Century Ireland," *Planning Perspectives* 8 (1993): 259–81.

78. T. Jones Hughes, "Historical Geography of Ireland from circa 1700," in G.L.H. Davies, ed., *Irish Geography: The Geographical Society of Ireland Golden Jubilee, 1934–1984* (Dublin, 1984), 155–56.

79. P. J. O'Connor, *Exploring Limerick's Past: An Historical Geography of Urban Development in County and City* (Newcastle West, 1987), 78.

80. W. H. Crawford, "The Influence of the Landlord in Eighteenth-Century Ulster," in Cullen and Smout, eds., *Comparative Aspects,* 200.

81. House of Commons Report, *Experimental Improvements on Crown Lands at King William's Town, Ireland* (London, 1834); D. Bowen, *Souperism: Myth or Reality?* (Cork, 1970), 67–106.

82. Cullen, *Ireland,* 77–82, 113–15; *The Parliamentary Gazetteer of Ireland* 1 (Dublin, 1846), 1: 413–14.

83. P.R.O.I., Pennefather Papers, 1745–1898, (D. 17,597–736; M.2,090–2,175; T. 7101–10), Wallop Papers, Deeds, and Leases Relating to the Irish Estates of the Wallop Family Hampshire County Record Office, England. (Box 99, Bundles 1 and 2).

84. Crawford, "Ulster Landowners," 123–26; J. FitzGerald, "The Organisation of the Drogheda Economy, 1780–1820" (M.A. thesis, National University of Ireland, 1972), 37–38, 81–97.

85. O'Brien, ed., *Catholic Ireland,* 73–92.

86. K. Whelan, "The Regional Impact of Irish Catholicism, 1700–1850," in Smith and Whelan, eds., *Common Ground,* 253–77.

87. K. Whelan, "The Catholic Parish, the Catholic Chapel, and Village Development in Ireland," *Irish Geography,* 16 (1983): 1–15.

88. Whelan, "Catholic Parish," 1–15; T. Jones Hughes, "Village and Town in Mid-Nineteenth-Century Ireland," *Irish Geography* 14 (1981): 99–106.

89. S. J. Connolly, "Union Government, 1812–1823," in Vaughan, ed., *Ireland under the Union,* 71; O. MacDonagh, "Ideas and Institutions, 1830–45," in Vaughan, ed., *Ireland Under the Union,* 213–14.

90. H. Burke, *The People and the Poor Law in Nineteenth-Century Ireland* (Littlehampton, 1987), 1–16.

91. R. B. McDowell, "Administration and the Public Services, 1800–70," in Vaughan, *Ireland under the Union,* 552–53; MacDonagh, "Ideas," 215–17.

92. McDowell, "Administration," 553.

93. P. O'Flanagan, "Settlement Development and Trading in Ireland, 1600–1800: A Preliminary Investigation," in Devine and Dickson, eds., *Ireland and Scotland,* 146–50.

94. W. A. McCutcheon, *The Industrial Archaeology of Northern Ireland* (HMSO, 1980), 2–6.

95. Young, *A Tour in Ireland,* 1: 56–57.

96. J. C. Beckett, "Eighteenth-Century Ireland," in Moody and Vaughan, eds., *Eighteenth-Century Ireland,* xlviii; J. L. McCracken, "The Social Structure and Social Life, 1714–1760," in Moody and Vaughn, *Eighteenth-Century Ireland,* 67; R.B. McDowell, "Ireland in 1800," in Moody and Vaughan, eds., *Eighteenth-Century Ireland,* 704.

97. C. Ó Gráda, "Industry and Communications, 1801–1845," in Vaughan, ed., *Ireland under the Union,* 150.

98. Ibid.; McCutcheon, *Industrial Archaeology,* 53.

99. L. M. Cullen, "Economic Development, 1750–1800," in Moody and Vaughan, eds., *Eighteenth-Century Ireland,* 179; Lewis, *Dictionary,* 11: 576.

100. Ó Gráda, "Industry and Communications," 148–49.

101. R. V. Comerford, "Ireland 1850–70: Post-Famine and Mid-Victorian," in Vaughan, ed., *Ireland under the Union,* 374–75.

102. Cullen, *Ireland,* 143–44.

103. J. Lee, "The Provision of Capital for Early Irish Railways, 1830–53," *Irish Historical Studies* 16 (1968–1969): 33–63; W. A. McCutcheon, "Transport, 1820–1914," in Kennedy and Ollerenshaw, eds., *Ulster,* 109–36; idem, *Industrial Archaeology,* 95–222.

104. M. Bence-Jones, *A Guide to Irish Country Houses* (London, 1988), xi.

105. W. Nolan, "Patterns of Living in Tipperary, 1750–1850," in Nolan and McGrath, eds., *Tipperary,* 288–324.

106. L. J. Proudfoot, "Landscaped Parks in Pre-Famine Ireland: A Regional Case-Study," in A. Verhoeve and J.A.J. Vervloet, eds., *The Transformation of the European Rural Landscape: Methodological Issues and Agrarian Change, 1770–1914* (Brussels, 1992), 230–37; idem, "Estate System," 523–43.

107. Robinson, *Plantation,* 72, 77.

108. Orme, *Ireland,* 136–38.

109. Proudfoot, "Landscaped Parks," 235.

110. Power, "Land, Politics, and Society," 38; Proudfoot, "Estate System," 536.

111. Morris, *Urban Form,* 176–77.

112. E. Malins and the Knight of Glin, *Lost Demesnes: Irish Landscape Gardening, 1660–1845* (London, 1976), 73–188.

113. Proudfoot, "Estate System," 536.

114. Cullen, *Emergence,* 43–44; B. de Breffny and R. ffolliott, *The Houses of Ireland* (London, 1975), 84.

Chapter 3. Duke of Devonshire's Irish Estate

1. J. Bateman, *The Great Landowners of Great Britain and Ireland* (reprint of the 4th [1883] ed.; Leicester, 1971), passim.

2. Estate Accounts 1818–1889 (N.L.I. L.P. Ms 6929).

3. Bateman, *Great Landowners*, 130.

4. The plantation scheme called for the confiscated lands to be divided into seignories of twelve thousand acres and decreasing proportions of eight, six, and four thousand acres. The lands were granted in fee farm to be held of the Crown in free and common socage. No undertaker was supposed to hold more than twelve thousand acres, and on an estate of that size he was required to settle ninety-one families including his own. See M. MacCarthy-Morrogh, *The Munster Plantation* (Oxford, 1986), 30–31, 247.

5. Ibid., 52.

6. Ibid., 141.

7. N. Canny, *The Upstart Earl* (Cambridge, 1982), 20.

8. For the following, see MacCarthy-Morrogh, *Munster Plantation*, 141–43, 156, 160–64, 169, 172, 175, 183, 242–47, 251, 254, 267, 273.

9. D. Townshend, *The Life and Letters of the Great Earl of Cork* (London, 1904), Appendix 2.

10. This estimate is derived from MacCarthy-Morrogh, *Munster Plantation*, Appendix: Land Acreage and Table 1, 287–92.

11. The Great Earl's grandson, Richard, inherited the title of earl of Cork and was created first earl of Burlington in 1664; See *Burke's Peerage, Baronetage, and Knightage*, 105th ed. (London, 1970), 1: 643–66.

12. E. Hewitt, ed., *Lord Shannon's Letters to His Son* (Belfast, 1982), xxviii; Premises Conveyed to Sir William Heathcote, 1738, and Alphabet of Lands Sold to Lord Duncannon (CW. [Currey] Ms L/9/11).

13. J. Pearson, *Stags and Serpents: The Story of the House of Cavendish and the Dukes of Devonshire* (London, 1983), 69 ff.

14. Thomas Knowlton to John Heaton, 20 Oct. 1808 (CW. [Currey] Ms L/5/4); Sir T. Osborne to Thomas Knowlton, 10 Nov. 1808 (ibid.); Deed of Conveyance, Osborne Premises, Dungarvan, 1809 (CW. [Currey] Ms L/9/18); P. O'Flanagan, "Rural Change South of the River Bride in Counties Cork and Waterford: The Surveyors' Evidence, 1716–1851," *Irish Geography* 15 (1982): 55.

15. This spittal land originally formed part of the endowments of the medieval lazars founded at Cashel and Tipperary.

16. Tithe Correspondence 1807–1836 (L.E.O. Ms C/1/36–7).

17. G. Bennett, *The History of Bandon and the Principle Towns in the West Riding of Cork* (Cork, 1869), 12–15; MacCarthy-Morrogh, *Munster Plantation*, 118, 253–54.

18. W. Fraher, *Dungarvan: An Architectural Inventory* (Dungarvan, 1984), 7–9; B. Graham, "The Towns of Medieval Ireland," in R. A. Butlin, ed., *The Development of the Irish Town* (London, 1977), 44, 55; S. Lewis, *A Topographical Dictionary of Ireland* (London, 1837), 1: 577–78, 2: 238; F. X. Martin, "Overlord Becomes Feudal Lord, 1172–85," in A. Cosgrove, ed., *A New History of Ireland*, vol. 2: *Medieval Ireland 1169–1534* (Oxford, 1987), 134.

19. Instructions Given by the Chief Secretary to Ireland with Reference to the Cities and Boroughs of Ireland Sending Representatives to Parliament, H. C. 1831–1832, *Reports and Plans*, 6: 9, 65, 145; Lewis, *Dictionary*, 1: 178–79, 577–78, 2: 283, 289, 727–28; D. O'Donoghue, *History of Bandon* (Bandon, 1970), 12; MacCarthy-Morrogh, *Munster*

Plantation, 260–61; M. V. Conlon, "The Borough of Youghal," *Journal of the Cork Historical and Archaeological Society* 50–51 (1945–1946): 112–14.

20. Lewis, *Dictionary* 1: 179; R. Lucas, *The Cork Directory for 1787–8* (Dublin, circa 1789), 109; C. Smith, *The Ancient and Present State of the City and County of Cork,* 2d ed. (Dublin, 1774), 239–40.

21. J. H. Andrews, "Land and People, c. 1780," in T. W. Moody and W. E. Vaughan, eds., *A New History of Ireland,* vol. 4: *Eighteenth-Century Ireland, 1691–1800* (Oxford, 1986), 259; J. C. Condon, "The Trade and Commerce of the Town of Youghal," *Journal of the Cork Historical and Archaeological Society* 50–51 (1945–1946): 117–24; L. M. Cullen, *Anglo-Irish Trade, 1660–1800* (Manchester, 1968), 14, idem, "Economic Development, 1750–1800," in Moody and Vaughan, eds., *Eighteenth-Century Ireland,* 184; S. Hayman, *The New Handbook of Youghal* (Youghal, 1868), 62–72; A. Marmion, *The Ancient and Modern History of the Maritime Ports of Ireland* (London, 1860), 547–48; A. R. Orme, "Youghal, County Cork—Growth, Decay, Resurgence," *Irish Geography* 5 (1966): 135–44.

22. C. Smith, *The Ancient and Present State of the County and City of Waterford* (Dublin, 1746), 51–2; MacCarthy-Morrogh, *Munster Plantation,* 230, 233–34.

23. P. O'Flanagan, "Population Change and Ethnicity in Munster Towns c. 1659–1851" (paper presented to the Urban History Conference, Port Stewart, County Londonderry, Northern Ireland, April 1987). In his more recent published version of this paper, O'Flanagan places more emphasis on the extent of this population growth; see P. O'Flanagan, "Urban Minorities and Majorities: Catholics and Protestants in Munster Towns c. 1659–1850," in W. J. Smyth and K. Whelan, eds., *Common Ground: Essays on the Historical Geography of Ireland* (Cork, 1988), 124–48.

24. H. Carter, *An Introduction to Urban Historical Geography* (London, 1983), 82–85; P. Clark, "Introduction: The Early Modern Town in the West: Research since 1945," in P. Clark, ed., *The Early Modern Town* (London, 1976), 1–42; R. Denis, "Stability and Change in Urban Communities: A Geographical Perspective," in J. H. Johnson and C. G. Pooley, eds., *The Structure of Nineteenth-Century Cities* (London, 1982), 253–82; D. Soudan, "Migrants and the Population Structure of Later Seventeenth-Century Provincial Cities and Market Towns," in P. Clark, ed., *The Transformation of English Provincial Towns, 1600–1800* (London, 1984), 133–68; P. Corfield, *The Impact of English Towns, 1700–1800* (Oxford, 1982), 99–123. See also T. Hershberg's critical review, "The Future of Urban History," in D. Fraser and A. Sutcliffe, eds., *The Pursuit of Urban History* (London, 1983), 428–48.

25. "State of Borough Representation in the Year 1784," *Northern Star,* 1–9 July 1796; "Population, Inhabitants, and Electors of Ireland," *Morning Post,* 23 Dec. 1790–11 Jan. 1791; "Return of the Amount of Hearth Money Paid by Several Cities, 1798–1800," *House of Commons Journal (Ireland)* 19 (1800), Appendix, dcclxi–dcclxiv; L. A. Clarkson, "An Anatomy of an Irish Town: The Economy of Armagh, 1770," *Irish Economic and Social History* 5 (1978): 28; Cullen, *Ireland,* 84–86.

26. Carter, *Urban Historical Geography,* 96–97.

27. A. Sheehan, "Irish Towns in a Period of Change, 1558–1625," in C. Bradley and R. Gillespie, eds., *Natives and Newcomers* (Dublin, 1986), 94.

28. Carter, *Urban Historical Geography,* 105–7.

29. Clarkson, "Anatomy," 27–28. O'Connor, for example, argues that in a nineteenth-century context, the minimum population cutoff point for urban status was five hundred; see P. O'Connor, *Exploring Limerick's Past* (Newcastle West, 1987), 86–87.

30. B. Scalé, Survey of the Duke of Devonshire's Irish Estates, 1773–1776, 4 vols., (CW. Ms).

31. "The Town of Bandonbridge as It Is Now Built" (circa 1615) (TCD Ms 1209, no. 42). See also "The Plot of the Towne of Bandon Bridge . . . as It Is Entended to Be Buylte," by Christopher Jefford, 1613 (TCD Ms 1209, no. 39). For an excellent discussion of the morphological growth of Bandon in the seventeenth century, see P. O'Flanagan, *Bandon,* Irish Historic Towns Atlas no. 3 (Dublin, 1988).

32. Carter, *Urban Historical Geography,* 171–83; J. Langton, "Residential Patterns in Pre-Industrial Cities: Some Case Studies from Seventeenth-Century Britain," *Transactions of the Institute of British Geographers* 65 (1975): 1–28; O'Flanagan, "Urban Minorities," 130; J. Patten, "Urban Occupations in Pre-Industrial England," *Transactions of the Institute of British Geographers,* n.s., 2 (1977): 296–313; G. Sjoberg, *The Preindustrial City Past and Present* (New York, 1960), 80–144; J. E. Vance, *This Scene of Man: The Role and Structure of the City in the Geography of Western Civilisation* (New York, 1977), 105–66, 201–70; P. Wheatley, "What the Greatness of a City Is Said to Be: Reflections on Sjoberg's *Preindustrial City,*" *Pacific Viewpoint* 4 (1963): 163–88.

33. MacCarthy-Morrogh, *Munster Plantation,* 255n.22; O'Flanagan, *Bandon,* 1–4.

34. Rental, General for 1760–1792 (N.L.I. L.P. Mss 6645–60).

35. J. Barry, "Henry Bowman. Reports on the Duke of Devonshire's Irish Estates, 1794–1797," *Analecta Hibernica* 22 (1960): 283–84.

36. P. Power, "An Old Map of Dungarvan Dated 1760," *Journal of the Waterford Archaeological Society* 14 (1911): 103–7; Smith, *Waterford,* 88.

37. Lewis, *Dictionary,* 2: 283; R. A. Butlin, "Urban and Proto-Urban Settlements in Pre-Norman Ireland," in R. A. Butlin, ed., *The Development of the Irish Town* (London, 1977), 11–27.

38. Martin, "Overlord Becomes Feudal Lord," in Cosgrove, ed., *Medieval Ireland,* 124; J. Watt, *The Church in Medieval Ireland* (Dublin, 1972), 142.

39. F. X. Martin, "Plantation Boroughs in Medieval Ireland, with a Handlist of Boroughs to c. 1500," in D. Harkness and M. O'Dowd, eds., *The Town in Ireland* (Belfast, 1981), 23–54; MacCarthy-Morrogh, *Munster Plantation,* 261.

40. Smith, *Waterford,* 52.

41. Barry, "Bowman," 276.

42. W. Conner to Sir A. Abdy, 8 Jan. and 14 Dec. 1773 (CW. [Currey] Ms L/9/7 Bundle: Irish Letters and Papers Relating to the Duke of Devonshire from About the Year 1772 to the End of 1776); Lewis, *Dictionary,* 2:285.

43. T. Jones Hughes, "Village and Town in Mid-Nineteenth Century Ireland," *Irish Geography,* 14 (1981): 99–106; O'Flanagan, "Urban Minorities," 134.

44. Lewis, *Dictionary,* 2:589; MacCarthy-Morrogh, *Munster Plantation,* 257, 260–62.

45. Barry, "Bowman," 282–83.

46. O'Flanagan, "Urban Minorities," 132–33.

47. Barry, "Bowman," 275–79; Orme, "Youghal," 135–38.

48. R. Caulfield, ed., *The Council Book of the Corporation of Youghal 1610–1659, 1666–1687, 1690–1800* (Guildford, 1878), 470, 472–73, 513–27; Conlon, "Borough," 114; Hayman, *New Handbook,* 60; Lewis, *Dictionary,* 2: 729–30; Scalé Survey, (CW. Ms); J. Bradley, "Planned Anglo-Norman Towns in Ireland," in H. B. Clark and A. Simms, eds., *The Comparative History of Urban Origins in Non-Roman Europe: Ireland, Wales, Denmark, Germany, Poland and Russia from the Ninth to the Thirteenth Centuries* (Oxford, 1985), 455; Orme, "Youghal," 127.

49. Condon, "Trade and Commerce," 120–21; "Description of the Town of Youghal," *Walker's Hibernian Magazine,* March 1778, 149–50; Hayman, *New Handbook,* pp. 64–76; Marmion, *Maritime Ports,* 547–48; Orme, "Youghal," 125, 135–38.

50. Caulfield, *Council Book,* 513–27.

51. Smith, *Cork,* 118–19; "Description," *Hibernian Magazine,* 148–50.
52. E. Hughes, "The Eighteenth-Century Estate Agent," in H. A. Cronne, T. W.
Moody, and D. B. Quinn, eds., *Essays in British and Irish History in Honour of James
Eadie Todd* (London, 1949), 185–99; D. Spring, *The English Landed Estate in the Nineteenth Century: Its Administration* (Baltimore, 1963), 3–4, 58–59; F.M.L. Thompson,
English Landed Society in the Nineteenth Century (London, 1963), 158–60.
53. George Bowles to Sir Beaumont Hotham, 31 Dec. 1788 (P.R.O.N.I. C.P.
T.3158/1691); John Heaton to Sixth Duke, 26 Aug. 1812 (CW. [Currey] Ms L/83/3).
54. For example, the report by William Greig on the Gosford estates in County
Armagh was commissioned at about the same time and with much the same end in
view. See F.M.L. Thompson and D. Tierney, eds., *General Report on the Gosford Estates
in County Armagh 1821 by William Greig* (Belfast, 1976).
55. Pearson, *Stags and Serpents,* 118–19.
56. Earl of Bessborough, ed., *Georgiana: Extracts from the Correspondence of Georgiana, Duchess of Devonshire* (London, 1955), 66–67, 116, 235, 243.
57. Ibid., 66–67.
58. Ibid., 116.
59. J. V. Beckett, *The Aristocracy in England, 1660–1914* (Oxford, 1986), 144; Pearson,
Stags and Serpents, 119; Hughes, "Estate Agent," 193; E. Richards, "The Land Agent,"
in G. E. Mingay, ed., *The Victorian Countryside* (London, 1981), 2:441.
60. Sixth Duke to G——, 18 Sept. 1814 (CW. Ms Sixth Duke's Correspondence,
Group I/119); Thompson, *Landed Society,* 167.
61. B. Currey to Sixth Duke, 20 July 1844 (CW. Ms Paxton Group, 233); B. Currey
to Sixth Duke, 24 Aug. 1844 (ibid., 251); Memorandum by J. Paxton, n/d (1844) (CW.
Ms Paxton Group, 231); D. Cannadine, "The Landowner as Millionaire: The Finances
of the Dukes of Devonshire, c. 1800–1926," *Agricultural History Review* 25 (1977): 82.
62. J. Paxton to S. Paxton, 27 Aug. 1844 (CW. Ms Paxton Group, 254).
63. See, for example, J. Paxton to S. Paxton, 20, 24, 25, 27, 28, and 29 Oct. 1844
(CW. Ms Paxton Group, 103–7); F. E. Currey to J. Paxton, 20 Feb. 1852, Letter Book:
Lismore, Tallow, and Miscellaneous 1849–1856 (N.L.I. L.P. Ms 7182); F. E. Currey to J.
Paxton, 11 Mar. 1852 (ibid.).
64. J. Paxton to Seventh Duke, 27 Jan. 1858 (CW. Ms Paxton Group, 100.44).
65. Cannadine, "Landowner as Millionaire," 82.
66. J. Paxton to Seventh Duke, 12 Feb. 1858 (CW. Ms Paxton Group, 100.42); Duke
of Bedford to Seventh Duke, 15 May 1858 (CW. Ms Sixth Duke's Correspondence
Group II, 4. 52); Duke of Bedford to Seventh Duke, 21 May 1858 (ibid., 4.54); Duke of
Bedford to Seventh Duke, 22 May 1858 (ibid., 4.55); Entries for 2 Mar., 23 Apr., 19
May, 21 May, and 2 June, 1858 (CW. Ms Seventh Duke's Diaries).
67. Thompson, *Landed Society,* 151–52.
68. A. Swanston to F. E. Currey, 5 Mar. 1858 (L.E.O. C/1/85 Pigeonhole B Correspondence: 1850–1859); L. J. Proudfoot, "The Management of a Great Estate: Patronage, Income and Expenditure on the Duke of Devonshire's Irish Property c. 1816 to
1891," *Irish Economic and Social History* 13 (1986): 50–51.
69. See, for example, entries for 30 Apr.–19 May 1859 (CW. Ms Seventh Duke's Diaries); 10 Apr.–26 Apr. 1860 (ibid.); 17 Mar.–28 Apr. 1862 (ibid.); Pearson, *Stags and
Serpents,* 116–46.
70. J. S. Donnelly, *The Land and the People of Nineteenth-Century Cork* (London,
1975), 182ff; Hughes, "Estate Agent," 192–93; Richards, "Land Agent," 453; Spring,
Landed Estate, 15; Thompson, *Landed Society,* 158.

71. W. Conner to Baron Hotham, 20 Nov. 1779 (CW. [Currey] Ms L/9/7 Bundle: Letters from the Duke of Devonshire's Irish Steward for the Years 1777–1780).

72. J. Heaton to Sixth Duke, 24 Aug. 1813 (CW. [Currey] Ms L/83/3 [2]).

73. H. Bowman to J. Heaton, 9 Jan. 1796 (P.R.O.N.I. C.P. T.3158/1734); J. Heaton to Sixth Duke, 26 Aug. 1812 (CW. [Currey] Ms L/83/3 [2]).

74. T. Knowlton to Sixth Duke, 10 Aug. 1820 (CW. Ms Sixth Duke's Correspondence, Group I/457); T. Knowlton to Sixth Duke, 23 Jan. 1820 (ibid., /418); J. Heaton to Sixth Duke, 26 Aug. 1812 (CW. [Currey] Ms L/83/3 [2]).

75. T. Knowlton to Sixth Duke, 4 Feb. 1820 (CW. Ms Sixth Duke's Correspondence, Group I /420); T. Knowlton to Sixth Duke, 10 Aug. 1820 (ibid., /457).

76. J. Abercrombie to Sixth Duke, 18 Apr. 1817 (CW. Ms Fifth Duke's Correspondence, 209); J. Abercrombie to Sixth Duke, 18 Dec. 1820 (ibid., /469); T. Knowlton to Sixth Duke, 28 Sept. 1812 (CW. Ms Sixth Duke's Correspondence, Group I / 80); T. Knowlton to Sixth Duke, 23 Jan. 1820 (ibid., /418); T. Knowlton to Sixth Duke, 4 Feb. 1820 (ibid., /420); J. Abercrombie to Sixth Duke, 9 Apr. 1817 (CW. Ms Fifth Duke's Correspondence, 208); J. Abercrombie to Sixth Duke, 18 Apr. 1817 (ibid., /209).

77. See, for example, H. Bowman to J. Heaton, 11 Aug. 1796 (CW. [Currey] Ms L/5 Bundle: Jan.–Dec. 1793 [sic]); T. Garde to J. Heaton, 15 Aug. 1796 (ibid.); T. Knowlton to J. Heaton, 13 Sept. 1797 (P.R.O.N.I. C.P. T.3158/1748); T. Knowlton to J. Heaton, 21 Apr. 1798 (ibid., /1763); T. Knowlton to J. Heaton, 5 June 1799 (ibid., /1789); T. Knowlton to J. Heaton, 7 April 1801 (ibid., /1814).

78. T. Garde to Fifth Duke, 15 June 1803 (CW. [Currey] Ms L/5 Bundle: Jan.–Dec. 1803).

79. B. English, "Patterns of Estate Management in East Yorkshire, c. 1840–c. 1880," *Agricultural History Review* 42 (1984): 29–48.

80. J. Abercrombie to Sixth Duke, 18 Apr. 1817 (CW. [Currey] Ms Fifth Duke's Correspondence, 209).

81. B. Currey to Sixth Duke, 20 Nov. 1839 (CW. Ms Sixth Duke's Correspondence, Group II, 4197); Richards, "Land Agent," 443; Spring, *Landed Estate,* 98–100; Thompson, *Landed Society,* 158–59.

82. Richards, "Land Agent," 443.

83. Donnelly, *Land and the People,* 10.

84. Thompson, *Landed Society,* 151–83.

85. "Memorandum . . . respecting the Duke of Devonshire's Affairs in Ireland, 5th/6th June, 1792" (CW. [Currey] Ms L/9/7).

86. Devon Commission, *Digest of Evidence,* part 1 (Dublin, 1847), 278.

87. Sixth Duke to Lord Duncannon, n/d, but 1837 (CW. [Currey] Ms L/83/4 [29] 1837); F. E. Currey to B. Currey, 25 May 1839 (CW. [Currey] Ms L/83/4 [30] 1839); W. S. Currey to Sixth Duke, 29 May 1839 (CW. [Currey] Ms L/83/4 [33] 1839–44).

88. See, for example, B. Currey to Col. W. S. Currey, 23 Feb. 1832 (L.E.O. C/1/2, Letters to Col. W. S. Currey, 1825–1834, 1836, 1839).

89. B. Currey to Sixth Duke, 20 Nov. 1839 (CW. Ms Sixth Duke's Correspondence, Group II /4197); F. E. Currey to Seventh Duke, 27 Aug. 1882, Copy Letter Book: F. A. Currey and C. H. Currey, 20 Mar. 1881–20 June 1889 (L.E.O. C/2/19); F. E. Currey to Seventh Duke, 22 Mar. 1884 (ibid.); F. E. Currey to Sir M. Barrington, 10 Sept. 1856, Letter Book: Lismore, Tallow, and Miscellaneous 1856–1869 (N.L.I. L.P. Ms 7189); F. E. Currey to J. Hollway, 8, 13, and 17 Dec. 1856 (ibid.); F. E. Currey to J. Hollway, 5 and 11 Feb. 1857 (ibid.); F. E. Currey to W. Currey, 24 Aug. 1861, Letter Book: W. Currey 1858–1863 (N.L.I. L.P. Ms 7190); F. E. Currey to W. Currey, 13 Feb. 1870, Letter Book: W. Currey 1864–1867 (N.L.I. L.P. Ms 7192).

90. B. Currey to Lord Morpeth(?), 2 July 1837 (CW. [Currey] Ms L/83/4 [29]); F. E. Currey to B. Currey, 30 Aug. 1837 (ibid.); Col. W. S. Currey to B. Currey, 3 Sept. 1837 (ibid.); F. E. Currey to B. Currey, 17 Dec. 1841 (CW. [Currey] Ms L/83/4 [37] Lismore 1842).

91. F. E. Currey to F. J. Howard, 3 Apr. 1857, Letter Book: Dungarvan 1850–1870 (N.L.I. L.P. Ms 7191); F. E. Currey to W. Currey, 4 Apr. 1857, Letter Book: W. Currey 1855–1858 (N.L.I. L.P. Ms 7188).

92. F. E. Currey to Seventh Duke, 23 and 25 May 1868, (Letter Book: W. Currey 1864–1867, N.L.I. L.P. Ms 7192).

93. F. E. Currey to Seventh Duke, 28 Feb. 1866 (ibid.); F. E. Currey to Seventh Duke, 31 Oct. 1867 (ibid.). For evidence of the continuing Fenian threat in and around Lismore over the ensuing years, see: F. E. Currey to Seventh Duke, 28 Dec. 1868 (ibid.); F. E. Currey to Seventh Duke, 28 Nov. 1869 (ibid.); Seventh Duke to F. E. Currey, 6 Dec. 1884 (L.E.O. C/1/85 Pigeonhole N: Letters to F. E. Currey and C. H. Currey, 1880–1889).

94. Seventh Duke to F. E. Currey, 1 July 1885 (ibid.).

95. Rental, General for 1765 (N.L.I. L.P. Ms 6646); G. J. Lyne, "Landlord-Tenant Relations on the Shelburne Estate in Kenmare, Bonane, and Tuosist, 1770–75," *Journal of the Kerry Archaeological and Historical Society* 12 (1979): 26.

96. Rental, General for 1805 (N.L.I. L.P. Ms 6677).

97. Rental, General for 1815 (N.L.I. L.P. Mss 6687–92); W. A. Maguire, *The Downshire Estates in Ireland, 1801–1845* (Oxford, 1972), 66–67; Richards, "Land Agent," 441.

98. Estate Accounts, 1841 (N.L.I. L.P. Ms 6935); Maguire, *Downshire Estates*, 66.

99. F. E. Currey to S. Berwick, 19 Aug. 1858, Letter Book: Lismore, Tallow, and Miscellaneous 1856–1869 (N.L.I. L.P. Ms 7189).

100. F. E. Currey to J. R. Berwick, 12 Oct. 1858 (ibid.).

101. A. Swanston to F. E. Currey, 5 Mar. 1858 (L.E.O. C/1/85 Pigeonhole B: Letters to F. E. Currey 1850–1859).

102. W. Currey to F. E. Currey, 19 Nov. 1856 (ibid.).

103. R. H. Power to D. Craig, 9 Jan. 1889, Copy Out-Letter-Book 27 Oct. 1880–17 May 1890 (L.E.O. C/2/2).

104. Fisheries Case (N.L.I. L.P. W. B. 12).

105. See, for example, T. Garde to J. Heaton, 31 May 1798 (P.R.O.N.I. C.P. T.3158/1764); T. Knowlton to J. Heaton, 9 Nov. 1798 (ibid., /1780); T. Knowlton to J. Heaton, 3 Jan. 1802 (ibid., /1832).

106. T. Garde to J. Heaton, 8 Jan. 1792 (ibid., /1700); T. Garde to J. Heaton, 6 May 1792 (ibid., /1706); T. Garde to J. Heaton, 20 Sept. 1792 (ibid., /1715); H. Bowman to J. Heaton, 29 Sept. 1792 (ibid., /1716).

107. T. Knowlton to J. Heaton, 21 Apr. 1798 (CW. [Currey] Ms L/5 Bundle: 1797–1799).

108. See, for example, T. Knowlton to J. Heaton, 9 Nov. 1798 (P.R.O.N.I. C.P. T.3158/1780); T. Garde to Fifth Duke, 20 Mar. 1799 (ibid., /1788); T. Knowlton to J. Heaton, 3 Jan. 1802 (ibid., /1832); T. Garde to Fifth Duke, 15 June 1803 (ibid., /1850); T. Garde to Fifth Duke, 15 June 1803[2] (ibid., /1851).

109. F. E. Currey to B. Currey, 9 May 1839 (CW. [Currey] Ms L/83/4 [30] 1839).

110. F. E. Currey to W. Currey, 6 June 1848, Letter Book: 1844, 1849–1851 (N.L.I. L.P. Ms 7183); F. E. Currey to W. Currey, 9 and 19 Jan. 1849 (ibid.); Estate Accounts 1818–1889 (N.L.I. L.P. Ms 6929).

111. D. P. Ronayne to Dr. P. Fogarty, 22 July 1837 (CW. [Currey] Ms L/83/4 [29]).

112. Col. W. S. Currey to B. Currey, 3 Sept. 1837 (ibid.).

113. T. Seward to Col. W. S. Currey, 6 Sept. 1837 (ibid.); Dr. P. Fogarty to Lord Morpeth, 19 Dec. 1837 (ibid.).

114. F. E. Currey to W. Currey, 19 Jan. 1849, Letter Book: 1844, 1849–1851 (N.L.I. L.P. Ms 7183); F. A. Currey to F. E. Currey, 1 Sept. 1879 (L.E.O. C/1/85 Pigeonhole K: Letters to F. E. Currey, 1870–1879).

115. W. Currey to F. E. Currey, 31 Oct. 1879 (ibid.); F. A. Currey to F. E. Currey, 10 Nov 1879 (ibid.); F. A. Currey to F. E. Currey, 1 Sept. 1879 (ibid.).

116. W. Currey to F. E. Currey, 31 Oct. 1879 (ibid.).

117. Bateman, *Landowners,* 137, 168; Maguire, *Downshire Estates,* 154–82.

118. Abstract of Receipts and Rents at Tollymore for One Year Ending 1 Nov. 1793 (P.R.O.N.I. Roden Mss MIC 147, reel 3, vol. 9); Earl of Roden to Mr. Moore, n/d, but 1794 (ibid., p. 207); Irish Accounts, 1795, (Courtenay Mss, Devon C.R.O., 1508M/Accounts/vol. 22).

119. See, for example, W. Carleton, *Valentine McClutchy, the Irish Agent. A Chronicle of the Castle Cumber Property* (London, 1845).

120. Donnelly, *Land and the People,* 173–78.

121. Rental, General for 1764 (N.L.I. L.P. Ms 6646).

122. "Incidental Receipts," Draft Ledger 1828–1829 (N.L.I. L.P. Ms 6960).

123. For example, the entry for 13 Dec. 1845, General Letting Book 1839–1847 (N.L.I. L.P. Ms7122); Variation in Rentals (Youghal), Draft Ledger 1833, 1833, 1838 (N.L.I. L.P. Mss 6965, 6966, 6969); Variation in Rentals (Tallow), Draft Ledger 1832, 1833 (N.L.I. L.P. Mss 6964–65); F. E. Currey to Seventh Duke, 1 Jan. 1868, Letter Book: F. E. Currey (N.L.I. L.P. Ms7192).

124. See, for example, H. Bowman to J. Heaton, 19 Apr. 1794 (CW. [Currey] Ms L/5 Bundle: Jan.–Dec. 1793).

125. Barry, "Bowman," 275–88.

126. T. Garde to J. Heaton, 8 Jan. 1792 (P.R.O.N.I. C.P. T.3158/1700).

127. Rental, General for 1813 (N.L.I. L.P. Ms 6683); Mr. Conner's Collection, 1772–1787 (CW. [Currey] Ms L/5 Box 1738–1812 Miscellaneous); D. Dickson, "An Economic History of the Cork Region in the Eighteenth Century" (Ph.D. diss., University of Dublin, 1977), 301.

128. Calculated from Rental, General for 1764 (N.L.I. L.P. Ms 6646), 1791 (ibid., Ms 6661) and 1813 (ibid., Ms 6683); Dickson, "Cork Region," 230.

129. D. Large, "The Wealth of the Greater Irish Landowners, 1750–1815," *Irish Historical Studies* 15 (1966): 21; A.P.W. Malcomson, "Absenteeism in Eighteenth-Century Ireland," *Irish Economic and Social History* 1 (1974): 18, 20, 28, 29.

130. Beckett, *Aristocracy,* 289; Cannadine, "Landowner as Millionaire," 95; G. E. Mingay, *English Landed Society in the Eighteenth Century* (London, 1963), 22–24.

131. Estate Accounts 1818–1889 (N.L.I. L.P. Ms 6929); Estate Accounts 1842, Variations in Rental, 140–156 (N.L.I. L.P. Ms 6936); Donnelly, *Land and the People,* 194–95.

132. All these figures have been derived from Estate Accounts 1818–1889 (N.L.I. L.P. Ms 6929).

133. B. Currey to Sixth Duke, 4 Nov. 1839 (CW. Ms Sixth Duke's Correspondence Group II/.4183); Poor Law Valuation Questionnaire, 10 Aug. 1880 (L.E.O. C/1/85 O); Finlay Dun, *Landlords and Tenants in Ireland* (London, 1881), 59.

134. W. E. Vaughan, "Landlord and Tenant Relations in Ireland between the Famine and the Land War, 1850–1878," in L. M. Cullen and T. C. Smout, eds., *Comparative Aspects of Scottish and Irish Economic and Social History, 1600–1900* (Edinburgh, 1977), 217–218.

135. Alexander Swanston to Francis Currey, 5 May 1852 (L.E.O. Ms C/1/85B); Alexander Swanston to Francis Currey, 3 July 1852 (ibid.).

136. L. M. Cullen, *An Economic History of Ireland since 1660,* 2d ed. (London, 1987), 108–14.

137. F. E. Currey to B. Currey, 1 Sept. 1843, Letter Book: B. Currey 1842–1844 (N.L.I. L.P. Ms 7183).

138. B. Currey to Sixth Duke, 29 Oct. 1846 (CW. Ms Sixth Duke's Correspondence Second Series 25.41).

139. B. Currey to Sixth Duke, 30 Sept. 1847 (ibid.); 1849—£5,826; 1850—£6,064; 1851—£6,610; 1852—£6,791; 1853 (half-year only)—£3,472, Estate Accounts 1818–1889 (N.L.I. L.P. Ms 6929); W. Currey to Sixth Duke, 12 June 1851 (CW. Ms Sixth Duke's Correspondence Second Series 25.81).

140. Cullen, *Ireland,* 136–40, 148.

141. Ibid., 113–17; Donnelly, *Land and the People,* passim; R. F. Forster, *Modern Ireland, 1600–1972* (London, 1988), 400ff; K. Theodore Hoppen, *Elections, Politics, and Society in Ireland 1832–1885* (Oxford, 1984), 112; B. Solow, *The Land Question and the Irish Economy, 1870–1903* (Cambridge, Mass., 1971), 51–88; W. E. Vaughan, *Landlords and Tenants in Ireland, 1848–1904* (Dundalk, 1984), 25–26.

142. F. Pyne to Seventh Duke, 17 Mar. 1881 (L.E.O. Ms C/1/85 N).

143. Entries for 1879–1881, Estate Accounts 1818–1889 (N.L.I. L.P. Ms 6929); Seventh Duke to F. E. Currey, 10 Oct. 1879 (L.E.O. C/1/85 I).

144. F. E. Currey to Marquis of Hartington, 2 Dec. 1880 (L.E.O. C/1/85 M); F. Pyne to Seventh Duke, 17 Mar. 1881 (L.E.O. Ms C/1/85 N).

145. C. H. Currey to Seventh Duke, 27 Nov. and 12 Dec. 1881, Copy Letter Book (L.E.O. C/2/19); F. E. Currey to Seventh Duke, 22 Mar. 1884 (ibid.); F. E. Currey to Seventh Duke, 15 Aug. 1881 (ibid.); F. E. Currey to Marquis of Hartington, 11 Dec. 1880 (L.E.O. C/1/85 M).

146. C. H. Currey to Seventh Duke, 11 Dec. 1882, Copy Letter Book (L.E.O. C/2/19); Entry for 1882, Estate Accounts 1818–1889 (N.L.I. L.P. Ms 6929).

147. Cullen, *Ireland,* 151–52; Forster, *Modern Ireland,* 405–8.

148. Ibid, 408–15; L. M. Gearey, *The Plan of Campaign* (Cork, 1986), Appendix 2.

149. Seventh Duke to F. E. Currey, 6 Dec. 1884 (L.E.O. C/1/85 N).

150. Seventh Duke to F. E. Currey, 25 May 1885 (ibid.); Seventh Duke to F. E. Currey, 1 July 1885 (ibid.).

151. Entries for 1886–1890, Estate Accounts 1818–1889 (N.L.I. L.P. Ms 6929); R. H. Power to Seventh Duke, 6 Nov. 1886 and 23 Nov. 1887, Copy Letter Book (L.E.O. C/2/19).

152. Rental, General for 1764 to 1791 (N.L.I. L.P. Mss 6646–61).

153. Dickson, "Cork Region," 428 et seq.

154. Ibid., chap. 7, passim; Condon, "Trade and Commerce," 120–21; Cullen, *Ireland,* 64–70; D. Dickson, *New Foundations: Ireland, 1660–1800* (Dublin, 1984), 123–24; S. Hayman, *New Handbook,* 67–72.

155. Lucas, *Cork Directory,* 108–9. On the utility of such directories for urban historical research, see Carter, *Urban Historical Geography,* 87–89; Dickson, "Cork Region," 560–61.

156. Sectional List 15, Lismore Papers, National Library of Ireland. Remedying the deficiencies in the data posed different problems. The erratic nature of the annual fluctuations in the arrears precluded any attempt at estimation, and accordingly the arrears graph has been left incomplete. The relative stability in the rent demand between 1835

and 1852 and again in the mid-1880s suggested that the missing rental data from these periods could be made good by substituting the average rent demand from the years immediately preceding and following the missing rentals. The gap in the rentals in the later 1850s coincided with a significant rent rise. Here the estimates are based on the average percentage of the overall rent demand represented by the Bandon rents in the years before and after the missing returns. The estimates for cash received were calculated in a similar way.

157. Calculated as the total of the combined value of the undifferentiated urban and rural tenancies at Youghal (the latter were excluded from the analysis), and the maximum range between the highest and the lowest average values at Bandon in the late 1850s.

158. A. Swanston to F. E. Currey, 5 May, 5 Aug., and 17 Sept. 1852 (L.E.O. C/1/85 B).

159. F. E. Currey to W. Currey, 7 Apr. 1858, Letter Book: F. E. Currey to W. Currey 1855–1858 (N.L.I. L.P. Ms 7188).

160. F. E. Currey to J. J. Byrne, 8 Oct. and 26 Oct. 1859, Letter Book: Dungarvan 1850–1870 (N.L.I. L.P. Ms 7191); F. E. Currey to J. J. Byrne, 29 May, 29 Aug., and 5 Sept. 1860, Letter Book: Youghal 1860–1880 (L.E.O. C/2/23).

Chapter 4. Mismanagement and Neglect

1. Quoted in D. Dickson, "An Economic History of the Cork Region in the Eighteenth Century" (Ph.D. diss., University of Dublin, 1977), 224n.30.

2. Ibid., 219, 228–35; E. Hughes, "The Eighteenth-Century Estate Agent," in H. A. Cronne, ed., *Essays in British and Irish History in Honour of James Eadie Todd* (London, 1949), 186, 193–94; G. J. Lyne, "Landlord-Tenant Relations on the Shelburne Estate in Kenmare, Bonane, and Tousist, 1770–75," *Journal of the Kerry Archaeological and Historical Society* 12 (1979): 26–48.

3. In the later case of Thomas Knowlton, the fifth duke offered him every opportunity to clear himself of all charges; see J. Heaton to Sixth Duke, 26 Aug. 1812 (CW. [Currey] Ms L/83/3 [2]).

4. J. V. Beckett, *The Aristocracy in England, 1660–1914* (Oxford, 1986), 151–54.

5. Sir R. Musgrave to J. Heaton, 13 Feb. 1792 (P.R.O.N.I. C.P. T.3158/1703).

6. For Conner's manipulation of leases, see in particular the Musgrave-Heaton correspondence of 1790–1792 (ibid., /1692 /1694 /1695 /1702 /1703).

7. J. G. Simms, "The Establishment of Protestant Ascendancy, 1691–1714," in T. W. Moody and W. E. Vaughan, eds., *A New History of Ireland*, Vol. 4: *Eighteenth-Century Ireland, 1691–1800* (Oxford, 1986), 19; L. M. Cullen, "Economic Development, 1691–1750," in Moody and Vaughn, eds., *Eighteenth-Century Ireland*, 167.

8. T. W. Moody, F. X. Martin, and F. J. Byrne, eds., *A New History of Ireland*, Vol. 8: *A Chronology of Irish History to 1976* (Oxford, 1982), 276, 279.

9. L. M. Cullen, *An Economic History of Ireland since 1660*, 2d ed. (London, 1987), 78–80.

10. Dickson, "Cork Region," 145ff.

11. See, for example, J. Barry, "Henry Bowman. Reports on the Duke of Devonshire's Irish Estates, 1794–1797," *Analecta Hibernica* 22, (1960): 275–76, and C. Maxwell, ed., *Arthur Young. A Tour in Ireland* (reprint, Cambridge, England, 1983), 174–78.

12. Tenures and Valuations, 1750–1760 (N.L.I. L.P. Ms 6155); Tenures and Valuations, 1792 (N.L.I. L.P. Ms 6156); Schedule of Leases, General, 1700–1802 (N.L.I. L.P. Ms 6177) (CW. [Currey] Ms L/4/14 and L/4/15).

13. See, for example, the lease for Margery Carr, 1751 in Copies of Counterpart Leases—Lismore, 1731–1757 (CW. [Currey] Ms L/4/15). Also see Barry, "Bowman," 284; Cullen, *Ireland,* 44–45, 77–79; and W. A. Maguire, *The Downshire Estates in Ireland, 1801–1845* (Oxford, 1972), 118–19. There is at least one reference to this type of concurrent lease on the estate, however; see W. Conner to Baron Hotham, 2 Sept. 1788 (CW. [Currey] Ms L/9/7 Bundle: Letters from the Duke of Devonshire's Irish Steward, William Conner, in the Years 1787–1790).

14. L. M. Cullen, *The Emergence of Modern Ireland, 1600–1900* (London, 1981), 43–51.

15. Barry, "Bowman," 284.

16. Ibid. P. J. O'Connor, *Exploring Limerick's Past: An Historical Geography of Urban Development in County and City* (Newcastle West, 1987), 58–63.

17. Lists of Tenants for Towns and Gardens of Bandon, Dungarvan, Lismore, Tallow, and Youghal, in Scalé Survey, 1773–1776, 4 vols. (CW. Ms). The data for Youghal is made less complete because the original list contains numerous entries that simply refer to "subtenants" without specifying the exact number.

18. H. Carter, *An Introduction to Urban Historical Geography* (London, 1983), 171–75; C.G.A. Clay, *Economic Expansion and Social Change: England 1500–1700, vol. 1: Towns and Trade* (Cambridge, 1984), 215–16; P. Corfield, *The Impact of English Towns, 1700–1800* (Oxford, 1982), 124–45.

19. Scalé Survey (CW. Ms); Rental General, 1768 and 1777 (N.L.I. L.P. Mss 6648 and 6649 [*sic*]); (CW. [Currey] Ms L/9/11 Bundle: Bernard Correspondence, 1787–1813); I. d'Alton, *Protestant Society and Politics in Cork, 1812–1844* (Cork, 1980), 102–3.

20. R. Lucas, *The Cork Directory for 1787–88* (Dublin, circa 1789), 109.

21. P. O'Flanagan, "Urban Minorities and Majorities: Catholics and Protestants in Munster Towns *c.* 1659–1850," in W. J. Smyth and K. Whelan, eds., *Common Ground: Essays in the Historical Geography of Ireland* (Cork, 1988), p. 136.

22. Ibid. 283–84.

23. Lismore, 11 percent; Youghal, 21 percent; Dungarvan, 1.6 percent.

24. Directions to Mr. Conner, 19 Sept. 1772 (CW. [Currey] Ms L/9/7 Bundle: Irish Letters and Papers Relative to the Duke of Devonshire from about the Year 1772 to the end of 1776); Barry, "Bowman," 276; Dickson, "Cork Region," 195–200.

25. List of Lease Proposals for Farms, 16 Mar. 1775 (CW. [Currey] Ms L/9/7 Bundle: Irish Letters and Papers Relative to the Duke of Devonshire from about the Year 1772 to the End of 1776); R. Donovan to Baron Hotham, 18 Jan. 1780 (CW. [Currey] Ms L/9/7 Bundle: Miscellaneous Irish Letters on the Duke of Devonshire's Affairs in the Years 1776–1783); W. Conner to Baron Hotham, 7 Feb. 1784, 5 Feb. 1785, and 4 Sept. 1786 (CW. [Currey] Ms L/9/7 Bundle: Letters from the Duke of Devonshire's Irish Steward, William Conner, in the Years 1784–1786).

26. Petition of Thomas and John Oliffe to Duke of Devonshire, 29 May 1785; J. Lysaght to Baron Hotham, 12 Nov. 1785; and J. Towell to Baron Hotham, 7 June 1786 (CW. [Currey] Ms L/9/7 Bundle: Miscellaneous Irish Letters on the Duke of Devonshire's Affairs in the Years 1783–1786); J. Towell to Baron Hotham, 7 Jan. 1787 (CW. [Currey] Ms L/9/7 Bundle: Letters, 1787–1790).

27. R. Musgrave to Baron Hotham, 29 Dec. 1783 (CW. [Currey] Ms L/9/7 Bundle: Miscellaneous Irish Letters on the Duke of Devonshire's Affairs in the Years 1783–1786); Dickson, "Cork Region," 195–96.

28. J. Towell to Baron Hotham, 7 June 1786 (CW. [Currey] Ms L/9/7 Bundle: Miscellaneous Irish Letters on the Duke of Devonshire's Affairs in the Years 1783–1786);

J. Towell to Baron Hotham, 7 Jan. 1787 and 20 Dec. 1788 (CW. [Currey] Ms L/9/7 Bundle: Letters, 1787–1790).

29. See, for example, the lease to Baggs, 26 May 1740 (CW. [Currey] Ms L/4/15).

30. Dickson, "Cork Region," 178–79.

31. Tenures and Valuations, 1750–1760 (N.L.I. L.P. Ms 6155), passim; Tenures and Valuations, 1792 (N.L.I. L.P. Ms 6156), passim.

32. Maguire, *Downshire Estates,* 133–36.

33. F.M.L. Thompson and D. Tierney, eds., *William Greig: General Report on the Gosford Estates in County Armagh 1821* (Belfast, 1976), 260.

34. Sir A. Abdy, Directions to Mr. Conner, 19 Sept. 1772 (CW. [Currey] Ms L/9/7 Bundle: Irish Letters and Papers Relative to the Duke of Devonshire from about the Year 1772 to the End of 1776); W. Conner to Sir Beaumont Hotham, 28 May 1778 (CW. [Currey] Ms L/9/7 Bundle: Letters from the Duke of Devonshire's Irish Steward in the Years 1777–1780); J. Sealy to Sir Beaumont Hotham, 18 Aug. 1786 (CW. [Currey] Ms L/9/7 Bundle: Miscellaneous Irish Letters on the Duke of Devonshire's Affairs in the Years 1783–1786); W. Conner to Sir Beaumont Hotham, 30 Dec. 1786 (CW. [Currey] Ms L/9/7 Bundle: Letters from the Duke of Devonshire's Irish Steward, William Conner, in the Years 1784–1786).

35. Dickson, "Cork Region," 34–35.

36. W. Conner to Sir A. Abdy, 10 Dec. 1774 (CW. [Currey] Ms L/5 Bundle: 1774–1791).

37. W. Conner to Sir Beaumont Hotham, 21 Dec. 1780 (CW. [Currey] Ms L/9/7 Bundle: Letters from the Duke of Devonshire's Irish Steward, William Conner, in the Years 1780–1783); D. Dickson, *New Foundations: Ireland 1660–1800* (Dublin, 1984), 103–6; idem, "Property and Social Structure in Eighteenth-Century South Munster," in L. M. Cullen and F. Furet, eds., *Ireland and France, 17th–20th Centuries: Towards a Comparative Study of Rural History* (Paris/Michigan, 1980), 129–38.

38. Dickson, "Cork Region," 227ff.

39. W. Conner to Sir Beaumont Hotham, 5 Feb. 1785 (CW. [Currey] Ms L/9/7 Bundle: Letters from the Duke of Devonshire's Irish Steward, William Conner, in the Years 1784–1786).

40. W. Conner to Sir Beaumont Hotham, 30 June 1786 (ibid.).

41. W. Conner to Sir Beaumont Hotham, 17 Mar. 1778 (CW. [Currey] Ms L/9/7 Bundle: Letters from the Duke of Devonshire's Irish Steward in the Years 1777–1780).

42. W. Conner to Sir Beaumont Hotham, 4 Sept. 1786 (CW. [Currey] Ms L/9/7 Bundle: Letters from the Duke of Devonshire's Irish Steward, William Conner, in the Years 1784–1786).

43. T. Garde to Sir Beaumont Hotham, 31 Jan. 1788 (CW. [Currey] Ms L/9/7 Bundle: Letters and Papers from Mr. Garde, Irish Law Agent for the Duke of Devonshire, c. 1777–1790).

44. C. Musgrave to Sir A. Abdy, 14 May 1774 (CW. [Currey] Ms L/9/7 Bundle: Irish Letters and Papers Relative to the Duke of Devonshire from About the year 1772 to the End of 1776); W. Conner to Sir A. Abdy, 17 Nov. 1774 (CW. [Currey] Ms L/5 Bundle: 1774–1791); T. Garde to Sir Beaumont Hotham, 29 Nov. 1776 (CW. [Currey] Ms L/9/7 Bundle: Irish Letters and Papers Relative to the Duke of Devonshire from about the Year 1772 to the End of 1776).

45. W. Conner to Sir Beaumont Hotham, 7 Feb. 1784, 28 Nov. 1784, 13 June 1785, 2 Aug. 1786, 27 Sept. 1786, 18 Oct. 1786, and 30 Dec. 1786 (CW. [Currey] Ms L/9/7 Bundle: Letters from the Duke of Devonshire's Irish Steward, William Conner, in the

Years 1784–1786); T. Garde to Sir Beaumont Hotham, 19 June 1787 (CW. [Currey] Ms L/9/7 Bundle: Letters and Papers from Mr. Garde, Irish Law Agent for the Duke of Devonshire, c. 1777–1790); W. Conner to Sir Beaumont Hotham, 13 Oct. 1787 (CW. [Currey] Ms L/9/7 Bundle: Letters from the Duke of Devonshire's Irish Steward in the Years 1787–1790); R. McDowell, *Ireland in the Age of Imperialism and Revolution* (Oxford, 1979), 79–83.

46. T. Garde to Sir Beaumont Hotham, 19 June 1787 (CW. [Currey] Ms L/9/7 Bundle: Letters and Papers from Mr. Garde, Irish Law Agent for the Duke of Devonshire, c. 1777–1790); 27 Geo. III, c. 15; Moody, Martin, and Byrne, *Chronology,* 283.

47. T. Garde to Sir Beaumont Hotham, 31 Jan. 1788 (CW. [Currey] Ms L/9/7 Bundle: Letters and Papers from Mr. Garde, Irish Law Agent for the Duke of Devonshire, c. 1777–1790).

48. H. Bowman to J. Heaton, 24 Aug. 1793 (CW. [Currey] Ms L/5 Bundle: Jan.–Dec. 1793).

49. T. Garde to Sir A. Abdy, 14 Dec. 1773 (CW. [Currey] Ms L/9/7 Bundle: Irish Letters and Papers Relative to the Duke of Devonshire from about the Year 1772 to the End of 1776).

50. T. Garde to Sir Beaumont Hotham, 5 June 1777, 7 Oct. 1778, 4 Dec. 1778, and 1 Feb. 1779 (CW. [Currey] Ms L/9/7 Bundle: Letters and Papers from Mr. Garde, Irish Law Agent for the Duke of Devonshire, c. 1777–1790); W. Conner to Sir Beaumont Hotham, 10 Apr. 1779 and 3 June 1779 (CW. [Currey] Ms L/9/7 Bundle: Letters from the Duke of Devonshire's Irish Steward in the years 1777–1780); T. Garde to Sir Beaumont Hotham, 11 May 1779 (ibid.); W. J. Smyth, "Estate Records and the Making of the Irish Landscape: An Example from County Tipperary," *Irish Geography* (1976): 38.

51. Dickson, "Cork Region," 240–42. These mills were attached to the manors of Lismore, Tallow, and Lisfinney, Inchiquin, Dungarvan and Coolfadda (Bandon) (Schedule of Leases, General, 1700–1802, N.L.I. L.P. Ms 6177). For a generally contrary view, see W. H. Crawford, "The Significance of Landed Estates in Ulster, 1600–1820," *Irish Economic and Social History* 17 (1990): 44–61.

52. W. Conner to Sir Beaumont Hotham, 15 May 1777 (CW. [Currey] Ms L/9/7 Bundle: Letters from the Duke of Devonshire's Irish Steward in the Years 1777–1780); T. Garde to Sir Beaumont Hotham, 1 June 1778 (CW. [Currey] Ms L/9/7 Bundle: Letters from Mr. Garde, Irish Law Agent for the Duke of Devonshire, c. 1777–1790); Memorial from M. Harris to the Duke of Devonshire, n/d, but circa Jan. 1780 (CW. [Currey] Ms L/9/7 Bundle: Miscellaneous Irish Letters on the Duke of Devonshire's Affairs in the Years 1776–1783).

53. Sir A. Abdy, Directions to Mr. Conner, 19 Sept. 1772 (CW. [Currey] Ms L/9/7 Bundle: Irish Letters and Papers Relative to the Duke of Devonshire from about the Year 1772 to the End of 1776); T. Garde to Sir A. Abdy, 14 Dec. 1773 and 17 May 1774 (ibid.).

54. T. Garde to Sir Beaumont Hotham, 22 Oct. 1775 (ibid.); W. Conner to Sir Beaumont Hotham, 27 Sept. 1777 (CW. [Currey] Ms L/9/7 Bundle: Letters from the Duke of Devonshire's Irish Steward in the Years 1777–1780); Memorial from M. Harris to the Duke of Devonshire, n/d, but circa Jan. 1780 (CW. [Currey] Ms L/9/7 Bundle: Miscellaneous Irish Letters on the Duke of Devonshire's Irish Affairs in the Years 1776–1783); W. Conner to Sir Beaumont Hotham, 14 Mar. 1781 and 30 June 1781 (CW. [Currey] Ms L/9/7 Bundle: Letters from the Duke of Devonshire's Irish Steward, William Conner, in the Years 1780–1783).

55. Sir R. Musgrave to Sir Beaumont Hotham, 10 Feb. 1786 and 25 Mar. 1786 (CW.

[Currey] Ms L/9/7 Bundle: Miscellaneous Irish Letters on the Duke of Devonshire's Affairs in the Years 1783–1786); Sir R. Musgrave to Sir Beaumont Hotham, 23 Jan. 1790 (CW. [Currey] Ms L/9/7 Bundle: Letters 1787–1790); Sir R. Musgrave to J. Heaton, 22 Dec. 1790 (P.R.O.N.I. C.P. T.3158/1694).

56. Sir R. Musgrave to J. Heaton, 14 Dec. 1790 (P.R.O.N.I. C.P. T.3158/1692), 22 Dec. 1790 (ibid. /1694), 11 Jan. 1792 (ibid. /1702), 13 Feb. 1792 (ibid. /1703); T. Garde to J. Heaton, 8 Jan. 1792 (ibid. /1700), 14 July 1792 (ibid. /1711), 19 July 1792 (ibid. /1712), 20 Sept. 1792 (ibid. /1715); Anonymous Letter from "Friends" to the Duke of Devonshire, 26 July 1792 (ibid. /1713).

57. Sir R. Musgrave to J. Heaton, 13 Jan. 1792 (CW. [Currey] Ms L/5 Bundle: Jan.–Dec. 1792).

58. T. Garde to J. Heaton, 10 Apr. 1792 (ibid.); T. Garde to J. Heaton, 28 June 1792 (CW. [Currey] Ms L/5 Bundle: Jan.–Dec. 1792); Dickson, "Cork Region," 294–98.

59. Sir R. Musgrave to Sir Beaumont Hotham, 7 Oct. 1783, 10 Feb. 1786, and 25 Mar. 1786 (CW. [Currey] Ms L/9/7 Bundle: Miscellaneous Irish Letters on the Duke of Devonshire's Affairs in the Years 1783–1786); Sir R. Musgrave to J. Heaton, 13 Feb. 1792 (CW. [Currey] Ms L/5 Bundle: Jan.–Dec. 1792).

60. Sir R. Musgrave to Sir Beaumont Hotham, 10 Feb. 1786 and 25 Mar. 1786 (CW. [Currey] Ms L/9/7 Bundle: Miscellaneous Irish Letters on the Duke of Devonshire's Affairs in the Years 1783–1786); W. Conner to Sir Beaumont Hotham, 13 Feb. 1790 (CW. [Currey] Ms L/5 Bundle: 1788–1791); T. Garde to J. Heaton, 28 June 1792 (CW. [Currey] Ms L/5 Bundle: Jan.–Dec. 1792).

61. T. Garde to J. Heaton, 28 June 1792 (CW. [Currey] Ms L/5 Bundle: Jan.–Dec. 1792).

62. Sir R. Musgrave to J. Heaton, 14 Dec. 1790 (P.R.O.N.I. C.P. T.3158/1692).

63. Anonymous "Friends" to the Duke of Devonshire, 26 July 1792 (CW. [Currey] Ms L/5 Bundle: Jan.–Dec. 1792); T. Garde to J. Heaton, 10 Apr. 1792, 14 July 1792, and 20 Sept. 1792 (ibid.).

64. W. Conner to Sir Beaumont Hotham, 15 May 1777 (CW. [Currey] Ms L/9/7 Bundle: Letters from the Duke of Devonshire's Irish Steward in the Years 1777–1780); G. Bowles to Sir Beaumont Hotham, 3 May 1788 and 31 Dec. 1788 (CW. [Currey] Ms L/5 Bundle: 1766–1773); W. Conner to Sir Beaumont Hotham, 8 Jan. 1789 and 21 Feb. 1789 (CW. [Currey]) Ms L/5 Bundle: 1788–1791). A marginal note (in a different hand) at the Tallow Mills entry in the 1790 Rental Account reads: "On asking Mr Conner if he was interested in it he said not when it was taken but after agreed to join them in building the mills" (Rental, General for 1790, N.L.I. L.P. Ms 6658).

65. T. Garde to J. Heaton, 28 June 1786 (CW. [Currey] Ms L/5 Bundle: Jan.–Dec. 1792); W. Conner to Sir Beaumont Hotham, 3 May 1788 (CW. [Currey] Ms L/5 Bundle: 1766–1773); J. Towell to Sir Beaumont Hotham, 20 Dec. 1788 (CW. [Currey] Ms L/9/7 Bundle: 1787–1790); G. Bowles to Sir Beaumont Hotham, 31 Dec. 1788 (ibid.); W. Conner to Sir Beaumont Hotham, 8 Jan. 1789 and 3 Feb. 1789 (CW. [Currey] Ms L/5 Bundle: 1788–1791); W. Conner to Sir Beaumont Hotham, 1 July 1789 (CW. [Currey] Ms L/9/7 Bundle: Letters from the Duke of Devonshire's Irish Steward, William Conner, in the Years 1787–1790).

66. W. Conner to Sir Beaumont Hotham, 18 Oct. 1786 (CW. [Currey] Ms L/9/7 Bundle: Letters from the Duke of Devonshire's Irish Steward, William Conner, in the Years 1784–1786); W. Conner to Sir Beaumont Hotham, 23 Oct. 1788 (CW. [Currey] Ms L/9/7 Bundle: Letters from the Duke of Devonshire's Irish Steward, William Conner, in the Years 1787–1790).

67. W. Conner to Sir Beaumont Hotham, 15 April 1787 (CW. [Currey] Ms L/9/7 Bundle: Letters from the Duke of Devonshire's Irish Steward in the Years 1787–1790); W. Conner to Sir Beaumont Hotham, 21 Feb. 1789 (CW. [Currey] Ms L/5 Bundle: 1788–1791).

68. T. Garde to J. Heaton, 20 Sept. 1792 (CW. [Currey] Ms L/5 Bundle: Jan.–Dec. 1792).

69. Rental, General for 1764–1765, 1768, 1777, and 1780–1791 (N.L.I. L.P. Mss 6646–6661); The State of William Conner's Account with His Grace the Duke of Devonshire in the Year Ending Ladyday 1770 (CW. [Currey] Ms L/45/95); Mr. Conner's Collection 1772–1787 (CW. [Currey] Ms L/5 Box 1738–1812 Miscellaneous).

70. Lismore District (Including Dungarvan, Tallow, Tipperary and Waterford), Chief Rents, Jointure Estate, Youghal District, Bandon District, Bandon Western District, and Jointure Estate (Western). From 1781 onward, Cork and Gillabbey, Ballyrafter, Ballygalane, Bandon Western, and Western Jointure were also separately identified.

71. Rental, General for 1764 (N.L.I. L.P. Ms 6646).

72. R. Musgrave to J. Heaton, 13 Feb. 1792 (P.R.O.N.I. C.P. T.3158/1703); T. Garde to J. Heaton, 16 April 1792 (ibid. /1705).

73. Rental, General for 1791 (N.L.I. L.P. Ms 6661).

74. Rental, General for 1764–1765, 1768, 1777, and 1780–1791 (N.L.I. L.P. Mss 6646–6661).

75. D. Large, "The Wealth of the Greater Irish Landowners, 1750–1815," *Irish Historical Studies* 15 (1966–1967): 33–35; Beckett, *Aristocracy,* 178–80.

76. Cullen, *Emergence,* chap. 4, passim. As, for example, at Castlewellan and Cookstown; see G. Camblin, *The Town in Ulster* (Belfast, 1951), 78, 81–82.

77. H. Bowman to J. Heaton, 4 Sept. 1792 (CW. [Currey] Ms L/5 Bundle: Jan.–Dec. 1792); T. Garde to J. Heaton, 20 Sept. 1792 (ibid.); Rental, General for 1791 (N.L.I. L.P. Ms 6661).

78. Among numerous examples, see Hotham's annotated reply on the reverse of the following: W. Conner to Sir Beaumont Hotham, 14 Apr. 1777, 17 Feb. 1778, 28 May 1778, 17 Sept. 1778, 3 June 1779, and 5 Dec. 1779 (CW. [Currey] Ms L/9/7 Bundle: Letters from the Duke of Devonshire's Irish Steward in the Years 1777–1780); W. Conner to Sir Beaumont Hotham, 7 June 1784, 18 June 1784, 5 Feb. 1785, 3 Dec. 1785, 19 Apr. 1786, and 15 Dec. 1786 (CW. [Currey] Ms L/9/7 Bundle: Letters from the Duke of Devonshire's Irish Steward in the Years 1784–1786).

79. W. Conner to Sir Beaumont Hotham, 22 May 1786 (ibid.); Dickson, "Cork Region," 221.

80. W. Conner to Sir Beaumont Hotham, 15 June 1778, 28 June 1778, and 29 Dec. 1779 (CW. [Currey] Ms L/9/7 Bundle: Letters from the Duke of Devonshire's Irish Steward in the Years 1777–1780).

81. W. Conner to Sir Beaumont Hotham, 24 Oct. 1775 (CW. [Currey] Ms L/9/7 Bundle: Irish Letters and Papers Relative to the Duke of Devonshire from about the Year 1772 to the End of 1776).

82. W. Conner to Sir Beaumont Hotham, 27 Nov. 1781 (CW. [Currey] Ms L/9/7 Bundle: Letters from the Duke of Devonshire's Irish Steward, William Conner, in the Years 1780–1783); W. Conner to Sir Beaumont Hotham, 19 May 1788 (CW. [Currey] Ms L/9/7 Bundle: Letters from the Duke of Devonshire's Irish Steward, William Conner, in the Years 1787–1790).

83. W. Conner to Sir Beaumont Hotham, 2 July 1785 (CW. [Currey] Ms L/9/7 Bundle: Letters from the Duke of Devonshire's Irish Steward, William Conner, in the Years 1784–1786).

84. W. Conner to Sir Beaumont Hotham, 16 Nov. 1776 (CW. [Currey] Ms L/9/7 Bundle: Irish Letters and Papers Relative to the Duke of Devonshire from about the Year 1772 to the End of 1776); W. Conner to Sir Beaumont Hotham, 28 June 1776, 28 May 1778, and 28 June 1778 (CW. [Currey] Ms L/9/7 Bundle: Letters from the Duke of Devonshire's Irish Steward in the Years 1777–1780); Cuthbert to W. Conner, 12 June 1778 (ibid.).

85. T. Garde to J. Heaton, 10 Apr. 1792 (CW. [Currey] Ms L/5 Bundle: Jan.–Dec. 1792).

86. W. Conner to Sir Beaumont Hotham, 4 Dec. 1775 (CW. [Currey] Ms L/9/7 Bundle: Irish Letters and Papers Relative to the Duke of Devonshire from about the Year 1772 to the End of 1776); Dickson, "Cork Region," 507.

87. Ibid., 509; E. O'Kelly, *The Old Private Banks of Munster* (Cork, 1959), 47–53.

88. Hugh and William Lawton's Answer to the Duke of Devonshire's Bill of Complaint, n/d, but circa Feb. 1776 (CW. [Currey] Ms L/9/7 Bundle: Irish Letters and Papers Relative to the Duke of Devonshire from about the Year 1772 to the End of 1776); Sir A. Abdy to T. Garde, 21 Jan. 1775 (CW. [Currey] Ms L/5 Bundle: 1774–1791); Case Copy, William Conner Against Lawton and Carleton, 12 Jan. 1776 (CW. [Currey] Ms L/9/7 Bundle: Irish Letters and Papers Relative to the Duke of Devonshire from about the Year 1772 to the End of 1776).

89. W. Conner to Sir Beaumont Hotham, 7 June 1784 and 2 Nov. 1784 (CW. [Currey] Ms L/9/7 Bundle: Letters from the Duke of Devonshire's Irish Steward, William Conner, in the Years 1784–1786).

90. Supposed State of Mr. Conner's Accounts, 22 Oct. 1784 (CW. [Currey] Ms L/5 Bundle: 1766–1773); Statement of Account, William Conner and the Fifth Duke of Devonshire, 1784 (ibid.).

91. W. Conner to Sir Beaumont Hotham, 5 Feb. 1785, 8 Mar. 1785, 13 June 1785, 2 July 1785, 23 Aug. 1785, 3 Dec. 1785, 7 Dec. 1785, and 8 Dec. 1785 (CW. [Currey] Ms L/9/7 Bundle: Letters from the Duke of Devonshire's Irish Steward, William Conner, in the Years 1784–1786).

92. The submission dates (in brackets) of Conner's surviving accounts are as follows: 1764 (July 1765); 1765 (May 1767); 1768 (Feb. 1770); 1777 (Dec. 1778); 1780 (Feb. 1783); 1781 (n/d); 1782–1784 (Feb. 1786); 1785–1786 (Feb. 1788); 1787 (Mar. 1788); 1788–1791 (Feb. 1797). See N.L.I. L.P. Mss 6646–61.

93. W. Conner to Sir Beaumont Hotham, 13 June 1785, 3 Dec. 1785, and 19 Apr. 1786 (CW. [Currey] Ms L/9/7 Bundle: Letters from the Duke of Devonshire's Irish Steward, William Conner, in the Years 1784–1786).

94. Among numerous examples, see: W. Conner to Sir Beaumont Hotham, 17 Sept. 1778, 20 Nov. 1779, 29 May 1780, 18 Sept. 1780, 11 May 1782, and 13 Jan. 1783 (CW. [Currey] Ms L/9/7 Bundle: Letters from the Duke of Devonshire's Irish Steward in the Years 1777–1780); W. Conner to Sir Beaumont Hotham, 13 Oct. 1787, 1 July 1789, 20 Oct. 1789, 9 Oct. 1789, 25 Nov. 1790, and 30 Jan. 1791 (CW. [Currey] Ms L/9/7 Bundle: Letters from the Duke of Devonshire's Irish Steward, William Conner, in the Years 1787–1790).

95. W. Conner to Sir Beaumont Hotham, 29 July 1786, and 15 Dec. 1786 (CW. [Currey] Ms L/9/7 Bundle: Letters from the Duke of Devonshire's Irish Steward, William Conner, in the Years 1784–1786).

96. W. Conner to Sir Beaumont Hotham, 22 June 1790 and 25 Nov. 1790 (CW. [Currey] Ms L/9/7 Bundle: Letters from the Duke of Devonshire's Irish Steward, William Conner, in the Years 1787–1790).

97. W. Conner to Sir Beaumont Hotham, 28 June 1777 (CW. [Currey] Ms L/9/7 Bundle: Letters from the Duke of Devonshire's Irish Steward in the Years 1777–1780); Sir R. Musgrave to J. Heaton, 13 Feb. 1792 (CW. [Currey] Ms L/5 Bundle: Jan.–Dec. 1792).

98. Sir R. Musgrave to J. Heaton, 14 Dec. 1790 (P.R.O.N.I. C.P. T.3158/1692); Sir R. Musgrave to J. Heaton, 22 Dec. 1790 (ibid. /1694); J. Heaton to W. Conner, 24 Aug. 1791 (ibid. /1696).

99. W. Conner to J. Heaton, 5 Sept. 1791 (CW. [Currey] Ms L/5 Bundle: 1788–1791).

100. Sir R. Musgrave to J. Heaton, 13 Feb. 1792 (CW. [Currey] Ms L/5 Bundle: Jan.–Dec. 1792); T. Garde to W. Conner, 16 June 1792 (ibid.).

101. Sir R. Musgrave to Sir Beaumont Hotham, 23 Jan. 1790 (CW. [Currey] Ms L/9/7 Bundle: 1787–1790); T. G. Lovett to Sir Beaumont Hotham, 26 Jan. 1790 (ibid.); J. Lovett to Sir Beaumont Hotham, 7 Mar. 1790 (ibid.); Sir R. Musgrave to J. Heaton, 14 Dec. 1790 (P.R.O.N.I. C.P. T.3158/1692); Sir R. Musgrave to J. Heaton, 13 Feb. 1792 (CW. [Currey] Ms L/5 Bundle: Jan.–Dec. 1792); Anonymous "Friends" to Fifth Duke, 26 July 1792 (ibid.); Memo by J. Heaton re W. Conner, 17 June 1792 (ibid.); Memo by J. Heaton "of information and advice to Mr. Conner," 11 July 1792 (P.R.O.N.I. C.P. T.3158/1710).

102. T. Garde to J. Heaton, 20 Sept. 1792 (CW. [Currey] Ms L/5 Bundle: Jan.–Dec. 1792); T. Knowlton to J. Heaton, 27 July 1799 (CW. [Currey] Ms L/5 Bundle: 1797–1799).

103. See, for example, Rental, General for 1764 (N.L.I. L.P. Ms 6646), 1784 (ibid., Ms 6650), and 1788 (ibid., Ms 6656); W. Conner to Sir Beaumont Hotham, 21 June 1783 (CW. [Currey] Ms L/9/7 Bundle: Letters from the Duke of Devonshire's Irish Steward, William Conner, in the Years 1780–1783); W. Conner to Sir Beaumont Hotham, 3 Feb. 1789 (CW. [Currey] Ms L/5 Bundle: 1788–1791).

104. C. Musgrave to W. Conner, 26 Nov. 1776 (CW. [Currey] Ms L/9/7 Bundle: Miscellaneous Irish Letters on the Duke of Devonshire's Affairs in the Years 1776–1783); W. Conner to Sir Beaumont Hotham, 28 Oct. 1780 (ibid.).

105. W. Conner to Sir A. Abdy, 8 Jan. 1773 (CW. [Currey] Ms L/9/7 Bundle: Irish Letters and Papers Relative to the Duke of Devonshire from about the Year 1772 to the End of 1776); L. M. Cullen, "Man, Landscape and Roads: The Changing Eighteenth Century," in W. Nolan, ed., *The Shaping of Ireland: The Geographical Perspective* (Dublin, 1986), 123–36; P. O'Flanagan, "Rural Change South of the River Bride in Counties Cork and Waterford: The Surveyors' Evidence, 1716–1851," *Irish Geography* 15 (1982): 60–61.

106. R. Grundy Heape, *Buxton under the Dukes of Devonshire* (London, 1948), 28–29.

107. J. Morrison, Estimate for Lismore Bridge, 4 Aug. 1771 (CW. [Currey] Ms L/5 Bundle: 1774–1791); J. Morrison to W. Conner, 6 Aug. 1771, 28 Apr. 1772, and 17 Aug. 1772 (ibid.); T. Ivory to Sir A. Abdy, 3 July 1773 (ibid.); T. Ivory, Observations Relative to the Bridge Proposed to Be Built Over the Blackwater at the Town of Lismore, 14 Feb. 1772 (ibid.); W. Conner to Sir A. Abdy, 8 Jan. 1773 (CW. [Currey] Ms L/9/7 Bundle: Irish Letters and Papers Relative to the Duke of Devonshire from about the Year 1772 to the End of 1776). Before their acceptance, Ivory's designs were first scrutinized—and criticized—by James Paine, the English architect responsible for the stable block at Chatsworth. See the Duchess of Devonshire, *The House* (London, 1982), 25, and F. Thompson, *Chatsworth: A Short History* (London, 1951), 27.

108. T. Ivory, Observations Relative to the Bridge Proposed to Be Built Over the Blackwater at the Town of Lismore, 14 Feb. 1772 (CW. [Currey] Ms L/5 Bundle: 1774–1791); J. Morrison to W. Conner, 28 Apr. 1772 (ibid.); T. Ivory to Sir A. Abdy, 14 Dec. 1773 (ibid.).

109. Messers Darley and Stokes to T. Ivory, 2 Dec. 1773 and 15 Jan. 1774 (ibid.); T. Ivory to Sir A. Abdy, 14 Dec. 1773, 16 Jan. 1774, and 15 Feb. 1774 (ibid.); General J. Gisborne to Sir A. Abdy, 3 Feb. 1774 (ibid.). The final cost was over £8,400. Memo by Messers Darley and Stokes to Duke of Devonshire, 6 Feb. 1776 (CW. [Currey] L/9/7 Bundle: Irish Letters and Papers Relative to the Duke of Devonshire from about the Year 1772 to the End of 1776).

110. Messers Darley and Stokes to T. Ivory, 2 Dec. 1773 and 15 Jan. 1774 (CW. (Currey Ms L/5 Bundle: 1774–1791); J. Morrison to Sir A. Abdy, 9 Jan. 1774 (ibid.); T. Ivory to Sir A. Abdy, 16 Jan. 1774 and 5 Feb. 1774 (ibid.); General J. Gisborne to Sir A. Abdy, 3 Feb. 1774 (ibid.); Memo by Messers Darley and Stokes to Duke of Devonshire, 6 Feb. 1776 (CW. [Currey] Ms L/9/7 Bundle: Irish Letters and Papers Relative to the Duke of Devonshire from about the Year 1772 to the End of 1776); Messers Darley and Stokes to Sir Beaumont Hotham, 6 Feb. 1776 (ibid.); T. Ivory to Sir Beaumont Hotham, 9 May 1776 (ibid.); W. Conner to Sir Beaumont Hotham, 9 July 1776 (ibid.); T. Ivory to Sir Beaumont Hotham, 28 Aug. 1776 (ibid.); W. Conner to Sir Beaumont Hotham, n/d, but circa Jan. 1778, 17 Mar. 1778, 11 Mar. 1779, 31 Mar. 1779, 10 Apr. 1779, and 3 June 1779 (CW. [Currey] Ms L/9/7 Bundle: Letters from the Duke of Devonshire's Irish Steward in the Years 1777–1780); T. Ivory to Sir Beaumont Hotham, 20 Dec. 1780 (CW. [Currey] Ms L/9/7 Bundle: Miscellaneous Irish Letters on the Duke of Devonshire's Affairs in the Years 1776–1783); F. E. Currey to W. Currey, 19 Dec. 1853 (Letter Book, W. Currey 1851–1855, N.L.I. L.P. Ms 7186).

111. T. Ivory to W. Conner, 15 Aug. 1772 (CW. [Currey] Ms L/5 Bundle: 1774–1791); T. Ivory to Sir A. Abdy, 7 Aug. 1773 (ibid.).

112. W. Conner to Sir Beaumont Hotham, 31 July 1775, 12 June 1776, 9 July 1776, and 15 Aug. 1776 (CW. [Currey] Ms L/9/7 Bundle: Irish Letters and Papers Relative to the Duke of Devonshire from about the Year 1772 to the End of 1776); W. Conner to Sir Beaumont Hotham, 24 Nov. 1777, 21 Mar. 1778, and 19 Feb. 1779 (CW. [Currey] Ms L/9/7 Bundle: Letters from the Duke of Devonshire's Irish Steward in the Years 1777–1780).

113. T. Ivory to Sir Beaumont Hotham, 28 Aug. 1776 and 5 Oct. 1776 (CW. [Currey] Ms L/9/7 Bundle: Irish Letters and Papers Relative to the Duke of Devonshire from about the Year 1772 to the End of 1776); W. Conner to Sir Beaumont Hotham, 16 Nov. 1776 (ibid.).

114. W. Conner to Sir Beaumont Hotham, 7 Mar. 1779 (CW. [Currey] Ms L/9/7 Bundle: Letters from the Duke of Devonshire's Irish Steward in the Years 1777–1780); W. Conner to Sir Beaumont Hotham, 23 Apr. 1781 (CW. [Currey] Ms L/9/7 Bundle: Letters from the Duke of Devonshire's Irish Steward, William Conner, in the Years 1780–1783); T. Ivory to Sir Beaumont Hotham, 23 May 1782 (CW. [Currey] Ms L/9/7 Bundle: Miscellaneous Irish Letters on the Duke of Devonshire's Affairs in the Years 1776–1783).

115. T. Ivory to Sir Beaumont Hotham, 20 Dec. 1780 and 24 Sept. 1781 (CW. [Currey] Ms L/9/7 Bundle: Miscellaneous Irish Letters on the Duke of Devonshire's Affairs in the Years 1776–1783); Rental, General for 1781 (N.L.I. L.P. Ms 6913[2]).

116. T. Ivory to Sir Beaumont Hotham, 23 May 1782 (CW. [Currey] Ms L/9/7 Bundle: Miscellaneous Irish Letters on the Duke of Devonshire's Affairs in the Years 1776–1783).

117. Sir R. Musgrave to J. Heaton, 13 Feb. 1792 (P.R.O.N.I. C.P. T.3158/1703); T. Garde to J. Heaton, 14 July 1792 (ibid. /1711).

118. E. Hewitt, ed. *Lord Shannon's Letters to His Son* (Belfast, 1982), xxviii, xxx–xxxi.

119. E. M. Johnston, *Great Britain and Ireland, 1760–1800* (Edinburgh, 1963), 322–27; A.P.W. Malcomson, "The Parliamentary Traffic of this Country," in T. Bartlett and D. W. Hayton, eds., *Penal Era and Golden Age* (Belfast, 1979), 138, 146–47.

120. Johnston estimates the number of freemen at fifty; see Johnston, *Great Britain,* 322. *Instructions* Given by the Chief Secretary to Ireland with reference to the Cities and Boroughs of Ireland Sending Representatives to Parliament, H. C. 1831–1832, *Reports and Plans,* 6:9, 145.

121. T. Garde to Sir Beaumont Hotham, 31 Jan. 1788 (CW. [Currey] Ms L/9/7 Bundle: Letters and Papers from Mr. Garde, Irish Law Agent for the Duke of Devonshire, c. 1777–1790).

122. W. Conner to Sir Beaumont Hotham, 17 Feb. 1778 (CW. [Currey] Ms L/9/7 Bundle: Letters from the Duke of Devonshire's Irish Steward in the Years 1777–1780).

123. W. Conner to Sir Beaumont Hotham, 17 Feb. 1778 (CW. [Currey] Ms L/9/7 Bundle: Letters from the Duke of Devonshire's Irish Steward in the Years 1777–1780); *Instructions,* 65.

124. W. Conner to Sir Beaumont Hotham, 17 Mar. 1778 (CW. [Currey] Ms L/9/7 Bundle: Letters from the Duke of Devonshire's Irish Steward in the Years 1777–1780); Hewitt, *Shannon's Letters,* xxxiv.

125. T. Knowlton to Sixth Duke, 28 Sept. 1812 (CW. Ms Sixth Duke's Correspondence Group I /77). "Close" boroughs were those under the complete control of one or two individuals, who were frequently also the major property owners in the town. See A.P.W. Malcomson, "The Parliamentary Traffic of this Country," Bartlett and Hayton, eds., *Penal Era,* 145.

126. Hewitt, *Shannon's Letters,* xxxv, xxxv–xxxvi.

127. Townsend Commons List. List of Commons, Apr.–May 1772 (P.R.O.N.I., T.2524/28), quoted in Hewitt, *Shannon's Letters,* 223.

128. Lord Shannon to Lord F. Cavendish, 29 Sept. 1767 (Copy) (CW. [Currey] Ms L/9/7 Bundle: Correspondence Relating to Bandon, 1766–1831); Article of Agreement with Mr. Bernard of Castle Bernard Made by Lord Shannon on Behalf of the Duke of Devonshire's Interest Regarding Bandon Corporation, 29 Sept. 1767 (Copy) (ibid.).

129. Hewitt, *Shannon's Letters,* xxxv, 240.

130. Malcomson, "Parliamentary Traffic," 140.

131. T. Bartlett, "The Townshend Viceroyalty, 1767–72," in Bartlett and Hayton, eds., *Penal Era,* 88–112; Hewitt, *Shannon's Letters,* xxxiii–iv.

132. W. Conner to Sir Beaumont Hotham, 12 June 1776 (CW. [Currey] Ms L/9/7 Bundle: Irish Letters and Papers Relative to the Duke of Devonshire from about the Year 1772 to the End of 1776); Hewitt, *Shannon's Letters,* 251.

133. W. Conner to Sir Beaumont Hotham, 21 Aug. 1783 (CW. [Currey] Ms L/9/7 Bundle: Letters from the Duke of Devonshire's Irish Steward, William Conner, in the Years 1780–1783); Sir R. Musgrave to Sir Beaumont Hotham, 25 Mar. 1786 (CW. [Currey] Ms L/9/7 Bundle: Miscellaneous Irish Letters on the Duke of Devonshire's Affairs in the Years 1783–1786).

134. W. Conner to Sir Beaumont Hotham, 17 Mar. 1778 (CW. [Currey] Ms L/9/7 Bundle: Letters from the Duke of Devonshire's Irish Steward in the Years 1777–1780); Hewitt, *Shannon's Letters,* 252–53.

135. W. Conner to Sir Beaumont Hotham, 12 June 1776 (CW. [Currey] Ms L/9/7 Bundle: Irish Letters and Papers Relative to the Duke of Devonshire from about the

Year 1772 to the End of 1776); W. Conner to Sir Beaumont Hotham, 21 Aug. 1783 (CW. [Currey] Ms L/9/7 Bundle: Letters from the Duke of Devonshire's Irish Steward, William Conner, in the Years 1780–1783); Sir R. Musgrave to Sir Beaumont Hotham, 7 Oct. 1783 (CW. [Currey] Ms L/9/7 Bundle: Miscellaneous Irish Letters on the Duke of Devonshire's Affairs in the Years 1783–1786); Hewitt, *Shannon's Letters*, xxxiii.

136. Sir R. Musgrave to J. Heaton, 22 Dec. 1790 (P.R.O.N.I. C.P. T.3158/1694).

137. W. Conner to Sir Beaumont Hotham, 12 June 1776 (CW. [Currey] Ms L/9/7 Bundle: Irish Letters and Papers Relative to the Duke of Devonshire from about the Year 1772 to the End of 1776); Colonel H. Cane to Sir Beaumont Hotham, 23 Sept. 1779 and 10 Aug. 1783 (CW. [Currey] Ms L/9/7 Bundle: Miscellaneous Irish Letters on the Duke of Devonshire's Affairs in the Years 1776–1783); Hewitt, *Shannon's Letters*, 253–54.

138. J. Pearson, *Stags and Serpents: The Story of the House of Cavendish and the Dukes of Devonshire* (London, 1983), 91–115; H. Stokes, *The Devonshire House Circle* (London, 1917), 90–92.

139. W. Conner to Sir Beaumont Hotham, 4 Sept. 1786 (CW. [Currey] Ms L/9/7 Bundle: Letters from the Duke of Devonshire's Irish Steward, William Conner, in the Years 1784–1786); T. Garde to Sir Beaumont Hotham, 31 Jan. 1788 (CW. [Currey] Ms L/9/7 Bundle: Letters and Papers from Mr. Garde, Irish Law Agent for the Duke of Devonshire c. 1777–1790).

140. W. Conner to Sir Beaumont Hotham, n/d, but Jan. 1778 and 10 Jan. 1778, 17 Feb. 1778, and 8 Aug. 1778 (CW. [Currey] Ms L/9/7 Bundle: Letters from the Duke of Devonshire's Irish Steward in the Years 1777–1780); W. Conner to Sir Beaumont Hotham, 19 May 1783, 4 June 1783, and 21 June 1783 (CW. [Currey] Ms L/9/7 Bundle: Letters from the Duke of Devonshire's Irish Steward, William Conner, in the Years 1780–1783); Sir R. Musgrave to J. Heaton, 13 Feb. 1792 (P.R.O.N.I. C.P. T.3158/1703); T. Garde to J. Heaton, 30 June 1792 (ibid. /1709); T. Garde to J. Heaton, 14 July 1792 (ibid. /1711).

141. W. Conner to Sir Beaumont Hotham, 5 Feb. 1785, 7 Dec. 1785, 5 June 1786, and 29 July 1786 (CW. [Currey] Ms L/9/7 Bundle: Letters from the Duke of Devonshire's Irish Steward, William Conner, in the Years 1784–1786).

142. Sir R. Musgrave to J. Heaton, 13 Feb. 1792 (P.R.O.N.I. C.P. T.3158/1703).

143. W. Conner to Sir Beaumont Hotham, 13 Feb. 1790 (CW. [Currey] Ms L/5 Bundle: 1788–1791).

144. T. Garde to Sir Beaumont Hotham, 31 Jan. 1788 (CW. [Currey] Ms L/9/7 Bundle: Letters and Papers from Mr. Garde, Irish Law Agent for the Duke of Devonshire c. 1777–1790).

Chapter 5. "For Power and Profit"

1. F. J. Carney, "Pre-Famine Irish Population: The Evidence from the Trinity College Estates," *Irish Economic and Social History* 2 (1975): 35–45; J. M. Goldstrom and L. A. Clarkson, eds., *Irish Population, Economy, and Society* (Oxford, 1981), 27; D. B. Grigg, *Population Growth and Agrarian Change: An Historical Perspective* (Cambridge, 1980), 116–17.

2. C. Ó Gráda, *Ireland Before and After the Famine: Explorations in Economic History, 1800–1925* (Manchester, 1988), 2–38.

3. T. Knowlton to J. Heaton, 2 July 1800 (CW. [Currey] Ms L/5 Bundle: 1800); T. Knowlton to J. Heaton, 11 Mar. 1801 (CW. [Currey] Ms L/5 Bundle: 1801).

4. H. Bowman to J. Heaton, 29 Jan. 1797 (CW. [Currey] Ms L/5 Bundle: Jan.–Dec. 1793).

5. Great Britain, Parliamentary Papers (1836, vols. 30–34), "Reports of the Commissioners for Inquiry into the Condition of the Poorer Classes in Ireland"; L. M. Cullen, *An Economic History of Ireland since 1660*, 2d ed. (London 1987), 119–20; S. Lewis, *Topographical Dictionary of Ireland* (London, 1837) 1: 179; W. K. Spillar, *A Short Topographical and Statistical Account of the Bandon Union* (Bandon, 1844), 34–37.

6. T. Garde to J. Heaton, 25 Sept. 1800 (CW. [Currey] Ms L/5 Bundle: 1800).

7. J. Barry, "Henry Bowman: Reports on the Duke of Devonshire's Irish Estates, 1794–1797," *Analecta Hibernica* 22 (1960): 275–88.

8. T. Garde to J. Heaton, 3 and 10 Apr. 1792 (CW [Currey] Ms L/5 Bundle: Jan.–Dec. 1792).

9. T. Knowlton to J. Heaton, 25 Jan. 1804 (CW. [Currey] Ms L/5 Bundle: Jan.–Dec. 1804).

10. Memorandum of Things Agreed with Mr. Garde to Be Attended to Respecting the Duke of Devonshire's Affairs in Ireland—June 5th and 6th 1792 (CW. [Currey] Ms L/9/7 Bundle: Bandon 1766–1831); Memorandum Taken Out by Mr. Garde and Mr. Bowman (CW. [Currey] Ms L/5 Bundle: Jan.–May 1793).

11. J. Abercrombie to Sixth Duke, 13 Jan. 1822 (CW. Ms Sixth Duke's Correspondence Group I/. 598).

12. J. Heaton to Sixth Duke, 26 Aug. 1812 (CW. [Currey] Ms L/83/3 [2]).

13. H. Bowman to J. Heaton, 5 Dec. 1792 (CW. [Currey] Ms L/5 Bundle: Jan.–Dec. 1792).

14. Barry, "Bowman," 279–80.

15. A.P.W. Malcomson, *John Forster: The Politics of the Anglo-Irish Ascendancy* (Oxford, 1978), 298–99.

16. Barry, "Bowman," 280.

17. Schedule of Tallow Town Leases, 1827 [*sic*] (N.L.I. L.P. Ms 6160).

18. Dungarvan Tenures, c. 1853 (N.L.I. L.P. Ms 6170).

19. Barry, "Bowman," 282.

20. R. Lloyd to T. Knowlton, 13 Nov. 1802 (CW. [Currey] Ms L/5 Bundle: Jan.–Dec. 1802).

21. R. Lloyd to T. Knowlton, 3 Dec. 1802 (CW. [Currey] Ms L/5 Bundle: Jan.–Dec. 1802).

22. R. Lloyd to T. Garde, 11 Feb. 1798 (CW. [Currey] Ms L/9/7 Bundle: Correspondence Relating to Bandon, 1766–1831).

23. Barry, "Bowman," 276–78.

24. H. Bowman, "Remarks on the Advantages that May Be Derived by Making a Canal Near Lismore, a Road Over the Mountains and Building an Inn at Lismore," (CW. [Currey] Ms L/5 Bundle: Jan.–May 1793).

25. Barry, "Bowman," 277.

26. Ibid.

27. H. Bowman to J. Heaton, 7 Nov. 1797 (CW. [Currey] Ms L/5 Bundle: 1797–1799).

28. Barry, "Bowman," 278.

29. H. Bowman to J. Heaton, 23 May 1793 (CW. [Currey] Ms L/5 Bundle: Jan.–Dec. 1793).

30. H. Bowman to J. Heaton, 24 Aug. 1793, 14 Sept. 1793, 17 May 1794, 30 June 1795, and 15 Aug. 1795 (ibid.).

31. Memorial—FitzGerald to Fifth Duke, 12 May 1810 (CW. [Currey] Ms L/9/11 Bundle: Miscellaneous Correspondence 1812–1818, Lismore Inn and Castle).

32. W. Jessop to J. Heaton, 19 June 1793 (ibid.); H. Bowman to J. Heaton, 24 Aug. 1793, 19 Apr. 1794, 17 May 1794, 10 July 1794, 30 June 1795, 23 July 1795, 15 Aug. 1795, and 3 Sept. 1795 (ibid.); T. Garde to J. Heaton, 27 July 1795 (ibid.); J. Hudson to J. Heaton, 6 Sept. 1797 (CW. [Currey] Ms L/5 Bundle: 1797–1799).

33. Lockage Accounts 1851–1890 (L.E.O. Ms A/6/1-28).

34. H. Bowman to J. Heaton, 9 Nov. 1796 (CW. [Currey] Ms L/5 Bundle: Jan.–Dec. 1793); Cullen, *Ireland*, 58–59; D. Dickson, "The Place of Dublin in the Eighteenth-Century Irish Economy," in T. M. Devine and D. Dickson, eds., *Ireland and Scotland, 1600–1850* (Edinburgh, 1983), 188; W. A. McCutcheon, "Transport, 1820–1914," in L. Kennedy and P. Ollerenshaw, eds., *An Economic History of Ulster, 1820–1939* (Manchester, 1985), 114.

35. Ibid.

36. Cullen, *Ireland*, 80; W. Nolan, "Patterns of Living in Tipperary, 1750–1850," in W. Nolan, ed., *Tipperary: History and Society* (Dublin, 1985), 293.

37. Among a fairly wide-ranging general literature but relatively few specific studies, see, for example, L. M. Cullen, *The Emergence of Modern Ireland, 1600–1900* (London, 1981), 61–82; M. E. Daly, "Irish Urban History: A Survey," *Urban History Yearbook* (Leicester, 1986), 64–65; A. A. Horner, "The Scope and the Limitations of the Landlord Contribution to Changing the Irish Landscape, 1700–1850," *Collected Papers Presented to the Permanent European Conference for the Study of the Rural Landscape* (Copenhagen, 1986), 71–77; P. J. O'Connor, *Exploring Limerick's Past: An Historical Geography of Urban Development in County and City* (Newcastle West, 1987), 36–85; and A. R. Orme, *The World's Landscapes*, vol. 4: *Ireland* (London, 1970), 138–48.

38. F.H.A. Aalen, *Man and the Landscape in Ireland* (London, 1978), 281–84; Cullen, *Emergence*, 68–72; O'Connor, *Limerick's Past*, 64–85, 88–96; Orme, *Ireland*, 143.

39. H. Bowman to J. Heaton, 23 July 1795, 9 Jan. 1796, 20 Feb. 1796, 11 Aug. 1796, 29 Jan. 1797, 7 Feb. 1797, and 30 Apr. 1797 (CW. [Currey] Ms. L/5 Bundle: Jan.–Dec. 1793); T. Garde to J. Heaton, 5 Apr. 1797 (ibid.); J. Panton to J. Heaton, 21 Nov. 1798 (CW. [Currey] Ms L/9/11 Bundle: Land Alphabets and Correspondence, 1798–1816).

40. H. Bowman to J. Heaton, 9 Feb. 1797 (CW [Currey] Ms L/5 Bundle: Jan.–Dec. 1793).

41. T. Knowlton to J. Heaton, 13 Sept. 1797 (CW. [Currey] Ms L/5 Bundle: 1797–1799).

42. T. Knowlton to J. Heaton, 20 Oct. 1797 (ibid.).

43. (CW. [Currey] Ms L/9/11 Bundle: Copy Correspondence 26 Oct. 1798–21 Mar. 1799, passim).

44. T. Knowlton to J. Heaton, 22 July 1799 and 27 July 1799 (CW. [Currey] Ms L/5 Bundle: 1797–1799); J. Panton to Mr. Shaw, 12 Dec. 1798 (ibid.).

45. D. McCartney, *The Dawning of Democracy: Ireland, 1800–1870* (Dublin, 1987), 1–25.

46. P. Jupp, *British and Irish Parliamentary Elections, 1784–1831* (Newton Abbot, 1973), 152–57.

47. P. Jupp, "Urban Politics in Ireland, 1801–31," in D. Harkness and M. O'Dowd, eds., *The Town in Ireland* (Belfast, 1981), 104–6.

48. Petition of the Inhabitants and Electors of Tallow to the Commissioners of Boroughs Disenfranchised by the Act of Union . . . 28 Apr. 1801 (P.R.O.N.I. C.P. T.3158/1815); T. Knowlton to J. Heaton, 6 July 1801 (CW. [Currey] Ms L/5 Bundle: 1801); T. Garde to J. Heaton, 11 and 31 July and 4 Aug. 1801 (ibid.); T. Knowlton to J. Heaton, 19 July 1803 (CW. [Currey] Ms L/5 Bundle: Jan.–Dec. 1803); McCartney, *Dawning*, 12.

49. H. Bowman to J. Heaton, 4 Feb. 1800 (P.R.O.N.I. C.P. T.3158/1799); J. Heaton to T. Knowlton, 4 July 1801 (CW. [Currey] Ms L/9/7 Bundle: Correspondence Relating to Bandon 1766–1831); "Mr. Garde's Statement Respecting the County of Waterford and the Borough of Dungarvan for the Consideration of His Grace the Duke of Devonshire . . . ," 2 Sept. 1801 (P.R.O.N.I. C.P. T.3158/1829); "Mr. Knowlton and Mr. Garde's Report in Regard to Power in Ireland," 3 Sept. 1801 (ibid. /1830).

50. W. Fraher, "The Reconstruction of Dungarvan, 1807–c. 1830: A Political Ploy," *Decies* 25 (1984): 5–10.

51. "Mr. Knowlton and Mr. Garde's Report in Regard to Power in Ireland," 3 Sept. 1801 (P.R.O.N.I. C.P. T.3158/1830).

52. T. Garde to J. Heaton, 8 Jan. 1792 (ibid. /1700).

53. T. Garde to J. Heaton, 20 July 1795 (ibid. /1729).

54. H. Bowman to J. Heaton, 12 Dec. 1797 (ibid. /1757).

55. W. B. Ponsonby to J. Heaton, 8 Mar. 1802 (ibid. /1833); T. Knowlton to J. Heaton, 18 July 1802 (ibid. /1844).

56. T. Knowlton to J. Heaton, 17 May 1803 (ibid. /1849).

57. T. Knowlton to J. Heaton, 1 Oct. 1806 (ibid. /1868); Barry, "Bowman," 284.

58. T. Knowlton to J. Heaton, 1 Oct. 1806 (P.R.O.N.I. C.P. T.3158/1868).

59. T. Knowlton to J. Heaton, 13 Aug. 1803, 3 Sept. 1803, and 20 Sept. 1803 (CW. [Currey] Ms L/5 Bundle: Jan.–Dec. 1803).

60. T. Knowlton to J. Heaton, 1 Oct. 1806 (P.R.O.N.I. C.P. T.3158/1868). The total cost of buying and shipping the materials was £2,678-6-4d. See "Dungarvan Works," Rental General, 1806 (N.L.I. L.P. Ms 6678).

61. "Dungarvan Works," Rental General, 1807 (N.L.I. L.P. Ms 6679); "Dungarvan Works," Rental General, 1808 (N.L.I. L.P. Ms 6673); "Dungarvan Works," Rental General, 1810 (N.L.I. L.P. Ms 6680); W. Fraher, *An Architectural Inventory of Dungarvan* (Dungarvan, 1984), 63–64; Fraher, "Dungarvan," 17–18.

62. B. M. Walker, ed., *Parliamentary Election Results in Ireland, 1801–1922* (Dublin, 1978), 12.

63. T. Knowlton to J. Heaton, 13 May 1807 (P.R.O.N.I. C.P. T.3158/1886); T. Knowlton to J. Heaton, 19 May 1807 (ibid. /1889); T. Knowlton to J. Heaton, 23 May 1807 (ibid. /1890); T. Knowlton to J. Heaton, 27 May 1807 (ibid. /1891).

64. Walker, *Election Results*, 16.

65. T. Knowlton to J. Heaton, 25 Apr. 1807 and 27 May 1807 (CW [Currey] Ms L/5 Bundle: Jan.–July 1807).

66. Memorial from the County Waterford Grand Jury to the Duke of Devonshire, 2 Oct. 1804 (CW. [Currey] Ms L/5 Bundle: Jan.–Dec. 1804).

67. J. Henry to General G. Walpole, 14 Apr. 1808 (CW. [Currey] Ms L/5 Bundle: Apr. 1808–May 1809).

68. T. Knowlton to J. Heaton, 20 Oct. 1808 (ibid.).

69. T. Knowlton to J. Heaton, 20 Oct. 1808 (CW. [Currey] Ms L/5 Bundle: Apr. 1808–May 1809); Fraher, "Dungarvan," 15.

70. Ibid.

71. Ibid.

72. T. Knowlton to J. Heaton, 20 Oct. 1808 (CW. [Currey] Ms L/5 Bundle: Apr. 1808–May 1809); "Dungarvan Works," Rental General, 1810, 1812, 1813 (N.L.I. L.P. Mss 6680, 6682, 6683); Lewis, *Dictionary*, 1:578.

73. Bridge Correspondence (N.L.I. L.P. Ms 7199).

74. T. Knowlton to Sixth Duke, 4 Feb. 1820 (CW. Sixth Duke's Correspondence Group I/. 420).

75. Bridge Correspondence (N.L.I. L.P. Ms 7199).

76. Malcomson, *Forster*, 69, 114, 282–83, 297–303.

77. T. Knowlton to J. Heaton, 25 Apr. 1807 (P.R.O.N.I. C.P. T.3158/1882).

78. T. Knowlton to J. Heaton, 12 Apr. 1807 (ibid. /1881).

79. T. Knowlton to J. Heaton, 22 Aug. 1807 (ibid. /1904); T. Knowlton to J. Heaton, 16 July 1807 (CW. [Currey] Ms L/5 Bundle: Jan.-July 1807); T. Knowlton to J. Heaton, 12 Sept. 1807 (CW. [Currey] Ms L/5 Bundle: Aug.–Dec. 1807); T. Knowlton to J. Heaton, 5 Dec. 1808 (CW [Currey] Ms L/5 Bundle: Apr. 1808–May 1809); Rental General, 1810 (N.L.I. L.P. Ms 6680); J. Heaton to Sixth Duke, 16 Feb. 1813 and 17 Mar. 1813 (CW. [Currey] Ms L/83/3 [2]).

80. T. Knowlton to J. Heaton, 17 May 1803 (CW. [Currey] Ms L/5 Bundle: Jan.–Dec. 1803).

81. T. Knowlton to J. Heaton, 7 Jan. 1807 and 13 May 1807 (CW. [Currey] Ms L/5 Bundle: Jan.–July 1807).

82. T. Knowlton to J. Heaton, 7 Jan. 1807 (ibid.).

83. T. Knowlton to J. Heaton, 13 May 1807 (ibid.).

84. T. Knowlton to J. Heaton, 10 June 1807 (CW. [Currey] Ms L/9/11 Bundle: Land Alphabets and Correspondence 1798–1816).

85. Fraher, "Dungarvan," 12, 19.

86. T. Knowlton to J. Heaton, 6 Jan. 1811 (CW. [Currey] Ms L/9/11 Bundle: Land Alphabets and Correspondence 1798–1816).

87. "Borough of Dungarvan," Disbursement Ledger 1821–1829 (N.L.I. L.P. Ms 6923).

88. Ibid. Malcomson, *Forster*, 312–13.

89. Untitled newspaper extract reporting admissions to freedom in Irish towns and cities in the seven years ending 7 Apr. 1829, ? Apr. 1829 (L.E.O. C/1/4 Bundle: Youghal Political and Election Correspondence 19 Nov. 1828–29 Oct. 1831).

90. Dungarvan Tenures, c. 1853 (N.L.I. L.P. Ms 6170).

91. O'Connor, *Limerick's Past*, 81, 84–85.

92. "Borough of Dungarvan," Disbursement Ledger 1821–1829 (N.L.I. L.P. Ms 6923).

93. Rental General, 1804–1813 (N.L.I. L.P. Mss 6675–6683); Rental General, 1811 (CW. [Currey] Ms L/9/11); Disbursement Ledger, 1815–1817 (1820) (N.L.I. L.P. Ms 6915).

94. T. Knowlton to J. Heaton, 7 Oct. 1800, 19 Oct. 1800, 25 Oct. 1800, and 20 Dec. 1800 (CW. [Currey] Ms L/5 Bundle: 1800); T. Knowlton to J. Heaton, 9 July 1801 (CW. [Currey] Ms L/5 Bundle: 1801); R. Lloyd to T. Knowlton, 13 Nov. 1802 (CW. [Currey] Ms L/5 Bundle: Jan.–Dec. 1802).

95. P. O'Flanagan, *Irish Historic Towns Atlas No. 3: Bandon* (Dublin, 1988), 6–7.

96. R. Lloyd to T. Knowlton, 15 Mar. 1802, 17 Mar. 1802, and 28 Mar. 1802 (CW. [Currey] Ms L/5 Bundle: Jan.–Dec. 1802); T. Knowlton to J. Heaton, 18 Mar. 1802, 27 Mar. 1802, 28 Mar 1802, and 7 Apr. 1802 (ibid.).

97. I. d'Alton, *Protestant Society and Politics in Cork, 1812–1844* (Cork, 1980), 124.

98. T. Knowlton to J. Heaton, 21 Apr. 1798 (CW. [Currey] Ms L/5 Bundle: 1797–1799); T. Garde to J. Heaton, 7 Mar. 1800 (CW. [Currey] Ms L/9/7 Bundle: Correspondence Relating to Bandon, 1766–1831).

99. Lord Bandon to Fifth Duke, 22 Sept. 1801 (ibid.).

100. R. Lloyd to T. Garde, 11 Feb. 1798 (CW. [Currey] Ms L/5 Bundle: 1797–1799).

101. "Extract of Lease and Survey of That Part of the Estate Held by Lord Bandon under the Duke of Devonshire," c. 1804 (CW. [Currey] Ms L/9/7 Bundle: Corre-

spondence Relating to Bandon 1766–1831); T. Knowlton to J. Heaton, 31 May 1807 (CW. [Currey] Ms L/9/11 Bundle: Lord Bandon's Correspondence 1807–1809).

102. W. Conner to T. Bernard, 8 Nov. 1787 (CW. [Currey] Ms L/9/11 Bundle: Bernard Correspondence 1787–1813).

103. "List of Bernard Correspondence, circa 1813" (ibid.).

104. Lord Bandon to Fifth Duke, 25 Aug. 1799 (CW. [Currey] Ms L/9/7 Bundle: Correspondence Relating to Bandon 1766–1831).

105. T. Knowlton to J. Heaton, 21 Apr. 1798 (P.R.O.N.I. C.P. T.3158/1763).

106. Lord Bandon to Fifth Duke, 25 Aug. 1799 and 22 Sept. 1801 (CW. [Currey] Ms L/9/7 Bundle: Correspondence Relating to Bandon 1766–1831); T. Knowlton to W. Ponsonby, 3 July 1802 (ibid.); Fifth Duke to Lord Bandon, 2 Oct. 1801 and 10 May 1802 (ibid.); T. Knowlton to J. Heaton, 11 May and 15 Oct. 1807 (ibid.).

107. T. Knowlton to J. Heaton, 19 Apr. 1806, 24 June 1806, and 18 July 1806 (CW. [Currey] Ms L/5 Bundle: Apr.–Dec. 1806); T. Knowlton to J. Heaton, 20 Aug. 1806 (CW. [Currey] Ms L/9/7 Bundle: Correspondence Relating to Bandon 1766–1831); A. B. Bernard to Fifth Duke, 17 Jan. 1805 (CW. [Currey] Ms L/9/11 Bundle: Bernard Correspondence 1787–1813).

108. (CW. [Currey] Ms L/9/11 Bundle: Bernard Correspondence 1787–1813), passim.

109. T. Knowlton to J. Heaton, 11 May 1807 (CW. [Currey] Ms L/9/7 Bundle: Correspondence Relating to Bandon 1766–1831); T. Knowlton to J. Heaton, 10 July 1807 (CW. [Currey] Ms L/9/11 Bundle: Lord Bandon's Correspondence 1807–1809).

110. (CW. [Currey] Ms L/9/11 Bundle: Bernard Correspondence 1787–1813), passim.

111. Walker, *Election Results*, 18.

112. Lord Bandon to Fifth Duke, 31 July 1811 (L.E.O. Ms C/1/19 Bundle: Correspondence of W. S. Currey Concerning the Borough of Bandon . . . 31 July 1811–21 Jan. 1827).

113. Paper Containing Copies of the Correspondence between T. Knowlton and S. Stawell, 25 Aug.–16 Sept. 1813 (ibid.); T. Knowlton to S. Stawell, 8 Sept. 1813 and 16 Sept. 1813 (ibid.); S. Stawell to T. Knowlton, 12 Sept. 1813 (ibid.); d'Alton, *Protestant Society*, 101–2; Walker, *Election Results*, 15–49.

114. "Mr. Knowlton and Mr. Garde's Report in Regard to Power in Ireland," 3 Sept. 1801 (P.R.O.N.I. C.P. T.3158/1830).

115. J. Heaton to Sixth Duke, 24 Aug. 1813 (CW. [Currey] Ms L/83/3 [2]).

116. J. Heaton to Sixth Duke, 26 Aug. 1813 (ibid.).

117. "Youghal Disbursements," Rental General, 1804–1813 (N.L.I. L.P. Mss 6675–6683); "Youghal Disbursements," Rental General, 1811 (CW. [Currey] Ms L/9/11); "Youghal Disbursements," Disbursement Ledger 1815–1817 (1820) (N.L.I. L.P. Ms 6195).

118. Youghal Rental, 1830 (N.L.I. L.P. Ms 6797).

119. d'Alton, *Protestant Society*, 105.

120. H. Bowman to J. Hudson, 12 Nov. 1796 (L.E.O. Ms C/1/1 Bundle: Youghal Correspondence 1 Dec. 1791–8 July 1812).

121. T. Knowlton to J. Heaton, 25 Oct. 1802 (CW. [Currey] Ms L/5 Bundle: Jan.–Dec. 1802).

122. T. Garde to J. Heaton, 9 Oct. 1802 (P.R.O.N.I. C.P. T.3158/1846).

123. T. Knowlton to J. Heaton, 29 Sept. 1807 (CW. [Currey] Ms L/9/7 Bundle: Youghal 1804–1807). Freemen could also be nominated by the aldermen in their capacity as past mayors, and were not made exclusively, as d'Alton implies, by the cur-

rent mayor. See Municipal Corporation Boundaries (Ireland), *Report and Plans* (London H. C., vol. 4, 1836 [1837]); d'Alton, *Protestant Society*, 103.

124. T. Knowlton to J. Heaton, 29 Sept. 1807 (CW. [Currey] Ms L/9/7 Bundle: Youghal 1804–1807).

125. T. Knowlton to J. Heaton, 6 Oct. 1807, 7 Oct. 1807, and 9 Oct. 1807 (ibid.); Mr. Lawton to J. Heaton, 25 Apr. 1807 (ibid.); T. Knowlton to J. Heaton, 10 Aug. 1808, 19 Aug. 1808, 8 Sept. 1808, and 18 Dec. 1808 (P.R.O.N.I. C.P. T.3158/1920/1921/1923/1932).

126. T. Knowlton to J. Hudson, 31 Dec. 1809 (L.E.O. Ms C/1/11 Bundle: Copy Correspondence Concerning Youghal 1809–1821).

127. T. Knowlton to Sixth Duke, 28 Sept. 1812 (CW. Ms Sixth Duke's Correspondence Group I/.77); J. Heaton to Sixth Duke, 24 Aug. 1813 (CW. [Currey] Ms L/83/3 [2]).

128. Earl of Shannon to Sixth Duke, 27 Aug. 1812 (CW. Ms Sixth Duke's Correspondence Group I/. 73).

129. d'Alton, *Protestant Society*, 124; Walker, *Election Results*, 21, 24.

130. J. Abercrombie to Sixth Duke, 13 Jan. 1822 (CW. Ms Sixth Duke's Correspondence Group I/598); (L.E.O. Ms C/1/11 Bundle: Copy Correspondence Concerning Youghal 1809–1821), passim.

131. "Mr. Knowlton's Instructions to Mr. Hudson," n/d, but circa 1812 (ibid.); T. Seward to J. Hudson, 24 May 1813, 12 Feb. 1816, and 21 Feb. 1816 (ibid.).

132. J. Abercrombie to Sixth Duke, 13 Jan. 1822 (CW. Ms Sixth Duke's Correspondence Group I/598).

133. T. Seward to J. Hudson, 18 Mar. 1815 and 12 Feb. 1818 (L.E.O. Ms C/1/11 Bundle: Copy Correspondence Concerning Youghal 1809–1821); J. Abercrombie to Sixth Duke, 13 Jan. 1822 (CW. Ms Sixth Duke's Correspondence Group I/598); d'Alton, *Protestant Society*, 105.

134. J. Abercrombie to Sixth Duke, 13 Jan. 1822 (CW. Ms Sixth Duke's Correspondence Group I/598).

135. Ibid. "Compensation," Disbursement Ledger, 1821–1829 (N.L.I. L.P. Ms 6923); d'Alton, *Protestant Society*, 107.

136. Ibid.

137. J. Abercrombie to Sixth Duke, 13 Jan. 1822 (CW. Ms Sixth Duke's Correspondence Group I/598).

138. The Duchess of Devonshire, *The House: A Portrait of Chatsworth* (London, 1982), 29–31; F. Thompson, *Chatsworth: A Short History* (London, 1951), 29–31.

139. Marquis of Hartington to "Dearest G.," 24 June 1810 (CW. Ms Fifth Duke's Correspondence, Sixth Duke's Group /1973); Marquis of Hartington to "Dearest G. M.," 26 June 1810 (ibid. /1975).

140. Account of Castle Rebuilding Expenses in 1812 and 1813, n/d (CW. [Currey] Ms L/9/11 Bundle: Miscellaneous Correspondence 1812–1818, Lismore Inn and Castle); "Lismore Works," Rental General, 1812 and 1813 (N.L.I. L.P. Mss 6682–6683); J. Pearson, *Stags and Serpents*, 119, 121–23.

141. Sixth Duke to "G.," 18 Sept. 1814 (CW. Ms Sixth Duke's Correspondence Group I/119).

142. Sixth Duke to "Ellie," 3 Sept. 1822 (ibid. /677).

143. Disbursement Ledger, 1815–1817 (1820) (N.L.I. L.P. Ms 6915).

144. Sixth Duke's Diary, entry for 31 Aug. 1822 (CW. Ms 767. 446/35).

145. Sixth Duke's Diary, entry for 20 Sept. 1822 (ibid. /38).

146. Sixth Duke's Diary, entry for 11 Sept. 1822 (ibid. /37).

147. These figures are derived from the entries in the Disbursement Ledger for 1821–1829 (N.L.I. L.P. Ms 6923). They are liable to be an overestimate as they include some sums, for example, for labor, that were expended on both rural and urban projects but which cannot be differentiated in the surviving accounts.

148. Sixth Duke's Diary, entry for 1 Sept. 1822 (CW. Ms 767. 446/36).

149. "Lismore Works," Disbursement Ledger, 1821–1829 (N.L.I. L.P. Ms 6923). Eight years later sundry houses were still being demolished in the New Walk "to improve the appearance of the town"; see Lismore and Tallow Rental, 1832 (N.L.I. L.P. Ms 6852).

150. Ibid.; Lismore and Tallow Rental, 1840 (N.L.I. L.P. Ms 6854).

151. "Variations in Rental," Draft Ledger for 1829–1833 (N.L.I. L.P. Mss 6961–65); "Variations in Rental," Draft Ledger, 1833 (N.L.I. L.P. Ms 6965); "Lismore Works," Draft Ledger, 1834 (N.L.I. L.P. Ms 6966).

152. Lismore and District Tenure Book, circa 1870 (N.L.I. L.P. Ms 6192); Draft Ledger, 1832 (N.L.I. L.P. Ms 6964).

153. "Bandon Works," Disbursement Ledger, 1821–1829 (N.L.I. L.P. Ms 6923); "Bandon Works," Draft Ledger, 1831 (N.L.I. L.P. Ms 6963).

154. O'Flanagan, *Bandon*, 6–7.

155. Printed Circular: "New Catholic Chapel and Parochial School at Dungarvan," 18 June 1829 (L.E.O. Ms C/1/7 Bundle: General Political Correspondence 9 June 1829–10 Aug. 1829).

156. W. S. Currey to B. Currey, 14 July 1832 (L.E.O. Ms C/1/30 Bundle: Dungarvan Political and Election Correspondence 3 Apr. 1832–26 Dec. 1833).

157. "Youghal Disbursements," Disbursement Ledger, 1821–1829 (N.L.I. L.P. Ms 6923); "Youghal Disbursements," Draft Ledgers for 1830, 1831, and 1832 (N.L.I. L.P. Mss 6962, 6963, 6964).

158. Remittances; Remittances by Sale of Estates; Works at Tallow, Lismore, and Kinnataloon; Quit Rents and Chiefries; Compensation; Taxes; Incidental Disbursements; Subscriptions, Schools, and Charities; Woods and Plantations; Law Charges; Drainage and Government Loan Instalments; Youghal Slob Enclosure; House Expenses; Gardens; Bandon Disbursements; Dungarvan Disbursements; Tithe Rent Charge; Management.

159. T. Knowlton to J. Heaton, 28 Aug. 1806 and 15 Sept. 1806 (CW. [Currey] Ms L/5 Bundle: Apr.–Dec. 1806).

160. F. E. Currey to Seventh Duke, 30 Oct. 1858, Letter Book, W. Currey 1858–1863 (N.L.I. L.P. Ms 7190).

161. J. Abercrombie to Sixth Duke, 6 Apr. 1817 (CW. Ms Fifth Duke's Correspondence, Sixth Duke's Group/. 207); B. Currey to W. S. Currey, 19 Nov. 1827 (L.E.O. Ms C/1/2 Bundle: General Correspondence 8 Feb. 1825–9 Dec. 1839).

162. For example, of the £2,414 total improvement expenditure at Tallow, Lismore, and Kinnataloon in 1823–1824, £708 (30 percent) was spent on labor, compared with £634 or 21 percent of the £3,039 spent in 1824–1825. See Disbursement Ledger, 1821–1829 (N.L.I. L.P. Ms 6923).

163. Bandon Rental, 1826–1835 (N.L.I. L.P. Ms 6158); Dungarvan Rental, 1826–1829 (N.L.I. L.P. Mss 6755–58); Dungarvan and Youghal Rental, 1830–1832 (N.L.I. L.P. Mss 6782, 6797–98); Youghal Rental, 1815–1829 (N.L.I. L.P. Ms 6792); Lismore and Tallow Rental, 1826 (N.L.I. L.P. Ms 6849); Lismore and Tallow Rental, 1827–1832 (N.L.I. L.P. Mss 6851–52).

164. F. O'Ferrall, *Catholic Emancipation: Daniel O'Connell and the Birth of Irish Democracy, 1820–1930* (Dublin, 1985), 120–21.

165. Ibid., 122–23.

166. Sixth Duke to the Roman Catholic Freeholders of County Waterford, 9 Sept. 1825 (L.E.O. Ms C/1/4 Bundle: Correspondence Concerning County Waterford Elections 16 May 1807–20 Oct. 1825).

167. W. S. Currey to Capt. Gumbleton, 22 Aug. 1825 (ibid.); R. Power to W. S. Currey, 25 Aug. 1825 (ibid.); W. S. Currey to Lord George Beresford, 28 Aug. 1825 (ibid.); W. S. Currey to Mr. Jackson, 2 Sept. 1825 (ibid.).

168. Quoted in O'Ferrall, *Catholic Emancipation*, 124.

169. J. Abercrombie to Lord Bute, 10 Mar. 1825 (L.E.O. Ms C/1/4 Bundle: Correspondence Concerning County Waterford Elections 16 May 1807–20 Oct. 1825); Sixth Duke to Roman Catholic Freeholders of County Waterford, 9 Sept. 1825 (ibid.).

170. "List of Freeholders Who Have Transgressed at Dungarvon [*sic*] or Before 17 Mar. 1826" (L.E.O. Ms C/1/5 Bundle: County Waterford Election Correspondence 25 Feb. 1826–30 May 1826); Memorial by W. S. Currey, 4 May 1826 (ibid.); J. Hudson to W. S. Currey, 18 June 1826 (L.E.O. Ms C/1/6 Bundle: County Waterford Election Correspondence 1 June 1826–26 June 1826).

171. Sir G. Hill to J. Abercrombie, 3 Sept. 1825 (L.E.O. Ms C/1/4 Bundle: Correspondence Concerning County Waterford Elections 16 May 1807–20 Oct. 1825).

172. R. W. Gumbleton to W. S. Currey, 3 May 1826 (L.E.O. Ms C/1/5 Bundle: County Waterford Election Correspondence, 25 Feb. 1826–30 May 1826).

173. T. Garvin, *The Evolution of Irish Nationalist Politics* (Dublin, 1981), 44; O'Ferrall, *Catholic Emancipation*, 128.

174. Ibid., 126–27.

175. Ibid, 127–29.

176. W. S. Currey to J. Swanston, 19 June 1826 (L.E.O. Ms C/1/6 Bundle: County Waterford Election Correspondence 1 June 1826–26 June 1826).

177. J. Keily to W. S. Currey, 24 June 1826 (ibid.); W. S. Currey to J. Keily, 24 June 1826 (ibid.).

178. W. S. Currey to J. Swanston, 19 June 1826 (ibid.); Mr. Bennett to H. Witham, 23 June 1826 (ibid.).

179. Note by W. S. Currey of Conversations with Rev. Mr. O'Donnell and the Rev. Mr. Foran, 17 June 1826 (ibid.); W. S. Currey's Notes on the Situation in the County Waterford Election, 18 June 1826 (ibid.).

180. Sixth Duke to J. Barron, 17 June 1829 (L.E.O. Ms C/1/7 Bundle: General Political Correspondence 9 June 1829–10 Aug. 1829).

181. B. Currey to W. S. Currey, 3 Aug. 1829 (L.E.O. C/1/8 Bundle: County Waterford By-Election Correspondence 3 Aug. 1829–25 Jan. 1830); J. Abercrombie to B. Currey, circa 6 Aug. 1829 (ibid.).

182. B. Currey to W. S. Currey, 3 Aug. 1829 and 5 Aug. 1829 (ibid.); J. Baldwin to H. Witham, 13 June 1829 (L.E.O. Ms C/1/7 Bundle: General Political Correspondence 9 June 1829–10 Aug. 1829).

183. "Instructions to Col. W. S. Currey," n/d, but post–7 Oct. 1829 (L.E.O. Ms C/1/8 Bundle: County Waterford By-Election Correspondence 3 Aug. 1829–25 Jan. 1830).

184. W. S. Currey to B. Currey, 20 June 1829 (L.E.O. Ms C/1/7 Bundle: General Political Correspondence 9 June 1829–10 Aug. 1829); B. Currey to W. S. Currey, 5 Aug. 1829 (L.E.O. Ms C/1/8 Bundle: County Waterford By-Election Correspondence 3 Aug. 1829–25 Jan. 1830).

185. B. Currey to W. S. Currey, 7 July 1829 (L.E.O. Ms C/1/7 Bundle: General Political Correspondence 9 June 1829–10 Aug. 1829).

186. J. Barron to W. S. Currey, 9 Jan. 1830 (L.E.O. Ms C/1/8 Bundle: County Waterford By-Election Correspondence 3 Aug. 1829–25 Jan. 1830); Walker, *Election Results*, 242.

187. G. Lamb to W. S. Currey, 14 June 1830 and 29 June 1830 (L.E.O. Ms C/1/29 Bundle: Dungarvan Political and Election Correspondence 26 Apr. 1829–26 Dec. 1831); Address from G. Lamb, "To the Gentlemen, Clergy, and Freeholders of Dungarvan," 5 July 1830 (ibid.); B. Currey to W. S. Currey, 6 July 1830 (ibid.).

188. J. Byrne to H. Witham, 9 Oct. 1829 (L.E.O. Ms C/1/8 Bundle: County Waterford By-Election Correspondence 3 Aug. 1829–25 Jan. 1830); Spoof Printed Election Address from Dominick Ronayne, 8 Dec. 1829 (ibid.).

189. W. S. Currey's "Calculation of the Number of Youghal Freemen Who Would Vote for the Duke's Friend, Mr. Ponsonby," n/d, but circa July 1829 (L.E.O. Ms C/1/14 Bundle: Youghal Political and Election Correspondence 19 Nov. 1828–29 Oct. 1831); Rough Draft of Letter from W. S. Currey to B. Currey, n/d, but circa July 1829 (L.E.O. Ms C/1/7 Bundle: General Political Correspondence 9 June 1829–10 Aug. 1829); J. Abercrombie to W. S. Currey, 10 Aug. 1829 (ibid.); d'Alton, *Protestant Society*, 106.

190. J. Swete to W. S. Currey, 7 May 1831 (L.E.O. Ms C/1/20 Bundle: Bandon Election Correspondence 14 Jan. 1830–26 Aug. 1831); d'Alton, *Protestant Society*, 102.

191. W. S. Currey to B. Currey, 25 May 1831 (L.E.O. Ms C/1/20 Bundle: Bandon Election Correspondence 14 Jan. 1830–26 Aug. 1831); J. Swete to W. S. Currey, 15 June 1831 (ibid.).

192. d'Alton, *Protestant Society*, 102–3.

Chapter 6. Changing Attitudes

1. Draft Ledger 1832–1858 (N.L.I. L. P. Mss 6964–77).

2. Sale Correspondence, 3 Sept. 1859–21 Aug. 1863, passim; Letter Book: F. E. Currey 1858–1863 (N.L.I. L.P. Ms 7190); L. J. Proudfoot, "Patrician Urban Landlords: Research on Patronal Relations in Nineteenth-Century 'Estate Towns' in the British Isles," in D. Denecke and G. Shaw, eds., *Urban Historical Geography* (Cambridge, England, 1988), 188.

3. Sixth Duke, Memorandum to Joseph Paxton, n/d, but circa July 1844 (CW. Ms Paxton Group 234.1).

4. R. F. Forster, *Modern Ireland, 1600–1972* (London, 1988), 337ff.

5. The total population figures and average houseful occupancy rates have been abstracted from the censuses, while the tenant population has been estimated by multiplying the total number of domestic houses recorded in the rental by the houseful multiplier. For the intercensal years, the houseful multiplier has been calculated as the average of the two nearest censuses.

6. H. Mason, "The Development of the Urban Pattern of Ireland, 1841–1881" (Ph.D. diss., Swansea, 1969), chap. 2 passim.

7. Mason, "Urban Pattern," Conclusion; Forster, *Modern Ireland*, 321.

8. L. A. Clarkson, "Population Change and Urbanisation, 1821–1911," in L. Kennedy and P. Ollerenshaw, eds., *An Economic History of Ulster, 1820–1939* (Manchester, 1985), 137–40, 151–53.

9. L. M. Cullen, *An Economic History of Ireland since 1660*, 2d ed. (London, 1987), 140–42, 147–48.

10. I. Slater, *Royal National Commercial Directory of Ireland* (Manchester, 1846).

11. Based on Slater, *Commercial Directory* for 1846, 1856, and 1870 (Manchester, 1846, 1856, 1870), and Pigot & Co., *City of Dublin and Hibernian Provincial Directory* (Dublin, 1824). The limitations to this type of source have been well described by Shaw and Horner. The simple enumeration of the individuals listed in these directories gives no idea of the size of each concern, its profitability, hinterland, or level of employment. Moreover, sectoral listing of the sort employed here can mask the fact that many businesses were multifunctional rather than specialist. The multiple entries that were consequently made in these directories by some enterprises seeking to advertise the full range of their services have frequently been construed as a deficiency, particularly where research has been concerned with the number of enterprises in a town rather than with the range of services they offered. In this instance, where the functional variety in each town is the prime concern, these multiple entries are significant in their own right, and no attempt has been made to adjust the figures downward to take account of them. See A. A. Horner, "Stability and Change in the Towns and Villages West of Dublin" (Ph.D. diss., Trinity College, Dublin, 1974), Appendix B passim; G. Shaw, *British Directories as Sources in Historical Geography*, Historical Geography Research Series, no. 8 (London, 1982).

12. Seventh Duke to F. E. Currey, 9 July 1872, 14 July 1872, and 17 July 1872 (L.E.O. C/1/85 D); H. C. Casserley, *Outline of Irish Railway History* (Newton Abbot, 1974), chap. 7 passim; K. A. Murray and D. B. McNeill, *The Great Southern & Western Railway* (Dublin, 1976), 36–41.

13. R. V. Comerford, "Ireland 1850–70: Post-Famine and Mid-Victorian," in W. E. Vaughan, ed., *A New History of Ireland, vol. 5: Ireland under the Union,* part 1: *1801–1870* (Oxford, 1989), 374–75; Cullen, *Ireland,* 140–44; K. Theodore Hoppen, *Elections, Politics, and Society in Ireland, 1832–1885* (Oxford, 1986), 436–40; C. Ó Gráda, "Industry and Communications, 1801–1845," in Vaughan, ed., *Ireland under the Union,* 150.

14. P. Connell, *Changing Forces Shaping a Nineteenth-Century Irish Town: A Case Study of Navan* (Maynooth, 1978), 8–19; Cullen, *Ireland,* 148–50; J. S. Donnelly, *The Land and the People of Nineteenth-Century Cork* (London, 1975), 13–14, 26–27.

15. C. Ó Gráda, "The Investment Behaviour of Irish Landlords 1850–1875: Some Preliminary Findings," *Agricultural History Review* 23 (1975): 153.

16. Estate Accounts 1818–1889 (N.L.I. L.P. Ms 6929).

17. B. Currey to Sixth Duke, 12 Oct. 1846 (CW. Ms Sixth Duke's Correspondence Second Series 25.40); B. Currey to Sixth Duke, 18 Dec. 1846 (ibid. 25.42).

18. T. Knowlton to J. Heaton, 4 Oct. 1806 (CW. [Currey] Ms L/5 Bundle: Jan.–Dec. 1806); T. Knowlton to J. Heaton, 16 July 1807 (P.R.O.N.I. T.3158/1901); Sir John Newport to Lord George Cavendish, 2 Oct. 1808 (ibid. /1924); T. Knowlton to J. Heaton, 20 Oct. 1808 (ibid. /1925); Estate Rental 1811 (CW. [Currey] Ms L/9/11); Rental General 1812 (N.L.I. L.P. Ms 6681–6682); Rental General 1813 (N.L.I. L.P. Ms 6683); Estate Accounts 1818–1889 (N.L.I. L.P. Ms 6929).

19. Sixth Duke to Lord Duncannon, circa 1840 (CW. [Currey] Ms L/83/4 1837).

20. B. Currey to Sixth Duke, 4 Nov. 1839 (CW. Ms Sixth Duke's Correspondence Group II/4183).

21. B. Currey to Sixth Duke, 30 Sept. 1847 (CW. Ms Sixth Duke's Correspondence Second Series 25.57).

22. B. Currey to Sixth Duke, 27 Feb. 1847 (ibid., 25.47).

23. B. Currey to Sixth Duke, 30 Sept. 1847 (ibid., 25.57).

24. B. Currey to Sixth Duke, 12 Oct. 1846 (ibid., 25.40).

25. B. Currey to Sixth Duke, 30 Sept. 1847 (ibid., 25.57); see also M. E. Daly, *The Famine in Ireland* (Dublin, 1986), 73–89.

26. F. E. Currey to Seventh Duke, 30 Oct. 1858, Letter Book: F. E. Currey 1858–1863 (N.L.I. L.P. Ms 7190).

27. Estimated by B. Currey to have already reached £120,000 by December 1843. See B. Currey, "Statement of Extraordinary Expenditure Beyond Income, 1817–1843," Jan. 1844 (CW. Ms Paxton Group, enclosed with 197.0); D. Cannadine, "Aristocratic Indebtedness in the Nineteenth Century: The Case Re-opened," *Economic History Review*, 2d ser., 30 (1977), passim; idem, "The Landowner as Millionaire: The Finances of the Dukes of Devonshire, c. 1800–c. 1926," *Agricultural History Review* 25, no. 2 (1977): 79–83; L. P. Curtis, "Incumbered Wealth: Landed Indebtedness in Post-Famine Ireland," *American Historical Review* 85, no.1 (1980): 332–67.

28. B. Currey to W. S. Currey, 19 Nov. 1827 (L.E.O. Ms C/1/2).

29. B. Currey, "Statement of Extraordinary Expenditure Beyond Income, 1817–1843," Jan. 1844 (CW. Ms Paxton Group, enclosed with 197).

30. J. Paxton, Memorandum on the Duke's Debts, n/d, but circa Jan.–July 1844 (ibid., 231).

31. Sixth Duke to J. Paxton, n/d, but circa Jan.–July 1844 (ibid., 234.1).

32. Sixth Duke to B. Currey, 18 July 1844 (ibid., 232).

33. B. Currey to Sixth Duke, 20 July 1844 (ibid., 233).

34. G. H. Cavendish to Sixth Duke, n/d, but circa July 1844 (ibid., 239); Sixth Duke to F. E. Currey, 29 Aug. 1844 (ibid., 256).

35. F. E. Currey to B. Currey, 2 Sept. 1844 (CW. [Currey] Ms L/83/4 (27) 1829).

36. J. Paxton to S. Paxton, 23 Feb. 1852 (CW. Ms Paxton Group 731).

37. Seventh Duke's Diaries, entries for 4 May 1859, 6 May 1859, 10 May 1859, 13 May 1859, and 15 May 1859 (CW. Ms); J. R. Berwick to F. E. Currey, 12 May 1859 (L.E.O. Ms C/1/85 B).

38. Seventh Duke's Diaries, entries for 2 Mar. 1858 and 23 April 1858 (CW. Ms); J. Paxton to Seventh Duke, 6 Mar. 1858 (CW. Ms Paxton Group 100.43).

39. J. Paxton to Seventh Duke, 27 Jan. 1858 (ibid., 100.44).

40. J. Paxton to Seventh Duke, 12 Feb. 1858 (CW. Ms Paxton Group 100.42); Duke of Bedford to Seventh Duke, 15 May 1858 (CW. Ms Sixth Duke's Correspondence Second Series 4.52); B. Currey, Memorandum Regarding Intended Sales, 20 May 1858 (ibid., 26.36); Duke of Bedford to Seventh Duke, 21 May 1858 (ibid., 4.54); Duke of Bedford to Seventh Duke, 22 May 1858 (ibid., 4.55).

41. J. Paxton to Seventh Duke, 12 Feb. 1858 (CW. Ms Paxton Group 100.42).

42. F. E. Currey to J. J. Byrne, 8 Oct. 1859 and 26 Oct. 1859, Letter Book: Dungarvan 1850–1870 (N.L.I. L.P. Ms 7191); F. E. Currey to J. J. Byrne, 29 May 1860, 29 Aug. 1860, and 5 Sept. 1860, Letter Book: Youghal 1860–1880 (L.E.O. C/2/23); F. E. Currey to M. Green, 31 May 1862 (ibid.).

43. F. E. Currey to W. Currey, 18 May 1860, Letter Book: F. E. Currey 1858–1863 (N.L.I. L.P. Ms 7190).

44. F. E. Currey to W. Currey, 5 May 1860 (ibid.).

45. F. E. Currey to W. Currey, 22 Nov. 1860 (ibid.).

46. G. H. Cavendish to Sixth Duke, n/d, but circa July 1844 (CW. Ms Paxton Group 239).

47. A. Swanston to F. E. Currey, 5 Mar. 1858 (L.E.O. C/1/85 B).

48. Figures derived from Estate Accounts 1818–1889 (N.L.I. L.P. Ms 6929).

49. See, for example, F. E. Currey to Seventh Duke, 14 Oct. 1861, Letter Book: F. E. Currey 1858–1863 (N.L.I. L.P. Ms 7190); Seventh Duke to F. E. Currey, 19 Oct. 1870, 4

Nov. 1870, and 20 Sept. 1872 (L.E.O. Ms C/1/85 D); Seventh Duke to F. E. Currey, 17 April 1873 and 1 Jan. 1874 (L.E.O. Ms C/1/85 E).

50. Seventh Duke to F. E. Currey, 19 Dec. 1873 (L.E.O. Ms C/1/85 H); Donnelly, *Land and the People*, 200–210; F.S.L. Lyons, *Ireland since the Famine* (London, 1971), 144–46; W. E. Vaughan, *Landlords and Tenants in Ireland, 1848–1904*, Studies in Irish Social and Economic History no. 2 (Dublin, 1984), 27–41.

51. Finlay Dun, *Landlords and Tenants in Ireland* (London, 1881), 59.

52. C. H. Currey to Duke of Argyll, 10 Jan. 1883 (L.E.O. Ms C/2/2).

53. C. H. Currey to Duke of Argyll, 26 Feb. 1883 (L.E.O. Ms C/2/2).

54. F. E. Currey to B. Currey, 2 Sept. 1844 (CW. [Currey] Ms L/83/4 (27) 1829); F. E. Currey to W. Currey, 19 Feb. 1858, Letter Book: W. Currey 1855–1858 (N.L.I. L.P. Ms 7188).

55. Estate Accounts 1818–1889 (N.L.I. L.P. Ms 6929); Estate Accounts 1839–1870 (N.L.I. L.P. Mss 6933–57); Draft Ledgers 1832–1870 (N.L.I. L.P. Mss 6964–89).

56. F. E. Currey to W. Currey, 23 Feb. 1860, Letter Book: F. E. Currey 1858–1863 (N.L.I. L.P. Ms 7190).

57. Draft Ledgers 1827–1833 (N.L.I. L.P. Mss 6959–65).

58. Draft Ledgers 1832–1833 (N.L.I. L.P. Mss 6964–65).

59. F. E. Currey to B. Currey, 20 Feb. 1839 (CW. [Currey] Ms L/83/4 [30] 1839); F. E. Currey to G. Hollwey, 21 Jan. 1852, 26 Jan. 1852, 11 Mar. 1853, 14 Apr. 1854, and 4 Aug. 1854, Letter Book: Lismore, Tallow, and Miscellaneous 1849–1856 (N.L.I. L.P. Ms 7182); F. E. Currey to W. Currey, 17 Feb. 1857, Letter Book: F. E. Currey 1855–1858 (N.L.I. L.P. Ms 7188); J. R. Berwick to F. E. Currey, 12 May 1859 (L.E.O. Ms C/1/85 B); F. E. Currey to W. C. Currey, 10 Aug. 1858 and 26 Mar. 1861, Letter Book: F. E. Currey 1858–1863 (N.L.I. L.P. Ms 7190); F. E. Currey to Seventh Duke, 29 Jan. 1859 and 20 July 1863 (ibid.); F. E. Currey to Seventh Duke, 3 Sept. 1873, Copy Letter Book (L.E.O. Ms C/2/18); F. E. Currey to G. Hollwey, 13 July 1878, 9 Aug. 1878, and 18 Apr. 1879, Copy Letter Book 1869–1880 (L.E.O. Ms C/2/1); J. R. Berwick to F. E. Currey, 23 Dec. 1881 and 4 Jan. 1882 (L.E.O. Ms C/1/85 N); J. R. Berwick to F. E. Currey, 9 June 1885 and 15 June 1885 (L.E.O. Ms C/1/85 P); R. H. Power to C. Tarrant, 28 May 1889, Copy Letter Book: 1880–1890 (L.E.O. Ms C/2/2).

60. F. E. Currey to W. Currey, 26 Dec. 1855, 28 Dec. 1855, 9 Mar. 1856, 14 Apr. 1856, and 16 May 1856, Letter Book: F. E. Currey 1855–1858 (N.L.I. L.P. Ms 7188); F. E. Currey to Seventh Duke, 4 Feb. 1864, Letter Book: F. E. Currey to W. Currey 1864–1871 (N.L.I. L.P. Ms 7192); F. E. Currey to J. R. Berwick, 15 Apr. 1869, Letter Book: Bandon 1851–1883 (N.L.I. L.P. Ms 7185).

61. F. E. Currey to B. Currey, 19 Dec. 1841 (CW. [Currey] Ms L/83/4 [37] 1842); F. E. Currey to Seventh Duke, 30 Oct. 1867, 8 Aug. 1868, and 21 Dec. 1868, Letter Book: F. E. Currey to W. Currey 1864–1871 (N.L.I. L.P. Ms 7192).

62. Draft Ledger 1851–1852 (N.L.I. L.P. Ms 6970); General Letting Book 1839–1847, *passim* (N.L.I. L.P. Ms 7122); Letting Book: Lismore and Tallow, *passim* (N.L.I. L.P. Ms 7125); Letting Book: Dungarvan, *passim* (N.L.I. L.P. Ms 7128).

63. F. E. Currey to W. Currey, 23 Feb. 1860, Letter Book: F. E. Currey 1858–1863 (N.L.I. L.P. Ms 7190); F. E. Currey to Seventh Duke, 6 July 1867 and 27 July 1867, Letter Book: F. E. Currey to W. Currey 1864–1871 (N.L.I. L.P. Ms 7192).

64. F. E. Currey to W. Currey, 17 Feb. 1857, Letter Book: F. E. Currey to W. Currey 1855–1858 (N. L. I. 7188); Seventh Duke to F. E. Currey, 6 Mar. 1877 (L.E.O. Ms C/1/85 H).

65. F. E. Currey to C. P. Cotton, 19 June 1884, Copy Letter Book: 1880–1890 (L.E.O. Ms C/2/2); J. R. Berwick to F. E. Currey, 9 Dec. 1882, 10 Dec. 1882, and 14 Dec. 1882 (L.E.O. Ms C/1/85 N).

66. F. E. Currey to J. R. Berwick, 23 Apr. 1883, Letter Book: 1883–1898 (L.E.O. Ms C/2/21); R. H. Power to D. Craig, 9 Jan. 1889 (ibid.).

67. Cannadine, "Landowner as Millionaire," 87; idem, *Lords and Landlords: The Aristocracy and the Towns, 1774–1967* (Leicester, 1980), 294–95.

68. Return of Towns Which Have Adopted the Act of 9 Geo. IV c.82 for Lighting, Cleansing, and Watching the Cities, Corporate, and Market Towns in Ireland, *Parliamentary Sessional Papers, Accounts and Papers*, 1836, vol. 47 (Miscellaneous), 629, 635; Return Showing Schedule of Towns in Ireland That Have Elected Town Commisoners under the Provisions of the Towns Improvement Act of [1854], *Parliamentary Sessional Papers, Accounts and Papers*, 1854–1855, vol. 18 (Ireland: Scotland), p. 588.

69. Return of Meetings Convened Under 9. Geo. IV c.82 for Making Provision for Lighting, Cleansing, and Watching the Cities, Corporate, and Market Towns of Ireland, *Parliamentary Sessional Papers, Accounts, and Papers*, 1843, vol. 50 (Ireland), p. 27.

70. Return of the Towns Which Have Adopted the Act of 9. Geo. IV c.82 and the Amount of Rate, *Parliamentary Sessional Papers, Accounts and Papers*, 1836, vol. 47 (Miscellaneous), p. 629; Return of the Number of Towns in Ireland Where Meetings of the Inhabitants Have Been Convened under the Provisions of the Act of 9 Geo. IV c.82, *Parliamentary Sessional Papers, Accounts and Papers*, 1846, vol. 42 (Ireland), p. 335.

71. Returns Showing the Schedule of Towns in Ireland That Have Elected Town Commissioners Under the Provisions of the Towns Improvement Act of [1854], *Parliamentary Sessional Papers, Accounts and Papers*, 1854–1855, vol. 18 (Ireland: Scotland), 588.

72. Bandon Rental 1826–1835 (N.L.I. L.P. Ms 6158); Dungarvan and Youghal Rentals 1832–1839 (N.L.I. L.P. Mss 6782–87); Return of the Towns Which Have Adopted the Act of 9. Geo. IV c.82 and the Amount of Rate, *Parliamentary Sessional Papers, Accounts and Papers*, 1836, vol. 47 (Miscellaneous), 629, 635–36, 641.

73. Entry for 9 June 1842, Bandon and Youghal Letting Book 1840–1843 (N.L.I. L.P. Ms 7127).

74. Entries for 5 May 1843 and 7 May 1843 (ibid.).

75. Entry for 9 June 1842 (ibid.); Entry for 7 Dec. 1851, Dungarvan Letting Book 1847–1858 (N.L.I. L.P. Ms 7128); F. E. Currey to J. R. Berwick, 7 June 1880, Letter Book: Bandon 1851–1883 (N.L.I. L.P. Ms 7185); R. H. Power to M. Healey, 7 Nov. 1885, Copy Letter Book: 1880–1890 (L.E.O. Ms C/2/2).

76. F. E. Currey to Seventh Duke, 23 Nov. 1859, Letter Book: F. E. Currey 1858–1863 (N.L.I. L.P. Ms 7190); F. E. Currey to W. Currey, 26 Mar. and 6 Nov. 1861 (ibid.).

77. For example, F. E. Currey to J. R. Berwick, 30 Jan. 1870, Letter Book: F. E. Currey (Bandon) 1851–1883 (N.L.I. L.P. Ms 7185). The threatened relocation by the Bandon merchant tenants in 1801 seems to have been exceptional (see chapter 5).

78. F. E. Currey to Mr. Rupert, 1 May 1851, Letter Book: Youghal 1848–1860 (N.L.I. L.P. Ms 7184).

79. Entries for 6 Oct. 1843, 4 June 1844, and 3 Dec. 1845, General Letting Book 1839–1847 (N.L.I. L.P. Ms 7122); entry for 11 Dec. 1851, Dungarvan Letting Book 1847–1858 (N.L.I. L.P. Ms 7128).

80. See, for example, Letting Book: Lismore and Tallow, passim (N.L.I. L.P. Ms 7125); R. H. Power to Mrs. M. Desmond, 22 Sept. 1888, Copy Letter Book: 1880–1890 (L.E.O. Ms C/2/2).

81. Entries for 2 Dec. 1844 and 28 Nov. 1858, Dungarvan Letting Book 1847–1858 (N.L.I. L.P. Ms 7128).

82. Dungarvan Tenants' Application Book, 1857–1861 (L.E.O. Ms T/6); Building Book, 1869 to 1879 (L.E.O. Ms T/23).

83. Calculated from Tallow District Valuation, c. 1865 [*sic*] (N.L.I. L.P. Ms 6190), and Lismore District Tenure Book c. 1870 [*sic*] (N.L.I. L.P. Ms 6192).

84. For example, Variations in Rental (Tallow), Draft Ledger 1832, 1833, 1834 (N.L.I. L.P. Mss 6964, 6965, 6966); Variations in Rental (Bandon), Draft Ledger 1836 (N.L.I. L.P. Ms 6968).

85. Total: 102, standard deviation: 0.61, Lismore and District Tenure Book c. 1870 [*sic*] (N.L.I. L.P. Ms 6192).

86. Youghal Town Tenure Book, post 1860 [*sic*] (N.L.I. L.P. Ms 6183).

87. Youghal Rental, 1828 et seq., (N.L.I. L.P. Ms 6795 et seq.); Dungarvan and Youghal Rentals, 1832–1833 et seq., (N.L.I. L.P. Ms 6782 et seq.).

88. A Schedule of Tallow Town Leases 1827 (N.L.I. L.P. Ms 6160).

89. Youghal Town Tenure Book post 1860 [*sic*], *passim* (N.L.I. L.P. Ms 6183); Bandon Tenure Book c. 1870 [*sic*], passim (N.L.I. L.P. Ms 6191).

90. Hoppen, *Elections*, 437–40.

91. F. E. Currey to Seventh Duke, 20 Jan. 1863, 7 Feb. 1863, 13 Feb. 1863, and 3 June 1863, Letter Book: F. E. Currey 1858–1863 (N.L.I. L.P. Ms 7190).

92. Hoppen, *Elections*, 117.

93. R. Stewart, *Party and Politics, 1830–1852* (London, 1989), 19–20.

94. J. C. Beckett, *The Making of Modern Ireland* (London, 1981), 308–17; N. Gash, *Politics in the Age of Peel* (London, 1977), 50–64.

95. Hoppen, *Elections*, 1–33.

96. Instructions Given by the Chief Secretary for Ireland with Reference to the Cities and Boroughs of Ireland, Sending representatives to Parliament, *Parliamentary Sessional Papers, Reports and Plans*, 1831–1832, vol. 6, 65–67, 145–50.

97. Hoppen, *Elections*, 1–12, 17–26.

98. P. O'Flanagan, "Urban Minorities and Majorities: Catholics and Protestants in Munster Towns, c. 1659–1850," in W. J. Smyth and K. Whelan, eds., *Common Ground: Essays in the Historical Geography of Ireland* (Cork, 1988), 124–48.

99. B. M. Walker, ed., *Parliamentary Election Results in Ireland, 1801–1922* (Dublin, 1978), 252.

100. Hoppen, *Elections*, 310–11.

101. W. S. Currey to J. E. Green, 14 Nov. 1832 (L.E.O. Ms C/1/16, Bundle: Youghal Election Correspondence, 1832).

102. (L.E.O. Ms C/1/30, Bundle: Dungarvan Election Correspondence, 1832–1833, passim); Stewart, *Party and Politics*, 42–43; Forster, *Modern Ireland*, 308–10.

103. F. E. Currey to W. S. Currey, 23 July 1837 (L.E.O. Ms C/1/22, Bundle: Bandon Election Correspondence, 1837); Hoppen, *Elections*, 282–84.

104. Lord Morpeth to B. Currey, 12 July 1837 (L.E.O. Ms C/1/22, Bundle: Bandon Election Correspondence, 1837); B. Currey to W. S. Currey, n/d, but circa July 1837 (ibid.).

105. J. Swanston to B. Currey, 13 July 1837 (ibid.).

106. B. Currey to W. S. Currey, 18 July 1837 (ibid.).

107. Sixth Duke to W. S. Currey, 17 July 1837 (ibid.).

108. B. Currey to W. S. Currey, 9 July 1832 (L.E.O. Ms C/1/30).

109. Hoppen, *Elections*, 83–85.

110. Figures calculated from Estate Accounts 1818–1889 (N.L.I. L.P. Ms 6929).

111. B. Currey to Sixth Duke, 8 Oct. 1832 (CW. Ms Sixth Duke's Correspondence Group II/2662).

112. Sixth Duke to B. Currey, 30 June 1837 (CW. [Currey] Ms L/83/4 [29]).

113. W. S. Currey to B. Currey, 3 July 1837 (ibid.).
114. F. E. Currey to B. Currey, 18 Sept. 1837 (ibid.); Hoppen, *Elections*, 284.
115. B. Currey to Sixth Duke, 17 Aug. 1837 (CW. [Currey] Ms L/83/4 [29]).
116. Hoppen, *Elections*, chap. 5 passim.
117. W. S. Currey to G. Ponsonby, 19 Nov. 1832 (L.E.O. Ms C/1/16).
118. R. G. Davies to the Mayor of Youghal, 15 Dec. 1832 (ibid.).
119. Hoppen, *Elections*, 392.
120. B. Currey to ? Wood, 1 Jan. 1834 (CW. Ms Paxton Group 2954.1).
121. G. Roche to W. S. Currey, 1 Jan. 1835 (L.E.O. Ms C/1/17).
122. B. Currey to Sixth Duke, 3 Jan. 1834 (CW. Ms Paxton Group 2954).
123. B. Currey's Instructions to W. S. Currey Regarding Dungarvan, 1 Jan. 1834
(CW. Ms Paxton Group 2954.2).
124. Stewart, *Party and Politics*, chap. 4 passim.
125. Sixth Duke to J. Abercrombie, 9 Dec. 1834 (L.E.O. Ms C/1/3).
126. James Abercrombie to Sixth Duke, 10 Dec. 1834 (ibid.).
127. B. Currey to ? Wood, 1 Jan. 1834 (CW. Ms Paxton Group 2954.1).
128. Ibid.
129. H. Bagge to W. S. Currey, 23 Jan. 1834 (L.E.O. Ms C/1/32).
130. Petition of [the] Electors of [the] Borough of Dungarvan to the Duke of Devonshire, 27 Jan. 1834 (L.E.O. Ms C/1/32); J. Dower to H. Witham, 30 Jan. 1834
(L.E.O. Ms C/1/32); H. Witham to J. Dower, n/d, but circa Feb. 1834 (ibid.).
131. A. Barry and K. Theodore Hoppen, "Borough Politics in O'Connellite Ireland:
The Youghal Poll Books of 1835 and 1837," *Journal of the Cork Historical and Archaeological Society* 83, no. 238 (1978), 106–46, and 84, no. 239 (1979), 15–43.
132. W. S. Currey to Lord Morpeth, 3 Dec. 1835 (L.E.O. Ms C/1/18); Hoppen, *Elections*, 310–11.
133. W. S. Currey to B. Currey, 10 Dec. 1834 (L.E.O. Ms C/1/17).
134. Barry and Hoppen, "Borough Politics," part 1, 106–121.
135. F. E. Currey to W. Currey, 26 Feb. 1851, Letter Book: F. E. Currey to W. Currey
1851–1855 (N.L.I. L.P. Ms 7186); Hoppen, *Elections*, 310.
136. W. Currey to F. E. Currey, 17 Nov. 1856 (L.E.O. Ms C/1/85 B).
137. W. Currey to F. E. Currey, 19 Nov. 1856 (ibid.).
138. F. E. Currey to Earl of Carlisle, 17 Mar. 1857, Letter Book: Dungarvan
1848–1886 (N.L.I. L.P. Ms 7191); F. E. Currey to F. J. Howard, 30 Mar. 1857 (ibid.);
F. E. Currey to T. Foley, 30 Mar. 1857 (ibid.).
139. F. E. Currey to F. J. Howard, 3 April 1857 (ibid.).
140. F. E. Currey to W. Currey, 4 Apr. 1857, Letter Book: F. E. Currey 1855–1858
(N.L.I. L.P. Ms 7188).
141. Hoppen, *Elections*, 436–55.
142. F. E. Currey to W. Currey, 10 Apr. 1859, Letter Book: F. E. Currey 1858–1863
(N.L.I. L.P. Ms 7190).
143. F. E. Currey to Seventh Duke, 20 Jan. 1863, 7 Feb. 1863, 13 Feb. 1863, and 3 June
1863 (ibid.); F. E. Currey to J. R. Berwick, 12 June 1863, Letter Book: Bandon 1851–1883
(N.L.I. L.P. Ms 7185); J. R. Berwick to F. E. Currey, 29 Oct. 1871 (L.E.O. Ms C/1/85 D).
144. Walker, *Election Results*, xi–xii, 328–29.
145. W. Currey to F. E. Currey, 1 Apr. 1878 (L.E.O. Ms C/1/85 K); F. A. Currey to
F. E. Currey, 9 Dec. 1878, 14 Dec. 1878, 27 Jan. 1879, 6 Mar. 1679, 13 Mar. 1879, 23
Mar. 1879, 13 June 1879, and 10 Nov. 1879 (ibid.); F. E. Currey to B. Whitney, 16 Jan.
1879 and 18 Jan. 1879, Copy Letter Book: 1869–1880 (L.E.O. Ms C/2/1).

146. F. E. Currey to Lt. Colonel Burke, 7 Aug. 1856, Letter Book: Lismore, Tallow, and Miscellaneous 1856–1869 (N.L.I. L.P. Ms 7189); F. E. Currey to Captain Barry, 21 Oct. 1863 (ibid.); F. E. Currey to Seventh Duke, 14 Nov. 1861, Letter Book: F. E. Currey 1858–1863 (N.L.I. L.P. Ms 7190); Cannadine, "Landowner as Millionaire," 94.
147. Ibid., 90, 97, graph 4.

Chapter 7. Property and Social Authority

1. A.P.W. Malcolmson, "Absenteeism in Eighteenth-Century Ireland," *Irish Economic and Social History* 1 (1974): 15–35.
2. A.P.W. Malcolmson, "The Parliamentary Traffic of This Country," in T. Bartlett and D. W. Hayton, eds., *Penal Era and Golden Age* (Belfast, 1979), 137–140.
3. Godfrey Lill to George Townshend, 9 and 10 July 1768 (Townshend Mss, N.L.I. Ms 394/41–2.).
4. A.P.W. Malcolmson, "The Newtown Act of 1748: Revision and Reconstruction," *Irish Historical Studies* 18 (1973): 335–36; idem, "Parliamentary Traffic," 150.
5. Ibid., 154–55.
6. Maurice FitzGerald to David Crosbie, 14 Aug. 1714 (T.C.D. Ms 3821/160); Philip Perceval to Lord Perceval, 11 July 1727 (Egmont Mss, B.L. Add. Ms 47032 fol. 27–28.).
7. Mrs Tighe to William Tighe, 10 Feb. 1790 (Tighe Mss, P.R.O.N.I. D.2685/1/1/17.).
8. Southwell to Marmaduke Coghill, 22 Apr. 1735, 14 Feb. and 11 Mar. 1736 (Southwell Mss, N.L.I. Ms 875.).
9. John Colclough to Caesar Colclough, 5 July 1795 (McPeake [Colclough] Mss, P.R.O.N.I. T.3048/C/18.).
10. A.P.W. Malcolmson, *John Foster: The Politics of the Anglo-Irish Ascendancy* (Oxford, 1978), 192–280; idem, "Parliamentary Traffic," passim.
11. Ibid., 149.
12. Compiled from the 1853 Report on Irish Markets and Fairs.
13. "Plan for the Improvement of the Estate of Edenderry, 5 Oct. 1810" (Downshire Mss, P.R.O.N.I. D.671/A5/6, pp. 5–6); *The Parliamentary Gazetteer of Ireland* (Dublin, 1846) 1:207, 368; 2:156, 338, 534, 715; 3:35; J. H. Gebbie, ed., *An Introduction to the Abercorn Letters (As Relating to Ireland 1736–1816)* (Omagh, 1972), 275.
14. Meredyth to Hill, 18 Feb. 1717 (Correspondence Minute Book 1707–1719, Downshire Mss, P.R.O.N.I. D.607/A/11.).
15. Meredyth to Hill, 31 Jan. 1720 (Correspondence Minute Book 1719–1726, Downshire Mss, P.R.O.N.I. D.607/A/12 no. 20.).
16. "Plan for the Improvement of the Edenderry Estate, 5 Oct. 1810" (Downshire Mss, P.R.O.N.I. D.671/A5/6, pp. 5–8.).
17. Ibid., 2.
18. Ibid.
19. *Parliamentary Gazetteer*, 1:205.
20. Ibid., 1:353–54.
21. Ibid., 1:413.
22. Ibid., 3:236.
23. Most recently summarized in S. A. Royle, "Industrialization, Urbanization, and Urban Society in Post-Famine Ireland, c. 1850–1921," in B. J. Graham and L. J. Proudfoot, eds., *An Historical Geography of Ireland* (London, 1993), 258–92.

24. *Parliamentary Gazetteer,* 2:159.
25. Ibid., 1:422.
26. Ibid., 2:320.
27. Ibid., 2:22.
28. Ibid., 1:371.
29. Ibid., 1:115–16.
30. Ibid., 2:305, 3:22.
31. Ibid., 1:115.
32. Ibid., 1:261.
33. County Cork, 1, folio 62, Ordnance Survey of Ireland, Six Inch Map, First Edition (Dublin, 1841).
34. *Parliamentary Gazetteer,* 3:75.
35. Ibid., 1:137–38.
36. Ibid., 1:48; 2:72, 83.
37. C. Costello, *Guide to Kildare and West Wicklow* (Naas, 1991), 56–57.
38. Ulster Architectural Heritage Society, *Guide to Historic Buildings . . . in the Towns and Villages of Mid Down* (Belfast, 1974), 14–16.
39. "Plan for the Improvement of the Edenderry Estate, 5 Oct. 1810" (Downshire Mss, P.R.O.N.I. D.671/A5/6, pp. 5–8; *Parliamentary Gazetteer,* 3:279–81; Gebbie, *Abercorn Letters,* 288, 300; E. MacLysaght, ed., *The Kenmare Manuscripts* (Dublin, 1942), 229–30.
40. *Parliamentary Gazetteer,* 2:457.
41. Ibid., 3:175.
42. L. Kennedy and L. A. Clarkson, "Birth, Death, and Exile: Irish Population History, 1700–1921," in Graham and Proudfoot, eds., *Historical Geography of Ireland,* 175.
43. L. J. Proudfoot, "Regionalism and Localism: Religious Change and Social Protest, c. 1700 to c. 1900," in Graham and Proudfoot, *Historical Geography of Ireland,* 211–15.
44. W. E. Vaughan and A. J. Fitzpatrick, eds., *Irish Historical Statistics: Population 1821–1971* (Dublin, 1978), 3.
45. J. S. Donnelly, "Landlords and Tenants," in W. E. Vaughan, ed., *A New History of Ireland, Vol. 5: Ireland under the Union, part 1, 1801–1870* (Oxford, 1989), 332–50; K. Theodore Hoppen, *Ireland since 1800: Conflict and Conformity* (London, 1989), 87–94.
46. Ibid.
47. W. E. Vaughan, *Landlords and Tenants in Mid-Victorian Ireland* (Oxford, 1994), passim.
48. Hoppen, *Ireland since 1800,* 87–94; M. Turner, "Rural Economies in Post-Famine Ireland, c. 1850–1914," in Graham and Proudfoot, eds., *Historical Geography of Ireland,* 293–337.
49. D. J. Hickey and J. E. Doherty, *A Dictionary of Irish History, 1800–1980,* 2d ed. (Dublin, 1989), 286–89.

Bibliography

1. Manuscript Material

a. *Chatsworth House, Derbyshire*
Devonshire Papers, CW. Ms:

Fifth Duke's Correspondence.
Sixth Duke's Correspondence (Groups I & II and Second Series).
Paxton Group (Correspondence).
Seventh Duke's Diaries.
Bernard Scalé, Survey of the Duke of Devonshire's Irish Estates, 1773–1775, 4 vols.

Papers deposited by Currey & Co at Chatsworth, CW. (Currey) Ms:

L	/	4	/	14	L	/	9	/	11	L	/	83	/	3
L	/	5	/		L	/	45	/	95	L	/	83	/	4
L	/	9	/	7				

b. *Lismore Castle, Waterford*
Devonshire Papers, A/6/1-2, C/1/1–C/2/23, T/6, T/23.

c. *National Library of Ireland*
Lismore Papers, N.L.I. Ms 6155–7213.
Southwell Papers, N.L.I. Ms 875.
Townshend Papers, N.L.I. Ms 394 41–42.

d. *Public Record Office for Northern Ireland*

Chatsworth Papers.   Shannon Papers.
Downshire Papers.   Tighe Papers.
McPeake [Colclough] Papers.   Villiers-Stuart Papers.
Roden Papers.

e. *Other Repositories*

British Library: Egmont Papers.
Devon County Record Office: Courtenay Papers.
Hampshire County Record Office: Wallop Papers.
Harvard University Library: Cork and Orrery Papers.
Public Record Office of Ireland (National Archives): Pennefather Papers.

2. Government Publications

Devon Commission, *Digest of Evidence,* part 1 (Dublin, 1847).

Great Britain, Parliamentary Papers (1836, vols. 30–34), *Reports of the Commissioners for Inquiry into the Condition of the Poorer Classes in Ireland.*

House of Commons *Report, Experimental Improvements on Crown Lands at King William's Town, Ireland* (London, 1834).

"Instructions Given by the Chief Secretary for Ireland with Reference to the Cities and Boroughs of Ireland, Sending representatives to Parliament," *Parliamentary Sessional Papers, Reports and Plans,* 1831–1832, vol. 6.

Ordnance Survey of Ireland, Six Inch Map, First Edition, County Cork, vol. 1, folio 62 (Dublin, 1841).

"Return of the Amount of Hearth Money Paid by Several Cities, 1798–1800," *House of Commons Journal (Ireland),* 19 (1800), Appendix, dccclxi–dccclxiv.

Return of Towns Which Have Adopted the Act of 9 Geo. IV c.82 for Lighting, Cleansing, and Watching the Cities, Corporate, and Market Towns in Ireland, *Parliamentary Sessional Papers, Accounts and Papers,* 1836, vol. 47 (Miscellaneous).

Return of Meetings Convened Under 9. Geo. IV c.82 for Making Provision for Lighting, Cleansing, and Watching the Cities, Corporate, and Market Towns of Ireland, *Parliamentary Sessional Papers, Accounts and Papers,* 1843, vol. 50 (Ireland).

Return of the Number of Towns in Ireland Where Meetings of the Inhabitants Have Been Convened Under the Provisions of the Act of 9 Geo. IV c.82, *Parliamentary Sessional Papers, Accounts and Papers,* 1846, vol. 42 (Ireland).

Return Showing Schedule of Towns in Ireland That Have Elected Town Commisoners Under the Provisions of the Towns Improvement Act of [1854], *Parliamentary Sessional Papers, Accounts and Papers,* 1854–1855, vol. 18 (Ireland: Scotland).

3. Newspapers

"Description of the Town of Youghal," *Walker's Hibernian Magazine,* March 1778.

"Population, Inhabitants, and Electors of Ireland," *Morning Post,* 23 Dec. 1790–11 Jan. 1791.

"State of Borough Representation in the Year 1784," *Northern Star,* 1–9 July 1796.

4. Period Works

Bateman, J. *The Great Landowners of Great Britain and Ireland* (Reprint of the 4th [1883] edition; Leicester, 1971).

Bennett, G. *The History of Bandon and the Principle Towns in the West Riding of Cork* (Cork, 1869).

Carleton, W. *Valentine McClutchy, the Irish Agent. A Chronicle of the Castle Cumber Property* (London, 1845).

Caulfield, R., ed. *The Council Book of the Corporation of Youghal 1610–1659, 1666–1687, 1690–1800* (Guildford, 1878).

Hayman, S. *The New Handbook of Youghal* (Youghal, 1868).

Larcom, T. A., ed. *The History of the Survey of Ireland Commonly Called the Down Survey, by Doctor William Petty, A.D. 1655–56* (Dublin, 1851).

Lewis, S. *Topographical Dictionary of Ireland* (London, 1837).

Lucas, R. *The Cork Directory for 1787–8* (Dublin, circa 1789).

Marmion, A. *The Ancient and Modern History of the Maritime Ports of Ireland* (London, 1860).

Pigot & Co. *City of Dublin and Hibernian Provincial Directory* (Dublin, 1824).

Slater, I. *Royal National Commercial Directory of Ireland,* for 1846, 1856, and 1870 (Manchester, 1846, 1856, 1870).
Smith, C. *The Ancient and Present State of the City and County of Cork,* 2d ed. (Dublin, 1774).
————. *The Ancient and Present State of the County and City of Waterford* (Dublin, 1746).
Spillar, W. K. *A Short Topographical and Statistical Account of the Bandon Union* (Bandon, 1844).
The Parliamentary Gazetteer of Ireland (Dublin, 1846).

5. Reference Works

Bence-Jones, M. *A Guide to Irish Country Houses* (London, 1988).
Burke's Peerage, Baronetage, and Knightage, 105th ed. (London, 1970).
Hickey, D. J., and J. E. Doherty. *A Dictionary of Irish History, 1800–1980,* 2d ed. (Dublin, 1989).
McEvoy, J. *County of Tyrone 1802: A Statistical Survey,* 2d ed. (Belfast, 1991).
Moody, T. W., F. X. Martin, and F. J. Byrne, eds. *A New History of Ireland,* vol. 7: *A Chronology of Irish History to 1976* (Oxford, 1982).
Newman, P. R. *Companion to Irish History . . . 1603–1921* (Oxford, 1991).
Pender, S., ed. *A Census of Ireland circa 1659, with Supplementary Material from the Poll Money Ordinances (1660–1661)* (Dublin, 1939).
Shaw, G. *British Directories as Sources in Historical Geography.* Historical Geography Research Series no. 8. (London 1982).
Simington, R. C., ed. *Books of Survey and Distribution.* 4 vols. (Dublin, 1944–1967).
————. *The Civil Survey.* 10 vols. (Dublin, 1931–1961).
Vaughan, W. E., and A. J. Fitzpatrick, eds. *Irish Historical Statistics: Population 1821–1971* (Dublin, 1978).
Walker, B. M., ed. *Parliamentary Election Results in Ireland, 1801–1922* (Dublin, 1978).

6. Theses

Carty, P. J. "The Historical Geography of County Roscommon." M.A. thesis, National University of Ireland, 1970.
Dickson, D. "An Economic History of the Cork Region in the Eighteenth Century." Ph.D. dissertation, University of Dublin, 1977.
FitzGerald, J. "The Organisation of the Drogheda Economy, 1780–1820." M.A. thesis, National University of Ireland, 1972.
Horner, A. A. "Stability and Change in the Towns and Villages West of Dublin." Ph.D. dissertation, Trinity College, Dublin, 1974.
Mason, H. "The Development of the Urban Pattern of Ireland, 1841–1881." Ph.D. dissertation, Swansea, 1969.
McCourt, E. "A Study of the Management of the Farnham Estates in County Cavan during the Nineteenth Century." M.A. thesis, University of Dublin, 1973.
Power, T. P. "Land, Politics, and Society in Eighteenth-Century Tipperary." Ph.D. dissertation, University of Dublin, 1987.
Proudfoot, L. J. "Urban Patronage and Estate Management on the Duke of Devonshire's Irish Estates (1764–1891): A Study in Landlord-Tenant Relationships." Ph.D. dissertation, Queen's University, Belfast, 1989.
Tod, A. M. "The Smiths of Baltiboys: A County Wicklow Family and Their Estate in the 1840s." Ph.D. dissertation, University of Edinburgh, 1978.

7. Articles and Monographs

Aalen, F.H.A. *Man and the Landscape in Ireland* (London, 1978).
———. "The Origin of Enclosures in Eastern Ireland." In N. Stephens and R. E. Glasscock, eds., *Irish Geographical Studies* (Belfast, 1970).
Abrams, P. "Towns and Economic Growth: Some Theories and Problems." In P. Abrams and E. A. Wrigley, eds., *Towns in Societies* (Cambridge, 1978).
Andrews, J. H. "Land and People, c. 1780." In T. W. Moody and W. E. Vaughan, eds., *A New History of Ireland*, vol. 4: *Eighteenth-Century Ireland, 1691–1800* (Oxford, 1986).
———. "The Struggle for Ireland's Public Commons." In P. O'Flanagan, P. Ferguson, and K. Whelan, eds., *Rural Ireland: Modernisation and Change, 1600–1900* (Cork, 1987).
Barry, A., and K. Theodore Hoppen. "Borough Politics in O'Connellite Ireland: The Youghal Poll Books of 1835 and 1837." *Journal of the Cork Historical and Archaeological Society* 83, no. 238 (1978), and 84, no. 239 (1979): 106–146.
Barry, J. "Henry Bowman. Reports on the Duke of Devonshire's Irish Estates, 1794–1797." *Analecta Hibernica* 22 (1960): 271–327.
Bartlett, T. "The Origins and Progress of the Catholic Question in Ireland, 1690–1800." In T. P. Power, and K. Whelan, eds., *Endurance and Emergence: Catholics in Ireland in the Eighteenth Century* (Dublin, 1990).
———. "The Townshend Viceroyalty, 1767–72." In T. Bartlett and D. W. Hayton, eds., *Penal Era and Golden Age* (Belfast, 1979).
Beckett, J. C. "Eighteenth-Century Ireland." In T. W. Moody and W. E. Vaughan, eds., *A New History of Ireland*, vol. 4: *Eighteenth-Century Ireland, 1691–1800.* (Oxford, 1986).
———. *The Making of Modern Ireland* (London, 1981).
Beckett, J. V. *Coal and Tobacco: The Lowthers and the Economic Development of West Cumberland, 1660–1760* (Cambridge, 1981).
———. *The Aristocracy in England, 1660–1914* (Oxford, 1986).
Bell, J., and M. Watson. *Irish Farming, 1750–1900* (Edinburgh, 1986).
Bessborough, Earl of, ed. *Georgiana: Extracts from the Correspondence of Georgiana, Duchess of Devonshire* (London, 1955).
Black, J. *Eighteenth-Century Europe, 1700–1789* (London, 1990).
Bowen, D. *Souperism: Myth or Reality?* (Cork, 1970).
Boyce, D. G. *Nationalism in Ireland* (London, 1982).
Boyle, E. "Linenopolis: The rise of the Textile Industry." In J. C. Beckett et al., eds., *Belfast: The Making of the City, 1800–1914* (Belfast, 1983).
Bradley, J. "Planned Anglo-Norman Towns in Ireland." In H. B. Clark and A. Simms, eds., *The Comparative History of Urban Origins in Non–Roman Europe: Ireland, Wales, Denmark, Germany, Poland, and Russia from the Ninth to the Thirteenth Centuries* (Oxford, 1985).
Buchanan, R. H. "Field Systems of Ireland." In A. R. H. Baker and R. A. Butlin, eds., *Studies of Field Systems in the British Isles* (Cambridge, 1973).
Burke, H. *The People and the Poor Law in Nineteenth-Century Ireland* (Littlehampton, 1987).
Burke, N. T. "An Early Modern Dublin Suburb: The Estate of Francis Augnier, Earl of Longford." *Irish Geography* 4 (1972): 365–383.
Butlin, R. A. "Land and People, c. 1600." In T. W. Moody, F. X. Martin, and F. J. Byrne, eds., *A New History of Ireland*, vol. 3: *Early Modern Ireland, 1534–1691* (Oxford, 1976).

————. "The Population of Dublin in the Late Seventeenth Century." *Irish Geography* 5 (1964–1968).

————. "Urban and Proto-Urban Settlements in Pre-Norman Ireland." In R. A. Butlin, ed., *The Development of the Irish Town* (London, 1977).

Camblin, G. *The Town in Ulster* (Belfast, 1951).

Cannadine, D. "Aristocratic Indebtedness in the Nineteenth Century: The Case Reopened." *Economic History Review*, 2d ser., 30 (1977): 624–650.

————. "The Landowner as Millionaire: The Finances of the Dukes of Devonshire, c. 1800–c. 1926." *Agricultural History Review* 25, no. 2 (1977): 77–97.

————. *Lords and Landlords: The Aristocracy and the Towns 1774–1967* (Leicester, 1980).

————. *Patricians, Power, and Politics in Nineteenth-Century Towns* (Leicester, 1982).

Canny, N. *The Upstart Earl* (Cambridge, England, 1982).

Carney, F. J. "Pre-Famine Irish Population: The Evidence from the Trinity College Estates." *Irish Economic and Social History* 2 (1975): 35–45.

Carter, H. *An Introduction to Urban Historical Geography* (London, 1983).

Casserley, H. C. *Outline of Irish Railway History* (Newton Abbot, 1974).

Clark, P. "Introduction: The Early Modern Town in the West: Research since 1945." In P. Clark, ed., *The Early Modern Town* (London, 1976).

Clarke, A. "The Irish Economy, 1600–60." In T. W. Moody, F. X. Martin, and F. J. Byrne, eds., *A New History of Ireland*, vol. 2: *Early Modern Ireland, 1534–1691* (Oxford, 1976).

Clarkson, L. A. "An Anatomy of an Irish Town: The Economy of Armagh, 1770." *Irish Economic and Social History* 5 (1978): 27–45.

————. "Armagh 1770: Portrait of an Urban Community." In D. Harkness and M. O'Dowd, eds., *The Town in Ireland* (Belfast, 1981).

————. "The Demography of Carrick-on-Suir, 1799." *Proceedings of the Royal Irish Academy* 87C, no. 2 (1987): 13–36.

————. "Irish Population Revisited, 1687–1921." In J. M. Goldstrom and L. A. Clarkson, eds., *Irish Population, Economy, and Society* (Oxford, 1981).

————. "Population Change and Urbanisation, 1821–1911." In L. Kennedy and P. Ollerenshaw, eds., *An Economic History of Ulster, 1820–1939* (Manchester, 1985).

Clay, C. G. A. *Economic Expansion and Social Change: England 1500–1700*, vol. 1: *Towns and Trade* (Cambridge, England, 1984).

Comerford, R. V. "Ireland 1850–70: Post-Famine and Mid-Victorian." In W. E. Vaughan, ed., *A New History of Ireland*, vol. 5: *Ireland under the Union*, part 1: *1801–1870* (Oxford, 1989).

Condon, J. C. "The Trade and Commerce of the Town of Youghal," *Journal of the Cork Historical and Archaeological Society* 50–51 (1945–1946): 117–124.

Conlon, M. V. "The Borough of Youghal." *Journal of the Cork Historical and Archaeological Society* 50–51 (1945–1946): 112–117.

Connell, K. H. *The Population of Ireland, 1750–1845* (Oxford, 1950).

Connell, P. *Changing Forces Shaping a Nineteenth-Century Irish Town: A Case Study of Navan* (Maynooth, 1978).

Connolly, S. *Religion and Society in Nineteenth-Century Ireland*, Studies in Irish Economic and Social History no. 3 (Dundalk, 1985).

Connolly, S. J. "Union Government, 1812–1823." In W. E. Vaughan, ed., *A New History of Ireland*, vol. 5: *Ireland under the Union*, part 1: *1801–1870* (Oxford, 1989).

Corfield, P. *The Impact of English Towns, 1700–1800* (Oxford, 1982).

Corish, P. J. "The Cromwellian Regime, 1650–60." In T. W. Moody, F. X. Martin, and F. J. Byrne, eds., *A New History of Ireland*, vol. 3: *Early Modern Ireland, 1534–1691* (Oxford, 1976).

Costello, C. *Guide to Kildare and West Wicklow* (Naas, 1991).

Cousens, S. H. "The Regional Variation in Emigration from Ireland between 1821 and 1841." *Transactions of the Institute of British Geographers* 37 (1965): 15–30.

⸻. "The Restriction of Population Growth in Pre-Famine Ireland." *Proceedings of the Royal Irish Academy* 64C (1964): 85–99.

Craig, M. *Dublin, 1660–1850* (Dublin, 1952).

Crawford, W. H. "The Influence of the Landlord in Eighteenth-Century Ulster." In L. M. Cullen and T. C. Smout, eds., *Comparative Aspects of Scottish and Irish Economic and Social History, 1600–1900* (Edinburgh, 1977).

⸻. "Landlord-Tenant Relations in Ulster, 1609–1820." *Irish Economic and Social History* 2 (1975): 5–21.

⸻. "The Significance of Landed Estates in Ulster, 1600–1820." *Irish Economic and Social History* 17 (1990): 44–61.

⸻. "Ulster Landowners and the Linen Industry." In J. T. Ward and R. G. Wilson, eds., *Land and Industry: The Landed Estate and the Industrial Revolution* (Newton Abbot, 1971).

Crotty, R. D. *Irish Agricultural Production: Its Volume and Structure* (Cork, 1966).

Cullen, L. M. *Anglo-Irish Trade, 1660–1800* (Manchester, 1968).

⸻. "Catholic Social Classes under the Penal Laws." In T. P. Power and K. Whelan, eds., *Endurance and Emergence: Catholics in Ireland in the Eighteenth Century* (Dublin, 1990).

⸻. "Economic Development, 1691–1750." In T. W. Moody and W. E. Vaughan, eds., *A New History of Ireland*, vol. 4: *Eighteenth Century Ireland, 1691–1800* (Oxford, 1986).

⸻. "Economic Development, 1750–1800." In T. W. Moody and W. E. Vaughan, eds., *A New History of Ireland*, vol. 4: *Eighteenth-Century Ireland, 1691–1800* (Oxford, 1986).

⸻. *An Economic History of Ireland since 1660.* 2d ed. (London, 1987).

⸻. *The Emergence of Modern Ireland, 1600–1900* (London, 1981).

⸻. "Man, Landscape, and Roads: The Changing Eighteenth Century." In W. Nolan, ed., *The Shaping of Ireland: The Geographical Perspective* (Dublin, 1986).

⸻. "The 1798 Rebellion in Wexford: United Irishman Organisation, Membership, Leadership." In K. Whelan, ed., *Wexford History and Society* (Dublin, 1987).

⸻. "The Social and Cultural Modernisation of Rural Ireland, 1600–1900." In L. M. Cullen and F. Furet, *Ireland and France 17th–20th Centuries: Towards a Comparative Study of Rural History* (Paris/Michigan, 1980).

Curl, J. S. *The Londonderry Plantation, 1609–1914* (Chichester, 1986).

Curtis, L. P. "Incumbered Wealth: Landed Indebtedness in Post-Famine Ireland." *American Historical Review* 85, no. 1 (1980): 332–367.

d'Alton, I. *Protestant Society and Politics in Cork, 1812–1844* (Cork, 1980).

Daly, M. E. "An Alien Entity? Attitudes to the City in Late-Nineteenth- and Twentieth-Century Ireland." *Etudes Irlandaises* 11 (1985): 181–194.

⸻. *The Famine in Ireland* (Dublin, 1986).

⸻. "Irish Urban History: A Survey." *Urban History Yearbook* (Leicester, 1986).

Daniels, S., and S. Seymour. "Landscape Design and the Idea of Improvement

1730–1914." In R. A. Dodgshon and R. A. Butlin, eds., *An Historical Geography of England and Wales* 2d ed. (London, 1990).

de Breffny, B., and R. ffolliott. *The Houses of Ireland* (London, 1975).

Dennis, R., and R. Prince. "Research in British Urban Historical Geography." In D. Denecke and G. Shaw, eds., *Urban Historical Geography: Recent Progress in Britain and Germany* (Cambridge, England, 1988).

———. "Stability and Change in Urban Communities: A Geographical Perspective." In J. H. Johnson and C. G. Pooley, eds., *The Structure of Nineteenth-Century Cities* (London, 1982).

Devonshire, Duchess of. *The House: A Portrait of Chatsworth* (London, 1982).

de Vries, Jan. *European Urbanisation, 1500–1800* (London, 1984).

Dickson, D. "Catholics and Trade in Eighteenth-Century Ireland: An Old Debate Revisited." In T. P. Power and K. Whelan, eds., *Endurance and Emergence: Catholics in Ireland in the Eighteenth Century* (Dublin, 1990).

———. "The Gap in Famines: A Useful Myth?" In E. M. Crawford, ed., *Famine: The Irish Experience, 900–1900* (Edinburgh, 1989).

———. *New Foundations: Ireland, 1660–1800* (Dublin, 1984).

———. "The Place of Dublin in the Eighteenth-Century Irish Economy." In T. M. Devine and D. Dickson, eds., *Ireland and Scotland, 1600–1850* (Edinburgh, 1983).

———. "Property and Social Structure in Eighteenth-Century South Munster." In L. M. Cullen and F. Furet, eds., *Ireland and France 17th–20th Centuries: Towards a Comparative Study of Rural History* (Paris/Michigan, 1980).

Doherty, C. "The Monastic Town in Early Medieval Ireland." In H. B. Clark and A. Simms, eds., *The Comparative History of Urban Origins in Non-Roman Europe: Ireland, Wales, Denmark, Germany, Poland, and Russia from the Ninth to the Thirteenth Centuries* (Oxford, 1985).

Donnelly, J. S. *The Land and the People of Nineteenth-Century Cork* (London, 1975).

———. "Landlords and Tenants." In W. E. Vaughan, ed., *A New History of Ireland,* vol. 5: *Ireland under the Union,* part 1: *1801–1870* (Oxford, 1989).

Dun, Finlay. *Landlords and Tenants in Ireland* (London, 1881).

English, B. "Patterns of Estate Management in East Yorkshire c. 1840–c. 1880." *Agricultural History Review* 42 (1984): 29–48.

Forster, R. F. *Modern Ireland, 1600–1972* (London, 1988).

Fraher, W. *An Architectural Inventory of Dungarvan* (Dungarvan, 1984).

———. "The Reconstruction of Dungarvan, 1807–c. 1830: A Political Ploy." *Decies* 25 (1984): 4–21.

Garvin, T. *The Evolution of Irish Nationalist Politics* (Dublin, 1981).

Gash, N. *Politics in the Age of Peel* (London, 1977).

Gearey, L. M. *The Plan of Campaign* (Cork, 1986).

Gebbie, J. H., ed. *An Introduction to the Abercorn Letters (As Relating to Ireland, 1736–1816)* (Omagh, 1972).

Gillespie, R. G. *Colonial Ulster: The Settlement of East Ulster, 1600–1641* (Cork, 1985).

Goldstrom, J. M., and L. A. Clarkson, eds. *Irish Population, Economy, and Society* (Oxford, 1981).

Graham, B. J. "The Definition and Classification of Medieval Irish Towns." *Irish Geography* 21, no. 1 (1988): 20–32.

———. "The Evolution of Urbanisation in Medieval Ireland." *Journal of Historical Geography* 5, no. 2 (1979): 111–127.

———. "The Towns of Medieval Ireland." In R. A. Butlin, ed., *The Development of the Irish Town* (London, 1977).

———. "Urban Genesis in Early Medieval Ireland." *Journal of Historical Geography* 13, no. 1 (1987): 3–16.

Graham, B. J., and L. J. Proudfoot. "A Perspective on the Nature of Irish Historical Geography." In B. J. Graham and L. J. Proudfoot, eds., *An Historical Geography of Ireland* (London, 1993).

Gribbon, H. D. "The Irish Linen Board, 1711–1828." In L. M. Cullen and T. C. Smout, eds., *Comparative Aspects of Scottish and Irish Economic and Social History, 1600–1900* (Edinburgh, 1977).

Grigg, D. B. *Population Growth and Agrarian Change: An Historical Perspective* (Cambridge, England, 1980).

Heape, R. Grundy. *Buxton under the Dukes of Devonshire* (London, 1948).

Herr, R. "Spain." In D. Spring, ed., *European Landed Elites in the Nineteenth Century* (Baltimore, n.d.).

Hershberg, T. "The Future of Urban History." In D. Fraser and A. Sutcliffe, eds., *The Pursuit of Urban History* (London, 1983).

Hewitt, E., ed. *Lord Shannon's Letters to His Son* (Belfast, 1982).

Hooker, E. R. *Readjustments of Agricultural Tenure in Ireland* (Chapel Hill, North Carolina, 1938).

Hoppen, K. Theodore. *Elections, Politics, and Society in Ireland, 1832–1885* (Oxford, 1984).

———. *Ireland since 1800: Conflict and Conformity* (London, 1989).

Horner, A. A. "Carton, Co. Kildare: A Case Study of the Making of an Irish Demesne." *Quarterly Bulletin of the Irish Georgian Society* 18 (1975): 45–104.

———. "Land Transactions and the Making of Carton Demesne." *Journal of the County Kildare Archaeological Society* 15 (1974): 387–396.

———. "The Scope and the Limitations of the Landlord Contribution to Changing the Irish Landscape, 1700–1850." *Collected Papers Presented to the Permanent European Conference for the Study of the Rural Landscape* (Copenhagen, 1986).

Hughes, E. "The Eighteenth-Century Estate Agent." In H. A. Cronne, ed., *Essays in British and Irish History in Honour of James Eadie Todd* (London, 1949).

Hughes, T. Jones. "Continuity and Change in Rural County Wexford in the Nineteenth Century." In K. Whelan, ed., *Wexford History and Society* (Dublin, 1987).

———. "The Estate System of Landholding in Nineteenth-Century Ireland." In W. Nolan, ed., *The Shaping of Ireland: The Geographical Perspective* (Dublin, 1986).

———. "Historical Geography of Ireland from circa 1700." In G.L.H. Davies, ed., *Irish Geography: The Geographical Society of Ireland Golden Jubilee, 1934–1984* (Dublin, 1984).

———. "Landholding and Settlement in County Tipperary in the Nineteenth Century." In W. Nolan, ed., *Tipperary: History and Society* (Dublin, 1985).

———. "Society and Settlement in Nineteenth-Century Ireland." *Irish Geography* 5 (1964–1968): 79–96.

———. "Village and Town in Mid-Nineteenth-Century Ireland." *Irish Geography* 14 (1981): 99–106.

Johnston, E. M. *Great Britain and Ireland, 1760–1800* (Edinburgh, 1963).

Jupp, P. *British and Irish Parliamentary Elections, 1784–1831* (Newton Abbot, 1973).

———. "Urban Politics in Ireland, 1801–31." In D. Harkness and M. O'Dowd, eds., *The Town in Ireland* (Belfast, 1981).

Kennedy, L., and L. A. Clarkson. "Birth, Death, and Exile: Irish Population History, 1700–1921." In B. J. Graham and L. J. Proudfoot, eds., *An Historical Geography of Ireland* (London, 1993).

Langton, J. "Residential Patterns in Pre-Industrial Cities: Some Case Studies from Seventeenth-Century Britain." *Transactions of the Institute of British Geographers* 65 (1975): 1–28.

Langton, J., and G. Hoppe. *Town and Country in the Development of Early Modern Western Europe*. Historical Geography Research Series no. 11 (London, 1983).

Large, D. "The Wealth of the Greater Irish Landowners, 1750–1815." *Irish Historical Studies* 15 (1966–1967): 21–45.

Lee, J. "The Provision of Capital for Early Irish Railways, 1830–53." *Irish Historical Studies* 16 (1968–1969): 33–63.

Lieven, D. *The Aristocracy in Europe, 1815–1914* (London, 1992).

Lowe, W. J. "Landlord and Tenant on the Estate of Trinity College, Dublin, 1851–1903." *Hermathena* 120 (1976): 5–24.

Lyne, G. J. "Landlord-Tenant Relations on the Shelburne Estate in Kenmare, Bonane, and Tousist, 1770–5." *Journal of the Kerry Archaeological and Historical Society* 12 (1979): 19–62.

Lyons, F.S.L. *Ireland since the Famine* (London, 1971).

MacCarthy, R. *The Trinity College Estates, 1800–1923* (Dundalk, 1992).

MacCarthy-Morrogh, M. *The Munster Plantation* (Oxford, 1986).

MacDonagh, O. "Ideas and Institutions, 1830–45." In W. E. Vaughan, ed., *A New History of Ireland*, vol. 5: *Ireland under the Union*, part 1: *1801–1870* (Oxford, 1989).

MacLysaght, E., ed. *The Kenmare Manuscripts* (Dublin, 1942).

McCartney, D. *The Dawning of Democracy: Ireland, 1800–1870* (Dublin, 1987).

McCracken, J. L. "The Social Structure and Social Life, 1714–1760." In T. W. Moody and W. E. Vaughan, eds., *A New History of Ireland*, vol. 4: *Eighteenth Century Ireland, 1691–1800* (Oxford, 1986).

McCutcheon, W. A. *The Industrial Archaeology of Northern Ireland* (HMSO, 1980).

———. "Transport, 1820–1914." In L. Kennedy and P. Ollerenshaw, eds., *An Economic History of Ulster, 1820–1939* (Manchester, 1985).

McDowell, R. B. "Administration and the Public Services, 1800–70." In W. E. Vaughan, ed., *A New History of Ireland*, vol. 5: *Ireland under the Union*, part 1: *1801–1870* (Oxford, 1989).

———. "Ireland in 1800." In T. W. Moody and W. E. Vaughan, eds., *A New History of Ireland*, vol. 4: *Eighteenth-Century Ireland, 1691–1800* (Oxford, 1986).

———. *Ireland in the Age of Imperialism and Revolution* (Oxford, 1979).

McGuire, J. "The Act of Union." In L. de Paor, ed., *Milestones in Irish History* (Cork, 1991).

Maguire, W. A. *The Downshire Estates in Ireland, 1801–1845* (Oxford, 1972).

———. "The 1822 Settlement of the Donegall Estates." *Irish Economic and Social History* 3 (1976): 17–31.

———. "Lord Donegall and the Sale of Belfast: A Case History from the Encumbered Estates Court." *Economic History Review*, 2d ser., 24 (1976).

McParland, E. "The Wide Streets Commissioners: Their Importance for Dublin Architecture in the Late Eighteenth and Early Nineteenth Century." *Quarterly Bulletin of the Irish Georgian Society* 15 (1972): 1–27.

Malcomson, A.P.W. "Absenteeism in Eighteenth-Century Ireland." *Irish Economic and Social History* 1 (1974): 15–35.

————. *John Foster: The Politics of the Anglo-Irish ascendancy* (Oxford, 1978).
————. "The Newtown Act of 1748: Revision and Reconstruction." *Irish Historical Studies* 18 (1973): 313–344.
————. "The Parliamentary Traffic of This Country." In T. Bartlett and D. W. Hayton, eds., *Penal Era and Golden Age* (Belfast, 1979).
Malins, E., and the Knight of Glin. *Lost Demesnes: Irish Landscape Gardening, 1660–1845* (London, 1976).
Martin, F. X. "Overlord Becomes Feudal Lord, 1172–85." In A. Cosgrove, ed., *A New History of Ireland*, vol. 2: *Medieval Ireland, 1169–1534* (Oxford, 1987).
————. "Plantation Boroughs in Medieval Ireland, with a Handlist of Boroughs to c. 1500." In D. Harkness and M. O'Dowd, eds., *The Town in Ireland* (Belfast, 1981).
Maxwell, C., ed. *Arthur Young: A Tour in Ireland* (reprint; Cambridge, England, 1983).
————. *Dublin under the Georges, 1714–1850* (Dublin, 1937).
Meenan, J., and D. Clarke, eds. *RDS: The Royal Dublin Society, 1731–1981* (Dublin, 1981).
Mingay, G. E. *English Landed Society in the Eighteenth Century* (London, 1963).
Mokyr, J. *Why Ireland Starved* (London, 1983).
Mooney, T., and F. White. "The Gentry's Winter Season." In D. Dickson, ed., *The Gorgeous Mask: Dublin, 1700–1850* (Dublin, 1987).
Morris, A.E.J. *History of Urban Form before the Industrial Revolution* (London, 1979).
Mortimore, M. J. "Landownership and Economic Growth in Bradford and Its Environs in the West Riding Conurbation, 1850–1900." *Transactions of the Institute of British Geographers* 46 (1969): 105–119.
Murray, K. A., and D. B. McNeill. *The Great Southern & Western Railway* (Dublin, 1976).
Neale, R. S. *Bath: A Social History, 1680–1850* (London, 1981).
Neely, W. G. *Kilcooley: Land and People in Tipperary* (privately published, 1983).
Nolan, W. *Fassadinin: Land, Settlement, and Society in South-East Ireland, 1600–1850* (Dublin, 1979).
————. "Patterns of Living in Tipperary, 1750–1850." In W. Nolan, ed., *Tipperary: History and Society* (Dublin, 1985).
O'Connor, P. J. *Exploring Limerick's Past: An Historical Geography of Urban Development in County and City* (Newcastle West, 1987).
O'Donoghue, D. *History of Bandon* (Bandon, 1970).
O'Ferrall, P. *Catholic Emancipation: Daniel O'Connell and the Birth of Irish Democracy, 1820–1930* (Dublin, 1985).
O'Flanagan, P. *Irish Historic Towns Atlas, no. 3: Bandon* (Dublin, 1988).
————. "Rural Change South of the River Bride in Counties Cork and Waterford: The Surveyors' Evidence, 1716–1851." *Irish Geography* 15 (1982): 51–69.
————. "Settlement Development and Trading in Ireland, 1600–1800: A Preliminary Investigation." In T. M. Devine and D. Dickson, eds., *Ireland and Scotland 1600–1850* (Edinburgh, 1983).
————. "Urban Minorities and Majorities: Catholics and Protestants in Munster Towns, c. 1659–1850." In W. J. Smyth and K. Whelan, eds., *Common Ground: Essays in the Historical Geography of Ireland* (Cork, 1988).
Ó Gráda, C. "Agricultural Rents, Pre-Famine and Post Famine." *Economic and Social Review* 7 (1974): 385–392.
————. "Industry and Communications, 1801–1845." In W. E. Vaughan, ed., *A New History of Ireland*, vol. 5: *Ireland under the Union*, part 1: *1801–1870* (Oxford, 1989).

————. "The Investment Behaviour of Irish Landlords, 1850–1875: Some Preliminary Findings." *Agricultural History Review* 23 (1975): 139–155.

————. *Ireland Before and After the Famine: Explorations in Economic History, 1800–1925* (Manchester, 1988).

————. "Poverty, Population, and Agriculture, 1801–1845." In W. E. Vaughan, ed., *A New History of Ireland,* vol. 5: *Ireland under the Union,* part 1: *1801–1870* (Oxford, 1989).

O'Kelly, E. *The Old Private Banks of Munster* (Cork, 1959).

Ollerenshaw, P. "Industry, 1820–1914." In L. Kennedy and P. Ollerenshaw, eds., *An Economic History of Ulster, 1820–1939* (Manchester, 1985).

Olsen, D. J. *Town Planning in London: The Eighteenth and Nineteenth Centuries* (New Haven, Conn., 1964).

Orme, A. R. *The World's Landscapes,* vol. 4: *Ireland* (London, 1970).

————. "Youghal, County Cork—Growth, Decay, Resurgence." *Irish Geography* 5 (1966): 121–149.

Osborough, O. S. "Catholics, Land, and the Popery Acts of Anne." In T. P. Power and K. Whelan, eds., *Endurance and Emergence: Catholics in Ireland in the Eighteenth Century* (Dublin, 1990).

Palmer, N. D. *The Irish Land League Crisis* (New Haven, Conn., 1940).

Patten, J. "Urban Occupations in Pre-Industrial England." *Transactions of the Institute of British Geographers,* n.s., 2 (1977): 296–313.

Pearson, J. *Stags and Serpents: The Story of the House of Cavendish and the Dukes of Devonshire* (London, 1983).

Pomfret, J. E. *The Struggle for Land in Ireland, 1800–1923* (Princeton, N.J., 1930).

Power, P. "An Old Map of Dungarvan Dated 1760." *Journal of the Waterford Archaeological Society* 14 (1911): 103–7.

Proudfoot, L. J. "The Estate System in Mid-Nineteenth-Century Waterford." In T. P. Power and W. Nolan, eds., *Waterford History and Society: Interdisciplinary Essays on the History of an Irish County* (Dublin, 1992).

————. "Landscaped Parks in Pre-Famine Ireland: A Regional Case-Study." In A. Verhoeve and J.A.J. Vervloet, eds., *The Transformation of the European Rural Landscape: Methodological Issues and Agrarian Change, 1770–1914* (Brussels, 1992).

————. "The Management of a Great Estate: Patronage, Income, and Expenditure on the Duke of Devonshire's Irish Property c. 1816 to 1891." *Irish Economic and Social History* 13 (1986): 32–55.

————. "Patrician Urban Landlords: Research on Patronal Relations in Nineteenth-Century 'Estate Towns' in the British Isles." In D. Denecke and G. Shaw, eds., *Urban Historical Geography* (Cambridge, England, 1988).

————. "Regionalism and Localism: Religious Change and Social Protest, c. 1700 to c. 1900." In B. J. Graham and L. J. Proudfoot, eds., *An Historical Geography of Ireland* (London, 1993).

Proudfoot, L. J., and B. J. Graham. "The Nature and Extent of Urban and Village Foundation and Improvement in Eighteenth- and Early-Nineteenth-Century Ireland." *Planning Perspectives* 8 (1993).

Richards, E. "The Land Agent." In G. E. Mingay, ed., *The Victorian Countryside,* vol. 2 (London, 1981).

Robinson, O. "The London Companies and Tenant Right in Nineteenth-Century Ireland," *Agricultural History Review* 18 (1970): 54–63.

————. "The London Companies as Progressive Landlords in Nineteenth-Century

Ireland." *The Economic History Review,* 2d ser., 15, nos. 1–3 (1962–1963): 103–118.

Robinson, P. *The Plantation of Ulster: British Settlement in an Irish Landscape* (Dublin, 1984).

Roebuck, P. "Rent Movement, Proprietorial Incomes, and Agricultural Development, 1730–1830." In P. Roebuck, ed., *Plantation to Partition* (Belfast, 1981).

Royle, S. A. "Industrialization, Urbanization, and Urban Society in Post-Famine Ireland, c. 1850–1921." In B. J. Graham and L. J. Proudfoot, eds., *An Historical Geography of Ireland* (London, 1993).

Sheehan, A. "Irish Towns in a Period of Change, 1558–1625." In C. Bradley and R. Gillespie, eds., *Natives and Newcomers* (Dublin, 1986).

Simms, J. G. "The Establishment of Protestant Ascendancy, 1691–1714." In T. W. Moody and W. E. Vaughan, eds., *A New History of Ireland,* vol. 4: *Eighteenth-Century Ireland, 1691–1800* (Oxford, 1986).

———. "The Restoration, 1660–1685." In T. W. Moody, F. X. Martin, and F. J. Byrne, eds., *A New History of Ireland,* vol. 3: *Early Modern Ireland, 1534–1691* (Oxford, 1976).

Sjoberg, G. *The Preindustrial City Past and Present* (New York, 1960).

Smyth, W. J. "Estate Records and the Making of the Irish Landscape: An Example from County Tipperary." *Irish Geography* 9 (1976): 29–49.

Solow, B. *The Land Question and the Irish Economy, 1870–1903* (Cambridge, Mass., 1971).

Soudan, D. "Migrants and the Population Structure of Later Seventeenth-Century Provincial Cities and Market Towns." In P. Clark, ed., *The Transformation of English Provincial Towns, 1600–1800* (London, 1984).

Spring, D. *The English Landed Estate in the Nineteenth Century: Its Administration* (Baltimore, 1963).

———. "Landed Elites Compared." In D. Spring, ed., *European Landed Elites in the Nineteenth Century* (Baltimore, n.d.).

Springett, J. "Landowners and Urban Development: The Ramsden Estate and Nineteenth-Century Huddersfield." *Journal of Historical Geography* 8 (1982): 129–144.

Stewart, R. *Party and Politics, 1830–1852* (London, 1989).

Stokes, H. *The Devonshire House Circle* (London, 1917).

Sutcliffe, A. *Towards the Planned City: Germany, Britain, the United States, and France, 1780–1914* (Oxford, 1981).

Thompson, F. *Chatsworth: A Short History* (London, 1951).

Thompson, F.M.L. *English Landed Society in the Nineteenth Century* (London, 1963).

Thompson, F.M.L., and D. Tierney, eds., *William Greig: General Report on the Gosford Estates in County Armagh 1821* (Belfast, 1976).

Townshend, D. *The Life and Letters of the Great Earl of Cork* (London, 1904).

Trainor, R. "Peers on an Industrial Frontier: The Earls of Dartmouth and Dudley in the Black Country, c. 1810 to 1914." In D. Cannadine, ed., *Patricians, Power, and Politics in Nineteenth-Century Towns* (Leicester, 1982).

Travers, P. *Settlements and Divisions: Ireland, 1870–1922* (Dublin, 1988).

Turner, M. "Rural Economies in Post-Famine Ireland, c. 1850–1914." In B. J. Graham and L. J. Proudfoot, eds., *An Historical Geography of Ireland* (London, 1993).

Ulster Architectural Heritage Society. *Guide to Historic Buildings . . . in the Towns and Villages of Mid Down* (Belfast, 1974).

Vance, J. E. *This Scene of Man: The Role and Structure of the City in the Geography of Western Civilisation* (New York, 1977).

Vaughan, W. E. "Agricultural Output, Rents, and Wages in Ireland, 1850–1880." In L. M. Cullen and F. Furet, eds., *Irlande et France, XVIe–XXe siecles* (Paris, 1980).

———. "An Assessment of the Economic Performance of Irish Landlords, 1851–1881." In F.S.L. Lyons and R.A.J. Hawkins, eds., *Ireland under the Union: Varieties of Tension* (Oxford, 1980).

———. "Landlord and Tenant Relations in Ireland between the Famine and the Land War, 1850–1878." In L. M. Cullen and T. C. Smout, eds., *Comparative Aspects of Scottish and Irish Economic and Social History, 1600–1900* (Edinburgh, 1977).

———. *Landlords and Tenants in Ireland, 1848–1904*. Studies in Irish Social and Economic History no. 2. (Dublin, 1984).

———. *Landlords and Tenants in Mid-Victorian Ireland* (Oxford, 1994).

———. *Sin, Sheep, and Scotsmen* (Belfast, 1983).

Wall, M. "The Penal Laws, 1691–1760." In G. O'Brien, ed., *Catholic Ireland in the Eighteenth Century* (Dublin, 1989).

———. "The Rise of a Catholic Middle Class in Eighteenth-Century Ireland." In G. O'Brien, ed., *Catholic Ireland in the Eighteenth Century* (Dublin, 1989).

Walsh, E. "Sackville Mall: The First One Hundred Years." In D. Dickson, ed., *The Gorgeous Mask: Dublin, 1700–1850* (Dublin, 1987).

Ward, D. "The Pre-Urban Cadaster and the Urban Pattern of Leeds." *Annals of the Association of American Geographers* 52 (1962): 150–66.

Watt, J. *The Church in Medieval Ireland* (Dublin, 1972).

Wheatley, P. "What the Greatness of a City Is Said to Be: Reflections on Sjoberg's *Preindustrial City*." *Pacific Viewpoint* 4 (1963): 163–88.

Whelan, K. "The Catholic Parish, the Catholic Chapel, and Village Development in Ireland." *Irish Geography* 16 (1983): 1–15.

———. "The Regional Impact of Irish Catholicism, 1700–1850." In W. J. Smyth and K. Whelan, eds., *Common Ground: Essays on the Historical Geography of Ireland* (Cork, 1988).

———. "The Role of the Catholic Priest in the 1798 Rebellion in County Wexford." In K. Whelan, ed., *Wexford History and Society* (Dublin, 1987).

Wilmot, S. *"The Business of Improvement": Agriculture and Scientific Culture in Britain, c. 1700–1870* (London, 1990).

Young, Arthur. *A Tour in Ireland . . . Made in the Years 1776, 1777, 1778 and . . . 1779*, vol. 2, part 2 (Dublin, 1780).

Index

Index

395

Munster Province: (*cont.*)
council of, 66; Defenders in, 38;
employment in, 30; estate cores in, 10;
leases in, 11; land sales in, 43; landowners
in, 24; linen production in, 28; plantation
of, 64, 66, 82, 135; population density in,
25, 171, 244; property in, 67; railways in,
295; rents in, 109; seignories in, 67; urban
population in, 16; woollen industry in, 29
Musgrave, Sir Richard, 145, 146, 163

Napoleonic Wars (1815), 15
Naas, 73
Navan, County, 16, 249
Neely, W. G., 9
New Birmingham, 55
new towns, 50, 182, 214, 308, 309, 312, 324
Newcastle West: estate in, 104
Newport, Sir John, 194
Newport-Pratt, 309
Newry Canal, 58, 182 (*see also* canals)
Newtownards, 307, 314
Nichols, William, 284
Nicol, William, 291
Nolan, W., 9
Northumberland, duke of, 3
Nottingham, 13
Nuremberg, 14

Oath of Abjuration, 35
O'Connell, Daniel: associates of, 284; and
Catholic Association, 40, 230; electoral
involvement by, 234; politics of, 43, 289;
son of, 284, 291
O'Connell, John, 291
O'Connor, P. J., 17, 53, 131, 200
Offaly, County (King's County), 44, 60, 62,
67, 68, 307
O'Flanagan, P., 9, 16, 71, 75, 133, 134, 201, 283,
284
Ó Gráda, C., 8, 26, 46, 171, 251
O'Loghlin, Michael, 284
Ordnance Survey Six-Inch maps, 60, 199, 312
Oriel, Lord, 313
Orme, A. R., 10
Ormond, duke of: estate of, 43
Orpin, Basil, 103 (*see also* Devonshire estates
law agents)
Orr brothers, 49
Orrery, 68; earls of, 96
Osborne, Sir Thomas, 187; estate of, 74

Palmer, N. D., 6
parliament, British, 56; Irish, 33, 34, 38, 50, 58,
184, 185, 305; Westminster, 41, 185

Parliamentary Commission (Borough
Representation, 1832), 161
Parnell, Charles Stewart, 114, 323
Paynes (agents), 96
Paxton, Sir Joseph, 91, 123, 256, 258
Penal Laws, 34–37, 54, 55, 127; Repeal of, 63,
320
Petty, family: estate of, 49
Piccadilly, 68
pig-iron production, 49 (*see also* industry)
Pilltown, 313
Pitt, William, the Younger, 39
plantations, 7, 17, 60, 64, 66, 135 (*see also*
Ulster and Munster)
Pomfret, J. E., 6
Ponsonby, family: estate of, 9
Ponsonby, George (Hon.), 210, 284
Ponsonby, John, 159–64
Ponsonby, William Brabazon, 159, 162
Poole, Thomas, 104
Poor Law Unions, 56
Poor Law valuation, 44
Poor Rate, 27, 44, 48, 113
Poor Relief (Ireland) Act (1838), 56
Popery Act (1704), 34, 35, 127 (*see also* Penal
Law)
Popham, Benjamin, 102 (*see also* Devonshire
estates law agents)
population, 15; decline of, 244, 320, 321;
estimates of, 25; fertility of, 27, 29; growth
of, 25, 27, 30, 31, 42, 63, 171; marriage, 27,
29; rural density of, 23, 25, 27, 28;
ruralurban migration, 31
Portadown, 17
Portland, duke of: estate of, 13
Portlaw, 29, 183
Portsmouth, 13
Power, R., 96, 230 (*see also* Devonshire estates,
agents)
Power, Thomas, 42
primate city, 72
Prosperous, 29
Protestant Ascendancy, 10, 41, 230, 282

railways, 59, 295, 309
Raleigh, Sir Walter, 65, 66, 67, 82, 149 (*see also*
landowners)
Rams, 305
Ramsden, family, 13 (*see also* landowners)
Reform Act (1832), 97, 169, 237, 239, 253
Registration Act (1704), 34 (*see also* Penal
Law)
Relief Act (1793), 192
Relief Bill (1825), 230, 233
Renaissance, 51, 61, 310

Urban Patronage and Social Authority: The Management of the Duke of Devonshire's Towns in Ireland, 1764–1891 was composed in 11/13.5 Adobe Garamond by Books International, Norcross, Georgia; printed on 60-pound Glatfelter Supple Opaque Recycled and bound by Thomson-Shore, Inc., Dexter, Michigan; and designed and produced by Kachergis Book Design, Pittsboro, North Carolina.